From an unfinished portrait by Louise Waterman Wise.

POEMS

(1904—1917)

BY

WILFRID WILSON GIBSON

34793

NEW YORK
THE MACMILLAN COMPANY
1917

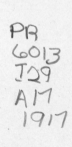

TO MY WIFE

CONTENTS

viii

CONTENTS

WOMENKIND

CONTENTS

FRIENDS

LIVELIHOOD

AKRA THE SLAVE

(1904)

So long had I travelled the lonely road,
Though, now and again, a wayfaring friend
Walked shoulder to shoulder, and lightened the load,
I often would think to myself as I strode,
No comrade will journey with you to the end.

And it seemed to me, as the days went past,
And I gossiped with cronies, or brooded alone,
By wayside fires, that my fortune was cast
To sojourn by other men's hearths to the last,
And never to come to my own hearthstone.

The lonely road no longer I roam.
We met, and were one in the heart's desire.
Together we came through the wintry gloam
To the little old house by the cross-ways, home;
And crossed the threshold, and kindled the fire.

POEMS

AKRA THE SLAVE

He thought to see me tremble
And totter as an oar-snapt reed,
When he spake death to me —
My courage, toppled in the dust,
Even as the head of cactus
The camel-keeper slashes
That his beasts may browse, unscathed,
The succulent, wounded green.
He thought to have me, broken,
And grovelling at his feet;
Mouthing and mumbling to his sandal-ties,
In stammering dread of death —
Ay! even as a king,
Who having from death's hand
Received his crown and kingdom,
For ever treads in terror of the hour
When death shall jog his elbow,
Twitch the purple from his shoulders,
And reclaim the borrowed crown.
But, little need have I to fear
The crouching, lean camp-follower,
Unto whose ever-gaping maw,
Day after day, I flung
The spoils of bow and arrow,
Ere I was taken captive —
I, who have often, at my mother's breast,
Awakened in the night-time,
To see death leering on me from the cave-mouth,
A gaunt and slinking shape
That snuffed the dying embers,
Blotting out the friendly stars —
I, who, a scarce-weaned boy,
Have toddled, gay and fearless,

Down the narrow jungle-track,
Through bodeful forest-darkness, panther-eyed;
And have felt cold snakes uncoiling
And gliding 'neath my naked sole,
From clammy slumber startled;
While, with sharp snap and crackle,
Beast-trodden branches strained behind me,
My father's hand scarce snatching me
Before the spring of crouching death!
But, naught of this the King could know.
He only knew that, on that far-off morning,
When first I came before him, captive,
Among my captive brothers,
And, as he lightly held, in idle fingers,
Above my unbowed head,
In equal poise
Death's freedom
Or the servitude of life,
I clutched at life:
And cared but little that his lips
Should curl, to see me, broken,
A slave among his slaves.
Yet, never slave of his was I;
Nor did I take my new life from his nod —
I . . . I who could have torn
The proud life out of him,
Before his guards could stay me . . .
Had she not sat beside him on her throne.

And he, who knew not then,
Nor ever, till to-day,
Has known me aught but slave,
Remembering that time,
Spake doom of death to me,
Idly, as to a slave:
And I await the end of night,
And dawn of death,
Even as a slave awaits . . .
Nay! as the unvanquished veteran
Awaits the hour of victory.

In silence, wheels the night,
Star-marshalled, over dreaming Babylon;
And none in all the sleeping city stirs,

Save the cloaked sentries on the outer walls
Who tread out patience 'twixt the gates of brass,
Numb with scarce-baffled slumber,
Or, maybe, some unsleeping priest of Bel,
A lonely warder of eternity,
Who watches on the temple's seventh stage,
With the unslumbering gods.
Yet, may not she, the Queen,
Whose beauty, slaying my body,
Brings my soul to immortal birth,
Although she does not know
Of my last vigil on the peak of life —
Yet, may not she awaken, troubled
By strange, bewildering dreams,
With heart a little fearful of the dawn
Of day, yet unrevealed?

There is no sound at all,
Save only the cool plashing
Of fountains in the courtyard
Without my lonely cell:
For fate has granted to me
This last, least consolation of sweet sound:
Though in the plains I perish,
I shall hear the noise of waters,
The noise of running waters,
As I die.
My earliest lullaby shall sing
My heart again to slumber.
And, even now, I hear
Stream-voices, long-forgotten, calling me
Back to the hills of home;
And, dreaming, I remember
The little yellow brooks
That ever, day and night,
Gush down the mountains singing,
Singing by the caves:
And hearkening unto them,
Once more a tiny baby,
A wee brown fist I dabble
In the foaming cool,
Frothing round my wrist,
Spurting up my arm,
Spraying my warm face;

And then again I chuckle,
As I see an empty gourd,
Fallen in the swirling waters,
Bobbing on the tawny eddies,
Swiftly out of sight.

And yet most clearly to remembrance comes
That far-off night, in early Spring,
When, loud with melted snow from Northern peaks,
The torrent roared and fretted;
While, couched within the cavern,
The clamour kept me wakeful;
And, even when I slept,
Tumbled, tumultuous, through my dreams,
And seemed to surge about me,
As the brawl of armèd men.
And once I sprang from slumber,
Hot and startled,
Dreaming that I felt
A warm breath on my cheek,
As if a jackal nuzzled me;
Or some dread, slinking foe
Made certain of my sleeping
Before he plunged the steel.
But nothing stirred within the glimmering cavern,
Where, all around me, lay my sleeping kindred;
And, when I stole without, with noiseless footsteps,
To rouse the smouldering watchfire into flame,
And cast fresh, crackling brushwood on the blaze,
I caught no glint of arms betwixt the branches,
Nor any sound or rumour, save
The choral noise of cold hill-waters,
Cold hill-waters singing,
Singing to the stars.
And so I turned me from the brooding night;
And, couched again upon the leopard-skins,
I slept, till dawn, in dream-untroubled sleep.
I woke to see the cold sky kindling red,
Beyond the mounded ash of the spent fire;
And lay, a moment, watching
The pearly light, caught, trembling,
In dewy-beaded spiders' webs
About the cave-mouth woven.
Then I arose;

And left my kindred, slumbering —
My mother, by my father,
And, at her breast, her youngest babe,
With dimpled fingers clutching at her bosom;
And, all around them, lying
Their sons and daughters, beautiful in sleep,
With parted lips,
And easy limbs outstretched
Along the tumbled bedskins:
And while they slumbered yet in shades of night,
I sprang out naked
Into eager dawn.
The sun had not yet scaled the eastern ridge:
And still the vales were hidden from my eyes
By snowy wreaths of swathing mist:
But, high upon a scar
That jutted sheer and stark,
In cold grey light,
There stood an antelope,
With lifted muzzle snuffing the fresh day;
When scenting me afar,
He plunged into the mist
With one quick, startled bound:
And, from the smoking vapour,
Arose a gentle pattering,
As, down the rocky trail,
The unseen herd went trotting
Upon their leader's heels.
And from the clear horizon
The exultant sun sprang god-like:
And on a little mound I stood,
With eager arms outstretched,
That, over my cold body,
The first warm golden beams
Of his life-giving light might fall.
And thus, awhile, I stood,
In radiant adoration tranced,
Until I caught the call of waters;
And, running downward to the stream,
That plunged into a darkling pool,
Where, in the rock was scooped a wide, deep basin;
Upon the glassy brink,
A moment, I hung, shivering,
And gazing down through deeps of lucent shadow;

And then I leapt headlong,
And felt the cloven waters
Closing, icy-cold, above me,
And, again, with sobbing breath,
Battled to the light and air:
And I ran into the sunshine,
Shaking from my tingling limbs
Showers of scintillating drops
Over radiant, dewy beds
Of the snowy cyclamen,
And dark-red anemone,
Till my tawny body glowed
With warm, ruddy, pulsing life.
And then again I sought the stream,
And plunged; and now, more boldly,
I crossed the pool, with easy stroke;
And climbed the further crag;
And, turning, plunged again.
And so, I dived and swam,
Till pangs of hunger pricked
My idle fancy homeward:
And eagerly I climbed the hill;
When, not a sling's throw from the cavern,
Stooping to pluck a red anemone,
To prank the wet, black tangle of my hair,
I heard a shout;
And looking up,
I saw strange men
With lifted spears
Bear down on me:
And as I turned,
A javelin sang
Above my shrinking shoulder,
And bit the ground before me.
But, swift as light I sped,
Until I reached the pool,
And leapt therein:
And he who pressed most hotly on my heels,
Fell stumbling after.
Still I never slackened,
Although I heard a floundering splash,
And then the laughter of his comrades:
And, as I swam for life,
Betwixt my thrusting heels,

Another spear that clove the crystal waters
Glanced underneath my body,
And in the stream-bed quivered bolt upright,
Caught in a cleft of rock.
With frantic arm I struck
Straight as a snake across the pool,
And climbed the further bank;
And plunging through deep brake,
Ran wildly onward,
Startling as I went
A browsing herd of antelope,
That, bounding, fled before me down the valley:
And after them I raced,
As though the hunter,
Not the hunted,
Until the chase sang in my blood,
And braced my straining thews.
I knew not if men followed,
Yet, on I sped, impetuously,
As speeds the fleet-foot onaga,
That breasts the windy morning,
With lifted head, and nostrils wide,
Exultant in his youth.
So, on and ever on,
Scarce knowing why I ran —
Enough for me to feel
Earth beaten back behind my heels,
And hear the loud air singing
The blood-song in my ears:
Till, stumbling headlong over
An unseen, fallen branch,
I rolled in a deep bed of withered leaves;
And lay, full-length in shuddering ecstasy
Of hot, tumultuous blood that rioted
Through every throbbing vein.
But when again, I breathed more easily,
And my wild, fluttering heart kept slower beat,
Hot-foot, my thoughts ran, wondering, backward:
And I arose and followed them
With swift and stealthy pace,
Until I reached the stream.
Along the bank I stole with wary step,
Until I came to where the waters
Narrowed, raging through a gorge,

Nigh the threshold of my home:
And across the thunderous flood,
From crag to crag I leapt:
And then I climbed a cedar,
From whose close ambush I could watch
Who came or went about the cavern-mouth.
I lay along a level branch:
And, through the thick, dark screen,
I peered with eager eyes:
But no one crossed my sight.
The whole land lay before me, drowsing
In deepest noonday slumber:
No twig stirred in the breathless blaze;
And underneath the boughs no serpent rustled:
And, in the earth and air,
Naught waked, save one lone eagle, nigh the sun,
With wings, unbaffled, beating
Up the blue, unclouded heavens.
A dreamless, suave security
Seemed brooding o'er the valley's golden slumber,
Whence rang or flashed no hint of lurking peril.
I dropped to earth,
And crouching low,
I stole yet nearer
Through the brake:
Till, drawing nigh the cavern-mouth,
I heard the sound of half-hushed sobbing:
And then I saw, within the gloom,
My mother and my sisters clustering round
My father's body, lying stark and dead,
A spear-wound in his breast.
And as I crept to them, they did not hear me,
Nor ever lift their heads;
But, shuddering, crouched together,
With drooping breasts half-hid in falling hair,
By that familiar form
In such strange slumber bound.
Only the baby, on her shoulder slung,
Saw me, and crowed me greeting,
As I stooped down to touch my weeping mother,
Who, turning suddenly,
With wild tear-fevered eyes;
Arose with whispered warning;
But, even then, too late.

Already, from behind,
Around my throat
An arm was flung;
And heavily I fell:
Yet, with a desperate wrench,
I slipped the clutch of my assailant:
And picking up a slingstone that lay handy,
I crashed it through his helm;
And dead he dropped.
And now upon me all his fellows thronged,
Like hounds about an antelope;
And gripped my naked limbs,
And dragged me down,
A struggling beast, among them:
And desperately I fought,
As fights the boar at bay,
When all the yelling pack,
With lathered lips, and white teeth gnashing,
Is closing in upon him,
And in his quivering flank, and gasping throat,
He feels the fangs of death:
Till, overcome at last,
They bound me hand and foot,
With knotted, leathern thongs;
And dragged me out to where, beneath the trees,
Trussed in like manner, with defiant eyes,
My brothers lay, already, side by side.
They laid me in the shade;
And flicked my wincing spirit
With laughter and light words:
"Now is the roe-buck taken!"
Then another,
On whose dark, sullen face there burned a livid weal:
"A buck in flight's a panther brought to bay!"
And then his fellow:
"True enough! and yet,
For such young thews they give good gold —
They give good gold in Babylon!"
And, laughing thus, they left us,
To lie through hours of aching silence,
Until, at length, the cool of evening fell;
When they returned from slumber;
And loosed the ankle-cords that we might stand;
And bade our mother feed us;

And she, with tender fingers, held
The milk-bowl to our parching lips;
And thrust dried dates betwixt our teeth;
And wept, to see us standing there,
With helpless hands, before her.
Then, bringing out their mules, they saddled them;
And tied us to the girths on either hand.
They drove my weeping sisters from the cavern;
And sought to tear my mother from her home;
But she escaped them;
And they let her bide
Amid the ruins of her life,
Whose light had dropped, so suddenly,
From out the highest heavens:
And, when I turned to look on her,
And win from her a last farewell,
I saw her, sitting desolate betwixt
Her silent husband and her wailing babe,
With still, strange eyes,
That stared upon the dead, unseeing,
While her own children went from her,
Scarce knowing that they left her, nevermore
To look upon her face.

Thus, we set out, as over
The darkening, Southern crags
The new moon's keen, curved blade was thrust:
My sisters trooping on before us,
Like a drove of young gazelles,
Which, in the dead of night,
With pards in leash, and torches flaring,
The hunters have encompassed.
They moved with timid steps,
And little runs;
Stumbling, with stifled cries;
And starting, panic-shot,
From every lurking shadow —
Behind them, terror's lifted lash:
Before them, ever crouching,
The horror of the unknown night —
While, as they moved before us,
The moonlight shivered off their shrinking shoulders
And naked, glancing limbs,
In shimmering, strange beauty.

And closely on their heels,
I, with my brothers, foremost in the file,
Marched, tethered 'twixt the plodding beasts,
Whose stolid riders sat,
Each with his javelin on the pummel couched,
In watchful silence, with dark eyes alert.
And once, nigh driven crazy
By the tugging of the thongs,
I sprang into the air,
As down a rocky steep we scrambled;
And strove to burst the galling bonds,
Or hurl my guards on one another;
But, all too sure of foot, the beasts,
And too securely girths and cords
Held me, and I stumbled.
Instantly a thong
Struck my wincing shoulders,
Blow on thudding blow.
I bit my lips; and strode on silently;
Nor fought again for freedom.
So on we journeyed through the night,
And down familiar mountain-tracks,
Through deep, dark forest,
Ever down and down;
Fording the streams, whose moon-bright waters flowed,
In eddies of delicious, aching cool,
About our weary thighs.
And, once, when in mid-torrent,
That swirled, girth-high about the plunging beasts,
A startled otter, glancing
Before their very hoofs,
Affrighted them; and, rearing,
With blind and desperate floundering,
They nearly dragged us down to death:
And, ere we righted,
With a fearful cry,
My eldest sister from the bevy broke;
And struck down-stream
With wild arm lashing desperately,
Until the current caught her;
And she sank, to rise no more.
And on again we travelled,
Down through the darkling woodlands:
And once I saw green, burning eyes,

Where, on a low-hung bough,
A night-black panther crouched,
As though to pounce upon my sisters;
But, the sudden crack of whips,
Startling him, he snarled;
And turned with lashing tail,
Crashing through dense brushwood.

When, once, again we came unto a clearing,
The night was near its noon:
And all the vales that lay before us
Were filled with moving, moonlit mists,
That seemed phantasmal waters
Of that enchanted world,
Where we, in dreams, sail over still lagoons,
Throughout eternal night,
And under unknown stars.
Still, on we fared, unresting,
Until the low moon paled;
When, halting on a mountain-spur,
We first looked down on Babylon,
Far in the dreaming West,
A cluster of dim towers,
Scarce visible to wearied eyes.
We camped within a sheltering cedar-grove;
And all the day, beneath the level boughs,
Upon the agelong-bedded needles lay,
Half-slumbering, with fleeting, fretful dreams
That could not quite forget the chafing cords,
That held our arms in aching numbness:
But, ere the noon, in sounder sleep I sank,
Dreaming I floated on a still, deep pool,
Beneath dark, overhanging branches;
And seemed to feel upon my cheek
The cool caress of waters;
While, far above me, through the night of trees,
Noon glimmered faintly as the glint of stars.
As thus I lay, in indolent ecstasy,
O'er me, suddenly, the waters
Curved, and I was dragged,
Down and down,
Through gurgling deeps
Of swirling, drowning darkness. . . .
When I awoke in terror;

And strove to sit upright;
But, tautly, with a jerk,
The thongs that held me to my brothers,
Dragged me back to earth.
Awhile I lay, with staring eyes, awake,
Watching a big, grey spider, crouched o'erhead,
In ambush 'neath a twig, beside her web,
Oft sallying out, to bind yet more securely,
The half-entangled flies.
And then, once more, I slumbered;
And dreamed a face leant over me,
More fair than any face
My waking eyes had ever looked upon.
Its beauty burned above me,
Not dusky like my sisters' faces,
But pale as the wan moon,
Reflected in a flood
Of darkly flowing waters,
Or as the creaming froth,
That, born amid the thunder of the fall,
Floats on the river's bosom in the sunshine,
Bubble after bubble,
Perishing in air.
So, a moment, over me,
With frail and fleeting glimmer
Of strange elusive, evanescent light,
The holy vision hovered.
And yet, whenever, with a fervent longing,
I sought to look into the darkling eyes,
The face would fade from me,
As foam caught in an eddy:
Until, at last, I wakened,
And, wondering, saw a pale star gleaming
Betwixt the cedar-branches.
And soon our captors stirred:
And we arose, to see
The walls and towers of Babylon, dark
Against the clear rose of the afterglow,
Already in the surge of shadows caught,
As night, beneath us, slowly Westward swept,
Flooding the dreaming plain that lay before us,
Vast, limitless, bewildering,
And strange to mountain-eyes.
As down the slope we went,

And when, at last, we left behind
The hills and singing waters,
A vague, oppressive fear
Of those dim, silent leagues of level land,
Fell on me; and I almost seemed
To bear upon my shoulders
The vaster dome of overwhelming night;
And, trembling like a child,
I looked askance at my two captors,
As they rode on in heedless silence,
Their swarthy faces sharp
Against the lucent sky.
And then, once more,
The old, familiar watchfires of the stars
Brought courage to my bosom;
And the young moon's brilliant horn
Was exalted in the sky:
And soon, the glooming wilderness
Awoke with glittering waters,
As a friendly wind sang unto me
Among the swaying reeds:
While, cloud on cloud,
The snowy flocks of pelican
Before our coming rose;
And, as they swerved to Southward,
The moonlight shivered off their flashing pinions.
So, on we marched, till dawn, across the plain;
And, on and on,
Beneath the waxing moon,
Each night we travelled Westward;
Until, at last, we halted
By the broad dull-gleaming flood
Of mighty, roaring Tigris;
And aroused from midnight slumber
The surly, grumbling ferrymen,
And crossed the swollen waters
Upon the great, skin rafts:
Then on again we fared,
Until the far, dim towers soared in the dawnlight;
And we encamped beside a stream,
Beneath dry, rustling palms.
And heavily I slumbered:
And only wakened once, at noon,
When, lifting up my head,

I saw the towers of Babylon burning blue,
Far off, in the blind heat:
And slept again, till sunset,
When we took our Westward course
Along the low bank of a broad canal,
That glimmered wanly 'neath a moonless sky.
Higher, and higher still,
As we drew slowly nearer,
Arose the vasty walls and serried towers,
That seemed to thrust among the stars,
And on embattled summits bear the night,
Unbowed beneath their burden,
As easily as, with unruffled brows,
And limber, upright bodies,
The village-daughters carry
At eve the brimming pitchers,
Poised upon their heads.
And when, above us, the wide-looming walls
Shut out the Western stars;
Beneath their shade, at midnight, we encamped,
To await till dawn should open
The city gates for us.
That night we did not sleep,
But, crouched upon the ground,
We watched the moon rise over Babylon,
Till, far behind us, o'er the glittering waste,
Was flung the wall's huge shadow,
And the moving shades of sentries,
Who, unseen above our heads,
Paced through the night incessantly.
Thus long we sat, hushed with awed expectation,
And gazing o'er the plain that we had travelled,
As, gradually, the climbing moon,
Escaping from the clustering towers,
Revealed far-gleaming waters,
And the sharp, shrill cry of owls,
Sweeping by on noiseless plumes,
Assailed the vasty silence,
Shivering off like darts
From some impenetrable shield.
And, as we waited,
Sometimes, fearfully,
I gazed up those stupendous, soaring walls
Of that great, slumbering city, wondering

What doom behind the bastioned ramparts slept,
What destiny, beneath the brooding night,
Awaited me beyond the brazen gates.
But, naught the blind, indifferent stars revealed,
Though towards the long night's ending,
Half-dazed with gazing up that aching height,
A drowsiness fell over me,
And in a restless waking-trance I lay,
Dreaming that Life and Death before me stood.
And, as each thrust towards me a shrouded cup,
Implacable silence bade me choose and drink.
But, as I stretched a blind, uncertain hand
To take the cup of death,
I wakened, and dawn trembled,
At last, beyond the Eastern hills,
And, star by star, night failed;
And eagerly the sun leapt up the sky,
And, as his flashing rays
Smote kindling towers and flaming gates of brass,
Across the reedy moat
A clattering drawbridge fell,
And wide the glittering portals slowly swung:
And there came streaming out in slow procession
A sleepy caravan of slouching camels,
Groaning and grumbling as they strode along
Beneath their mountainous burdens,
Upon whose swaying summits,
Impassively, the blue-robed merchants sat.
They passed us slowly by,
And then we took the bridge,
And, while our captors parleyed with the guards,
Who stood, on either hand,
With naked swords,
I turned my head,
And saw for the last time, far Eastward,
The cold, snow-brilliant peaks,
Beyond my dim, blue, native hills.
And, as I looked, my thoughts flew homeward,
And I, one dreaming moment,
Stood by my mourning mother in the cavern
Of desolation, looking on the dead.
And then, between the brazen gate-posts,
And underneath the brazen lintel,
At last we entered Babylon.

Before us, yet another wall arose,
And, turning sharply
Down a narrow way,
The living breath of heaven seemed shut from us
As though beneath the beetling crags
Of some deep mountain-gorge —
By cliffs of wall, on either hand,
That soared up to the narrow sky,
Which with dim lustre lit
The shimmering surface of enamelled brick,
Whereon, through giant groves,
Blue-coated hunters chased the boar,
Or 'loosed red-tasselled falcon
After flying crane.
But soon we reached another gate,
Sword-guarded, and we entered,
And plunged into the traffic
Of clamorous merchantmen,
Speeding their business ere the heat of day.
And as we jostled, slowly,
Through bewildering bazaars,
The porters and the idler wayfarers
All turned to look upon our shame,
With cold, unpitying eyes,
And indolent, gaping mouths,
Or jested with our captors,
Until we left the busier thoroughfares,
And walked through groves of cypress and of ilex,
Where not a sound or rumour troubled
The silence of the dark-plumed boughs
And glimmering deeps of peace,
Save only the cool spurt of waters
That, from a myriad unseen jets,
Fretted the crystal airs of morning,
And fell in frolic showers
Of twinkling, rainbow drops,
That plashed in unseen basins;
And through the blaze of almond-orchards,
Tremulous with blossom
That flickered in a rosy, silken snow
Of falling petals over us,
And wreathed about our feet
In soft and scented drifts;
Beneath pomegranate trees in young, green leaf,

And through vast gardens, glowing with strange flowers,
Such as no April kindled into bloom
Among the valleys of my native hills.
We came unto a court of many fountains,
Where, leaping off their jaded mules,
Our captors loosed the thongs that held us,
But left our wrists still bound.
And one with great clay pitchers came,
And over our hot bodies, travel-stained,
Poured out cool, cleansing waters
In a gurgling, crystal stream,
And flung coarse robes of indigo
About our naked shoulders.
And here we left behind us
The maidens and the younger boys,
And passing through a gateway,
Came out upon a busy wharf,
Where, southward, midway through the city,
The broad Euphrates flows,
His dark flood thronged with merchant-dhows,
And fishing-boats of reed and bitumen,
Piled high with glistering barbel, freshly-caught;
And foreign craft, with many-coloured sails,
And laden deep with precious merchandise,
That, over wide, bewildering waters,
Across the perilous world,
The adventurous, dark-bearded mariners,
Who swear by unknown gods in alien tongues,
Bring ever to the gates of Babylon.
We crossed the drawbridge, round whose granite piers
Swirled strong, Spring-swollen waters,
Loud and tawny,
And, through great brazen portals,
Passed within the palace gates,
When first I saw afar the hanging-gardens,
Arch on arch,
And tier on tier,
Against a glowing sky.
Two strapping Nubians, like young giants
Hewn from blue-black marble
By some immortal hand in immemorial ages,
Led us slowly onward.
The dappled pard-skins, slung across their shoulders,
Scarcely hid the ox-like thews,

Beneath the dark skin rippling,
As they strode along before us.
Through courts of alabaster,
And painted corridors,
And chambers fair with flowery tapestries
They led us, wondering, till at last we came
Into a vast, dim hall of glimmering gold,
The end of all our journeying.
And, as we halted on the threshold,
My eyes could see but little for a moment,
In the dusky, heavy air,
Through the ceaseless cloud of incense,
Rising from the smouldering braziers
To the gold, grey-clouded dome,
Tingling strangely in my nostrils,
As I came from morning airs;
Then slowly filling them with drowsy fume
When, looking up with half-dazed eyes,
I saw the King upon his golden throne:
And through my body
Raged rebellious blood,
In baffled beating
At my corded wrists,
As if to burst the galling bonds,
That I might hurl that lean, swart face,
So idly turning towards us,
With thin curled lips,
And cold, incurious eyes,
To headlong death —
Yea! even though I tumbled
The towers of Babylon round about my head.
And, when our captors bowed their foreheads low
Obsequious to the throne,
I stood upright,
And gazed my loathing on that listless form —
The gay, embroidered robe,
The golden cap, that prankt the crispèd locks,
The short, square beard, new-oiled and barbered —
But, in a flash,
A heavy blow
Fell on my head,
And struck me to my knees
Before the sleek, indifferent king.
And then, on either hand,

With gripping palms upon my shoulders set,
The Nubians towered above me
Like mighty men of stone.
And savagely I struggled,
Half-stunned, to rise again;
When, as I vainly battled
In their unrelenting clutch,
My eyes lit for the first time on the Queen,
Who sat upon the daïs, by her lord
Half-shadowed, on a throne of ivory,
And all the hate died in me, as I saw
The face that hovered over me in dream,
When I had slept beneath the low-boughed cedar:
The moon-pale brows, o'er which the clustered hair
Hung like the smoke of torches, ruddy-gold,
Against a canopy of peacock plumes:
The deep brown, burning eyes,
From which the soul looked on me in fierce pity.
And, as I gazed on that exultant beauty,
The hunter and the slayer of men
Was slain within me instantly,
And I forgot the mountains and my home;
My desolate mother, and my father's death;
My captive sisters . . . and the thronèd King!
I was as one, that moment,
New-born into the world
Full-limbed and thewed,
Yet, with the wondering heart
Of earth-bewildered childhood.
And, unto me, it seemed
That, as the Queen looked down on me,
There stole into her eyes
Some dim remembrance of old dreams,
That in their brown depths flickered
With strange, elusive light,
Like stars that tremble in still forest-pools.
One spake —
I scarce knew whom, nor cared —
And bade me choose,
Before the throne,
Between a life of slavery,
Or merciful, swift death —
Death, that but a moment since,
I would have dragged, exulting, on me —

And with my eyes still set on the Queen's face,
I answered:
" I will serve ":
And scarcely heeded that my wrists were loosed.

And, huddled in a stifling hut,
That night, among my fellows,
I could not sleep at all:
But gazed, wild-eyed, till dawn upon that face,
Which hovered o'er me, like the moon of dreams;
And seemed to draw the wandering tides of life
In one vast wave, which ever strove
To climb the heavens wherein she moved,
That it might break in triumphing foam about her.
Not then, nor ever afterwards,
Was I a slave, among my fellow-slaves,
But one, who, with mean drudgery,
And daily penance serves
Before a holy altar,
That, sometimes, as he labours, his glad eyes
May catch a gleam of the immortal light
Within the secret shrine;
Yea! and, maybe, shall look, one day, with trembling,
On the bright-haired, imperishable god.
And, even when, day after day,
I bore the big reed baskets, laden
With wet clay, digged beyond the Western moat,
Although I seemed to tread,
As treads the ox that turns the water-wheel,
A blindfold round of servitude,
My quenchless vision ever burned before me:
And when, in after days, I fed
The roaring oven-furnaces;
And toiled by them through sweltering days,
Though over me, at times, would come
Great longing for the hill-tops,
And the noise of torrent-waters:
Or when, more skilled, I moulded
The damp clay into bricks;
And spread the colour and the glaze;
And in strength-giving heat of glowing kilns
I baked them durable,
Clean-shaped, and meet for service:
My vision flamed yet brighter;

And unto me it seemed
As if my gross and useless clay were burned
In a white ecstasy of lustral fire,
That, in the fashioning of the house of love,
I might serve perfectly the builder's need.
Thus, many months, I laboured;
Till, one day, at the noontide hour of rest,
I lay; and with a sharpened reed —
As temple-scribes write down the holy lore
On tablets of wet clay —
On the moist earth beside me,
I limned a young fawn, cropping
A bunch of tender, overhanging leaves.
And, as I slowly drew,
I dreamt a little sadly of the days,
When I, too, roamed, untethered,
And drinking in, unquestioning,
The sunshine and the air,
And all the rapture of the earth that turns,
New every morning to the wondering sun,
Refashioned in still nights of starry dews:
But one, the while, unseen of me,
Watched my unconscious hand, approving:
And I was set, next morning,
Among the craftsmen, who so deftly limned
The hunts and battles for the palace walls.
And, happily, with them I lived
A life of loving labour, for each line
Flowed from the knowledge of my heart:
I drew the startled ostrich
Fleeing from the far-flung noose:
The brindled lynx; the onaga
In dewy-plashing flight;
The bristling boar, at bay,
Crouched in a deadly ring of threatening spears,
With streaming nostrils, and red eyes ablaze;
The striped hyæna; the gaunt, green-eyed wolf;
The skulking jackal; the grey, brush-tailed fox;
The hunting leopard and the antelope,
In mid-chase tense,
With every thew astrain;
The dappled panther; the brown-eyed gazelle,
Butting with black horns through the tangled
        brake;

The nimble hare, alert, with pricked-up ears;
The tiger, crouched, with yellow eyes afire;
The shaggy mountain-goat,
Perched on the utmost crag,
Against the afterglow of lucent ruby,
Or, poised with bunching hoofs
In mid-spring over a dark, yawning chasm;
Or the black stallion, with his tameless troop,
Fording a mountain-river in the dawn.
And, sometimes, as we toiled,
A terrible fleeting rapture
Would come upon me, when the Queen
Passed by us with her maidens;
Or paused, a moment, gazing,
With tranced and kindling eyes upon our labours:
But never did I dare, at any time,
To lift my eyes to hers,
And look, as soul on soul,
As on the day her beauty brought to birth
The strange new life within me.
In silence she would ever leave us;
And ever with her passing perished
The light and colour of my work;
So that my heart failed, daunted by that glimpse
Of the ever-living beauty.
And, sometimes, I would carve in ruddy teak,
Or ivory, from the Indian merchants bought,
Or in the rare, black basalt, little beasts
To please the idle fancies of the King;
Or model in wet clay, and cast in bronze,
Great bulls and lions for the palace-courts;
Or carve him seals of lapis-lazuli,
Of jasper, amethyst and serpentine,
Chalcedony — carnelian, chrysoprase,
Agate, sardonyx, and chalcedonyx —
Green jade, and alabaster;
Or cut in stones that flashed and flickered
Like a glancing kingfisher,
Or, in the sun-filled amber,
The kite with broad wings spread,
Or little fluttering doves that pecked
A golden bunch of dates:
And then of these in settings of fine gold
Made fillets, rings and ear-rings.

Thus, one day,
Dreaming, as ever, of the Queen,
I wrought a golden serpent for her hair:
And when I brought it to the King, next morn,
Where he sat brooding over chess,
He bade me bear it to the Queen, myself,
And so, I went unto her, where she sat,
Among her singing maidens, at the loom,
Weaving a silken web of Tyrian dye.
I laid the trinket at her feet, in silence:
And she arose, and set it in her hair,
Whose living lustre far outshone
The cold, dead metal I had fashioned,
As she stood before me, dreaming,
In her robe of flowing blue;
Then looked a moment on me with kind eyes.
And though she spoke no word,
I turned, and fled, in trembling,
Before the light that shivered through me,
And struck my soul with shuddering ecstasy:
And, still, through many days,
Although I did not look again
Upon those dreaming eyes,
Their visionary light
Within my soul, revealed eternity.

Thus, have the mortal years
Flowed onward to the perfect end —
This day of days,
That never night shall quench,
Nor darkness vanquish:
And, at dawn,
I die.

And yet, this morning, as I slowly climbed
The steep, ascending stages
That lead up to the hanging-gardens —
Where, tier on tier,
The great brick arches bore
Their April wealth of blossoms,
Plumed with palm and dusky cypress —
I little knew that I
Who came to carve a garland
Round a fountain's porphyry basin,

Should scale so soon the utmost peak of life.
Throughout the morn I toiled,
Until an hour ere noon —
For no one, save the King and Queen,
May walk in those high gardens, after midday —
When, underneath a cypress shade,
I paused, a moment, resting;
And looking down upon the basking city,
Beneath me slumbering deeply —
Garden on garden glowing, grove on grove,
Like some green fabric, shot with myriad hues,
And chequered with white clusters of flat roofs,
Aquiver in clear heat:
And then I gazed up through the aching azure,
At the restless kites that hover
Ever over Babylon:
And, as I watched one broad-winged bird that hung
Above the seven-coloured pyramid
Of Bel's great temple,
With wide pinions spread,
As though it kept eternal vigil over
The golden image in the golden shrine,
I thought of eagles poised
Above the peaks of glittering snows,
Beyond the Eastern plains.
Half-dreaming, thus, I lay,
Lulled by the tinkling waters,
Till, unawares, sleep slowly overcame me;
And noonday drifted by:
And still, I slept, unheeding:
And, in my sleep,
I looked on Beauty in a quiet place
Of forest gloom and immemorial dream:
When, something rousing me from slumber,
With waking eyes that yet seemed dream-enchanted,
I looked upon the Queen,
Where, in a secret close,
Set thickly round with screens of yew and ilex,
She stood upon the dark, broad brim
Of a wide granite basin, gazing down,
With dreaming eyes, into the glooming cool,
Unraimented, save of the flickering gleam,
Reflected from the lucent waters,
That flowed before her silently:

And slowly, from her feet,
The cold light rippled up her body, till,
Entangled in the meshes of her hair,
It flooded the calm rapture of her face:
When, dreaming still, she lifted up her eyes,
Unseeing; and I looked upon her soul,
Unveiled, in naked immortality,
Untrammelled by the trappings of brief time,
And cloaks of circumstance.
How long I looked upon the perfect beauty,
I cannot tell —
Each moment, flowing to eternity,
Bearing me further from time's narrow shores;
Though, yet, a little while,
From those unshadowed deeps time sought to hold me.

Suddenly, I felt
A ghostly arrow pierce my life;
And I leapt up, and turning,
I saw the King beside me,
With steely, glittering eyes
Shooting barbèd anger,
Though he coldly spake,
With evil, curling lips:
" Slave, thou art dead! "
And yet I did not quail:
But, looking 'twixt his brows,
I answered: and he blenched before my words:
" Nay!   I have seen:
" And am newborn, a King! "
And then his craven fingers
Went quaking to his wagging beard,
As if he felt my clutch upon his throat:
Yet, though, with one quick blow,
I might have hurled him down to death,
I never stirred:
And, eyeing me, he summoned
The negro-eunuchs, who kept watch below:
But I, ere they could spring up the first stage,
Went forth to meet them;
And they bound my wrists.

And so, down from the hills, my life has flowed,
Until, at fullest flood, it meets the sea.

With calm and unregretful heart, I wait
Till dawn shall loose the arrow from the bow.
I, who, with eager, faltering hand have sought
To fashion a little beauty, in the end,
Have looked on the perfect beauty, and I die —
Even as the priest, who, in the heart of night,
Trembling before the thunder-riven shrine,
Looks on the face of God, and perishes.
I die . . .
And yet, maybe, when earth lies heavily
Upon the time-o'ertoppled towers,
And tumbled walls, and broken gates of brass;
And the winds whisper one another:
"Where, Oh! where is Babylon?"
In the dim underworld of dreaming shades,
My soul shall seek out beauty
And look, once more,
Upon the unveiled vision . . .
And not die.

Night passes: and already in the court,
Amid the plash of fountains,
There sounds the pad of naked feet approaching.
With slow, deliberate pace,
As though they trod out all my perished years,
The Nubians come, to lead me out to death.
Slowly the great door opens;
And clearer comes the call of waters;
Cool airs are on my brow . . .
Lo! . . . in the East, the dawn.

1904.

STONEFOLDS

(1906)

The ragged heather-ridge is black
Against the sunset's frosty rose;
With rustling breath, down syke and slack,
The icy, eager north-wind blows.

It shivers through my hair, and flicks
The blood into my tingling cheek;
And with adventurous urging pricks
My spirit, that in drowsy reek

Of glowing peats had dreamt too long,
Crouched in the cosy ingle-nook,
Till life seemed vainer than the song
The kettle sings upon the crook —

Till life seemed vainer than the puff
Of steam that perished in hot air —
A fretful fume, a vapour stuff
Of gusty passion, cloudy care.

But as, once more, I watch the stars
Re-kindle in the glittering west,
Beyond the fell-top's naked scars,
Life rouses in me with new zest.

The immortal wakens in my blood
Beneath the wind's relentless thresh;
And universal life at flood
Breaks through the bonds of bone and flesh.

I scale the utmost peak of night,
The eternal breath upon my face;
Till, borne on plumes of singing light,
I lose myself in starry space.

STONEFOLDS

Persons:

Nicholas Thirlwall, *an old shepherd.*
Rachel Thirlwall, *his wife.*
Ruth Thirlwall, *his daughter.*
Ralph Moore, *a young shepherd, Nicholas' nephew.*

Scene: The living-room of Stonefolds, a shepherd's house on the
fells. A door opens on to the yard, another to the back of
the house. Nicholas, an infirm, old man, sits on the settle
by the peat-fire with his back to the outer door. His wife,
Rachel, moves about putting things away in a cupboard,
tending the fire, etc. A clock in the corner ticks loudly.
Storm rages without.

Nicholas. Is Ralph there?

Rachel.   Nay, he's gone back to the fold.

Nicholas. If only I might go with him! It's strange
The year's lambs should be born, and I not there.
The labouring ewes will miss my hand to-night;
Though Ralph's a careful fellow, he is young;
And six-and-fifty lambings have I seen.
It's hard, it's hard that I sit crippled here
When there's so much to do — so much to do!
That I, who should be tending the young lambs,
As helpless as a yeanling crouch and shake
Beside the peats, and shudder at the night.

Rachel. It's a wild night! See how beneath the door
The snow has silted. It's a perilous night
For young things to be born. Hark to the wind!

Nicholas. Ay, it's the lambing-storm.

Rachel.   I'll set a pan
Of milk upon the hob, for Ralph may bring
Some motherless lamb to tend before the fire.

Nicholas. It's hard, it's hard that all may help but me —

While I have seen so many young things born,
So many perish in my time. Worn out,
Useless and old, I sit before the fire
Warming my hands that once were never cold,
And now are never warm. I sit and shake
Like quaking-grass, and cannot even rise
To shift my seat, or turn my hand to aught,
When there's so much to do.

    [*A noise as of some one knocking the snow off his boots
    against the threshold.*]

                      What's that?

RACHEL.   It's Ralph.

    [*The door opens, and Ralph comes in, white with snow, carry-
    ing a lanthorn, and a new-born lamb wrapped in his
    plaid. He looks about him, as though expecting to see
    someone with* NICHOLAS *and* RACHEL; *then, with a
    sigh, he sets down the lanthorn on the table, and carries
    the lamb to the hearth, and lays it on the rug before the
    fire, while* RACHEL *fills a bottle with warm milk.*]

  RALPH.   The old lame ewe is dead. I've brought her lamb
To lie before the fire; but it is weak
And like to die.

    NICHOLAS.   Had I but tended her!

    RALPH.   The ewe was old.

    NICHOLAS.   Ay, ay, the ewe was old,
And so must die, and none pay any heed!
I, too, am old — I, too, am growing old.

    RALPH [*to* RACHEL, *who is kneeling by the lamb*].   You keep
    the yeanling warm till I come back,
I doubt that it can live; but I must go.

               [*Takes his lanthorn and goes out.*]

    RACHEL.   Ralph's a good lad and has a tender heart.

    NICHOLAS.   Ay, he's a careful fellow. He should wed.
At his age I'd been wed hard on a year.

    RACHEL.   But Ralph will never wed.

    NICHOLAS.   Why should he not?
He is a likely lad. Why should he not?

    RACHEL.   It's just a year to-night since Ruth left home.

    NICHOLAS.   Ruth! What of Ruth? The lass has made her
    bed,
And she must lie upon it now.

RACHEL. Poor Ruth!
Yet, Ralph will never wed.
NICHOLAS. How can you tell?
RACHEL. I watch him as he sits before the fire
Each night in his own corner, with still eyes
That gaze and gaze into the glowing peat
Until they burn as fiercely as the flame
On which they feed; and sometimes, suddenly,
His fingers grip the settle till it shakes;
And when I speak he heeds not, till the light
Has perished from his eyes, and, dull as ash,
They look upon the crumbling peats once more.
NICHOLAS. A woman's fancies! Ralph is not a boy
To peak and pine because a silly wench,
Who, if she'd had but wit, might be his wife,
Flits one fine night. O Ruth! to give up Ralph
For that young wastrel, Michael! Ralph must wed
The sooner if he broods. A wife and babes
Will leave him little time for idle brooding.
He's not the fool his father was.
RACHEL. Poor Ruth!
Yet, Ralph will never wed. At other times,
I see him sit and hearken all night long
As though he fretted for some well-known foot —
Listening with his whole body, like a hare —
Bolt-upright on the settle; every nerve
Astrain to catch the never-falling sound
Of home-returning steps. Only last night
I watched him till my heart was sore for him.
He seemed to listen with his very eyes,
That gleamed like some wild creature's.
                    [*The clock strikes.*] It's gone ten.
Come, Nicholas, I will help you to your bed.
NICHOLAS. Nay, nay! I'll not to bed to-night. Why, lass,
I have not gone to bed at lambing-time
Since I could hold a lanthorn! That must be
Nigh sixty years; and I'll not sleep to-night.
Though I be as much use asleep as waking
Since my legs failed me, yet I could not sleep.
I can but sit and think about the lambs
That in the fold are opening wondering eyes,
Poor new-born things!
RACHEL. This one lies very still.
I'll get more peats to heap upon the fire.

It's cold, maybe.   [*Goes through the inner door.*]
    NICHOLAS.   It's weak, and like to die.

> [*The outer door slowly opens, and* RUTH *enters, wearily, with
> hesitating steps.   She is dressed in a cloak, and is cov-
> ered with snow.   She pauses uncertainly in the middle
> of the room, and looks at her father, who, unaware of
> her presence, still sits gazing at the lamb, which opens
> its mouth as if to bleat, but makes no sound.*]

    NICHOLAS.   Poor, bleating beast!   We two are much alike,
At either end of life, though scarce an hour
You've been in this rough world, and I so long
That death already has me by the heels;
For neither of us can stir to help himself,
But both must bleat for others' aid.   This world
Is rough and bitter to the newly born,
But far more bitter to the nearly dead.
    RUTH [*softly*].   Father!
    NICHOLAS [*not hearing her, and still mumbling to himself*].
        I've seen so many young things born,
So many perish!

> [RACHEL *enters, and, seeing* RUTH, *drops the peats which
> she is carrying and folds her to her breast.*]

    RACHEL.   Ruth!   My child, my child!
    NICHOLAS [*still gazing into the fire*].   Why harp on Ruth?
        The lass has made her bed. . . .
    RUTH [*tottering towards him and kneeling on the rug by his
        side*].   Father!
    NICHOLAS.   What, is it Ruth?   [*Fondling her.*]
                                        My child, my child!
Why, you are cold; and you are white with snow!
You shiver, lass, like any new-born lamb.

> [RACHEL *meanwhile strips off* RUTH'S *cloak, and fills a cup
> with milk from the pan on the hob.*]

    RUTH.   I thought I never should win home.   The snow
Was all about me.   Even now my eyes
Are blinded by the whirling white that stung
My face like knotted cords, and in my ears
Rustled of death — of cold, white, swirling death.

I thought I never should win home again
With that wild night against me. How I fought!
I was so weary, I was fain at whiles
To strive no more against the cruel night,
And could have lain down gladly in a drift,
As in my bed, to die . . . had I not known . . .
Yet, knowing, I dared not. But I am dazed.
    RACHEL [*holding the cup to* RUTH'S *lips*]. Come, drink this
      milk. 'Twas heated for the lambs.
I little knew that for my own poor lamb
I set it on the hob an hour ago!
    RUTH [*seeing for the first time the lamb on the hearth*]. The
      lambs? I had forgotten — I am dazed.
This is the lambing-time; and Ralph . . .
                        and Ralph . . .
    NICHOLAS. Is in the fold, where I should be if I . . .
    RUTH [*bending over the lamb*]. Ah, what a night to come into
      the world!
Poor, motherless thing! and those poor, patient mothers!
I might have known it was the lambing-storm.

    [*She moans and almost falls, but* RACHEL *stays her in her
      arms.*]

    RACHEL. Child, you are ill!
    RUTH.   Yes, I am near my time.
    RACHEL [*raising her from the ground and supporting her*].
      Come, daughter, your own bed awaits you now,
And has awaited you these many nights.
Come, Ruth. [*They move slowly across the room.*]
    RUTH.   I thought I never should win home.
    NICHOLAS [*as they pass into the inner room*]. Yes, I have seen
      so many young things born,
So many perish! Rachel! They are gone;
And we're alone again, the lamb and I.
Poor beast, poor beast, has she forgotten you
Now that her own stray lamb is home again?
You lie so still and bleat no longer now.
It's only I bleat now. Maybe, you're dead,
And will not bleat again, or need to bleat,
Because you're spared by death from growing old;
And it can scarce be long till death's cold clutch
Shall stop my bleating too.

[*He sits gazing into the fire, and dozes. Time passes. The cry of a new-born babe is heard from the next room.*]

NICHOLAS [*mumbling, half asleep*]. Yes, I have seen
So many young things born, so many perish!

[*He dozes again. After a while* RACHEL *enters, carrying a baby wrapped in a blanket, which she lays on the rug before the fire.*]

RACHEL.   See, Nicholas! Wake up! It is Ruth's child.
NICHOLAS [*waking*].   Ruth's child! Why, Ruth is but a child
herself!
RACHEL.   Don't sleep again, for you must watch the babe
While I go back to Ruth again.   She lies
So still and cold; and knows naught of the child.
Unless she rouse, she cannot last till day.
                              [*Goes into the other room.*]
NICHOLAS.   So many young things perish; and I, so old,
Am left to sit all day with idle hands,
And can do naught to save them.

[*The knocking of snowy boots against the threshold is heard again.   The door opens, and* RALPH *enters with his lanthorn.*]

                              Is that Ralph?

[RALPH *goes towards the lamb, but, seeing the child, stands gazing in amazement.*]

RALPH.   Uncle, what babe is this?
NICHOLAS.   Lad, Ruth is home.
RALPH.   Ruth has come home! I knew that she would come.
She could not stay, though held so long from me,
For I have ever called her in my heart,
By day and night, through all the weary year.
I knew — I knew that she would come to-night
Through storm and peril, and within the fold
My heart has gone out to the labouring ewes,
And new-born lambs, and all weak, helpless things.
And yet I might have killed her! — though I sought
Only to draw her to my shielding breast.
She might have fallen by the way, and died,
On such a night! She shall not stray again.

The love that drew her from the perilous night
May never let her go.

[RACHEL, *entering, is about to speak, but seeing* RALPH, *pauses.*]

RALPH [*to* RACHEL]. Ruth has come home!
And we shall never let her go again.
RACHEL [*speaking slowly*]. Ay, Ruth is home.

[*Going to the hearth and taking the child in her arms.*]

You poor, poor, motherless babe!

[RALPH *gazes at her as though stunned, then bends over the lamb.*]

RALPH. It's dead. I must go back now to the fold.
I shall be there till morning.

[*He crosses to the door and goes out.*]

RACHEL [*calling after him*] Ralph! your plaid!

[*She follows to the door and opens it. The snow drifts into the room*].

RACHEL. He's gone without his lanthorn and his plaid.
God keep him safe on such a night! Poor Ralph!
Ruth's babe no longer breathes.

[*Laying the child by the dead lamb.*]

To-night has death
Shown pity to the motherless and weak,
And folded them in peace. How sweet they sleep!
NICHOLAS. We two have seen so many young things born,
So many perish; yet death takes us not.
Wife, bar the door; that wind blows through my bones.
It's a long night. [*Clock strikes.*]
What hour is that?
RACHEL.   It's one;
The night is over.
NICHOLAS.   Yet another day!

THE BRIDAL

Persons:

HUGH SHIELD, *a young shepherd.*
ESTHER SHIELD, *his bride.*
ANN SHIELD, *his mother.*

Scene: The living-room of Bleakridge, a lonely shepherd's cot-
tage on the fells. In one corner is a four-post bed on which
ANN SHIELD, an old, bed-ridden woman, lies sleeping, unseen
behind the closed curtains. On the table in the middle of the
room a meal is spread. The latch clicks, the door opens, and
HUGH SHIELD enters, glancing towards the bed, then turns
to hold open the door for ESTHER SHIELD, who follows him
into the room.

HUGH. Wife, welcome home!

> [*Embracing her, and leading her to a chair.*]

Come, rest, for you are tired.
ESTHER. No, I'm not weary. [*Looking towards bed.*]
Does your mother sleep?
HUGH [*crossing to bed and peering betwixt the curtains*]. Ay,
she sleeps sound, and we'll not waken her,
For she is ever fretful when she wakes.
It would not do to break the news . . .
ESTHER. The news!
Did she not know we were to wed to-day?
HUGH. She did not know I was to wed at all.
ESTHER. Hugh! Why did you not tell her?
HUGH. I don't know.
I would have told her when I spoke to you —
Just seven nights since — it seems so long ago! —
But when I breathed your name she put me off
Ere I had told my will. She's sorely failed,
And wanders in her speech. A chance word serves
To scare her like a shadow-startled ewe,

And send her old mind rambling through the past
Till I can scarce keep pace with her. Next morn
I spoke, and still she would not hear me out,
And yet she ever liked you, lass, and naught
She spoke against you; only her poor wits
Are like a flock of sheep without a herd;
And so she mumbled idle, driftless things;
Unless it were a mother's jealous fear
That made her cunning, and she sought to turn
My thoughts from you.   Old people aye dread change.
    ESTHER. You should have told her ere we wedded, Hugh.
    HUGH.   When I arose this morn, I went to her
To tell her, but she slept; and when I set
Her breakfast on the table by her bed,
I would have waked her, and stretched out my hand
To rouse her, and the words were on my lips;
And yet, I didn't touch her, spoke no word.
I was afraid to speak, I don't know why.
'Twas folly, lass, and yet I could not speak.
    ESTHER. You should have told her.
    HUGH.   Well, it doesn't matter;
For we are wedded, Esther. I'm no boy,
That I must ever ask my mother's leave
Ere I do aught. I left her sleeping still;
And when she waked, she'd think me with the sheep;
And sup her meal in peace; and little know
Into what fold I wandered, and with whom!
    ESTHER. You should have told her, Hugh. She will be wroth
To wake and find you wed. If you were frightened
To tell her then, how will you tell her now?
    HUGH. 'Twas not her wrath I feared. I scarce know why
I did not tell her; for I would have wed
Though she had bidden me " Nay " a thousand times.
Lass, do you think a word would hold me back,
Like a cowed collie, when I would be forth?
Not all the world could keep me from you, lass,
Once I had set my heart on you.   D'you think
I should have taken " Nay," lass, even from you!
    ESTHER. Ay, you are masterful; and had your way
To church ere scarce I knew it; and, yet, Hugh,
You had not had your way so easily
Had it not been my way as well!
    HUGH.   Ay, lass,
Naught could have held us from each other — naught,

And naught shall ever part us.

ESTHER [*glancing towards the bed*].   Hugh, she stirs.
Your voice has wakened her.

ANN [*from the bed*].   ·   Hugh, are you there?

HUGH [*going towards the bed*].   Ay, mother.

ANN.   Lad, what hour is it?

HUGH.   Nigh noon.

ANN.   I did not wake till you had gone this morn.
I must have slumbered soundly, though I slept
But little in the night.   I could not sleep.
I lay awake, and watched the dark hours pass;
They seemed to trail as slowly as the years
On which I brooded, and did naught but brood,
Though my eyes burned for slumber — those dark years
So long since passed!   I did not sleep till dawn;
And then I dreamt again of those dark years;
And in my dream they seemed to threaten you.
And when I waked the clock was striking nine,
And you were gone.   I must have slept again,
For you are here.   I did not hear the latch.

HUGH.   Mother, I spoke to you the other eve
Of Esther — but you did not heed . . .

ANN.   My dream!
Hugh, lad, I heard your words with fearful heart,
Yet, could not speak.   Son, you must never wed.

HUGH.   What say you, mother!   Am I yet a boy —
A pup to bring to heel with "must" and "shall"?
Mother, this cur's beyond your call!

ANN.   Nay, lad,
I don't bid you for bidding's sake; nor yet
Because I dread another mistress here.
Hugh, son, my mother's heart would have you wed;
Yet this same heart cries out to hinder you.
Believe me, for your happiness I speak.
You must not wed.

HUGH.   Hush, mother!   Don't speak now.

[*He motions to* ESTHER, *who comes forward to the bed*.]

ANN [*turning towards* ESTHER].   Is some one there?   You
        should have told me, Hugh.
Who is it, lad; for my old eyes are weak,
And the light dazzles them?   I know the face.
Is't Esther Ord?

HUGH. No, Esther Shield, my bride.
ANN [*after a pause*]. Then it's too late! Had I but spoken
    then,
Or held my tongue for ever!
HUGH. That were best.
Don't heed her, lass. She doesn't know what she says.
  ANN. Would that I didn't know, had never known!
O son, it's you who do not know. But now,
It is too late, too late. How could I think
That you would wed, and never breathe a word!
And yet, I might have known, I might have known!
You have your father's will.
HUGH. Ay, mother, words
Are naught to me but words: and all your words
Would never stay me when my heart was set.
If 'twas my father's way, I am his son.
  ANN. You are his son. Would, lad, that you were not!
HUGH. Mother!
  ANN. You're right, son, I will say no more.
I should have spoken then, or not at all.
It's now too late to speak.
  ESTHER. It's not too late.
HUGH [*slowly*]. Esther says truly. It's not yet too late.
You shall speak on now; it's too late to leave
Your thought unspoken, mother. You have said
Too much — too little to keep silence now.
The gate's unbarred; you cannot stay the flock.
  ANN. Have I not kept my counsel all these years?
Nay, I'll not speak now; it's too late, too late.

[*Turning to* ESTHER.]

Esther, my lass, I would you had not heard.
I wish you well, though you may doubt it now —
I wish you well with all my heart. Come nigh
That I may kiss you.
  ESTHER. It is not too late.
If you have any mercy in your heart,
Speak out your mind as though I were not here.
  HUGH. Ay, you shall speak out now.
  ANN. Then I shall speak.
Maybe it's not too late. I shall speak out
As I would one had spoken out to me
Upon my bridal-morn. If my words seem

Too fierce, too bitter, it's because they spring
From a fierce, bitter heart.   O Esther, lass,
'Twere better you should die than your young heart
Grow old and fierce and bitter — better far
That it should break, and you should die, than live
To grow old in black bitterness and wrath
As I have done.   I have not much life left,
But I would save you, lass, with my last breath,
If any word can fend off destiny.
And, Hugh, my son, though I speak bitter things
To your unhappiness, I only seek
To snatch you from disaster.   You have said
That words are weak: yet, I have nothing else.
You will not hate a poor, old woman, Hugh,
Because she snatches at a wisp of straw
To save the son who drowns before her eyes?
I must speak out the bitter, galling truth,
Though you should hate me, son, for evermore.

    HUGH.   Say on: I shall not hate you.   Speak out all
If it will ease you.

    ANN.   Naught can bring me ease
Save death, and death bides long.   Yet, I will speak.
You did not know your father, Hugh; he died
When you were in your cradle.   You have heard
How, on a hurdle, he was brought home dead
From Thirlwall Crags; for folk have told you this,
Though I have never breathed his name to you.
They wondered how he fell.   He did not fall.
And when I never spoke of him, they thought
That I was dumb with sorrow.   It was hate
That held me mute.   How should I mourn him dead
Whom I had hated living!   Don't speak, Hugh,
Till I have told you all.   Then you shall judge.
I scarce have breath to tell the tale; and yet,
'Twill soon be told; and if you hate me, son,
As I did hate your father, I fear not,
For I am too nigh death; and soon shall lie,
Unmindful of your hate as he of mine.
I could not hate you, son, although you bear
His name, and though his blood runs in your veins.
When first I knew him he was much like you —
As tall and broad and comely, and his eyes
The same fierce blue, his hair the same dull red.
Ay, you are like your father to your hands —

Your big, brown, cruel hands! You have his grip.
And he was just about your age; and lived
Here with his father, a fierce, silent man —
Mad Hugh the neighbours called him — whose wife died
Ere she could weary of her wedding-gown.
Folks said that fear had killed her. Yet, when Hugh,
Your father, wooed, I could not say him nay,
Though he was like his father. I was young,
And loved him for his very fierceness; proud
Because he was so big and strong; and yet,
I ever feared him; and, poor, trembling fool,
'Twas fear that drove me to him; and we wed
When old Hugh died. The day he brought me home —
Home to this self-same house, I shrank from him
Because I feared him, and he saw my fear.
I feared the passion in his wild, blue eyes,
And loathed his fiery love — so nigh to hate.
But I was his; and there was none to speak
As now I speak, or, on that very morn,
I should have left him. Ah, had I but known!
I was so young. A bitter year wore through,
And you were born, son: still I could not die,
Though fear was ever on me, and he knew
I feared him, and for that he hated me.
Have patience, lad; the tale is well-nigh told.
One day, when his hand touched me, I shrank back.
He saw, and sudden frenzy filled his eyes;
He clutched me by the throat with savage grip,
And flung me fiercely from him; and I fell
Against the hearthstone, and knew nothing more,
Till, coming to myself again, I found
That he was gone; and all the room was dark.
The night had fallen; and I heard you cry —
For you were in your cradle, Hugh — and rose,
Though all my body quivered with keen pain,
To suckle you. Next morn they brought him in,
Dead on a hurdle. When I swooned and fell,
They thought that grief had killed me; but, even then,
I could not die, and came to life again,
And wakened on this bed I have not left
So many years. The folk were good to me,
And as they tended you I heard them talk,
And wonder how your father came to fall;
Yet, I spoke naught of him, because I knew

He hadn't fallen; but headlong to death
Had leapt, afraid his hand had murdered me.
Ay, panic drove him. . . . You must hear me out.
Don't speak yet, lad. I have not much to say.
But you are all your father!

    HUGH.   I shall speak!
Say, mother, have I ever done you ill?

    ANN.   No, son, you ever have been good to me,
Because I knew you, and I did not fear you.
Yet, you are all your father. When a babe
I knew it, for your little fist would smite
The breast from which it fed in sudden wrath.
When you were barely weaned, a shepherd brought
A poor, wee, motherless lamb for you to tend;
And though you loved it with your hot, young heart,
And hugged it nigh to death; and, day or night,
Would not be parted from it; yet one morn,
When it shrank from your fierce caress, your hands
In sudden fury clutched its throat, and nigh
Had strangled it, ere it was snatched from you.
That day I vowed that you should never wed
If I might stay you. But I speak too late.
'Twere as much use to bid the unborn babe
Beware to breathe the bitter breath of life!

    HUGH. It is not yet too late. [*Turning to* ESTHER.]
                  Lass, you have heard.

    [*Going to the door and throwing it open.*]

The door is open; you are free to go.
Why do you tarry? Are you not afraid?
Go, ere I hate you. I'll not hinder you.
I would not have you bound to me by fear.
Don't fear to leave me; rather fear to bide
With me who am my father's very son.
Go, lass, while yet I love you!

    ESTHER [*closing the door*]. I shall bide.
I have heard all; and yet, I would not go,
Nor would I have a single word unsaid.
I loved you, husband; yet, I did not know you
Until your mother spoke. I know you now;
And I am not afraid.

    [*Taking off her hat, and moving towards the table.*]
           Come, take your seat.

THE SCAR

Persons:

ABEL FORSTER, *a shepherd.*
MARGARET FORSTER, *his wife.*

Scene: The Scar, a shepherd's cottage on the fells. ABEL FORS-
TER is seated with his back to the open door, gazing with un-
seeing eyes into a smouldering peat-fire, the dull glow from
which is the only light in the room. The pendulum of the
hanging-clock is silent and motionless, and the choral voice
of the moorland-burn and the intermittent hunting-cry of the
owl are the only sounds that break the frosty silence of the
night. Presently, a step is heard on the threshold, and MAR-
GARET FORSTER enters, wrapped in a shawl which covers the
bundle she is carrying in her arms. As she sinks wearily into
a chair by the door, ABEL looks up at her, uncertainly; then
fixes his eyes again on the fire, from which he does not raise
them while speaking.

ABEL. So, you are back!
MARGARET. Yes, I am back.
ABEL. I knew,
Sooner or later, you would come again.
I have expected you these many nights,
But thought to see you sooner, lass.
MARGARET. And yet,
You could not know: I did not know myself;
And even at the door I almost turned.
ABEL. Yet, you are here.
MARGARET. Yes, I am here to-night;
But where the dawn shall find me I don't know.
ABEL. You would not go again! Lass, do you think
My door shall ever stand ajar for you
To come and go when it may please your whim?
MARGARET. No; if I go again, I don't come back.
ABEL. You shall not go.
MARGARET. Ah! have you not learned aught

47

From the long months that taught so much to me?

ABEL. Ay, lass, I have learned something. Do not leave me.
You, too, have learned, you say; and have come home.
Why go again into the world to starve
While there is food and shelter for you here?
But you will bide. We shall forget the past.
Let us forgive each other. . . .

MARGARET.   I don't come
To crave forgiveness — nor would I forget.

ABEL. Why have you come then? Were you hunger-driven?
O lass, I hoped . . .

MARGARET.   No, I don't come to beg;
Nor would I starve while I have hands to work.
I lacked nor food nor shelter since I left.

ABEL. Then, why have you returned?

MARGARET.   I have come back
Because I am the mother of your son.

> [*She rises from her seat and throws back her shawl, reveal-*
> *ing a baby at her breast.*]

ABEL [*looking up*]. My son! Ah, Margaret! Now I under-
    stand.
To think I didn't know!

MARGARET.   The boy was born
A month ago.

ABEL.   Your babe has brought you home.
You will not go again. You have come back
Because you could not quite forget!

MARGARET.   I've come
Because the babe is yours. I would not keep
Your own from you; nor would I rob the child
Of home and father.

ABEL.   Had you no other thought?
Had you forgotten in so brief a while
How we had loved, lass?

MARGARET.   We knew naught of love.

ABEL. Did we not know love when we wedded?

MARGARET.   No!
It was not love, but passion wedded us;
And passion parted us as easily.

ABEL. Ay, passion parted us. Yet, surely, love
Brings us again together. We were young
And hasty, maybe, when we wed; but, lass,

I have awaited these seven weary months
For your return; and with the sheep by day,
Or brooding every night beside the hearth,
I have thought long on many things.   The months
Have brought me wisdom; and I love.   I knew
You would return; for you, too, have found love.
    MARGARET.   Is this your wisdom?   Little have you learned.
You are as hasty as the day we wed!
I, too, have brooded long on many things.
Maybe, my wisdom is no more than yours,
But only time will tell.   Who knows!   I've lived
And laboured in the city these long months;
And though I found friends even there, and folk
Were good to me; and, when the boy was born,
A neighbour tended me — yet, to my heart,
The city was a solitude; I lived
Alone in all that teeming throng of folk.
Yet, I was not afraid to be alone;
Nor, in my loneliness, did I regret
That we had parted; for the solitude
Revealed so much that else I had not learned
Of my own heart to me.   But, when, at length
I knew another life within me stirred,
My thoughts turned homewards to the hills; it seemed
So pitiful that a baby should be born
Amid that stifling squalor.   As I watched
The little children, starved and pinched and white,
Already old in evil ere their time,
Who swarmed in those foul alleys, and who played
In every gutter of the reeking courts,
I vowed no child of mine should draw its breath
In that dark city, by our waywardness
Robbed of the air and sun, ay, and the hills,
And the wide playground of the windy heath:
And yet, I lingered till the boy was born.
But, as he nestled at my breast, he drew
The angry pride from me; and, as I looked
Upon him I remembered you.   He brought
Me understanding; and his wide, blue eyes
Told me that he was yours; and, while he slept,
I often lay awake and thought of you;
And wondered what life held for this wee babe.
And sometimes in the night . . .
    ABEL.   Have you, too, known

The long night-watches? Since you went away,
Each morning, as I left the lonely house,
My heart said: surely she will come to-day;
And when each evening I returned from work,
I looked to meet you on the threshold; yet,
By night alone within the silent house
I longed for you the sorest. Through lone hours
My heart has listened for your step, until
I trembled at the noises of the night.
I am no craven, yet, the moor-owl's shriek
At midnight, or the barking of a fox,
Or even the drumming of the snipe ere dawn
Has set me quaking. Ay, night long, for you
The door was left ajar. And, hour by hour,
I've listened to the singing of the burn
Until I had each tinkling note by heart.
Though I have lived my life among the hills,
I never listened to a stream before.
Yet, little comfort all its melody
Could bring my heart; but now that you are back
It seems to sing you welcome to your home.
You have come home. You could not quite forget.

    MARGARET.   I have forgotten naught; and naught I rue:
Yet, when the weakness left me, I arose
To bring your babe to you.

    ABEL.   Naught but the babe?

    MARGARET.   Lad, shut the door; for I am cold; and fetch
Some peats to mend the fire; it's almost out.
You need a woman's hand to tend you, lad.
See, you have let the clock run down!

    ABEL.   My heart
Kept bitter count of all those lonely hours.
Margaret, your wisdom is no less than mine;
And mine is love, lass.

    MARGARET.   Only time will tell.

WINTER DAWN

Persons:

STEPHEN REED, *a shepherd.*
ELIZABETH REED, *Stephen's wife.*
MARY REED, *Stephen's mother.*

Scene: Callersteads, a lonely shepherd's cottage on the fells. A candle burns on the window-sill, though the light of dawn already glimmers through the snow-blinded panes. ELIZABETH REED paces the sanded floor with impatient step. MARY REED sits crouched on the settle over the peat-fire; ELIZABETH'S baby sleeping in a cradle by her side.

ELIZABETH.   The men are long away.
MARY.   Have patience, lass;
They'll soon be back; they've scarce been gone an hour.
It's toilsome travelling when the drifts are deep;
And William is no longer young.   Fear naught,
They'll bring back Stephen with them safe and sound.
    ELIZABETH.   You know he could not live through such a night.
    MARY.   Nay, none may know but God.   I only know
That I have heard my father many times
Tell over and over, as though it were some tale
He'd learned by heart — for he was innocent
And helpless as a babe for many years
Before death took him — how, when he was young,
A hundred sheep were buried in the drifts
Down Devil's Sike, yet not an ewe was lost,
Though five days passed ere they could be dug out;
And they had cropped the grass beneath their feet
Bare to the roots, and nibbled at their wool
To stay the pangs of hunger, when, at last,
The shepherds found them, nearly starved, poor beasts.
If the frost hold, sheep live for many days
Beneath a drift; the snow lies on them light,
So they can draw their breath, and keep them warm;
But when the thaw comes it is death to them,
For they are smothered 'neath the melting snow.

I've heard my father speak these very words
A thousand times; and I can see him now,
As, huddled in the ingle o'er the fire,
With crazy eyes and ever-groping hands,
He sat all day, and mumbled to himself.
If silly sheep can keep themselves alive
So many days and nights, a shepherd lad,
With all his wits to strive against the storm,
Would never perish in a day and night;
And Stephen is a man. . . .
  ELIZABETH.   If Stephen lived,
He would not bide from home a day and night;
He could not lose his way across the fell,
Unless the snow o'ercame him.
  MARY.   Yet, maybe,
He sheltered 'neath a dyke, and fell asleep;
And William and his man will find him there.
  ELIZABETH. Ay, they will find him sleeping sure enough,
But from that slumber who shall waken him?
  MARY. Nay, lass, you shall not speak so! Stephen lives,
The mother's heart within me tells me this:
That I shall look upon my son again
Before an hour has passed.
  ELIZABETH.   A wife's love knows
Its loss ere it be told; and in my heart
I know this night has taken him from me.
My husband's eyes shall never look again
In mine, nor his lips ever call me wife.
You cannot love him as I love him. . . .
  MARY.   Lass!
  ELIZABETH. Because he is your son, you love him, woman;
But I, for love of him, became his bride.
  MARY. Lass, don't speak so. Your son cries out to you.
Take him within your arms, and comfort him
Until his father comes.
  ELIZABETH.   Poor babe, poor babe!
Your father nevermore will look on you,
And hug you to his breast, and call you his.
Nay! shut your eyes!
   [To MARY.] O woman, take the boy!
I cannot bear to look into those eyes
So like his father's! Hark! did you hear aught?
  MARY. Some one is on the threshold. See who comes.
  ELIZABETH. No! No! I dare not. Give me back the child,

And open you the door.   Quick, woman, quick!
Surely strange fingers fumble at the latch!

> [*As she speaks, the door slowly opens, and* STEPHEN *enters
> wearily, with faltering step, and groping like a blind
> man.* ELIZABETH *runs to meet him, but he passes her
> unseeing, and walks towards the hearth.*]

ELIZABETH.   Stephen!   [*Shrinking as he passes her.*]   It is
   not he!
MARY.   My son!   My son!
STEPHEN [*speaking slowly and wearily*].   Ay, mother, are you
   there?   I cannot see you.
Why have you lit no candle?   Fetch a light.
This darkness hurts my eyes.   I scarce could find
The track across the fell.   Did you forget
To set the candle on the window-sill?
Or maybe 'twas the snow that hid the flame.
The master kept me late, because my task
Was but half-done; and, when I left the school,
The snow was deep, and blew into my eyes,
Pricking them like hot needles.   I was tired,
And hardly could win home, it was so dark;
Yet, that strange darkness burned my eyes like fire,
And dazzled them like flame, and still they burn.
But why do you sit lightless?   Fetch a light,
That I may see.   It must be very late.
I seemed to wander through an endless night;
And I am weary and would go to bed.
   MARY.   Son, sit you down.   The snow has blinded you.
You will see better soon.

> [*Handing him a pot from the hob.*]
      Come, drink this ale;
It's hot, and will put life in your cold limbs.
Your supper awaits you; you are very late.

> [*To* ELIZABETH.]

Lass, speak a word to him!
   ELIZABETH.   It is not he!
   MARY.   Ay, lass, it's he.   The snow's bewildered him;
He dreams he is a little lad again.
But speak you to him; he will know your voice.
Your word may call his wits again to him.
   ELIZABETH.   No!   No!   The night has taken him from me.
This is not he who went out yesterday,

My kiss upon his lips, to seek the sheep,
And bring them into shelter from the storm.
My husband's eyes shall never look in mine
Again, nor his lips ever call me wife.
This is not he!
    STEPHEN.   Why do you bring no light?
The darkness hurts my eyes. Do you not heed?
I never knew such darkness. It is strange,
I feel the glow, yet cannot see the peats.
    MARY.   Lass, speak a word!
    ELIZABETH.   Stephen! . . . He doesn't hear me.
    STEPHEN.   Whom do you speak with, mother? Is father back
Already from the mart? But I forget —
It must be late; 'twas dark ere I left school —
So strangely dark; it scorched my eyes like fire.
    MARY.   Son, don't you know Elizabeth?
    STEPHEN.   The lass
With big, brown eyes who sits by me at school?
Ay, ay, I know her well; but what of her?
    MARY.   Do you not know Elizabeth, your wife?
    STEPHEN.   Mother, I am too weary for your jest;
And my eyes hurt me. I would go to sleep.
Light me to bed. Why do you bring no light?
    MARY.   Ah, God, that he had slept to wake no more!
    ELIZABETH.   What say you, woman? Have you not your son?
It's I have lost my husband, and my babe
Is fatherless.
    MARY.   No, he may know the babe!
You take the boy and lay him in his lap.
Maybe his child will bring him to himself.
Son, do you not remember your poor babe?
    STEPHEN.   My baby brother, Philip? But he died
So long ago; what makes you speak of him?
Yes, I remember well the day he died,
And how the snow fell when they buried him.
The mare could scarce make headway through the drifts,
And plunged and stumbled, and the cart sank oft
Over the axle-tree; and when, at last,
We reached the church, the storm closed in again,
And happed the little coffin in white flakes,
Ere they had laid it in the grave. To-night
'Twas such a storm. I must have lost my way,
The night has seemed so long, and I am tired.
Mother, a light! The darkness hurts my eyes.

You do not heed.

MARY.   At least you know me, son!
God give you light, ay! even though it blind
Your eyes to me forever, so that you
May know your wife and child!

ELIZABETH.   My little babe!
He has forgotten us and does not love us.
The cruel night has taken him from us.
Don't cry, my son. He'll pay no heed to you.
Last night your father and my husband died.

STEPHEN. I am so weary, mother. Bring a light.

MARY. Son, take my hand. I'll lead you to your bed.
Maybe, a healing sleep will make you whole,
And bring your wandering spirit home again.

ELIZABETH. No, no! It's I must lead him! He is mine.
The night has taken my husband, but the dawn
Has brought him back, a helpless child, to me.
He fumbles in the darkness; yet, my love
Shall be a light to lead him to the end.
Come, Stephen, take my hand.

STEPHEN.   Elizabeth!
What are you doing from home on such a night?
You have a gentle touch; I'll come with you.
It seems the snow has blinded me; but you
Will lead me safely through this dazzling dark.
Come, lass, for I am weary, and would sleep.

MARY [*as* ELIZABETH *and* STEPHEN *pass out of the room*].
   Ay, you must lead him to the end. Though sleep
May heal his sight, it cannot heal his mind,
Or lift the deeper darkness from his soul.
My poor, old father lives again in him;
And he, my son, so young and hale, must tread
The twilight road to death. Ah God! Ah God!
Through me the curse has fallen on my son!
Yet, when the madness on my father fell,
He was a frail, old man, and nigher death;
And Stephen is so young and full of life.
Nay! Surely, it's the storm has stricken him!
Elizabeth, your poor heart spoke too true:
The bitter night has widowed you, your babe
Is fatherless, and you must lead my son
Through the bewildering dark. But yesterday
It seems I guided his first baby steps!
Ay, you must lead him; you are young and strong,

And I am old and feeble, and my hand
Would fail him ere he reached the journey's end.

[*The baby cries out, and* MARY *takes him in her arms.*]

Poor babe, poor babe!   A bleak dawn breaks for you!

[*A sound of footsteps on the threshold.*]

The seekers are returning.   William comes;
And I must tell him that his son is home.

THE FERRY

Persons:

JOHN TODD, *an old ferryman.*
ROBERT TODD, *his son.*
JANE TODD, *Robert's wife.*

Scene: The living-room of the ferry-house — a door opening on to the river-bank, another to the inner room. It is evening in early spring, and the ceaseless roar of the river in flood sounds through the room. JOHN, *seated at a cobbler's bench, works by candle-light.* JANE, *coming from the inner room, takes a chair to the fireside, and sits down with her knitting. The outer door opens, and* ROBERT *enters.*

ROBERT. The river's in full-spate.
JANE.   Ay, how it roars!
JOHN [*looking up from his work*]. The snow has melted on
    the fells.
JANE.   That wind
Will puff the candle out. Lad, shut the door.
JOHN. It's fresh, and smells of spring. 'Twas such a
    night. . . .
ROBERT. Wife, I'll away down to the Traveller's Rest.
JANE. Well, don't be late.
JOHN.   But what about the boat?
ROBERT. The boat is safe enough; I've made her fast.
JOHN. Ay, lad, but what if any one should hail,
And you not here to answer to their call?
I cannot take the oars; you know that well.
ROBERT. The devil himself could never cross to-night;
That water is too big.   [*Goes out.*]
JOHN.   'Twas such a night
That Margaret hailed, and did not hail in vain.
I did not fear the flood.
JANE.   You cannot hear
How loud it roars. Your ears are dull with age.
You could not cross to-night.

JOHN.   If Margaret called,
Old as I am, I'd take the oars my hands
Have touched not these long years.   If Margaret called —
But she will call no more.   *[Bends over his work.]*
  JANE.   You could not cross.
  JOHN.   I would that Robert had not gone to-night.
  JANE.   Why, he's a steady lad; there's little harm.
  JOHN.   Ay, lass; and yet, I wish he had not gone.
If any one should hail, and he not here!
  JANE.   No one will hail to-night.
  JOHN.   'Twas such a night
That Margaret hailed.
  JANE.   'Twas cruel madness then.
  JOHN.   She knew that I would come.
  JANE.   More shame to her
That she should call you to nigh-certain death!
  JOHN.   How can you speak of Robert's mother so!
She knew my arm was strong.   She came that night
Home from the city, after many years.
She stood upon the bank and called my name,
And I, above the roar of waters, heard,
And took the oars and crossed to her, though twice
The river caught me in its swirl, and strove
To sweep me to the dam.   But I was strong,
And reached the other bank; and in she stepped,
And never seemed to think of fear.   Her eyes
Were on me, and I rowed her home, though death
Clutched at the boat, and sought to drag us down;
For I was young and strong.   That May we wed;
And by the next spring-floods the boy was born,
And she lay dead — and I, so young and strong!
My strength that brought her through the roaring spate
Could not hold back that silent-ebbing life.

                         [Bends over his work.]

  JANE.   Yes, I have heard the story many times.

  *[Silence falls on the room save for the roar of the river.
   After a while, JOHN lifts his head as though listening.]*

  JOHN.   Hark!   What is that?
  JANE.   It's nothing but the flood.
  JOHN *[still listening]*.   She calls!

JANE.   Who calls?
JOHN.   Do you hear naught?
JANE.   Nay, naught.
There's naught to hear — only the river's roar.

[JOHN *bends again over his work, and is silent for a while;
but often lifts his head as though listening. At last he
speaks.*]

JOHN. Can you hear naught, lass? Some one hails the boat.
JANE. It's but your fancy. How could you hear aught
With your deaf ears, when I can scarcely catch
My needles' click — the river roars so loud!
JOHN. I heard a voice.
JANE.   I tell you it was naught.
No voice could cross that flood. If any called,
That roar would drown their cry. You could not hear.
But no one would be fool enough to call
On such a night as this.
JOHN.   I heard a voice.
I would that Robert had not gone to-night. . . .
JANE. What could he do if he were here?
JOHN.   I crossed
On such a night.
JANE.   Ay, ay, but Robert's wed.
JOHN [*starting up*]. Hark, hark, she calls! I hear the voice
     again.
JANE [*rising and laying a hand on his arm*]. Nay, father!
Sit thee down. There's no one calls.
Your memory tricks you. It's the river's roar
That rings in your old head, and mazes you.

[JOHN *sits down again at his bench.*]

It sounds as though it sought to drag the banks
Along with it — and all! You'd almost think
That it was round the house!

[*Goes to the door and opens it and looks out.*]

                         How fierce and black
Among the rocks it threshes 'neath the moon!
It makes me shudder though we're high and dry.

[*Closes the door.*]

JOHN. Did you see no one on the other bank?
JANE. No one was there to see. Who should there be?

[JOHN *bends again over his work; then stops, and sits gazing into the fire, still listening.*]

JOHN [*rising and speaking slowly*]. Lass, some one hails the
boat; and I must go,
For Robert is not here.
JANE [*rising too, and holding him by the arm as he turns to-
wards the door.*] You go! You go!
What would you do, you poor, old crazy man?
'Twould break you like a straw!
JOHN.   Yes, I am old;
But Robert is not here.
JANE.   If he were here
He could do naught. The flood would crush the boat
Like any eggshell!
JOHN.   Robert should be here.
Hark, hark, the voice again! Lass, I must go.

[*He tries to move towards the door, but* JANE *takes him by
the arms and forces him back into his seat.*]

JANE. You crazed, old man! Sit down. What would you
do?
You need not hurry to your death; fear not,
'Twill come ere you are ready! Sit you down.
You're feeble in my hands as any babe.
What could you do against that raging flood?
JOHN. Yes, I am weak, who once was young and strong.
But Robert should be here.
JANE.   I'll fetch him home.
If you'll sit quiet till I come again.

[JOHN *gazes silently into the fire, then closes his eyes as if
asleep.*]

JANE. He's quiet now; the silly fit has passed.
Yet, I will go for Robert. It were best
That he should come. I think I should go crazed
Betwixt the flood and his fond, doting talk.
I fear I don't know what. It's that old man
Has filled me with his fancies; but he sleeps

Sound as a babe. I'll go for Robert now,
And be back ere he wakes.

> [*Throws a shawl over her head, and goes out softly, closing
> the door behind her.* JOHN *sits for a while with his eyes
> still shut; then starts up suddenly, and stands listening.*]

JOHN. She calls! She calls!

> [*Moves to the door and throws it open.*]

I come! I come!

> [*Shading his eyes with his hand and gazing into the night.*]

She awaits me on the bank,
Beyond the raging waters, in the light.
Margaret, I come!

> [*He goes out, leaving the door open. The clank of a chain
> being unloosed is heard; then nothing save the thresh of
> the river. Some moments pass; then voices are heard on
> the threshold.*]

ROBERT [*outside*]. The door is open, lass.
You should not leave it so.
JANE [*entering*]. I shut it close.
Father! He is not here! He's gone!
ROBERT. Gone where?
JANE. Robert, the boat! the boat! [*They rush out together.*]
ROBERT [*his voice heard above the roar of the waters*]. The
boat's gone too!
Quick, to the dam!
JANE [*as they pass the door*]. He seemed to sleep so sound.

> [*The candle gutters out in the draught from the open door,
> and nothing is heard but the noise of the waters.*]

ON THE THRESHOLD

Persons:

PHILIP RIDLEY, *a young shepherd.*
ALICE RIDLEY, *his bride.*
ELLEN HALL, *an elderly woman.*

Scene: Cragshields, a cottage on the fells. Through a little win-
dow to one side of the hearth a far-off lough is seen, glitter-
ing in the April sunshine. Now and again, the call of the
curlew is heard. PHILIP RIDLEY *and his wife are seated at*
breakfast near the open door.

ALICE.   No more of love, lad!   We are wedded folk
With work to do, and little time enough
To earn our bread in; and must put away
Such lovers' folly.
　　PHILIP.　　　　　Can you say so, lass,
Hearing the curlew pipe down every slack!
Their mating-call runs rippling through my blood.
Hark, do you hear how shrill and sweet it is!
Does it stir naught in you?   You have no heart
If that can leave you cold which thrills me through
Till every vein's a-tingle.
　　ALICE.　　　　　　Shut the door,
And sup your porridge ere it cools.   You know
Even the curlew cannot live on love.
He's a wise bird, and soon will sober down.
He courts but in due season, and his voice
Keeps not the wooing note the whole year long.
So must we settle down, lad.   Do you think
Old William Hall and his goodwife who dwelt,
For sixty years, together in this house,
Before our coming, as the neighbours tell,
Lived like young lovers through so many years?
　　PHILIP.   But we've not mated, lass, as curlew mate;
Our love shall know no season.   I have heard
That William and his wife were hard and cold,

62

And seldom spoke save with a bitter tongue.

ALICE.   And yet, they dwelt beneath this very roof
Together sixty years — as we may dwell!
They must have wed as young as we, and come
Home to this hearth as full of foolish hope.
I shudder when I think of those long years.

PHILIP.   Don't think of them, for they are naught to you.

ALICE.   Had they no children, then?

PHILIP.   But one, a lass;
And she was led astray.   They cast her out,
And barred the door upon her one wild night;
And what became of her none ever knew.
The neighbours ne'er heard tell of her again.

ALICE.   I wonder if she lives, poor soul!   And yet,
I'd bar the door on any child of mine. . . .

PHILIP.   You wouldn't, Alice.   You don't know your heart.
We'll speak no more of them.   The past is past,
And throws no shadow on our lives; no ghost
Of old unhappiness shall haunt our home.
The years hold no such bitterness for us;
And naught shall come between us and our love.

ALICE.   Now you are at your foolish talk!   It's time
That you were with the sheep.   If you have naught
To turn your hand to, I have more to do
Than may be done ere bedtime.   Shift your seat
Till I have cleared the table, lad.

PHILIP.   No, lass,
I must away; but, ere I go, one kiss
To keep my heart up through the morning!

ALICE.   Go,
You foolish lad!   You're still a boy.

PHILIP.   Time mends
The folly that is youth — if it be folly
To live and love in happiness and hope;
For we are young but once; and, as you say,
We have full sixty years in which to grow
Wise, cold and crabbed, if we should live as long
As William and his wife.

          [*To his collie.*]   Down, Nelly, down!
I will be back ere noonday.

                    [*Goes out, closing the door behind him.*]

ALICE.   Sixty years!
It's a long while to dwell in bitterness.

I wonder if they ever loved as we
When they were young.   Maybe they did, until
Their daughter's trouble soured their hearts — and yet,
Surely, if they had loved! . . . Ah, well, the years
Must bring what they will bring, and we abide
The winter, though it freeze the springs of love.

> [*She turns to her work of scrubbing and sweeping. After a
> while, the door opens noiselessly; and* ELLEN HALL
> *stands on the threshold, unseen of* ALICE, *who is bend-
> ing over the hearth.*]

ELLEN [*gazing about her absently*].   The dresser stood against
the other wall.

> [*Seeing* ALICE, *who looks up suddenly in amazement.*]

Forgive me that I did not knock.   So long
I raised this latch a dozen times a day,
Undreaming that the hour would ever come
When I should need to knock, that, when, once more,
I stood upon the threshold, I forgot
The years that stood between me and my home,
And that I came a stranger to this house.
Forgive me. . . .
    ALICE.   Nay, come in, and take a seat.
We are newcomers to these parts. . . .
    ELLEN.   Had you
Been born and 'bred within a mile or so,
You would not know me, lass; for you are young;
And it is forty years since I left home.
But you shall know me ere I take a seat
Beneath your roof.   If you will ask me then. . . .
You start at that!   I see that you have heard
My tale already.   I am Ellen Hall,
The outcast whom the neighbours told you of.
But I must go.   Forgive me that I brought
My shadow in your house.   I meant no harm.
I only wished to see my home once more.
    ALICE.   Nay, nay, come in, and rest; for you are tired.
You must not go with neither bite nor sup.
I'll set the kettle on the bar. . . .
    ELLEN.   Nay, lass,
I will not eat nor drink, but I would rest

A little while, for my old feet have found
The fell-road long and heavy, though my heart
Grew young again, breathing the upland air.
Let me not hinder you: just do your work
As though I were not here.   I'll not bide long.

[After a pause.]

Lass, do you love your man?
    ALICE.   I wedded him.
    ELLEN.   Though your reproof be bitter, it is just;
But I have lived so long on bitter words
That I, long since, have lost the taste of them.
I did not speak the word in wantonness;
For as I look upon you where you stand
In your fresh bloom of youth, old memories stir
Within me; for your eyes are kind.   My heart
That has not spoken out so many years
A moment longed to tell its tale to you,
The tale it never told to any heart;
But it shall keep its silence to the end,
For you are proud and happy in your youth,
As I was proud and happy once.   Ay, lass,
Even I was young and comely in my time —
Though you may smile to hear it now, as then
I should have smiled. . . . Nay, lass, I do not blame you!
Forgive a lonely woman, frail and old,
Whom years and grief have brought to foolishness.
    ALICE.   Nay, nay, I didn't smile.   I'd hear your tale
If you would tell it me.   'Twill ease your heart
To pour its sorrow in another's ear.
But if you would keep silence, breathe no word.
Yet, bide till you are rested.
    ELLEN.   Thank you, lass.
A silence that has lasted forty years
May not be broken in a breathing space.
It isn't easy, speaking; yet, I'll speak
Because your eyes are kind, and nevermore
Shall look upon me when the tale is told.
I haven't much to tell, for you have heard
The neighbours' talk; and yet, lass, none may know
The heart's true story save the heart itself;
And they who speak, not knowing the full truth,
May twist on idle tongues unwittingly
What little of the truth is theirs.   You know

It was my sin, as folk account it sin,
To love beyond my station — ay, to love
Unquestioning, undoubting, unafraid —
To love with the fierce faith and simple might
And courage of a young girl's innocence.
In sweet, blind trustfulness and happy pride,
As many a maid has loved, nor lived to rue.
Yet, I don't blame him: he was passion's fool —
Ay, one of those from whom hard fate withholds
The wonder and the tenderness of love —
Though I believed he loved me as I loved,
And as I love him yet — ay, even yet!
Blindly I loved him — blinded by the light
Of my own love, my love that still. . . . But you,
Unless you love, you will not understand;
For only love brings knowledge. You have heard
How, when he left me, I was turned from home.
Abandoned in my trouble, I was thrust
On the cold mercy of a winter night.
This very door was barred against my woe —
I still can hear that bolt shot after me —
Although I never turned. Nay, speak no word!
I crave no pity; for I loved, and love
Brooks no compassion from a happier heart.
And I remember little of that night;
It scarcely seemed to matter when so much
Was gone from me that all should go. To me
My parents had been ever shrewd and harsh
As to each other. They had never known
The tenderness of love; for they had wed
In wanton passion which had left them cold,
To live for sixty years on bitter words;
For they were over eighty when both died,
As though they had been lovers, on one day.
Spare all the fresh young pity of your heart
For those whom chance has tethered without love
To tread together the same path of life
Till death release them.

  ALICE.   Did you ne'er return?
  ELLEN. Love's outcasts don't come back.
  ALICE.   Might not the years
Have softened their hard hearts? They would relent. . . .
  ELLEN. Time brings no understanding without love;
Love cannot spring from barrenness; the soil

That does not quicken to the breath of spring
Will bear no blade of green in winter days.
I pitied them; and, had my child but lived,
I had forgiven them with all my heart.
    ALICE.   Ah! they were cruel! but you, what could you do?
    ELLEN.   I lived — but not as idle tongues have lied.
I loved him, lass; and if your heart is true
To love, 'twill know that I speak truly. Yet,
What can the happy know of love! O lass,
You are too fresh and fair to have known love!
    ALICE.   Yet, I love Philip.
    ELLEN.   Nay, you cannot love!
They don't know love who have not starved for love,
And worked their fingers to the bone for love,
And lived for love, without love's recompense,
Death holding within easy reach the while
The escape and solace of forgetfulness.
Still, you may love — for, even unto me,
Love once was happiness. Forgive me, lass;
It is so long since I knew happiness.
You have not idle hands; but then you toil
For him you love and who loves you again,
While I have laboured only for my love
Of him who never loved me, and to whom
I was a broken trinket, cast aside,
Forgotten, for he wedded years ago.
Forgive me, if I weary you; so long
My heart has brooded in its solitude
On all these things, oft shaping them to words
For its own comfort — for even words give ease
To aching and intolerable thought —
Although it could not utter them aloud,
That, now they find a vent, they teem, a spate
Enough to drown your patience.
    ALICE.   Nay, speak on.
    ELLEN.   I have dwelt long in grey and narrow streets,
A stranger among strangers, where men snatch
A starveling living from each other's clutch;
Ay, I have toiled in cities where men grind
Their brothers' bones for bread, where life is naught
But labour and starvation to the end.
Lass, may your kind eyes never need to grow,
As mine have grown, accustomed to the sight
Of the evil and the wretchedness and want

That huddle in dark alleys; yet even there
Love shines, though cooped in stifling misery,
A candle in a garret.   To the poor,
Life is not easy underneath the sun,
But in the dark and reeking city ways
It's more relentless, grim and terrible —
The endless struggle.   Lass, I never thought
To look upon the hills of home again,
Or tread the ling, or breathe the living air
That I had breathed, a heedless child; but when
By chance I heard my parents both were gone
To where the shadow of a daughter's shame
Might never vex their slumber, my heart yearned
To gaze once more o'er the familiar fells
Where I had first found love.   So I set out,
Hoping to come and go ere the new herd
Should take possession.   As I crossed the crags,
I saw the smoke curl o'er the chimney-stack,
And knew I came too late.

ALICE.   Nay, not too late!
You have not come too late!

ELLEN.   I nigh turned back.
I had not meant to cross the threshold-stone;
But as I climbed the brae-top, and looked forth
Over the sweep of bent and heath, and breathed
The morning air, and gazed upon the loughs
A-shimmer in the sun, and heard the call
Of curlew down the slacks, and felt the spring
Of heather under-foot, I — who had thought
So little of these things when I had lived,
A careless lass, among them, but had come
To hanker after them in city streets —
Was filled with strange forgetfulness, and moved
As in a trance, scarce knowing what I did,
Till I had raised the latch, and saw your eyes
In wonder fixed on mine.   But I must go
Before your man comes in.

ALICE.   No, you must bide.
This is your home.   You must not go again
Back to the city.   You are old and weak;
And I and Philip are both young and strong
To work for you, if you will live with us.

ELLEN.   With all my heart I thank you, lass, and yet,
I may not bide.   Though I am old and weak,

I would tread out my pathway to the end.
It is too late, too late to turn aside;
Nor would I if I could, since I have fared
So far along the solitary way.
I could not rest at ease in idleness.
Yet, I shall go to take up work again
With kindlier memories of my home, and when
Once more the narrow alleys on me close,
I shall remember some one living here
Whom love has given understanding. Life
Be good to you — yes, I can wish you this,
Though you have all that life withheld from me.
I don't know what the future holds, and yet,
Whatever may befall you, this is sure:
You shall not know the utmost bitterness;
Life cannot be all barren, having love.
From the full knowledge of my heart I speak
As one who through the perilous night has come
To you, upon the threshold of your day,
The dawnlight on your brow. Lass, fare you well!
    ALICE.   Farewell! and yet, I grieve that you should go
Back to the struggle who have brought to me
The secret you have wrung from life.
                    [*Kissing her.*]   Farewell!
You have revealed to me my happiness.
    ELLEN.   Your kiss brings comfort, daughter.   Fare you well!

    [*She goes out, and* ALICE *stands in the doorway, gazing after
       her for a while. Presently a gate clashes hard by, and*
       PHILIP *approaches.*]

    PHILIP.   What do you look on, lass — so rare a light
Burns in your deep, brown eyes! What do you see?
Have you been listening to the curlew's call?
    ALICE.   No: I have heard a voice from out the past;
And my eyes look down all the happy years
That you and I must travel, side by side.

1906.

DAILY BREAD

(1908–1909)

All life moving to one measure —
Daily bread, daily bread —
Bread of life, and bread of labour,
Bread of bitterness and sorrow,
Hand-to-mouth, and no to-morrow,
Dearth for housemate, death for neighbour . . .

" Yet, when all the babes are fed,
Love, are there not crumbs to treasure? "

TO

JANE HAY

SAINT ABB'S HAVEN,
1908.

As one, at midnight, wakened by the call
Of golden-plovers in their seaward flight,
Who lies and listens, as the clear notes fall
Through tingling quiet of the frosty night —
Who lies and listens, till the wild notes fail;
And then, in fancy, following the flock
Fares over slumbering hill and dreaming dale,
Until he hears the surf on reef and rock
Break, thundering; and all sense of self is drowned
Within the mightier music of the deep,
And he no more recalls the piping sound
That startled him from dull, undreaming sleep:
So I, first waking from oblivion, heard,
With heart that kindled to the call of song,
The voice of young life, fluting like a bird,
And echoed that wild piping; till, ere long,
Lured onward by that happy, singing-flight,
I caught the stormy summons of the sea,
And dared the restless deeps that, day and night,
Surge with the life-song of humanity.

DAILY BREAD

THE HOUSE OF CANDLES

Scene: GRISEL STARK'S *cottage.* GRISEL STARK *lies unconscious on the bed. Two neighbours,* BARBARA WILSON *and*
REBECCA WOOD, *stand watching her, and whispering together.*

BARBARA.   The house was dark;
And so I knew, at once,
That something was amiss.
  REBECCA.   The house was dark?
  BARBARA.   No blink of light
The window showed —
The window that had blazed, each night, for years.
I stood a moment, wondering, at my door;
And then I crossed the roadway,
And listened on the threshold,
Before I dared to knock;
Though what I feared
I could not tell.
It seemed so strange
To find the house in darkness —
No candles in the window,
And not a glimmer 'neath the door.
And when with quaking heart
At last I knocked
And no one answered me,
I raised the latch
And entered.
The room was dark and silent —
So silent that I felt
As though I'd stumbled suddenly
Into the house of death.
The fire was out,
And not a candle lit;

75

And you know how the candles blazed,
Night-long, these many years.
   REBECCA. She must have burned a fortune out in candles.
   BARBARA. And when, at last,
I'd fumbled for the matches,
And struck a light,
It only served to show
The candlesticks burnt empty;
And naught I saw of Grisel,
Before it flickered out,
Although I felt her in the room,
And feared lest I should touch her
In the dark.
And so I ran to fetch my lamp,
And, in its friendly light,
I looked about me with a braver heart
And quickly found her
Stretched before the hearth.
At first I thought her dead,
And shrank from her;
For she was ever cold and proud with all,
And I had never touched her hand before.
And, as I looked on that lean hand outstretched,
I wondered if that hand
Had done the thing —
The thing that gossip told of it,
When first she came to Morton.
It frightened me;
And, as I watched,
I seemed to see the fingers crooking
To clutch a baby's throat;
And yet I could not draw my eyes from them,
Until I realised
That only in my fancy they had stirred.
For still the hand lay, limp and white;
And soon I was myself again,
And pity drove out fear;
And bending down to lift that fallen head
I found that still she breathed.
I loosed her bodice;
Then I fetched my man;
And we together lifted her,
And laid her on the bed —
It took us all our time;

For, though she is so slight,
She was a dead-weight in our hands,
As though we lifted more than one weak body —
As if some dreadful burden bore her down.

REBECCA. God knows what sins are on her!
How dared you touch her, neighbour?
'Twas madness, surely.

BARBARA. I could not leave her lying helpless.
And, maybe, she is innocent.
We know that babes die often,
Though only God knows why.
My firstborn, Robert, died. . . .

REBECCA. The innocent are not afraid of darkness,
Nor waste a heifer's price
On candles in a twelvemonth.

BARBARA. She never stirred,
When we had laid her on the bed;
And nothing I could do would rouse her.
I sent my man to fetch the doctor;
But he can scarcely come
Ere daybreak, even if my man
Should chance to find him in.
'Twere dreadful, should she die,
Before the doctor comes.

REBECCA. If she's to die, she'll die
Whether he comes or not.
It's strange that such as she
Should have an easy end.

BARBARA. O neighbour, you are hard!
What would you have?

REBECCA. A murderer. . . .

BARBARA. Nay, you shall not in this house!
Nothing was known.

REBECCA. But you yourself have said,
These many times. . . .
I heard it from your lips.

BARBARA. Perhaps we have all wronged her.
May she not be as innocent
Of her poor baby's death,
As it. . . .

REBECCA. As it! How can you tell
That even it was innocent?

BARBARA. The babe!

REBECCA. A bastard brat,

You may be sure!
Else, where is her goodman?
A woman's not worth much
Who comes, alone, from God knows where,
To a strange village, and sets up a house,
Where she, within a month, is brought to bed;
And cannot name the father of her child.

    BARBARA.   Cannot?   How do you know?
Has she told aught to you?

    REBECCA.   To me!
Nay, not a word;
For she was ever close.
But you know well enough,
No man was ever seen to cross her threshold,
By day at all events.
God knows what moths her candles singed!
Had she been all she should be,
What need for secrecy?
Her silence proves her guilt;
And her dead brat. . . .

    BARBARA.   A babe is still a babe,
Whoever be its father.

    REBECCA.   Ay . . . and yet
She hadn't too much love for it,
To throttle . . .

    BARBARA.   Nay, you shall not, neighbour, here!

    REBECCA.   Why not?
It's common knowledge.
You know, as well as I do,
How all the village whispered,
When it died,
That she had strangled it.

    BARBARA.   Still, naught was known.

    REBECCA.   Why, I have heard you speak the thing
Right out with your own lips,
In Farmer Thompson's field,
And Grisel hoeing not ten yards away!

    BARBARA.   But I was young and thoughtless,
And I've borne children of my own
Since then . . .
And seen my firstborn die.
Oh, when we're young, we're hard of heart,
Till we ourselves have felt
A baby's fingers clutching at the breast.

REBECCA. Ah, who is hard and cruel now?
You twit me that I'm barren,
And yet, I thank the Lord
That I'm not such as she
Whom you befriend.
Although I brought my man no child,
At least I bore no nameless children.

BARBARA. Forgive my heedless words!
You will not, neighbour?
It's ever careless words that hurt past healing.
The thought of me
Will rankle in your heart,
Because my heart,
That bears no grudge against you,
Let slip an idle word,
Beyond recall.
But you,
Though you have been denied so much,
Have been spared something, too;
You have not stood
Beside your firstborn's grave.

REBECCA. Your patient stirs.
You'd better keep your tenderness for her,
And not waste words on me.
You know the saying:
" Least said, is soonest mended."

[She turns, as if to go.]

BARBARA. Ay, she wakens.
But you're not going now?

REBECCA. Why should I stay?

BARBARA. You would not go and leave me,
Alone with her?
If she should die!

REBECCA. If she's to die, she'll die.
Fear not, she's not the sort
To go before her time.

BARBARA. I dare not bide alone.

REBECCA. You dare not — you!
Oh, the brave mothers!
Must the barren wife
Lose her night's rest
To tend two shiftless mothers?
For she,
The helpless wanton on the bed,

And you,
Who stand a-tremble by her side,
Are mothers both;
While I —
I'm but a barren woman,
Hard of heart.
    BARBARA.   I never said so, neighbour.
But go,
I do not need you.
I, who have brought to birth,
Can look on death alone, if need be.
I fear no longer.
Shut the door behind you.
    REBECCA.   Nay, but I'll stay.
    BARBARA.   Bide if you will,
But don't come nigh the bed.
    REBECCA.   Don't fear,
I would not soil my hands.
    BARBARA.   Your heart is soiled past cleansing.
But it's no time for words.
She'll die while we are wrangling.
She tries to speak.

    [GRISEL STARK *raises herself on the bed and looks about her.*]

    GRISEL.   Oh!
The great light!
    BARBARA.   The light?
It's but my lamp.
It hurts your eyes . . .
    GRISEL.   Nay, do not move it.
It's not the lamp I mean.
The light is in my heart.
The candles all are quenched;
Yet I fear nothing now.
But where am I?
    BARBARA.   You're on your bed,
In your own house.
    GRISEL.   But you —
How do you come here —
You and your lamp?
I never heard the latch.
    BARBARA.   Nay, you've been ill.
I saw the house in darkness;

And feared that something was amiss.
And so I entered,
To find you stretched, unconscious, by your hearth.
   GRISEL.   I must have fallen then.
Yes, I've been ill for years;
But I am better now,
And I shall ail no more.
You say the house was dark;
Yet it was full of light —
The light within my heart —
The light that quenched the candles and my fears.
I, who have dwelt in darkness,
Know the light,
As you can never know it.
Since he died,
My little babe,
So many years ago,
My heart has dwelt in darkness.
And though fear ever kindled
Pale candles to dispel the night,
But little they availed;
Nor even noon could drive away
That darkness from my heart —
My heart so choked with bitterness.
Since my babe died . . .
Nay, neighbour, don't shrink back!
These hands have never done a baby hurt.
I know what's in your mind;
I heard those dreadful whisperings,
In years gone by;
Though then I answered nothing.
But, oh! if you have felt
A newborn baby, cold against the breast,
You'll know I speak the truth.
   BARBARA.   I know.
   GRISEL.   Still . . . you were right to shrink:
Although my hands are clean.
I killed the babe —
I killed it, in my heart,
Ere it was born.
I poisoned it with hate —
My hate of him who had forsaken me.
Why don't you shrink from me,
Now all is told?

Your eyes are kind;
And I can talk with you
As I have talked with no one.
But, who's that —
There, in the shadow . . .
Though it matters little;
For I would have the whole world see
The light that floods my heart.
When first I left my home,
To hide my shame from friendly eyes,
And came into this countryside,
And thought to bear the pang
And burden of my misery
More easily, 'mid strangers,
My heart was black against . . .
But, even now,
Why should I name that name,
Which once was all-in-all to me!
And, that dark month
Before his child was born,
I brooded on my wrongs;
And nursed hate in my bosom,
Until there was no room
For any other care within my heart.
Ah, shut your ears,
If you would hear no more!
For I must tell out all.
Your brow is smooth:
I think you could not hate:
And few have known such hate as mine.
His child,
Within my womb,
Because it was his child —
Ay, even it,
My hatred would not spare,
But ever prayed
That it might never look upon the light,
Nor draw a mortal breath;
Though I myself must perish
To keep the life from it.
My time came;
And I went through all, alone.
Nay, spare your pity, neighbour!
'Twas my will.

I kept you all at bay,
To serve my evil ends.
And little I remember of those days,
Save as a dream of anguish,
Until the morn I woke
To feel a lifeless baby at my breast —
Whose eyes had never looked upon the light —
Whose lips had never drawn a mortal breath —
And knew my prayer was answered,
Though I lived;
For death had passed me by,
And left me to my punishment —
To live . . .
Knowing myself a murderer in my heart,
Although my hands were clean.
And, since that hour,
The babe has haunted me!
And I have never dared
To be alone with darkness,
A moment, lest those eyes,
Which I denied the light of heaven,
Should burn out from the dark on me.
I strove to keep the night at bay
With flickering candles,
But, in vain,
Because my own breast still was dark.
The night was in my heart,
My stubborn heart,
That could not yet forgive.
But, when I came from work to-day,
  was so spent,
  scarce could lift the latch,
Or cross the threshold-stone;
And could not eat nor sup;
  ust having strength to light my candles,
Before I fell asleep,
Beside the hearth.
How long I slept,
  cannot tell.
  wakened with a start,
To find the room in darkness —
The candles all burnt out.
And I was frightened;
For it was long since I had looked

On utter night;
And now,
I seemed to look in my own heart.
I feared to breathe;
And then for the first time
Since I had been forsaken,
The thought of him came to me,
Without a breath of hate;
And pity stole like light into my heart;
And, in a flash,
The room was filled with light.
And, as I wondered whence
The sudden glory sprang,
My little babe
Before me, laughing, stood,
With arms outstretched,
And happy, kindling eyes —
His little body filled with living light.
And, as I stooped . . .
To snatch him to my breast,
I fell . . .
And knew no more . . .
Till, in the night,
I saw you, standing by the bed.
But, nay!
There is no night,
Since I have cast out fear;
And I shall dread the darkness nevermore.
But . . . I am weary . . .
And would sleep . . .
You need not watch with me;
For I fear nothing now . . .
I who have come through midnight . . .
And look . . . upon . . . the dawn.
The light . . . the light! . . .
My babe . . . my newborn babe!

[*She sinks back exhausted, moaning.*

BARBARA.   She cannot last long now;
The end is nigh.
I fear he'll be too late.
    REBECCA.   Too late?

What could he do if he were here?
She's far beyond the need of doctors.

[*A noise of wheels is heard without; the door opens, and the breath of morning sweeps through the room.*]

ON THE ROAD

REUBEN APPLEBY.
JESSIE APPLEBY, *his wife.*
PETER NIXON, *a stonebreaker.*

REUBEN APPLEBY *and his wife sit under a hedge by the highway.*
  REUBEN *is eating bread and cheese, while* JESSIE *is feeding*
  her baby with milk out of a bottle.

  REUBEN. " Married! " he says,
And looks at me quite sharply —
" A boy like you! "
And civilly I answered:
" Not such a boy, sir;
I am nineteen, past."
" Nineteen! " says he, and laughs;
" And you a husband, with a wife to keep —
A wife and family, I suppose."
" We have a baby, sir."
" A baby! and you're just a child yourself!
What right have you to marry,
And bring into the world
A tribe of helpless children
To starve, and beg, and steal? "
With that he took his children by the hand,
And walked away.
I could have flung his money after him,
But I had laboured for it
And was hungry,
And knew that you were famished;
And the boy must have his milk.
What right! —
I could have flung . . .
  JESSIE.   Then, you had flung away
Your baby's life!
  REUBEN.   Ay, lass, that stopt me,

And the thought of you;
And so, I took the sixpence,
And bought the bread and cheese and milk.
  JESSIE. You brought it just in time.
He'd cried himself to sleep;
But in my arms he lay so still and white,
That I was frightened.
  REUBEN. You were famished, lass.
  JESSIE. Yes; I was done.
I scarce could hold him,
Though he's light —
So thin and light.
But, when I laid him down, he cried so,
I could not bear . . .
  REUBEN. Well, he looks happy now.
He's drinking like a fish.
The milk will make him fat again.
But you eat nothing, Jessie.
  JESSIE. I cannot eat.
  REUBEN. You cannot?
  JESSIE. Not just now.
  REUBEN. Jessie, you must;
You'll die of hunger.
  JESSIE. I'm not hungry now;
But only weary.
After, perhaps . . .
  REUBEN. What right had I to marry!
What right had he —
He, with his wife and children,
To speak to me like that?
I could have flung . . .
  JESSIE. Nay, lad; don't vex yourself
With thought of such as he.
How can it matter what he said to you,
Now that it's over,
And the boy is fed?
  REUBEN. His money bought the milk —
Ay, and the bread and cheese.
  JESSIE. And do they not taste sweet?
You seem to relish them.
  REUBEN. They're well enough.
But, would not any food taste sweet,
After starvation?
And I'd worked for it.

JESSIE. How could it be his money,
If you'd earned it?
REUBEN. True, lass.
Still, you eat nothing.
JESSIE. I cannot eat.
REUBEN. It's ill work tramping all the livelong day,
With naught but hunger in the belly,
As we did yesterday;
And then, at night,
To shelter 'neath a stack;
And lie, and think —
Too cold and tired to sleep —
To lie, and think,
And wonder if to-morrow
Would bring us bite and sup;
Envying the very beasts that they could feed
Upon the hay that bedded us.
And still, 'twas good to rest
From tramping the hard road.
But, you were plucky, lass;
And trudged so bravely.
JESSIE. Yet I could have dropped,
Had I not hoped to get him milk ere night.
REUBEN. Poor babe!
He cried all day.
My sleeve was wet with tears.
JESSIE. 'Twas a hard road, and long.
REUBEN. The road is hard and long the poor must travel.
JESSIE. Ay, and the end?
REUBEN. The end?
Where the end lies, who knows?

[*A pause.*]

Wife, he spake truly;
I'd no right to marry —
No right to wed, and bring into the world . . .
JESSIE. What's that you say?
You're wearied of me, husband?
REUBEN. Nay, wife, you know . . .
Still, he spake truly.
I never thought of it like this before;
I never should have thought of it at all,
Had he not spoken;

I'd not wits enough.
But now, I see;
I had no right to marry,
And bring into the world
A baby . . .
   JESSIE.   Don't you love your son?
   REUBEN.   Love him!
I wouldn't see him starve.
I had no right . . .
Yet, when we married,
Things looked so different, Jessie.
I earned my weekly wage,
Enough to live on,
And to keep a wife on;
And we were happy in our home,
Together, weren't we, wife?
   JESSIE.   Ay, we were happy, Reuben.
   REUBEN.   And then, the baby came,
And we were happier still;
For, how could we foresee
Bad times would follow,
And work be slack;
And all the mills be stopt;
And we be bundled out of house and home,
With naught to do
But take the road,
And look for work elsewhere?
It's a long looking . . .
Nay, but he spake truly . . .
I had no right . . .
   JESSIE.   Nay, Reuben, you talk foolishness;
Your head is light with fasting.
An empty belly makes an empty head.
Leave idle talking to the rich;
A poor man can't afford it.
And I've no patience with such folly.
   REUBEN.   Nay, it's not folly, lass,
But truth, the bitter truth.
Is it not true, we're on the road,
I, and my starving wife and babe?
   JESSIE.   Nay, husband; see!
He's drunk the milk;
And sleeps so sweetly.
   REUBEN.   But you're ill.

JESSIE.　Ill?
Nay, I'm well enough.
　　REUBEN.　Yet you're too ill to eat.
　　JESSIE.　Nay, I was only tired.
But I'll eat now, lad,
If you've left me aught!
See how it goes!
　　REUBEN.　I had no right . . .
　　JESSIE.　Not if you did not love me!
　　REUBEN.　You know . . .
　　JESSIE.　How can I tell?
You talk so strangely;
And say that you'd no right to wed me . . .
Why did you wed me, then?
　　REUBEN.　Because I couldn't help . . .
I could not do without you.
I did not think . . .
How could I think, when I was mad for you?
　　JESSIE.　And yet you had no right?
　　REUBEN.　Right!　What thought I of right?
I only thought of you, lass.
Nay, but I did not think . . .
I only felt,
And knew I needs must have you.
　　JESSIE.　You loved me . . .
Then, was love not right enough?
Why talk of right?
Or, have you wearied of us —
Your wife and son?
Poor babe!
He doesn't love us any longer.
　　REUBEN.　Nay, wife, you know . . .

　　　[PETER NIXON, *an elderly man, gaunt and bent with labour,*
　　　comes slowly down the road, with his stonebreaker's ham-
　　　mer on his shoulder.　He glances at REUBEN *and* JESSIE,
　　　in passing; hesitates, then turns, and comes towards
　　　them.]

　　PETER.　Fine morning, mate and mistress!
Might you be looking for a job, my lad?
Well . . . there's a heap of stones to break, down yonder.
I was just on my way . . .
But I am old:

And, maybe, a bit idle;
And you look young,
And not afraid of work,
Or I'm an ill judge of a workman's hands.
And when the job's done, lad,
There'll be a shilling.
And there's worse work than breaking stones for bread.
And I'll just have a nap,
While you are busy,
And, maybe, sleep away the afternoon,
Like the old, idle rascal that I am.
Nay, but there's naught to thank me for.
I'm old;
And I've no wife and children,
And so, don't need the shilling.
But you are young;
And you must work for it,
While I sit by and watch you
And keep you at it.
I like to watch folk working,
For I am old and idle.
Perhaps I'll sleep a bit, with one eye open;
And when you think I'm nodding,
I'll come down on you like a load of metal.
Don't fear!
I'll make you earn it;
You'll have to sweat,
Before that shilling's yours;
Unless you're proud —
Too proud to work . . .
Nay?
Well, the heap's down yonder —
There, at the turning.
Ah, the bonnie babe!
We had no children, mistress.
And what can any old man do with shillings,
With no one but himself to spend them on —
An idle, good-for-nothing, lone old man?

[*He leads them to the turning of the road.*]

THE BETROTHED

Persons:

DEBORAH GREY, *Edward Grey's mother.*
FRANCES HALL, *betrothed to Edward Grey.*

*Scene: A fishing village, on the return of the Boats from the sea-
son's fishing in foreign waters.* DEBORAH GREY'S *cottage.*
DEBORAH GREY, *an infirm, middle-aged woman, sits by the
hearth.* FRANCES HALL *enters, and sits down with her knitting.*

DEBORAH.   Why, Frances, you're not gone
To watch the Boats come in?
When I was but a wench,
With lad aboard a homing boat,
I could not rest, nor work,
For days and days before,
But spent my whole time on the quay,
To catch the first glimpse of his sail;
And little recked, although my mother chided.
But you . . .
    FRANCES.   The Boats are not in sight yet.
    DEBORAH.   They're due to-day, lass, surely?
And, if you tarry here,
You'll miss the first sight of the sails,
That brings such sweet relief
Unto the anxious heart.
How often have I stared
Upon the far horizon,
Until it seemed his sail
Would never sweep in sight;
And, in the end,
I looked in vain.
    FRANCES.   In vain!
I, too, shall look in vain.
    DEBORAH.   Why, Frances, lass,
What ails you?
Is this a brave girl's heart?

Though, in the end,
I looked in vain,
Good hope was ever in my breast,
Until I knew.
A woman who gives way to foolish fears
May bring about the thing she dreads.
O lass, cast out that thought,
Lest it should bring his boat in peril!
He will return.
Tell that unto your heart,
Till it believes.
Your doubt may breed disaster.
But, away!
You should be with the other women-folk,
As I would be,
If I could crawl as far.
Your eager eyes
Should welcome the first speck that swims in sight,
And know it for his sail.

FRANCES. Nay, I would stay with you.
We soon shall hear
When any boat's in sight.

DEBORAH. One scarce would think you had a lover, Frances.
In my young days,
No girl could keep indoors,
Knowing the Boats were due.
Yet, here you sit
So calmly, knitting.

FRANCES. If I don't knit,
What can I do?

DEBORAH. What can . . .

FRANCES. I only knit,
Because I dare not think.

DEBORAH. You dare not think?

FRANCES. But you . . .
You have no mercy . . .
Nay, forgive me!
I did not mean to hurt . . .
And yet,
If you had only let me knit in peace.

DEBORAH. In peace?

FRANCES. And now,
I cannot even knit.
Why should I knit for him?

DEBORAH. For Edward?

FRANCES. Yes, for him.
Why should I,
Knowing that I knit in vain?

DEBORAH. What ails you, lass?
Do you not love my son?

FRANCE. Do I not love him?
Love him . . . woman . . . love!
Why, you know naught of love
To question this!
Have you no eyes, no heart?
Ah, God!
I thought the dullest would have seen . . .
And you, his mother . . .
And you once were young!
But you are young no longer.
You look on Edward as a child.
Still, you were young once,
And have loved, you say . . .

DEBORAH. Yes, lass, I loved.
God knows, none ever was more true to love . . .

FRANCES. Then you should know the terror and despair.

DEBORAH. At your age, Frances, love, to me,
Was naught but happiness and hope.

FRANCES. You have not loved!

DEBORAH. Yes, I have loved!
I, too, have known the terror and despair;
But never looked to meet it ere its time.
I doubted naught,
Until disaster fell.
I did not go half-way to meet disaster.

FRANCES. And yet, disaster came?

DEBORAH. Disaster came . . .
But I had known some happiness.
My maiden days of love
Were one long, happy dream.
Your heart should know no care now.
What can it dread?

FRANCES. If I but knew!

DEBORAH. You foolish girl!
When you know more of life,
You will not spend your heart so easily
On idle fancies.
'Twill be time enough

To meet your trouble, when it comes.
I know, and none knows better,
The bitterness life brings.
And still, we better naught by dark foreboding,
And brooding on unknown . . .
    FRANCES. It's the unknown I dread.
    DEBORAH. Nay, lass,
Enough of this!
There's naught to fear.
Your lover, even now, is on his way,
And strains his eyes to catch the earliest glimpse . . .

        [A noise of voices and running footsteps without.]

Hark, lass!
They cry:
The Boats!
The Boats in sight!
Why do you tarry, lass?
Away with you!
Oh, would that I could go
To meet my son!
    FRANCES. The Boats are still far off.
I cannot go yet.
    DEBORAH. You must! Away!
Why, what would Edward think,
Were you not there,
The first to greet him
As he steps ashore?
    FRANCES. I nevermore shall greet him . . .
    DEBORAH. Woman, peace!
I am his mother.
Could I fail to know,
If death had taken him?
The sea could not withhold
Such knowledge from me for a single hour.
He is not drowned . . .
May he forgive my lips that slipt the word!
Your folly goaded me.
And, surely, never word of mine
Can bring my son in peril!

                    [FRANCES goes out.]

And yet, I too, have feared . . .
Nay, surely, I have come
Unto the end of all my misery!

Life cannot hold fresh woe in store.
My days began in happiness;
And now, it seems,
Though I have passed through terrors and despairs,
That I shall come again to happiness,
Before the end.
Nay, there is naught to dread.
My son is hale and hearty,
And comes to wed a lass who loves him;
And she, I know, is true to him;
And such a handy girl
Will make the best of wives.
And I, one day,
Shall nurse his child upon my knee.

                              [Shouting without.]

The Boats are in!
I know that cry!
How oft my heart has leapt with hope to hear it;
Then fallen dead,
When no one came to answer my heart's cry.

[A long pause, during which DEBORAH *sits gazing at the fire.]*

But I'll not think of that now.
Edward comes —
My son comes home —
And with him comes the hope
Of all my happiness.
For, surely, life . . .
How long it takes to get the nets ashore . . .
But I hear footsteps coming . . .
They stop short.
Some one has crossed his threshold, and won home.
Joy has come home to some one's heart.
Again, a rush of feet . . .
But they have passed the door.
I might have known 'twas not his foot.
And still, I thought
That no one could have beaten my boy home.
Surely, by now, the nets are out,
And all made trim and ship-shape.
And yet,
He does not come.
Some one must keep him . . .

Some one . . . I forget!
Nay, I'm no longer all-in-all to him.
Why should he haste,
With Frances by his side?
Two never trod a road as quick as one.
I must be patient still . . .
But hark!
A woman's step . . .
A woman's . . .
And . . . alone!
She stops, thank God!
Nay . . . she comes slowly on.
O God, that she may pass!
She stops . . .
She only stops for breath.
She will go by.
Perhaps, poor soul, her lover has been drowned —
Her lover,
Or her husband . . .
Or her son.
I wonder who . . .
And still
She lingers . . .
I hear no sound.
Could I but rise!
She stirs at last.
Ah, God! she's drawing nearer;
Her foot is on the threshold . . .

[FRANCES *enters, slowly, and sinks wearily into a chair, without speaking.*]

DEBORAH.   You come, alone?
FRANCES.   I come, alone.
DEBORAH.   The Boats are in?
FRANCES.   The Boats are in.
DEBORAH.   All in?
Say, lass, that one has not yet reached the harbour.
Have pity!
FRANCES.   All are in.
DEBORAH.   No boat is missing?
FRANCES.   *The Family's Pride* has foundered.
DEBORAH.   But that was not his boat.
He was not on her, lass, when she went down?

Speak, lass!

FRANCES. He was not on her.
Her crew went down with her . . .
But he . . .

DEBORAH. He is not drowned?

FRANCES. He is not drowned.

DEBORAH. Thank God!
And yet, he stays . . .
What keeps him, Frances?
Will he soon be home?
Are all the nets not out yet?
And you . . .
Do you but come before him?
You frightened me;
You walked so slowly;
And you looked . . . you look . . .
O woman, tell me that he follows you!

FRANCES. He does not follow.

DEBORAH. Oh, you'll drive me crazed!
Have you no heart!
Speak out.
And tell me quickly
What keeps my son from me.

FRANCES. How should I know what keeps your son from you?

DEBORAH. He is not dead?

FRANCES. He is not dead.

DEBORAH. And yet he bides from home.
O woman, speak!
For pity's sake,
Tell all you know —
For you know something;
And I'm strong;
I've gone through much.
Speak out the truth.

FRANCES. There is not much to tell.
He left the Boats,
Ere they put out for home.
He gave no reason.
He only asked his mates
To let you have his share,
When they should make the season's reckoning.
He said he needed naught;
As he had done with fishing,
And never would return.

DEBORAH. My son!
And they knew nothing of the way he went?
    FRANCES. Nothing!
They tried to turn him:
But in vain.
Woman . . . your son . . .
    DEBORAH. He left no word for you?
    FRANCES. Nay, not a word.
He had no thought for me . . .
Nor for his child.
    DEBORAH. His child?
    FRANCES. His child, that, even now,
Within my womb . . .
    DEBORAH. Ah, God, had I but known!
Had I but known!
He is his father's son.
    FRANCES. Woman, what's that you mutter?
Were you not married . . . you?
    DEBORAH. Yes, I was wedded,
Ere my boy was born.
But that meant little:
For his father left me,
Ere Edward saw the light.
He went away,
Without a word;
And I have not set eyes on him again.
He may be living still,
For all I know.
    FRANCES. And you . . .
You let me love his son.
    DEBORAH. His son?
But Edward was my son as well.
He never knew his father;
And could I dream
He'd follow in his steps?
Believe me, or believe not,
As you will,
This thing my heart could never have foreseen.
I have been blind and foolish, maybe, lass,
Because I loved my son;
Yes, I was blind,
And you must curse me for that blindness,
And not for any evil purpose.
If I had seen,

I should have told you all;
Ay, even though my words estranged
My only son from me.
Ah, God, that he had died,
Ere this could happen!
But time re-tells the old and bitter tale
I know too well already.
That he . . .
You say
The Family's Pride went down with all her men;
And Martha Irwin is left desolate
Of all her sons;
And still I envy her.
Her sons have gallantly gone down to death,
But mine . . .
I would that he, too . . .
I would that he . . .
    FRANCES.   Nay, woman, hush!
For he may still return.
And yet you say
His father came no more.
    DEBORAH.   He came no more.
    FRANCES.   Then there is nothing left for me,
But death . . .
And I . . . I loved him . . .
    DEBORAH.   No love is spent in vain.
Don't talk of death.
    FRANCES.   What else is left me, woman?
    DEBORAH.   Life!
    FRANCES.   Life . . . without him!
Ah, God, I love him still!
And life without him were a living death.
And I would rather lie
Cold in my grave,
If I must die.
    DEBORAH.   You must not die.
    FRANCES.   Who bids me live?
    DEBORAH.   The child.
    FRANCES.   His child!
Far better I should die
Than it be born to misery.
    DEBORAH.   'Twas even so I talked,
Before my boy was born;
And yet, I lived.

FRANCES. And what has life been worth to you?
DEBORAH. I have not found much happiness in life;
And now all that I've worked for,
The happiness I thought within my reach,
That I have laboured after all these years,
Is snatched from me;
And, in the end,
I find no peace.
And still, have I not worked?
And work is something more than happiness;
It's life itself.
I have not flinched from life,
But looked it in the face.
My son was born to me in bitterness,
And he has passed from me again
In bitterness.
And yet, meanwhile,
I've found my life worth living.
I have worked;
And I am old,
And broken ere my time —
The woman's life
Is not an easy one, at best.
But you are strong;
And unto her who labours for a child
Life cannot be all barrenness.
Ay, you must live life out.
You cannot see the end;
And happiness, that slips me, at the last,
May still be yours.
The child may be your child and mine —
Not Edward's and his father's.
We two have loved,
And we will both be faithful to the end.
I have not many years to live out,
But I would not die now;
For I yet hope to nurse
My grandchild on my knee.
Life has denied me much;
But you will not deny me this?
Have pity on me,
Old and desolate.
Would you forsake me, lass?
FRANCES. I will not leave you.

THE FIRSTBORN

Persons:

DAVID ELLIOT.
MIRIAM ELLIOT, *his wife.*

Scene: DAVID ELLIOT'S *cottage.* MIRIAM ELLIOT *stands by the
open door, looking out.*

MIRIAM.   The Boats are in;
And I . . .
I dare not go to meet him.
I wouldn't have him hear the tidings
From other lips than mine —
His wife's . . .
And yet,
How shall I tell him —
I, his wife!
How shall I say:
" Husband, you have no son;
For I, his mother —
I have let him die
While you were toiling for him on the deep? "
Perhaps they'll break the news to him,
Before he . . .
Nay, but he must learn it here —
Here, in his home,
And only from my lips,
Lest he should blench, and tremble, in the street,
Or turn upon the speaker in blind fury.
I think he'll not be fierce with me:
Though he's so passionate,
And loves the child
Beyond all else.
He knows I, too,
Love . . .
And yet,
When all is told,

I nevermore shall dare
To look into his eyes.
His step . . .
He comes.
    DAVID [*entering*].   Well, wife, I'm home.
Have you no word of welcome?
Come, kiss me, wife.
    MIRIAM.   Nay, not till you know all.
    DAVID.   Know all . . .
Then it is true . . .
Wife, I know all.

                           [*Kisses her.*]

    MIRIAM.   Some one has told you?
    DAVID.   Nay;
I did not learn it, Miriam,
From mortal lips.
Before we reached the quay,
My heart already feared;
And when I saw no face among the throng
To welcome me,
I knew the boy was dead —
That he had died
The night I saw him, cradled in the foam.
    MIRIAM.   You saw him, David!
    DAVID.   Yes, I saw him, wife,
Aslumber in the hollow of a wave.
'Twas on a Friday night,
A fortnight since . . .
    MIRIAM.   The night he died!
    DAVID.   Yes, wife; I saw him die.
    MIRIAM.   You saw him die?
    DAVID.   'Twas on the Friday night
When we sailed out,
Beneath a cloudy moon,
To shoot the nets,
As, standing in the bow,
I watched the heaving waters,
My glance lit on a patch of foam
That held my gaze
Until it took a baby's form.
And all at once
I knew that it was he,
Our little David,
Who lay sleeping there.

And as the moon flashed out
I saw, more clearly,
His dear, white dimpling body —
One wee arm,
Curled on his breast,
The other, stretched towards me,
Although he seemed to sleep;
And, on his brow, his hair,
As ruddy as the new-dipt sails —
Your hair he had, wife,
Though his eyes were mine —
His ruddy hair gleamed brightly,
Unwetted by the waves.
And as I looked on him,
My heart went cold.
And still I could not draw my eyes away,
Until the moon went in,
And he had slipt from sight,
Although I strained across the glooming waters
For one more glimpse of that foam-cradled form.
And then we reached the fishing ground;
And I — I turned to work,
Although my heart was sore —
My heart, that knew too surely
All was not well with them I loved.

    MIRIAM.   That night,
I watched beside him as he slept;
One little arm was curled upon his breast,
The other stretched towards me;
His ruddy hair drooped o'er his brow.
He slept.
But in the end . . .

    DAVID.   Ah, God, I know!
For, as we hauled the nets,
I saw his body, tangled in the mesh —
His little body, struggling,
Frail and white,
Among the silver herring.
My heart stood still.
I could not stir,
Nor utter cry.
But, as the nets came in,
I knew that there was nothing in the mesh
Save lashing fish;

And, as we shook it out,
Naught flashed beneath the moon,
Or tumbled in the hold,
Save the live quivering heap of silver herring.
A heavy catch they said.
But I — how should I know?

MIRIAM.   Ah, husband, how he struggled
Ere he died!
He fought so hard —
So hard for life. . . .
And I. . . .
I could do nothing for him —
I, his mother.
David, you know my love for him.
My heart has well-nigh died with him.
You do not blame . . .

DAVID.   Nay, wife;
For he was taken in the nets;
And I, his father,
Could not set him free.
We could do nothing, Miriam.
Once again,
I saw him, ere the dawning,
And once more,
He nestled in the hollow of a wave,
Foam-white amid the foam.
His little hands were clasped upon his breast,
And then I knew he slumbered peacefully,
And would not wake again.
The day broke,
And I never saw him more.

MIRIAM.   He slumbered peacefully;
His little hands were clasped upon his breast,
I watched with him till dawn.

DAVID.   And my heart watched with you.

MIRIAM.   And we are left without him.

DAVID.   But we are left together, wife —
We two . . .

MIRIAM.   We two . . .
And we three were so happy,
Together, husband!
Oh, why should he leave us?
For he was always happy,
Till the end . . .

DAVID.　Yes, he was always happy;
His little life was full of happiness.
Perhaps it's for the best
That he's not lived to look,
As all must look,
Some day or other, on unhappiness.
He brought so much;
And, though he's gone so suddenly,
He has not taken all away with him.
We still have memories.
　　MIRIAM.　But memory is bitter.
　　DAVID.　Can thought of him be anything but sweet?
Do you remember, wife, when he was born,
Two years ago,
How I was out at sea?
My heart was filled with fear for you,
And hankered to be home.
The wind and tide
Were dead against us:
But my will was strong,
And when I saw our chosen signal —
A snow-white kerchief by the chimney-stack —
Waving me welcome, with the welcome word,
That you were safely through,
And unto me a son was born —
Wife, I was mad for home,
And crazed to run the boat
Against the odds of wind and water,
Though other signals warned us from the shore.
What did I care!
My mates were daft with fear,
And cried out, we'd be dashed to death
Upon the Devil's Tooth,
But more they feared my eyes —
My eyes that saw your signal,
Aflutter with fair welcome;
And we rode in,
Against the odds of wind and wave;
And folk ran down to greet us,
As if we had been snatched from death;
Though I —
I did not heed them,
But leapt ashore,
And ran to you —

To you, who'd come through peril, too,
And won safe into harbour.
And then I saw the babe,
Our little son,
That snuggled to your breast,
And nestled in my heart.

    MIRIAM.   My bosom yearns for him . . .
Your heart will evermore be empty.

    DAVID.   Nay, wife, nay!
Shall not your breast and mine
Be ever full of love of him?
Sweet memories of him
Shall nestle in our hearts,
For evermore,
And we have still each other.

    MIRIAM.   And our son.

" THE FAMILY'S PRIDE "

Persons:

MARTHA IRWIN, *a widow.*
KATHERINE IRWIN, *her daughter.*
AGNES IRWIN, *her daughter-in-law.*
EMMA PRUDDAH, *a neighbour.*

Scene: MARTHA IRWIN'S *cottage at dawn.*

KATHERINE.   She has not stirred,
Nor spoken all the night,
Though I have never left her.
    EMMA.   I could not sleep for thinking of her face.
My man still slumbers soundly;
And, it's so many nights
Since he has stretched his body on a bed,
I would not waken him.
There's little rest for men at sea,
Cramped in a narrow bunk,
Betwixt the watches,
For an hour or so.
And he has slept beside me,
All night long,
As soundly as a boat becalmed.
And it was good to see him
Sleeping there,
As I recalled the wakeful nights
I'd lain alone.
It's weary waiting for your man's return;
But, when he comes again . . .
    KATHERINE.   She has not stirred,
Nor spoken once,
Nor lifted up her eyes
The livelong night;
Nor can I rouse her now.
And she has taken neither bite nor sup.
Agnes, John's wife,

And Michael's lass have been,
Though they, poor wenches,
Were distraught themselves.
But nothing rouses her;
And she has scarcely breathed,
Since first I broke the news to her,
And told her that her sons were drowned.
She stayed at home,
While I went down
To meet the Boats,
Saying, that wives and maids
Should be the first to welcome
The men on their return.
    EMMA.   'Twas well she did not go.
    KATHERINE.   When first I heard the tidings,
I was stunned,
And stood awhile, dumfounded.
Then I remembered . . .
And I shook myself,
And ran straight home to her,
Lest she should hear of her sons' death
From any stranger's lips.
She stood upon the threshold,
'Waiting them,
A smile of welcome on her face.
But when she saw me come, alone,
She caught her breath,
And looked into my eyes,
And spoke to me,
Ere I could utter aught:
" And has the sea kept all? "
And I . . .
I could but answer, " All! "
She asked no more,
But turned upon her heel,
And went indoors,
And sat down by the hearth.
She has not stirred,
Nor spoken since to me;
Though once I heard her
Murmur to herself
Her dead sons' names,
Slowly, as though she feared
Lest they should slip her memory.

" John, William, Michael, Mark, and little Pete,"
She murmured to herself;
And neither stirred nor spake again.

    EMMA.   It's well that you are left her.

    KATHERINE.   My name she did not breathe.
I'm naught to her;
She never cared for me.
Her sons were all-in-all to her.
I grudged them not her whole heart's love . . .
My brothers! . . .
Now I've none but her,
And she has no one left
To keep life in her heart.

    EMMA.   Nay, do not say so;
You're her daughter, lass.

    KATHERINE.   Her sons were all-in-all,
And they are dead.
'Twas strange she never asked me how they died;
She must have seen them drowning
In my eyes.
And I have told her nothing more,
For she has asked me nothing.
And yet, what should she ask?
What was there left to tell her heart?
Her mother's heart knew all,
Ere aught was told.

    EMMA.   Lass, 'twas a cruel storm.
My husband scarce escaped.
The Family's Pride . . .

    KATHERINE.   Nay, spare me, neighbour, now.
I cannot listen to that tale again —
I, who have looked upon that face all night,
And harkened for a word from those dumb lips.
Had she but wept,
Or spoken once to me,
I might have helped her somewhat,
Even I.
Oh, how I long to lay that aching brow
In slumber on my breast.
And yet,
I dare not lay my hand on her,
Lest she turn round on me,
And realise
That only I am left her.

EMMA [*going to the door*].   Agnes comes,
And brings her babe with her.
Perhaps the boy will rouse your mother.

[*To* AGNES, *as she enters.*]

Lass, lay him in her lap.
He'll rouse the spark of life in her,
And wake her from her brooding on the dead.

[AGNES *goes forward without speaking, and lays the
child in its grandmother's lap.* MARTHA IR-
WIN *gazes at it, then takes it to her breast,
looking up at* AGNES.]

MARTHA.   Yes, I will tend the boy,
While you go down . . .
To meet your husband, Agnes.
Lass, away!
The Boats will soon be in,
And you will be the first to greet . . .
My son . . . your husband . . .
For he's yours . . .
As well as mine . . .
And I must share with you.
The Boats will soon be in,
And soon my eyes shall look upon my sons —
My bonnie sons . . .
John, William, Michael, Mark,
And little Pete . . .
Though even Peter is not little now;
He's a grown man,
Though he's my youngest son.
And still . . .
It seems but such a little while
Since I held John,
My eldest,
In my arms,
As now . . .
I hold his son.
But . . . lass . . . away!
To greet . . . your husband . . .
And . . . my son . . .
    AGNES.   O God, have pity!

EMMA.   She does not know what she is saying;
Her grief has been too much for her.

MARTHA.   Away . . . away . . .
You'll be too late . . .
But, Katherine,
Stay with me . . .
I think . . .
I've suddenly grown old,
And I would have you with me . . .
Till . . . they come.

EMMA.   Look to the child!
She doesn't know . . .
'Twill fall!

AGNES.   Nay, but I have it safe.

EMMA.   The end is not far off.

KATHERINE.   Come, mother,
Lay your head upon my bosom.

MARTHA.   Ah, daughter, is that you?
Yes, I am weary . . .
And would rest awhile . . .
I hope they'll come
Before it's cold . . .
And you have. set five plates?
And not forgotten Peter's knife?
The Boats will soon be in . . .
And I shall look upon my sons,
Once more, before I die . . .
For I am nigh death, Katherine . . .
Hark . . . they come . . .
Their feet are on the threshold . . .
Katherine, quick . . .
Fling the door wide . . .
That I . . . may look . . .
On them . . .
My sons . . .
My sons . . .
Oh!

KATHERINE.   Death has pitied her.

THE GARRET

Persons:

ISAAC OXLEY.
ADAH ROBSON.

Scene: A garret in the slums, furnished only with a bed. It is almost midnight; but ADAH ROBSON, *with her hat and jacket on, and an old carpet-bag by her side, sits on an empty box by the window, in the light reflected from the lamps in the court below. Presently a step is heard on the stairs; the door opens, and* ISAAC OXLEY *enters.*

ISAAC.   You . . . Adah . . . here!
ADAH.   Yes, Isaac, I have come.
ISAAC.   Come . . . Adah . . . come?
But how've you come so far?
ADAH.   Much of the way I walked;
And only took the train,
When I could trail no farther.
ISAAC.   'Twas a long way for you to come alone.
And how, lass, did you find me —
You, who had never seen a bigger town
Than Morton, with its one long straggling street?
ADAH.   I had the letter with me that you wrote,
So long ago.
And folk were good to me.
And, when I was dumbfounded by the noise,
And by the throngs of people
That, like a never-ending flock of sheep,
Met in a narrow lane,
Daft with the yapping of the dogs,
Scurried and jostled round me,
Some one would pity my bewilderment,
And put me on the way;
Though many that I asked
Had never even heard of Barker's Court.
But all of them were kind,

113

And did their best to help me.

    ISAAC. How long have you been here?

    ADAH. Close on three hours.

    ISAAC. So long!

    ADAH. I could have cried,
I was so wearied;
And after all,
When I got here, to find you out!

    ISAAC. I'm sorry, lass.
If I'd but known . . .

    ADAH. The neighbours could not tell me where you
       were;
But thought that night
Would bring you home.

    ISAAC. Home, lass!
It's well that you won hither,
Safe through the streets.
Were you not frightened, Adah?

    ADAH. Though sore bewildered,
I was not afraid.
The folk were kind.

    ISAAC. Ay, folk are kind enough,
As far as words go,
And are always willing
To squander breath on strangers;
For city-folk are not like hill-folk, Adah.
But why did you leave home?

    ADAH. To come to you . . .
But you're not pleased to see me.

    ISAAC. Yes, lass; you know . . . but . . .

    ADAH. Mother died last week,
And I have no one else to turn to.
And, Isaac, when you went away,
You said you'd come again for me;
And that is nigh a year since.
I waited for you;
Yet you never came.
And when my mother died,
I had no home;
And so I thought . . .
But, maybe, I did wrong
To come to you like this.
But you . . .
You said . . .

And still you did not come;
And only wrote one letter.
Why did you never come for me?
You said you would.
When you had found . . .
   ISAAC.   When I had found a home for you.
But I have found no home.
   ADAH.   Yet this . . .
   ISAAC.   This is no home for you —
This empty garret.
   ADAH.   It's bare;
Still, we soon . . .
   ISAAC.   We soon!
Nay, you must not stay here;
You must go back again.
   ADAH.   I must go back?
   ISAAC.   You must go home.
   ADAH.   I have no home . . .
I thought . . .
But I did wrong to come.
Forgive me, Isaac; yet . . .
   ISAAC.   O Adah, lass,
There's nothing to forgive.
But you can never live here —
Here in this reeking hell.
And I . . .
How could I bear to see you starve . . .
   ADAH.   To see me starve!
Why should I starve?
For I am strong;
And I can work.
   ISAAC.   When I came to the city first,
I, too, was strong;
And I could work;
And yet,
I starve.
   ADAH.   Starve, Isaac!
Oh, but you are thin and worn!
While you were standing in the dark,
I did not see;
But now the light falls on you,
You look famished.
Are you not working, Isaac?
Are you ill —

Too ill to work?
    ISAAC. Nay, Adah, I'm not ill,
Save for the want of work.
    ADAH. A man like you,
Who used to work . . .
    ISAAC. Ay, lass,
While there was work for me.
You know how hard I toiled at home,
Until my father died,
And Stephen married;
And there was room for me no longer;
And not a cottage in the countryside
That I could get,
For love or money,
To make a home
For you and me.
And I was forced to turn my back
On all familiar things —
On all that I'd grown up with,
And all that had not changed,
Since first I blinked in daylight;
To leave my friends,
And go out into the world,
To seek my fortune among strangers —
A stranger among strangers —
To seek my fortune!
    ADAH. And have you not found . . .
    ISAAC. My fortune?
Ay, here is my fortune, lass,
This empty garret
In the mouth of hell.
    ADAH. Yet, when you left,
You were so full of hope,
And said that in the city
There would be work enough;
Ay, and a home for us.
    ISAAC. Yes, I was hopeful,
For I was strong,
And full of meat,
And did not know in cities strong men starve —
Starve in the midst of plenty,
And wander, homeless,
In a maze of houses.
    ADAH. But, wherefor . . .

ISAAC. Because there is no work for them.
" If a man toil not, neither shall he eat."
It's a just law, I thought,
While I could labour,
And eat my fill.
But when there was no work for me,
And I saw many who had never worked,
Rich, and full-fed, and happy,
While old men starved,
Because work failed them,
Things seemed quite different.
You know that life's not easy
For us poor country folk at any time;
Still, at the worst,
Up ere the dawn, and labouring till dark,
We somehow scrape along
On hard-won earnings;
For while there's work, there's hope;
But when work fails . . .
 ADAH. And you have had no work,
Since you left home?
 ISAAC. Nay, none that I call work.
 ADAH. How have you lived?
 ISAAC. You know I'd saved a pound or two
Towards our home . . .
 ADAH. But that would never serve . . .
 ISAAC. Nay, 'twas soon gone;
Though I spent sparingly enough, God knows!
I should have died without it.
It's hungry tramping through the streets all day
From works to works,
And standing in the throng
Outside the factory gates,
Still hoping against hope, that when they open,
I, too, may be allowed to slip inside.
But times are bad;
And when the gates close to,
I ever find myself among the crowd,
Shut out from work and bread.
 ADAH. How have you lived?
 ISAAC. Why, lass, I hardly know —
An odd job here and there;
Enough to put a copper in the pocket;
Still, never fit work for a man like me.

These hands, lass, were not made
To open carriage doors —
These arms to carry papers —
And this big, hulking body,
To scramble in the gutter
With starveling boys for life!

    ADAH.   Nay, surely!

    ISAAC.   O Adah, you must go away from here;
For here men starve;
Ay, men and women starve;
And starving folk are ill to live with.
Such sights I've seen!
I did not think that hell could hold such sights.
But here, where hundreds hunger,
And wander shelterless at night,
Or sleep beneath dark arches,
Or on cold benches, wrapped in soaking fog,
Here . . . here is hell! . . .
Go . . . go . . . before . . .

    ADAH.   O Isaac, you are ill!

    ISAAC.   Nay, I'm not ill!

    ADAH.   Yet you seem faint.

    ISAAC.   Naught ails me — save starvation.
One cannot trudge all day
Without a bite . . .

    ADAH.   Oh, you are famished!
And I'm hungry too,
For I've had little since I left.
I thought to find you sooner,
And then together . . .

    ISAAC.   You are hungry, Adah!
And I have naught to offer,
Not a crust.
The cupboard is quite empty,
As empty as my pocket.
I have not earned a copper all day long.

    ADAH.   But I've some money, Isaac,
Though not much;
Still, a few shillings.
There was little left
When mother died.
Yet, while there is a penny,
Why should we sit and hunger?
I'll go and buy some food,

If there's a bite to get at such an hour.
    ISAAC. Yes, there is always food to get . . .
For money.
    ADAH. Then I will go . . .
    ISAAC. Nay, you shall not go down
Into that hell at such a time of night.
I'll get the food.
    ADAH. But you're too weak.
    ISAAC. Nay, I am strong enough . . .
It is not far.
    ADAH. Then take the purse.
    ISAAC. Nay, lass; it's safer here;
And sixpence is enough to buy a feast.
It's long since I've had silver in my hand.
Would God that I had earned it!
I hardly like to take your money.
    ADAH. O Isaac, I am famished!
    ISAAC. I'll not be long.

> [*He goes out, and is heard hurrying downstairs.
> ADAH takes off her hat and jacket, and un-
> packs her bag, laying her scanty stock of clothes
> and other belongings on the bed; then, unfold-
> ing a parcel, she takes out a cheap tin clock and
> winds it up, and sets it on the mantelpiece,
> where it ticks loudly in the vacant silence.
> After a while ISAAC returns, carrying a basin
> of coffee and a chunk of bread, which he lays
> on a box beside ADAH.*]

    ADAH. So quickly!
    ISAAC. 'Twas not far;
And I came back as quickly as I could,
Lest it should get too cold,
And filled with fog.
Come, take a drink,
While there's some heat in it;
'Twill do you good.
    ADAH. Nay, you drink first.
You need it more than I.
    ISAAC. Nay, lass, it's yours.
And I — I have no cup.
I paid a penny for the basin;
But they will make that good again,

When I return it.

    ADAH. You'd not take it back —
The first thing that you've bought to set up house with!
If you've no cup,
Can we not drink together from the basin,
As man and wife
In their own home?
We are not strangers.

    ISAAC. Set up house . . .
As man and wife . . .
Together . . .
In their home . . .
Nay, lass,
That cannot be.
You shall not starve for my sake.
Oh, had you seen the faces round the stall —
The hungry faces in the flare
Of naphtha, and the eyes
That glared out from the shadows greedily;
And as I passed them with the coffee,
The cold, blue lips that drank up the rich steam,
As though they feasted . . .

    ADAH. And you'd naught for them!

    ISAAC. To one poor girl I gave
A penny of your money;
A child, almost, she seemed!
But she was naught but skin and bone, and rags —
And oh, such eyes;
I little thought I'd live to see
That look in any girl's eyes.
But when the body starves,
The best of us are weak;
And there's small blame
To such as she.

    ADAH. Come drink your coffee, lad.
It's long since we two supped together.

    ISAAC. A merry meeting this!
Hark!
What is that?
A clock!
Where did it come from?

    ADAH. Don't you know it, Isaac?
I brought it with me;
It's my very own.

They could not take it from me.
I'd paid for it at Morton Fair
With my own money.
And, while you were gone,
I took it from my bag,
And wound it up.
Things seemed more homelike
When I heard it ticking.

    ISAAC.   Homelike . . .
Ay, Adah, there's a kind of comfort
In listening to the ticking of a clock.
That coffee's made another man of me.
This garret never seemed like home before.
Yet, since you came, somehow . . .
But you must go to-morrow.

    ADAH.   Go . . . Isaac . . . where?

    ISAAC.   I do not know.
I only know,
If you stay here,
You'll starve.

    ADAH.   And if I go, I'll starve.
Why should we starve apart?
But we'll not starve, lad,
If we stick together.
We'll win through somehow.
Though there's none for you,
There may be work for me;
And better times will come,
And bring you work.

    ISAAC.   I've trudged the streets,
All day . . .

    ADAH.   But that day's gone;
And has not even it brought something to you?

    ISAAC.   Ay; though it's been a black and bitter day —
The ending's brave.
If there were no to-morrow . . .

    ADAH.   We don't know what to-morrow brings.

    ISAAC.   To-morrow!
Lass, have I not said
Unto my heart each night
To-morrow will bring work?
And yet, to-morrow
Comes ever empty-handed.

    ADAH.   Nay, surely, Isaac,

Yesterday your garret
Was bare save for the bed and this old box.
Now have you not a clock and basin
To start housekeeping with?
    ISAAC. And you?
    ADAH. If you will let me stay . . .
    ISAAC. If I will let you . . . let you . . .
O lass, I cannot let you go again,
Though we should starve . . .
    ADAH. We shall not starve . . .
But live and work together.   [*The clock strikes.*]
    ISAAC. It's a brave clock.
    ADAH. What! three, already!
And to-morrow comes.
The day is not far off,
Though it is dark.
    ISAAC. Ay, lass;
And now, at home, the village cocks
Will all be stretching their long necks, and crowing.

THE SHIRT

Scene: A room in tenements, near the railway. CAROLINE AL-
DER *sits by the fire, sewing.* ISA GREY *is standing near her,
gazing at the blaze. The clank and rumble of wagons being
shunted sounds loudly through the night-air.*

 CAROLINE. Ay, lass, the shirt's for Will;
I'll not be sorry when it's finished,
Though it's the last I'll make for him.
 ISA. The last?
 CAROLINE. You'll make the next, I trust.
You surely don't expect, my girl,
I'll still be making for him, when he's married?
You're much mistaken . . .
 ISA. Nay! . . .
But, when you said the last, somehow . . .
 CAROLINE. The very last!
And well I mind the first I made,
Or ever he was born,
Nigh twenty year ago;
And I was but a lass, like you;
And, as I sewed it, by the fire,
His father sat and watched me; and we talked . . .
We talked of him . . .
His father always hoped 'twould be a boy;
And yet, before he came
To wear the shirt, I'd made for him . . .
 ISA. His father never saw him?
 CAROLINE. Nay; he'd not leave his engine,
Although the fireman leapt . . .

             [A pause.]

But 'twas a dainty shirt!
For I had eyes in those days,
And nimble fingers too —
You never saw the like.
Why, this would make a score of it;
He's grown a bit since then!
See, what a neck and shoulders —

His father's, to an inch!
You'll have your work set . . .
　　Isa. Yes, it's big enough.
　　Caroline. He's just his father's spit and image;
And he's his father, in more ways than one.
I've never had a wrong word from his lips.
However things have gone with him,
He always comes in just as he went out.
You're lucky, lass, as I was . . .
Though I . . .
And now I've made his shirts for twenty year,
Just twenty year, come Michaelmas.
He's aye slept snugly in my handiwork.
At one time, I could scarce keep pace with him;
He sprouted up so quickly;
And every year, I've had to cut them bigger,
Till now that he's a man, fullgrown . . .
And still, to-night, somehow, I almost wish
That I was hemming baby-shirts again,
His father, sitting by me, as I sewed . . .
But you will soon be stitching, lass . . .
　　Isa. I wonder . . .
How clearly we can hear the trains, to-night!
　　Caroline. Perhaps the air is frosty;
Though I have always seemed to hear them clearer
Since ; . . since his father . . .
　　Isa. I hate to hear them clanking.
　　Caroline. Ay, lass; but you'll get used to it,
Before you've lived here long.
I couldn't sleep at night without it now.
Once, when I stayed at Mary's,
I could not sleep a wink . . .
The quiet seemed so queer . . .
I missed the clank . . .
　　Isa. I never shall get used to it.
I hate that clanking . . .
I wish that Will would leave the shunting . . .
　　Caroline. Ay, coupling's chancy work;
But life's a chancy thing, at best.
And other jobs are bad to get;
And he's a steady lad.
　　Isa. Yet, if he slipped!
　　Caroline. There's little fear of him;
He's always been surefooted, from a boy;

And such a nerve!
I've seen him walk the tiles . . .
    ISA.   To think that he'll be at it all night long!
    CAROLINE.   Well, he must take his shift among the
        rest.
It's hard, at first, to miss your man, at night;
But, wives must needs get used to it.
My man was often gone from me,
The day and night together;
And it was on the night-shift . . .
He hadn't slept a wink for days,
For he'd been sitting up with me —
The doctor thought I'd scarce pull through —
But he'd to go, and leave me.
I never saw him more.
They'd buried him, and all,
Ere I was out of bed again.

                                   [*Pause.*]

But, that was long ago —
Nigh twenty year —
And now, his son's a man;
And soon to marry.
There, lass: it's almost done:
I've just one button now . . .
    ISA.   I'll sew it on.
I've never done a stitch for him.
    CAROLINE.   Nay! it's the last I'll make for him:
And no one else must have a hand in it.
You'll have enough to do,
Before you've long been married . . .
    ISA.   I wonder . . .
    CAROLINE.   Wonder, lass!
What's wrong with you to-night?
You seem so . . . why, you're all atremble!
    ISA.   The trains have stopped . . .
I cannot hear a sound.
    CAROLINE.   Ay, lass: it's queer . . .
But soon they'll start again.
I never knew such quiet . . .
    ISA.   That they would all start clanking!
I cannot bear the silence . . .
    CAROLINE.   It's time that you were getting home to
        bed:
You're overwrought to-night.

ISA. I wish I knew . . .
There's not a sound yet . . .
CAROLINE. Nay, lass, hark!

[*An express thunders by, shaking the houses.*]

ISA. Well, I'll be getting home.
Goodnight!
CAROLINE. Goodnight!
There, that's the last stitch done.
Is't not a brave shirt, lass!
It's ready for him when he comes.

[ISA *goes out, and down the stairs.*]

She's overwrought a bit.
About the time that I was wed . . .
It's strangely quiet now again . . .
I never knew . . .
They must have finished shunting . . .
Yet . . .

[*She stands, listening, as a hurrying step is heard on
the stairs, and* ISA *bursts into the room, panting.*]

CAROLINE. What's wrong, lass!
ISA. Will! O, Will!
CAROLINE. Speak, woman, speak!
ISA. They're bringing him . . .
I met them in the street . . .
O Will! O Will!
CAROLINE. His son . . . too . . .

[CAROLINE *picks up the shirt which has fallen from
her hand. They stand silent, waiting: and
there is no sound in the room, until the shunting of wagons starts again, when* ISA *puts her
fingers to her ears, and sinks to the ground.*]

ISA. 'Twill never stop again;
I'll always hear . . .

THE MOTHER

Persons:

ROSE ALLEN, *a young widow.*
HER CHILD.
ANNIE FEATHERSTONE, *Rose Allen's sister.*

Scene: A lonely moorland cottage, in the early morning. The child sleeps on the bed. ANNIE FEATHERSTONE is tending the fire when ROSE, dressed as for a holiday, enters from the other room.

ANNIE. You are not going, surely,
After all!
    ROSE. Why not?
The boy is better.
    ANNIE. Better, Rose?
    ROSE. Well, he's no worse to-day than yesterday.
    ANNIE. I think he's worse.
    ROSE. You think?
You always think the worst of everything.
Don't you remember . . .
    ANNIE. I remember much.
    ROSE. Then you must know
How often you've cried " wolf! "
Already, Annie.
Had you but children of your own,
You'd know how little makes them sick,
How quickly they recover;
And would not fret yourself
At every baby ailment,
Nor see a tragedy
In every prick or scratch.
He sleeps,
And little ails a child when he can sleep.
    ANNIE. But how he tosses!
It's no healthy slumber.
His hands are hot and restless,

His brow's afire —
Come, feel it.
    ROSE.   Why, that's nothing, Annie.
It's the old story —
Spinster's children . . .
You know the rest.
    ANNIE.   I know the rest.
    ROSE.   Ah, well!
But you should know a mother
Has something else to do
Than break her heart, whenever
A fractious baby pukes and pules,
Or sit and weep her eyes out
At every scratch and tumble.
How should we get through life,
If we paid heed
To every whine and whimper?
But even you
Will learn in time, perhaps,
And . . .
    ANNIE.   Even I!
    ROSE.   Yes, even you.
But don't be angry with me,
And think that I don't love my child.
You know how much I love him,
Though he's so troublesome;
And how I've worked
My fingers to the bone
To keep him, since his father died.
My life is hard enough, God knows!
And must I miss the little fun life offers?
I get so little pleasure;
And Morton Fair comes only once a year.
But you are hard,
And you'd deny me this.
Ah, well!
Then I must stay.
    ANNIE.   I would deny you nothing, child.
    ROSE.   You call me " child! "
Then you are angry.
But I'll not quarrel with you.
Child!
Yes, I'm young —
I wedded young —

But you are old and wise,
And never cared for fairings.
There's but twelve months betwixt us,
And yet, what years and years!
A widow and a mother, too,
I am not half as old.
I wonder if I'll ever be . . .
    ANNIE.   Nay you will never be as old as I . . .
    ROSE.   Never?
How can you know?
Do you foretell my death?
Shall I not live to see the year out?
    ANNIE.   Though you should live to see
A hundred years out,
You will still be young.
    ROSE.   Ah, now I understand you.
You frightened me at first
With your long face and solemn words.
You mean my heart is young,
And think I'm thoughtless.
Yet, a girl
Can hardly go through all that I've gone through,
And still be thoughtless.
Annie, I know life
As you have never known it.

                                  [The clock strikes.]
Is that five?
But I must go.
If I'm to catch the train.
It's full three hours' fast walking.
I've stood too long already,
Chattering.
Well, lass, good-bye.
    ANNIE.   You have not kissed the boy " good-bye."
    ROSE.   He sleeps so soundly,
I'll not waken him.
Now, lass, you see
That I'm the careful mother after all,
And I deny myself for him.
How sweet he sleeps!
I'll bring him home a fairing
Which he will like far better
Than all your precious kisses.

And now you're angry with me,
Though I meant nothing, Annie.
You must not worry so.
You know I love him,
And would bide at home,
Did I not know I leave him
In safe hands.
Still, if you mind . . .
    ANNIE.   I do not mind.
    ROSE.   Good-bye, then.
I could not leave the boy in better hands.

                                  [Goes out.]

    ANNIE.   And she has gone through all,
And yet,
Knows naught!
Life has not touched her,
Though a man has spent
His whole heart's love on her;
And she has stood
Beside her husband's deathbed;
And borne his child within her womb,
Yet, she's unchanged,
And still a child,
As ignorant of life as her poor babe.
While I, whom life denied
All, save the yearning,
I am old at heart.
Life fed her to the full,
While I went hungry for the crumbs.
Already I am old and famine-worn,
While she is young and careless.
Passion has brought no tenderness to her;
She never has known love —
Nay, though she drank a strong man's love,
His very life-blood, yet,
She knew not what she drank.
She drained that draught
As though 'twere water,
And soon forgot the cup,
When it was empty,
And broken at her feet.
And now the crystal spring of baby-love

Is spilt in vain for her,
While I am parched,
And thirst for one sweet drop.
Ah, God, have I not thirsted!
And yet the cup
Has ever passed my lips,
Untasted . . .
Now I never shall drink life.
His love had not been spent, in vain,
On me,
Had life but let him love me,
As I loved.
But he . . .
He was so happy in his love,
And I — I loved
To see him happy in his love.
And still my selfish heart
Was often sore
That he could be so happy,
While I . . .
And yet,
He never knew of my unhappiness,
For Rose was all the world to him;
And I,
But Rose's shadow —
She, ever fresh and fair,
And I, so gloomy;
And he loved the light,
And never knew his star was cold at heart.
Thank God, he did not know —
Not even in the end!
What would not I have given for the right
To stand beside him at the last,
And hold his hand in mine —
To lay that weary head upon my bosom!
I burned with love for him.
And still, denied all else,
Had it been mine
To bring him balm and quiet in the end,
And spend on him a mother's tenderness,
I should have been content . . . I think . . .
And yet,
Had things been otherwise,
Was not my heart

His heart's true mate?
But he . . .
His child another bore him,
And scarcely knew that 'twas his child —
His child, that should have brought into her breast
The milk of tenderness,
And to her heart, the light of understanding.
His child, and fatherless!
But motherhood to her meant little.
A cold and careless wife,
So is she now a careless mother.
The pangs and labouring
Of travail taught her nothing.
She rose from off her bearing-bed
As easily as she had left
The deathbed of her love.
'Twas I, indeed,
Who bore the pangs of travail
To bring his child to birth —
Ay, even as on me
Fell the whole burden of the husband's death.

[*The child wakens and stirs restlessly.*

THE CHILD.   Mother!
ANNIE.   Yes, son.
He does not know me.
And am not I his mother!
She only bore his body . . .
    THE CHILD.   Mother, a drink.
    ANNIE.   And she . . .
She is not here!
Drink this, my son.
You are his son . . . and mine!
Your young soul was brought forth
Of my great love for him,
The father of your soul.
Have I not mothered it,
And nurtured its young life
With my heart's love,
And fed it on the milk of tenderness?
He sleeps again, our child.
Her eyes he has;
But when he sleeps,

She has no part in him.
Then he is all his father . . .
And all mine —
All mine, all mine,
My babe, my babe!
He sleeps . . .
And yet . . .
I fear . . .
He lies so still.
O God, and I,
His mother,
Can do naught,
Alone and helpless,
In this wilderness!
Had she not gone . . .
But I,
What can I do?
I dare not leave him, yet scarce dare to bide.
If there were but a neighbour . . .
But where could I seek help . . .
If help there be at all
For him in this world now?
He stirs again.
Nay, I must stay with him,
My babe, my babe!
Don't fear;
I'll not forsake you!
And, in the end,
You shall not lack a mother's hand
Upon your brow,
Nor lack a mother's bosom
On which to lay your head.
   THE CHILD.   Mother . . .
A drink . . .
   ANNIE.   Your thirst is quenched.
Those lips will never breathe that word again.
Much have I craved of life . . .
And it is given to me
To close your eyes in death.
My child, my child!
Now you are ours, all ours . . .
All his . . . and mine!

[*The day wears slowly through as* ANNIE *watches*

*by the dead child.   In the late afternoon the
door opens, and* ROSE ALLEN *enters.*]

ROSE.   Am I not a good mother?
I've left the Fair half over.
I could not stay,
For something made me anxious.
Your words kept dinning in my ears,
And spoilt the fun;
And so I left quite early;
And yet,
I did not quite forget my boy,
Though I'm so careless, Annie.
I bring a fairing for him —
See!
A jumping . . .
Does he sleep?
He lies so very still.
ANNIE.   Yes, he sleeps sound.

THE FURNACE

Persons:

JACOB PRINGLE, *a stoker.*
ELEANOR PRINGLE, *his wife.*
THEIR CHILDREN.
BESSIE PURDHAM, *a neighbour.*

Scene: A room in tenements. JACOB PRINGLE, *his head and body swathed in bandages, lies on the bed, unconscious, moaning incessantly.* ELEANOR PRINGLE, *with her young baby at her breast, stands near the door, talking to* BESSIE PURDHAM. *The other two children, aged three and two years, stand silent by the bed, gazing wonderingly at their father.*

    BESSIE.   I heard the doctor go;
And so I've come
To see if I may help you.
    ELEANOR.   There's nothing more to do.
    BESSIE.   I thought, perhaps . . .
    ELEANOR.   There's nothing more to do.
The doctor and the nurse did all they could,
Before they left.
They only went,
When they could do no good by staying.
They said they'd come again to-night,
If he . . . if he . . .
    BESSIE.   Nay, don't take on so, woman.
Your man will soon be well again.
Keep a brave heart within you.
    ELEANOR.   The doctor says there's little hope.
    BESSIE.   'Twas strange to bring him here.
    ELEANOR.   Here, to his home?
Does it seem strange to you
To bring him home?
Where would you have him taken?
They brought him home . . . Ah, God!
    BESSIE.   The hospital . . .
    ELEANOR.   It was too far.

135

The doctor said:
'Twas not worth while
To take him such a journey,
When there was little hope.
And so,
They did not pass the door,
To bear him among strangers,
But brought him in,
And laid him on the bed.
'Twas not worth while . . .
And so they brought him home,
Home to his wife and children.
'Twas not worth while . . .
    BESSIE.   How did it happen?
    ELEANOR.   None can tell.
They found him on his face
Before the furnace-door,
The life well-nigh burnt out of him;
His head, and breast, and hands . . .
Oh, it's too terrible to think of, neighbour!
    BESSIE.   He must have fainted.
    ELEANOR.   None will ever know,
Unless . . .
But, he's not spoken since.
He only moans, and moans;
The doctor says that he's not conscious,
And cannot feel it much,
And mayn't come to himself again.
If he should never speak!
    BESSIE.   'Twas strange that he . . .
He seemed so strong . . .
    ELEANOR.   They say his shovel
Had tumbled in the furnace, and the heat
Had crumpled it like paper;
And it was almost melted;
And he himself had only fallen short.
His head, and breast, and hands . . .
Oh, how he moans!
The doctor says he cannot feel much;
And still he moans, and moans.
He has not spoken . . .
If he should never speak . . .
If he should not come to himself . . .
If he . . . Ah, God!

And he so young!

BESSIE. How old's your husband?

ELEANOR. Twenty-three next March.

BESSIE. So young! And you?

ELEANOR. Just twenty, turned.

BESSIE. Why, you are only children,
The pair of you!

ELEANOR. Yet he's a father,
I, a mother . . .
A father . . . and his children —
What can his children do,
If he should leave them,
And they, but babes,
And Winter coming on?

BESSIE. He may be well before then;
And they've you.

ELEANOR. What can I do without him?

BESSIE. You can but do your best.
If only they'd been boys . . .
Still, keep a brave heart, woman;
For, surely, at the worst,
The masters will do something;
And there'll be money . . .

ELEANOR. Money . . . woman . . . money!
I want naught with their money.
I want my husband,
And my children's father.
Let them pitch all their money in the furnace
Where he . . .
I wouldn't touch a penny;
'Twould burn my fingers.
Money . . .
For him!

BESSIE. You wouldn't have your children starve?
Money is bread . . .

ELEANOR. Nay; but I'll work for them:
They shall not want,
While I can lift a finger.
He loves them,
And has slaved so hard for them.
If he can work no more,
Am I not strong to work?
He is so proud of them.
And oft when he comes home . . .

Ah, God, they brought him home!
And he has never spoken;
He has no word for them —
He who was always cheery,
And dandled them, and danced them,
And tossed them to the ceiling.
Look, how they wait, poor babes!
They cannot understand
Why he should say no word,
But only moan, and moan . . .
Ah, how he moans!
He tries to speak, I think.
If he should speak!

 JACOB [*in a hoarse whisper*]. The big, red, gaping
   mouth . . .

 ELEANOR. Ah, God, he's wandering!

 BESSIE. He thinks he's at the furnace.

 JACOB. I feed, and feed, and feed it,
And yet it's never full;
But always gaping, gaping,
And licking its red lips.
I feed it with my shovel,
All night long.
I shovel without ceasing;
But it just licks the coke up in a twinkling,
And roars, and roars for more.
I cannot feed it faster;
And it's angry.
I shovel all night long,
Till I can scarcely stand.
The sweat pours out of me;
And then it licks the sweat up with its breath,
And roars more fiercely.
My eyes are coals of fire;
My arms can scarcely lift
Another shovelful . . .
Oh, how it roars, and roars! It's angry
Because I cannot feed it fast enough.
The red tongue licks the shovel,
As though it would devour it.
The shovel is red-hot . . .
It melts . . . it melts . . .
It's melting in my hands . . .
I cannot drop it . . .

My hands are full of molten iron.
Water . . . Ah, God!
My hands . . . my hands!
Oh!

ELEANOR.   And there is nothing I can do for him!
I am his wife:
And still, I can do nothing.
The doctor said, there was no more to do.
They left me naught to do for him.

BESSIE.   Nay, lass, there's nothing to be done.
He's quiet now.
Perhaps he'll sleep.

JACOB.   The great, red eyes . . .
They burn me through and through.
They glare upon me all night long;
They never sleep:
But always glower on me.
They never even blink;
But stare, and stare . . .
I cannot look upon them any longer —
I cannot face them . . . still . . .
Ah, God, I cannot shut them out!
They burn right through my eyelids,
And set my eyes afire.
My eye-lids are red-hot,
And scorch my eyes . . .
My eyes, my eyes!
Oh, I would tear them out . . .
But I . . . I cannot lift my hands;
They're full of molten iron.
My hands!
Oh!

BESSIE.   He seems quite spent.
Perhaps the worst is over.

ELEANOR.   Oh, would to God . . .

JACOB.   The big, red, gaping mouth . . .
It gapes,
And licks its lips,
And roars, and roars for food.
I cannot breathe,
Its hot breath stifles me.
It puffs at me,
Then tries to suck me in —
Into that roaring hell.

It gapes . . . it gapes . . .
For me!
I cannot feed it fast enough;
And it is angry,
And roars, and roars with hunger.
Some night the red tongue will shoot out and lick me
Into that blazing hell-mouth —
Will lick me to a cinder,
A handful of white ash.
It will shoot out . . .
Ah, God!
The fiery tongue
Is all about me now;
It wraps me round and round,
And licks me in.
At last the furnace has me —
The furnace that I feared.
I burn . . .

    ELEANOR.   That he should suffer so!
Ah, God, that he might . . .

      THE ELDEST CHILD.   Mother, what's a furnace?

      ELEANOR.   Ah, child, that you should hear!
I scarcely knew you listened.
A furnace is the mouth . . .
Nay, it's a fire —
A big, big fire.

    CHILD.   A fire?
But why is Daddy frightened?
I do not fear the fire.
I sit quite close,
And warm my hands.
I'd love a big, big fire,
And would not be afraid of it:
So, why is Daddy?
I've often sat upon his knee,
Quite close,
And watched the pretty flames.
He never told me he was frightened,
Or I'd have held his hand.

    ELEANOR.   And he will nevermore
Sit by the hearth,
His children on his knee,
And listen to their prattle.
He was proud . . .

BESSIE.   He does not moan so much,
And hardly moves.
I think . . .
But, hark!
He tries to speak again.
His voice is weaker;
He can scarcely whisper.
JACOB.   O mother, do you see the little flame
That leaps above the bars,
And dances in and out?
Look how he dances, dances,
Upon the red-hot coals.
Oh, now, he's gone —
He must have heard me talking.
But there he is again:
And laughing at me,
And waving his red cap.
BESSIE.   The worst is over.
He's easier now.
ELEANOR.   His mind is wandering back to his old
        home.
He's heard the child;
And thinks that he's a child, too.
JACOB.   I love to watch the fire;
And when I am a man,
I'll mind a furnace, mother,
And feed it all day long;
And watch it blaze;
And listen to its roaring.
Look, mother, do you see the little flame,
That runs right down into that deep, red hollow;
And waves to me to follow after?
I'd like to follow him,
And run right down —
Right down that golden lane,
Among the dancing flames,
And dance with them.
Ah, there he is;
And laughing at me,
And waving his red cap . . .
And dancing . . . dancing . . .   [*A pause.*]
CHILD.   O mother, look,
The fire has gone quite out;
And I am cold.

BESSIE.   He moans no longer . . .
ELEANOR.   He seems more easy . . .
He does not stir . . .
How quiet he has grown . . .
It's strange, he lies so still,
So suddenly . . .
That he would speak to me!
BESSIE.   Ay, he is easy now;
But he will never stir again, nor speak . . .
ELEANOR.   Jacob!
CHILD.   He is not frightened now.

THE CHILD

Persons:

Amos Woodman.
Joan Woodman, *his wife.*

Scene: A garret in the slums. It is afternoon and a gleam of sunshine, struggling through the grimy window, reveals the nakedness of the room, which is quite bare of furniture. In one corner Joan Woodman *crouches by a heap of rags and straw, on which is lying the dead body of her child. She is a young woman, but looks older than her years, being worn and haggard with want and suffering. The door opens and* Amos Woodman *enters, wearily. He is lame and coughs almost incessantly. As he pauses on the threshold, his wife rises and goes towards him.*

Joan.   He's gone.
Amos.   Forgive me, Joan.
Joan.   Forgive you, Amos?
Amos.   Ay, forgive me —
Forgive me that I left you with the child.
I could not bear
To sit and watch him dying,
When there was nothing I could do to save him.
    Joan.   'Twas better that you went.
It is not good to see a baby die . . .
And yet . . .
When all was over,
I knew 'twas best.
    Amos.   Best, wife?
    Joan.   Yes, husband;
For he suffers nothing now.
    Amos.   Ah, how he suffered!
And I,
His father,
Could do naught to ease him.
He cried for bread;

143

And I — I had no bread —
I had no bread to give him.
Perhaps it's best . . .
And yet . . .
If he'd but lived . . .
   JOAN.   Lived, Amos?
It's not good to see a baby starve —
To watch him wasting day by day,
To hear him crying . . .
   AMOS.   Yes, he cried for bread —
And I, his father, had no bread to give him.
I would have worked these fingers to the bone,
To save him —
To the bone!
They're little else already.
But times are bad,
And work is slack,
And so I needs must watch my baby starving —
Must sit with idle hands and see him starving —
Must watch him starve to death;
His little body wasting day by day;
The hunger gnawing at his little life;
His weak voice growing weaker.
He cried for bread . . .
   JOAN.   He'll cry no more.
He feels no hunger now;
And wants for nothing.
   AMOS.   Ay, he's quiet . . .
We'll never hear his voice again.
If he'd but lived . . .
Yet he is free from pain now,
And will not thirst nor hunger any more.
And though, if no help comes,
We two must starve.
The hunger will no longer gnaw our hearts,
Knowing that he's beyond the clutch of hunger.
   JOAN.   Ay, we must starve, it seems,
If you have found no work;
Though I am free now . . .
Free to seek for work.
He does not need me now;
And nevermore will need me.
Ah, God, I'm free . . .
Free!

Amos. They only look at me,
And shake their heads;
Though I was strong once, wife,
And I could work,
When there was work to get.
But times are bad,
And work is slack;
And I must needs sit idle.
While he was dying —
While he was dying for the want of food —
The hands that should have earned his bread were idle.
I gave him life,
Yet could not feed the life that I had given.
    Joan. Ay, Amos, you were always steady,
And ever worked well;
And I, too, have worked;
And yet we've not a penny in the world,
And scarce a bite to eat.
Reach down the loaf
And cut yourself a slice;
You've eaten naught all day.
    Amos. And you, wife?
    Joan. Nay, I cannot eat just now.
He drank the milk,
But could not touch the bread;
He was too ill to eat.
    Amos. And when he cried to me for bread,
I had no bread to give him.
Wife, how should I eat bread
When I'd no bread to give him till too late?

[*They sit for a while silent on an upturned empty
orange-box by the window.*]

    Joan. Your cough is worse to-day.
You've eaten naught,
And sit so still,
Save when the coughing takes you.
    Amos. Wife, I was thinking.
    Joan. Thinking!
Nay, lad, don't think;
It is not good to think,
At times like these.
I dare not —

I, who bore him,
And gave him suck.
    AMOS.   Wife, I was thinking of a little child.
    JOAN.   Of him?
    AMOS.   Nay, not of him,
But of a happy child,
Who played and paddled daylong in the brook
That ran before his father's cottage.
And, as I thought,
I seemed to hear the pleasant noise of waters —
The noise that once was in my ears all day,
Though then I never heard it,
Or, hearing, did not heed.
Yes, I was thinking of a happy child —
A happy child . . .
And yet, of him;
For, as I listened to the sound,
It seemed to me the baby that we loved
No longer lay upon that heap of rags,
Lifeless and cold,
But, somewhere, far away,
Beyond this cruel city,
Among the northern hills,
Played happily the livelong day,
Paddling and splashing in the brook that runs
Before a cottage door.
O wife, do you not hear the noise of water —
Of water, running in and out,
And in and out among the stones,
And tumbling over boulders?
He does not hear it,
For he's far too happy.
O wife, do you not hear the noise of water —
Of water, running, running . . .

     [*The room slowly darkens as they sit, hand in hand,
       gazing at the sky beyond the chimney-stacks.*]

THE NIGHT-SHIFT

Persons:

JENNY CRASTER, *Robert Craster's wife.*
TAMAR CRASTER, *Robert Craster's mother.*
MAGGIE THOMSON, *a neighbour.*
LIZZIE THOMSON, *her daughter.*

Scene: ROBERT CRASTER'S *cottage, in the early morning.* JENNY
CRASTER *lies in bed, her newborn baby by her side. Her eyes
are closed, and she seems barely conscious.* TAMAR CRASTER
stands at the door talking with MAGGIE THOMSON.

> TAMAR.   My son!
> But, hush!
> She must not hear;
> 'Twould be the death of her.
> 'Twill take her all her time, poor lass,
> To pull through as it is.
> And, if she heard, her husband . . .
> But it's not true . . .
> Oh, say it is not true!
>   MAGGIE.   Ay, Tamar, it is true enough;
> And there's but little hope
> That any man will leave the pit alive.
>   TAMAR.   My son!
> She must not hear a whisper;
> The news would kill her, and her newborn babe.
>   MAGGIE.   Sooner or later,
> She must know, poor soul!
>   TAMAR.   Ay, but not yet;
> For she's in need of sleep.
> When there's no help,
> And she must know,
> Then 'twill be time enough
> To break the news to her.
> Perhaps, when she has slept a bit,
> She will be strong to bear much
> That's now beyond her strength.

147

MAGGIE.   Well, I'm away!
My man has gone already
To see if there's a chance of doing aught.
Thank God, he's on the day-shift!
If he'd been in the pit . . .
But he was sleeping soundly,
Beside me, snug in bed,
Until the rumbling roused us;
When he leapt up and ran
Nigh naked to the pit.
I had to stay and hush the children
To sleep again;
The noise had startled them.
And then I came to tell you.
There's scarce a body left
In all the village.
The cottages were empty,
And every door ajar,
As I came by;
For all the women-folk
Have run to the pit-head.
And I must go;
I cannot stay behind,
Not knowing what is happening.
If there is any news,
I'll bring you word;
Although it's feared
There's little hope of rescue.

[*She goes out, closing the door behind her.*

TAMAR.   Robert, my son!
But I must breathe no word,
Lest she should hear.
She must not know my son's in peril;
For he's her husband.
The women-folk are gathered round the shaft —
Poor wives and mothers,
Waiting and watching,
And hoping against hope.
Would that I, too, watched with them —
A mother 'mid the mothers —
To share with them what little hope there may be.
But I must bide at home,

Alone with her I dare not speak to,
Or breathe a word of all my fears to.
Nay, I must keep them to myself,
Even though my heart . . .
My son's in danger,
Yet I dare not go . . .
No longer he belongs to me alone;
For he's her husband and a father now:
And I must stay
To tend his wife and son.
    JENNY [*opening her eyes and speaking in a whisper*].
        Is Robert not home yet?
    TAMAR. Nay, daughter . . .
He's not home yet.
    JENNY. What time is it?
    TAMAR. It's nearly . . .
Nay . . .

    [*She goes to the clock on the wall and holds the
        pendulum until it stops.*]

The clock has stopt.
    JENNY. I thought I heard it ticking;
Though now I cannot hear it.
Still, it seems almost light;
And he should not be long.
How pleased he'll be to have a boy!
I hope that they'll not tell him,
Before he reaches home.
I'd like to see his face,
When first he learns
That he's the father of a son.
He'll soon be home . . . be home . . .
My babe!
He'll be so pleased.
I hope . . .
That they'll not tell him . . .
    TAMAR. Nay . . . they'll not tell.
But you must not talk now,
For you're too weakly,
And should save yourself.
Until . . .
    JENNY. Until he comes.
Yes, I'll lie very quiet,

And save myself that I may see him,
When he first learns . . .
But there's a sound of tapping . . .
Do you not hear it?
   TAMAR.   Nay, lass, I hear nothing.
   JENNY.   I thought it was the clock.
   TAMAR.   The clock has stopt.
   JENNY.   It must be in my head then.
It keeps on tapping . . . tapping . . .
He'll soon be home.
But I'm so tired,
And cannot keep awake.
I'll sleep . . .
Till he comes home.
And, Tamar, you'll be sure to waken me
The moment he comes home?
You'll not forget?
   TAMAR.   Nay, lass, I'll not forget.
   JENNY [*drowsily sinking back into unconsciousness*].
      It keeps on tapping . . . tapping . . .
Tap . . . tap . . . tap . . . tap . . .
   TAMAR.   Till he comes home . . .
Ah, God, how shall I tell her!
For I must tell her soon;
I cannot keep it from her long.
And I, his mother,
Must be the first to tell his wife
That he . . .
But he may come yet . . .
And she must know naught now.
For she's too weakly,
And 'twould kill her outright;
And, after all,
He may come home again,
Before there's any need to tell her **aught.**
When there's no help,
And she must know,
Then 'twill be soon enough . . .
She'll have a longer spell than I
To bear it . . .
She is young!
And I . . . I seem quite old,
So suddenly!
She said she heard a sound of tapping . . .

She might have heard my heart almost,
It beat so loudly at my side
While she was speaking of my son,
Her husband,
And wondering, poor soul . . .
But, may he not come safe home after all?
She may speak truly, when she says
He'll soon be home.
And yet . . .
She heard a sound of tapping . . .
While I heard nothing —
Nothing save my heart,
My old heart dinning in my ears.

    JENNY [*sitting up suddenly in bed and gazing into va-*
        cancy]. Hark!
There it is again . . .
A sound of tapping . . .
I hear it tapping, tapping . . .
Like a pick . . .
Tap . . . tap . . . tap . . . tap . . .

    TAMAR. A pick . . .
Ah, God!
Nay, daughter; there is nothing.
You must lie quiet now,
Or you . . .

    JENNY. Tap . . . tap . . .
It goes on tapping, tapping,
In the dark . . .
It's dark . . . so dark;
And I can scarcely breathe,
The darkness lies so heavily upon me,
As though I wandered somewhere underground,
With all the earth above me,
With great rocks hanging overhead,
So close that my hair brushes them,
Although I cannot see them;
And I can touch them with my hand . . .
Oh, they are falling, falling . . .
I've pulled them down on me . . .
The great black rocks . . .

               [*She sinks back exhausted.*]

    TAMAR. Nay, lass, you're lying in your bed,

Your own warm bed,
Beside your little son.
    JENNY [*drowsily*].   My little son!
When he comes home
He'll be so pleased . . .
But still I hear a sound
Of tapping . . .
Tap . . . tap . . . tap . . . tap . . .

                            [*She dozes over.*]

    TAMAR. My son!
Nay, there's no hope,
For she hears something . . .
Something that I cannot.
The wife's heart hears
What the old mother's may not,
Because it beats too loudly.

      [*She sits for a while gazing into the fire.*]

    JENNY [*sitting up again suddenly*]. Will no one stop
      that tapping?
I cannot sleep for it.
I think that some one is shut in somewhere,
And trying to get out.
Will no one let them out,
And stop the tapping?
It keeps on tapping, tapping . . .
Tap . . . tap . . . tap . . . tap . . .
And I can scarcely breathe,
The darkness is so thick.
It stifles me,
And weighs so heavily upon me,
And drips, and drips . . .
My hair is wet already;
There's water all about my knees.
I cannot see it,
But I feel it creeping,
Higher and higher,
Cold as death, about me:
I cannot see it,
But I hear it swishing
At every step,
And feel it dripping cold —

The darkness dripping down upon me,
So cold, so cold.
And yet . . . I cannot breathe . . .
The darkness is so thick, so hot:
It's like a furnace-blast
Upon my brow;
And weighs so heavily,
As though great rocks were hanging overhead!
And dripping, dripping . . .
I cannot lift my feet,
The water holds them,
It's creeping . . . creeping . . .
My wet hair drags me down.
Ah, God!
Will no one stop that tapping . . .
I cannot sleep . . .
And I would sleep
Till he comes home . . .
Tap . . . tap . . . tap . . . tap . . .

[*Sinks back exhausted.*]

TAMAR.   O God, have mercy on her . . . and on me!
She hears,
And yet,
She knows not what she hears.
But I,
Though I hear nothing,
I know all.
Robert, my son!
    JENNY [*starting up again*].   I cannot breathe
The darkness is so thick —
So thick and hot,
It stifles me . . .
Ah, God! Ah, God!
The darkness is ablaze.
The rocks are falling, falling . . .
The great, black, dripping rocks . . .
And I am falling . . .

[*A pause.*]

And there's some one tapping,
As though they would be in.
Why don't you let him in?
It is my husband;

He would see his son —
His firstborn son.
Can you not hear a tapping, tapping?
It's like the tapping of a pick . . .
Tap . . . tap . . .
But it grows fainter:
Now I cannot hear it.
The darkness has come down on me.
I sink . . . I sink . . .

　　　　　　　　　　　　　[She lies back exhausted.]

　　TAMAR.　She does not hear it now.
And now . . . it almost seems
As if . . . my heart had stopt . . .
I cannot breathe . . .
But she is sleeping soundly,
And sleep will give her strength.
She's scarcely slept,
Since he was born —
The poor wee babe! —
And he is sleeping too.
I would that I were in as deep a slumber,
For I am weary . . .
Yet, how could I sleep?
They sleep,
Because they do not know,
But I . . . I know.
Robert, my son!

　　　[She sits gazing into the fire.　After a while JENNY
　　　　wakens and looks about her.]

　　JENNY.　My little son,
Your father'll soon be home.
He'll be so pleased . . .
But he should be home now,
For it is light.
Has Robert not come home yet?
　　TAMAR.　Not . . . yet . . .
　　JENNY.　What time . . .
　　TAMAR.　The clock has stopt.
　　JENNY.　I wonder what can keep him.
It is light . . .

TAMAR. Nay, woman, it's not light yet.
It's dark . . . quite dark . . .
You're weakly still;
And you've been wandering;
And now you're talking foolishness.
You must not speak;
But go to sleep again,
And waken well and strong.
    JENNY. It seems quite light . . .
    TAMAR. Nay . . . it is dark . . . God knows!
    JENNY [*drowsily*]. I think that I could sleep again —
Sleep . . . till he comes.

> [*She sinks into a deeper slumber.* TAMAR *sits for a while, gazing into the fire with vacant eyes. Suddenly she speaks, her voice little more than a whisper, and tries to rise, but falls forward on to the hearthrug, and lies motionless.*]

    TAMAR. It's dark . . . quite dark . . .
Robert . . . my son!

> [*Time passes; presently a sound of voices is heard without; the door opens quietly, and* MAGGIE THOMSON *enters, followed by her daughter,* LIZZIE.]

    MAGGIE. Tamar . . . where are you?
Quick, lass, . . . she's fallen!
She must have fainted . . .
The shock . . .

> [*They turn* TAMAR'S *face to the light and loosen her bodice.*]

O God!
She does not breathe;
Her heart has failed her.
And I —
I left her here alone . . .
His mother . . .
    LIZZIE. The clock has stopt.
    MAGGIE. Look to the wife . . .
She may . . .

LIZZIE.   She's sleeping quietly.
MAGGIE.   Poor Jennie!
And her babe is fatherless.
LIZZIE.   He's snuggled to her breast,
And sleeping soundly.
A fine big boy he is.

AGATHA STEEL

Persons:

ZILLAH PAXTON.
AGATHA STEEL, *her daughter.*

Scene: A room in tenements. It is evening; and ZILLAH PAX-
TON, an elderly woman, sits by the fire, with folded hands;
when the door opens and AGATHA STEEL enters.

    ZILLAH. You, Agatha!
You startled me . . .
I heard the staircase creaking;
But little dreamt 'twas your foot.
I never thought to look on you again.
Since you and Jim went off, so suddenly,
Without a word, and only newly wedded,
It seemed I'd heard the last of you.
You went without a word to me —
Without a word to me, your mother!
And you've not written me a line —
A single line in all these years —
Three years, at least:
And I, for all you cared,
I might have been both dead and buried.
And you say nothing now!
Have you no tongue at all?
I'm glad to see your face, although it looks . . .
But you — you must be ailing, daughter,
To look like that!
Have you come back to me, because you're ailing,
Come back to me . . .
Speak, woman!
    AGATHA. Nay . . . I'm well enough.
    ZILLAH. Well? Nay, you're ailing, Agatha.
A mother's eye is quick . . .
But, where is Jim?
Is he not with you, lass?

AGATHA.   I don't know where he is.

ZILLAH.   You don't know where!
He has not left you, daughter?

AGATHA.   He's left me for another woman.

ZILLAH.   A curse . . .

AGATHA.   Nay! you've no right to curse him.

ZILLAH.   Right!   I've no right to curse the man
Who leaves my daughter, his own wedded wife . . .
Have I, your mother . . .

AGATHA.   You've no right:
For you, my mother, let me wed him.

ZILLAH.   I let you!   Why, what else was there to do?
The thing was past my mending,
Before I even heard of it.

AGATHA.   You know that is not true.
I married him for your sake:
You drove me to it,
Though you knew I loathed him.

ZILLAH.   For my sake!   I — I drove you!
So I'm to bear the blame of your ill-doing,
Because I tried to do the best for you,
And save you from the gutter!

AGATHA.   The best for me . . . the best!
To make me wed the man I hated!

ZILLAH.   You did not always hate him.

AGATHA.   True . . . yet, I think,
I never really loved him.

ZILLAH.   More shame to you!

AGATHA.   Perhaps, and still,
Even I would not have married him.
But you — you knew him,
And you let me wed him,
Though I was your own daughter, just a child.
Yea, I was young, God knows!
But he . . .
He always had a way with him:
And I was in his arms, before I knew.
And then . . .
I loathed him, loathed him!
And you . . . you knew . . . and yet . . .

ZILLAH.   What else was left?
Would you have had . . .

AGATHA.   Ay! anything but this.
But you . . . you cannot understand.

You have not changed, while I . . .
   ZILLAH.   Changed, Agatha?
   AGATHA.   And yet, how should you change?
You've not gone through what I have.
Still, it is strange to think three years
Should make no difference, when, to me . . .
But you . . . you speak, as you spoke then —
Then, when you scolded me, and said,
The Beals had always been respectable:
And so, I married him:
And I have been respectable:
And clung unto the man who hated me,
Until he shook me off.
   ZILLAH.   But you're his wife . . .
   AGATHA.   Oh, mother, will you never understand!
Yes, I'm his wife, his wedded wife:
And I've been faithful to him,
Been faithful to the husband that I hated,
Though he was ever faithless.
Yes, mother, I, your daughter,
Have been respectable.
I've not disgraced you, mother.
   ZILLAH.   Ah, lass, you're bitter;
But, it's little wonder,
Since you're forsaken.
Jim was always wild . . .
   AGATHA.   Wild!
   ZILLAH.   From a boy . . .
And still, I never thought . . .
A curse . . .
   AGATHA.   Nay! bless him, rather,
That he, at least, has left me.
   ZILLAH.   Ay! maybe, you're well rid of him,
If he's been cruel . . .
   AGATHA.   Cruel, woman!
You know that he was drunk the night we married.
He's scarce been sober, since.
And, when a man's in drink . . .
But, that's past now:
We'll talk no more about it.
A blow is neither here nor there,
If only you're respectable!
   ZILLAH.   But, how've you lived these years?
   AGATHA.   God knows!

He never did a stroke of work;
But, lived upon the little I could earn.
We've travelled all the countryside:
For, when I'd worked my fingers to the bone,
To get a home together,
He'd always break it up;
And drag me out again,
To trail behind him to another town.

    ZILLAH.   You've had no children, daughter?

    AGATHA.   Children . . . ah, God!

    ZILLAH.   Dead, Agatha!
Perhaps, it's well . . .

    AGATHA.   It's well that I should bear three stillborn
        babies!

    ZILLAH.   Stillborn! Ah, daughter!

    AGATHA.   If only one had lived . . .
But he . . . he killed them . . .
Ay! I'm bitter.

    ZILLAH.   You've cause enough: he's used you cruelly.
Three stillborn babes!

    AGATHA.   Mother, you understand!

    ZILLAH.   Ay, Agatha!
My first was stillborn . . .

    AGATHA.   I never knew.

    ZILLAH.   And yet, your father, lass,
Was always good to me.
Ay! he was ever kind . . .
But, Jim has used you cruelly.

    AGATHA [*rising*].   Well . . . now, it's over!
And I have some hope . . .
But, I must not stay talking here.
It's time . . .

    ZILLAH.   You would not go again?
Where can you go?
You'll live here, surely, now?

    AGATHA.   Nay! anywhere but here.
He'll likely weary of his mistress —
Poor soul, I pity her!
And seek again his wife to keep him.
He'd come here, first . . .
What startles you?

    ZILLAH.   I thought I heard a step.

    AGATHA.   Oh! I've no fear he'll come yet;
She's young, and strong . . .

ZILLAH. I did not think 'twas Jim,
But Richard.
AGATHA. Richard? Who?
ZILLAH. Yes, Agatha, you've given me no chance
To tell you that I'd wed again.
AGATHA. You . . . married!
ZILLAH. Ay, a year ago,
To Richard Paxton.
AGATHA. Mother! not to him!
ZILLAH. Why not . . .
AGATHA. You've married him . . .
And, yet, you knew that he was never steady!
ZILLAH. Well, life's a lonely thing without a man:
And you had left me, daughter:
You left, without a word: and never wrote:
You didn't care, though I was dead, and buried.
Why should you mind . . .
And there's small blame to them
Who drink too much, at whiles.
There's little else the poor can get too much of:
And life, at best, is dull enough, God knows.
Sometimes, it's better to forget . . .
And . . . it's a lovely dizziness.
AGATHA. You! Mother!
ZILLAH. Ay! you'll blame me.
But, Richard is not always kind . . .
AGATHA. Nay, mother, I don't blame you:
It's better to forget.
Forgive me if I spoke too harshly:
I am not bitter, now.
But I must go.
ZILLAH. Where will you go?
AGATHA. I cannot tell — but, far away from here . . .
That I, too, may forget . . .
Yes; even I!
Since I am free;
And there is hope within me
That I may bear a living child.

MATES

Persons:

MARTIN AYNSLEY, *a pitman.*
CHARLOTTE AYNSLEY, *his mother.*
GRACE HARDY, *his betrothed.*

Scene: CHARLOTTE AYNSLEY'S *cottage.* CHARLOTTE AYNSLEY
and GRACE HARDY *stand by fire, talking together.*

CHARLOTTE. Nay, lass! I cannot turn him;
He pays no heed to me:
He'll have his will, for all that I can say.
He's just his father over.
    GRACE. But, have you said . . .
    CHARLOTTE. Said! Have I not said all to him
A mother's heart can say —
A heart left mateless,
And with one son left . . .
How could I leave a single word unspoken,
To save the only son that's left me —
To save him from the death
That overtook his father and his brothers,
That night . . .
When I . . .
I slumbered soundly;
And never dreamt of danger,
While they, my husband and my sons . . .
And Martin —
Though 'twas only by a hair's breadth
That he himself escaped,
And came to me again —
Yet, he'll not leave the pit,
For all my pleading.
Perhaps if you . . .
    GRACE. Nay! but I've talked, and talked, with him;
And he would answer nothing.
I could not win a word from him.

Will you not try again?
    CHARLOTTE. Try, daughter, try!
What is there left to try?
How could I leave a stone unturned!
Do I not lie awake the livelong night,
To think of ways and means
To keep him from the pit?
I've scarcely slept a wink since . . .
Since that night —
That night I slept so soundly . . .

                                         [*Pause.*]

It seems as though he could not break with it —
The pit that all his folk have worked in.
It's said, his father's grandfather
Was born at the pit-bottom —
Ay, daughter! born and died there:
For, two days after he was married,
They found him, crushed beneath a rock,
Dead, in the very shaft —
The very shaft in which his mother bore him:
For womenfolk worked in the pits in those days,
Young girls, and mothers near their time,
And little children, naked . . .
    GRACE. But is there nothing else that Martin
Would care to try his hand at?
    CHARLOTTE. Have I not offered, lass,
To set him up in any trade he fancies?
This very morn, when he came in,
I said I'd buy a horse and cart,
With stock-in-trade for him to hawk:
For hawking's scarce a job
That needs a man brought up to it.
At least, I thought that he . . .
    GRACE. What did he say?
    CHARLOTTE. He only laughed at first;
But, when I pressed him, shrugged his shoulders,
You know the way he has with him,
And looked me straight betwixt the eyes —
Looked at me with his father's eyes —
And then he said:
" Nay, mother! I'm a pitman;
And I must take my chance among my mates."
He's just his father over . . .

GRACE. That was all?

CHARLOTTE. All, daughter! Was it not enough?
There's nothing more to say.
He will not leave the pit,
Although his father, and his brothers . . .
And he, himself . . .
I never shall sleep soundly any more —
Though sound I slept that night,
While they were dying . . . I . . .

GRACE. I'll speak with him again.
Perhaps . . .

CHARLOTTE. Ay, lass; he'll listen to you,
If he'll pay heed to any one.

GRACE. Oh, Charlotte, do you think that I . . .
When you, his mother . . .
Do you think he cares . . .
He cares so much for me?
If I could only turn him!
And yet, if he'll not heed . . .

CHARLOTTE. It seems, I've lost my hold:
He's broken from my apron-strings,
It's your turn now;
And you must try your strength with him.
He's stubborn; but he's fond of you;
And when his heart is set on anything,
He's just his father over.
When Stephen first walked out with me,
His mother bade . . .
But Martin's stirring;
I must get his bait.
Ay! even while we talk of him, he's dressing
To go upon the night-shift.
Talk! Talk!

GRACE. Yet, I must try to save him.
If I could only turn . . .

CHARLOTTE. Pray God, you may!
There's still a chance;
Though I . . .
It's your turn now.
I'm only Martin's mother;
But, you . . .
When Stephen wooed me, I was more to him . . .
And you'll be more to Martin . . .
How he whistles!

His heart, at least, is light enough.
And, in a moment he'll be out.
I'll leave you here to wait for him,
And speak with him, alone;
And if he asks for me,
Say that I'm seeking coals —
Coals! seeking coals!
God knows their cost . . .
Sometimes I cannot bear to see a fire,
And think of all the burning lives . . .
He'll soon be out.
His bait is on the table;
Though I'll be back before he leaves.
    GRACE. Nay, do not go.
What can I say to him!
    CHARLOTTE. Your heart will tell you, if you love . . .
But, here he comes.

    [*She picks up the scuttle and shovel and goes out.*
    MARTIN AYNSLEY *enters from the inner room.*]

    MARTIN. Mother, this button . . .
You here, lass!
I thought I heard my mother's voice,
But did not know who talked with her.
Has she gone out?
I wanted . . .
    GRACE. Come, lad, I'll sew the button on.
    MARTIN. You, Grace!
Well, you've got nimble fingers.
But, mother, lass . . .
    GRACE. She'll not be long.
Come nearer to the window:
Nay, but you must stand quietly,
Or you'll be pricked, in no time.
    MARTIN. Nay, then, I'd best be quiet,
For I shall often want you . . .
I play the deuce with buttons.
You're not afraid, lass, when you think of all . . .
    GRACE. Nay, I'll not mind the buttons;
They'll be the least . . .
    MARTIN. The least?
    GRACE. If wives had naught to do for men,
But sew on buttons,

They would thank their stars.
But, maybe, some one else than I
Will sew yours on for you.
    MARTIN.   Why, Grace, who else?
    GRACE. Who knows!
The chance is, you'll go buttonless,
For any stitch that I . . .
    MARTIN. What ails you, lass?
You would not have your husband . . .
    GRACE. My husband! Nay; I'll tend my husband:
'Twas you that I was speaking of.
    MARTIN. Well: I don't understand you:
But if you keep your husband's buttons on,
Then I'll go snug and decent.
    GRACE. Lad, don't you be too sure.
    MARTIN. Too sure! Why, Grace!
But you, you cannot help yourself.
I've set my heart upon you:
And mother says I'm stubborn.
    GRACE. And if I'm stubborn, too?
    MARTIN. You, Grace! But you don't know me!
    GRACE. And, are you sure you've naught to learn of me?
    MARTIN. I'm sure you're mine, beyond all help.
You're true to me . . .
    GRACE. God knows, I'm true . . .
But still . . . it's not too late . . .
    MARTIN. Come, woman! no more foolishness,
You're stitched to me as firmly as this button
That you've sewn on so strongly.
    GRACE. As firmly! yes: I sewed it on:
But I can snip it off with much less labour.
    MARTIN. Not if I hold the scissors!

                        [Snatches them up.]

Nay! you may tug, and tug:
Your work will stand it easily:
'Twill not give way, though you should tug my shirt off.
Your work's too good: and you are mine, as surely . . .
But, lass, enough of this.
If I had only known that you were here,
I would . . . yet, you and she —
You seemed to have enough to talk of,
Without me . . .

GRACE. Ay! we'd much to talk of.

MARTIN. When only half awake, I heard you at it;
And lay, and wondered what 'twas all about.
You womenfolk must always chatter, chatter:
You've got such restless tongues.

GRACE. And yet, it is the men that keep them wagging.

MARTIN. The men?

GRACE. Foolhardy, heedless men,
That don't care how they break the women's peace.

MARTIN. Ah, now, I understand! There's more than
              buttons!
I've little need to ask what kept you talking.
You've put your heads together: but, it's useless.
I cannot leave the pit, though you should talk till doomsday:
So let no more be said.

GRACE. For my sake, Martin!

MARTIN. Your sake, Grace?
There's little I'd not do for you, you know, lass, but not this.
You would not have me cowardly, for your sake?
How should I face my mates, if I forsook them?
You would not have me spend my days,
A cur, with tail betwixt his legs,
And slinking round the nearest corner,
Whenever my old mates went by
To take their usual shift?
Nay; I will hold my head up,
A man, among the men,
For your sake — ay! for your sake!

GRACE. And who would dare to call you coward —
Who, knowing all you've been through?

MARTIN. There's one who knows what I've been
              through,
Who'd call me coward.

GRACE. Who, lad?

MARTIN. Can you ask?
One, Martin Aynsley.

GRACE. Ay . . . and yet . . .
If you care naught for me,
Think of your mother, Martin.
You know she's lost her husband,
And all her sons but you;
And cannot rest, while you are in the pit.

MARTIN. You know I care for you; and think of her;
And yet, I'm sure of one thing,

Though you may little think it now,
If I forsook the pit,
The time would surely come
When you would both despise me in your hearts.
    GRACE. Nay, Martin!
    MARTIN. Grace, I know:
It's sure as death.
I cannot leave the pit.
My father died,
And I will die, a pitman.
You wouldn't have me throw up work
That I was born and bred to:
You surely wouldn't have me
Throw over all my mates —
The lads I went to school with,
That I've grown up with,
Played and worked with,
And had such larks . . .
There's not too many of them left now . . .
But all there are went through that night with me.
Before that night,
Perhaps, I might have left them;
But now, how could I!
Nay, I'll take my chance.
    GRACE. Then some one else must sew . . .
    MARTIN. Hark!
    GRACE. What d'you hear?
    MARTIN. I thought I heard him whistling.
    GRACE. Who, lad?
    MARTIN. I thought 'twas Nicholas, my mate:
But that was not his whistle.
He always whistles for me,
Every night at Jackson's Corner;
And we go to work together.
    GRACE. Ay! he'd whistle you to death . . .
And you . . . you'd follow . . .
    MARTIN. Shame upon you, lass!
How can you talk like that!
You know as well as I do
That, but for him, I'd be a dead man now.
'Twas he alone who dragged me —
Who dragged me from the death
That overtook my father and my brothers.
Grace, he did not forsake me:

Shall I desert him now?
He sought me, at the first alarm,
And we two fled together,
Before the creeping choke-damp,
Until it gained upon us,
And I was overcome,
And dropped, to die:
When Nicholas picked me up,
And bore me in his arms,
Along the stifling galleries —
Stumbling over dead and dying
Every step he staggered.
Though he could scarcely struggle
Against the damp himself,
He bore me into safety;
And kept the spark of life in me,
Till we at last were rescued.

GRACE.   And yet, you'd go through that again?
MARTIN.   If need be, lass, with Nicholas.
GRACE.   You love him more than me.
MARTIN.   Nay, Grace! you know . . .
GRACE.   Yet you'll not even leave the pit for my sake,
While you would go to death for his.
MARTIN.   I'd go to death for him;
But I'd not be a coward
For your sake, even, Grace.
GRACE.   Then you must choose between us.
MARTIN.   Grace!
GRACE.   Ay! you must choose, and now!
I cannot lead your mother's life,
Or my own mother's, either.
You know that in the dead of night
My father and my brothers
Were lost with yours . . . and I . . .
Who saw them brought in, one by one,
And laid upon their beds,
With faces covered . . .
How could I ever rest at all,
With that remembrance in my heart,
While you were in the pit —
With dread for ever on me,
That you, too, would be brought,
And laid, a broken bundle, at my feet,
Or never come at all to me again?

How could I live,
With ears for ever listening for the rumble
Of fresh disaster?
With eyes for ever wide with dread to see
The flames leap up the shaft?
How could I sleep . . .   [*A shrill whistling is heard.*]
He whistles you — your mate!
And who am I to keep you?
Forsake me now for him . . .
And I . . . and I . . .
   MARTIN.   Grace!
   GRACE.   Nay, Martin! you must choose . . .
He whistles louder . . .
He's impatient . . .
Hark!
Now you must choose between us.
   MARTIN.   The choice is made, lass;
I choose him — and you!

> [*He takes her in his arms, snatches a kiss, and goes out.*]

   GRACE [*gazing after him*].   The choice is made . . .
He knows I cannot break with him.
And I must sew . . . [*calling after him*].
You've gone without your bait!
Martin!

> [*She picks up the basket and can, and runs out after
> him.*]

THE OPERATION

Persons:

WILLIAM LOWRY, *a printer.*
HESTER LOWRY, *his wife.*
LETTY LOWRY, *their daughter.*

Scene: A room in tenements, late at night. WILLIAM LOWRY *sits with his coat off, in an armchair, smoking, and reading a newspaper. The door opens, and* HESTER LOWRY *enters. Over her arm is a basket, laden with purchases, which she lays on the table with a sigh.*

WILLIAM.   You're late to-night.
You should have let me come with you:
That basket's heavy, wife.
HESTER.   'Twas not the basket, William:
I was kept.
WILLIAM.   What kept you, wife?
The shops would not be thronged, to-night.
HESTER.   I finished with the shops, three hours ago.
I had to wait my turn.
WILLIAM.   Your turn?
Who kept you waiting?
HESTER.   The doctors, husband.
WILLIAM.   Doctors, wife?
HESTER.   I thought 'twas time to have the thing away;
And so I went to see.
The doctors shook their heads;
And said, next week, it might have been too late . . .
WILLIAM.   Too late?   What ails you, wife?   I never
knew . . .
HESTER.   They say it's cancer.
They were very kind;
And wanted me to stay, to-night,
And have it done, at once.
They'd hardly let me leave.
I said, I must come home to see you first.

171

They'll take me in to-morrow.

WILLIAM. To-morrow, wife! And I . . . I never
    knew.
You must have guessed, before you went . . .

HESTER. Yes, lad; I knew: and 'twas no shock to me;
I've known so long.

WILLIAM. So long! . . . and never told me!
But, lass, the pain . . .

HESTER. Ay; it was bad to bear.
At first I scarce could keep from crying out;
But, as the years went by . . .

WILLIAM. The years! You've had the pain for years?

HESTER. Ay, off and on.
It's full eleven years, since first I felt it.

WILLIAM. And, from the first, you knew . . .

HESTER. I knew.
My father died of it.

WILLIAM. Eleven years! And never breathed a word,
Nor murmured once, but patiently . . .

HESTER. I come of fisherfolk, who live on patience.
It's little use for any man
To be impatient with the sea.

WILLIAM. And I . . . I never guessed.
I've seen you, day by day,
And slept, each night, beside you in the bed;
And yet, you never breathed a word . . .

HESTER. Nay, lad; I've kept the thing from you:
'Twould not have eased the pain to share it.
You slept the sounder, knowing nothing;
Though, there were times the gnawing was so bad,
I could have torn . . .

WILLIAM. And I slept on unknowing!
You never even wakened me.
And every little ache I've had,
I've made a pretty song about it!

HESTER. You've made a song!
And what about the time your arm was caught . . .
Was caught in the machine, and you were hanging . . .
Were hanging by the flesh, a mortal hour!

WILLIAM. Nay; Michael held me up upon his back.

HESTER. But, all that time your arm was in the wheels;
And you . . . you never murmured, once, they say;
But, only laughed, and jested;
Although they had to take a chisel,

And cut each cog out separately,
Before the flesh was freed.
How you could bear the strain and jar,
And never once lose heart,
I cannot think; and your poor arm . . .
Your poor, poor arm, with all the sinews torn . . .

WILLIAM. I've never really played the fiddle since:
I've got tc make the notes, that used to come.
But you, wife, all these years . . .
And I slept on . . .

HESTER. 'Twould not have eased . . .

WILLIAM. But, if I'd known,
You should have had the doctor at the first.

HESTER. I knew you could not spare me then:
Those were not easy times!
You, laid off idle through your accident,
And Letty, but a baby:
And we had both enough to do,
To keep the home together.
I hoped, at least, to keep things going;
Till I should be past doing things.
The time has come . . .
But I . . . I've saved a bit:
And Letty's thirteen past,
And finished schooling,
And old enough to manage for you.
Is she in bed?

WILLIAM. She went an hour ago.
She wanted sorely to wait up for you;
But she was sleepy, so I wouldn't let her.

HESTER. Ay, she's been at it all day long;
And she's a handy lass,
And will do well enough for you,
Until . . . until . . .

WILLIAM. Does Letty know?

HESTER. Nay, she knows nothing, William;
And I'll not tell her now till morning.
I would not spoil her sleep.
Poor child, she little dreams!
But she's a plucky girl,
And I have taught her everything:
And she can cook, and scrub, and wash,
As well as any woman.
You'll scarcely miss me . . .

WILLIAM.   Wife!

HESTER.   I've seen to all your clothes,
And there are shirts and stockings
To last for many weeks,
To last until . . .
I mayn't be long away.

WILLIAM.   O, wife, it's terrible . . . I cannot think . . .
It seems so strange that all these years . . .

HESTER.   You never saw my father:
He suffered long, poor fellow,
But never rightly knew that it was cancer,
Till very nigh the end.
It laid him low at last,
When he was far from home,
After the herring in the Western seas.
The doctor said he must return by train,
But he'd not leave his boat;
And so his mates set sail,
(The season just begun,
And catches heavier than they'd been for years)
And brought him home.
And, when the *Ella* neared the harbour,
He left his bunk, and took the tiller,
And brought her in himself.
Though, in his heart, he knew it was the last time,
Yet he'd a smile for us;
And when the boat was berthed,
He looked my mother bravely in the eyes,
And clasped her hand, and they went home together.
He never rose again:
The doctors could do nothing:
But he was brave and gay until the end;
And always smiled, and said it did not hurt,
Although his teeth were clenched,
And his strong fingers clutched the bedclothes tightly.

WILLIAM.   And you're his daughter, wife!

HESTER.   But I've cried out before I'm hurt too sorely.
Next week, the doctors said, it might have been . . .
It's taken in the nick of time,
And I will soon be well again.
Folk go through such, and worse, each day:
It's naught to make a fuss about.
I've only one more night to bear the pain . . .
And then . . .

WILLIAM. Ay, wife, you'll soon be well again,
With such a heart in you.
And yet, if you had gone too long . . .
You should have told me at the first,
And let us fend . . .
  HESTER. My father brought his boat in.

[*The inner door opens, and* LETTY *stands in the door-
    way, in her night-dress.*]

  LETTY. Is mother not home yet?
Oh, there you are!
You stayed so long to-night,
I've been asleep and dreaming!
Oh, such a dreadful dream!
I dreamt that you . . .
But you are safe and sound!
You are not ailing, mother?
  HESTER. Lass, I'm as well as I have been for years.
But you'll catch cold:
You'd better get to bed again.
  LETTY. But, I shall dream.
  HESTER. Nay, you'll sleep sound, to-night.

[LETTY *kisses her father and mother good-night and
    goes back to the bedroom.*]

THE CALL

Persons:

SETH HERDMAN, *a fireman.*
MARY HERDMAN, *his mother.*
CHRISTOPHER BELL, *a fireman.*

*Scene: The engine-house of a fire-station. The men are gathered
in knots, talking in subdued voices, scarcely audible above the
racket of the street. SETH HERDMAN paces backwards and
forwards, impetuously, by himself, when CHRISTOPHER BELL
approaches him, holding out his hand.*

CHRISTOPHER. The best of luck!
SETH. I fear there's little hope.
CHRISTOPHER. Nay, keep your heart up. You can
    never tell.
When my first lass was born, my wife had long been ailing:
There seemed to be no chance for her:
And now, though she's the mother
Of six brave, sonsy lasses,
She's heartier than she's been in all her life.
SETH. The doctor says . . .
CHRISTOPHER. But even doctors don't know everything.
Your wife was always plucky,
And she'll surprise them yet.
You must be plucky, too.
Your mother tends her — and you know your mother!
And only think, if all goes well upstairs,
How proud you'll be!
For I'm a father, and I know.
There's not a prouder man in all the world.
SETH. If all goes well . . .
CHRISTOPHER. You'll be the happiest man . . .
There'll be no doing with you!
SETH. If I but knew!
CHRISTOPHER. The waiting's a sore trial.
But think, what luck we're not called out to-night!

176

It would be hard to go . . .

SETH. It's harder still to stand here, doing nothing,
While she . . . I'd bear it better,
If only I'd a job to tackle —
A job that left no time for thinking.
I'd rather be upon a blazing roof,
Than standing idle, with such thoughts at work,
While she . . .

CHRISTOPHER. Ay, lad, I understand.
Uncertainty's the devil.
But dwell upon the lucky chance,
And maybe, 'twill be yours:
And then you'll be the happiest of men.
You cannot think the difference children make:
No house is home, unless there's children in it.
My girls are always in my mind:
And yet, whenever I go in,
It's fresh delight to see them,
And take them in my arms.
They're more to me than I can tell you;
I'm always dull at saying
The thing that's in my heart:
But they have brought so much to me,
And just made all the difference to my life —
Ay, to my life and work —
For now I've them to work for.
Though I was never slack, they hearten me;
And when I hear the cry
That there are children in a burning house,
I always think of them,
And see their faces in the flames,
Their arms stretched out to me;
And hear their little voices calling, " Daddy! "
Then naught could hold me back.

SETH. Ay, you were always reckless.

CHRISTOPHER. Not reckless, lad. No father dare be
        reckless.
Upon the toppling walls,
Amid the flames and smoke,
I always know they're 'waiting me at home,
That I must win through all to them.
And when at last, perhaps at dawn,
I'm free to cross my threshold,
Drenched, stifled, scorched and scalded,

To see them lying quietly,
In dreamless slumber, clean and sweet!
   SETH.   If but the bell would sound,
And call us out to tackle
The biggest blaze . . .
   CHRISTOPHER.   Nay, lad, you don't know what you're
      saying.
That thought's not worthy of you:
For you're no coward in the face of danger.
The waiting's hard to bear;
But she bears more than you.
   SETH.   It's her I think of;
She bears all . . . while I . . .
I can do nothing . . . nothing!
The doctor said . . . Ah, God!
If she should not win through!
   CHRISTOPHER.   Lad, at the worst, I know that you'll be
      brave.
But, see, your mother . . . Courage!

> [MARY HERDMAN *enters hurriedly, and goes up to*
> SETH, *and takes him in her arms, without speak-*
> *ing.*]

   SETH.   Mother!
   MARY.   My son!
   SETH.   Is there no hope?
   MARY.   The babe's alive.
   SETH.   And she . . . and she . . .

> [*The fire alarm sounds, and all the men spring to the*
> *engine.*]

Thank God, there's work!
Come, lads.

THE WOUND

Persons:

HETTY DROVER, *Phillip Drover's wife.*
SUSAN WELCH, *her mother.*
JOHN RIDDLE, *a ship's riveter.*

Scene: A room in tenements. HETTY DROVER *stands near the
window, gazing out with unseeing eyes. She has a wound on
her brow, and another on her hand; but seems oblivious of
them. A footstep on the stairs arouses her; and she hastily
pulls her hair over her brow, hides her hand beneath her
apron; and moves towards the cradle in which her baby is
sleeping. The door opens; and* SUSAN WELCH *enters.*

    HETTY.   You, mother!
    SUSAN.   I've just come . . .
Why, daughter, what's amiss?
You look so pale . . .
And, oh! your brow is bleeding —
A dreadful wound . . .
Nay! do not touch it, woman.
Your hand bleeds, too!
    HETTY.   It's nothing.
    SUSAN.   Nothing!
A wound like that — you call it nothing!
But, I must bind it up, instead of talking.
Words won't heal wounds,
Though often they're the cause of them.

      [*She takes some old linen from a drawer; fills a basin
          with water, and washes, and binds the wound while
          she is talking.*]

Ah, what a gash! your poor, poor brow!
How you could come by such a wound,
I cannot think . . .
    HETTY.   I fell.

SUSAN. You fell? How did you come to fall?
HETTY. I hardly know.
SUSAN. You hardly know?
HETTY. I think I must have slipt; and struck the fender;
And clutched the bars, in falling:
My hand is burnt,
Although I did not feel it then.
SUSAN. You think you slipt! And then you call it noth-
    ing —
A wound like that, clean to the bone!
But, maybe, you are dazed a bit;
I shouldn't wonder if . . .
When did it happen, daughter?
HETTY. Long ago . . .
SUSAN. It cannot be so long; the wound still bleeds.
HETTY. Long . . . long ago . . .
I don't know what I'm saying!
An hour ago, perhaps.
SUSAN. An hour ago? Then Phillip had not gone?
HETTY. Nay . . . he'd not gone . . .
SUSAN. How comes it that he left you, lass,
In such a state as this?
HETTY. Oh, but I'm dazed!
And don't know what I'm saying.
He'd left, long, long before.
SUSAN. What set him off so early?
He hasn't far to go.
The Yard would scarce be open.
HETTY. I don't know why he went.
Perhaps, he thought he'd take a turn . . .
SUSAN. On such a morning, daughter!
HETTY. Why not? A drop or two of rain
Is neither here nor there with menfolk.
'Twould take a pretty splash, I fancy,
To keep my man indoors.
But, I know nothing where he went.
I only know he'd gone . . . long, long before . . .
Why, woman, can you think he'd go —
He'd go, and leave me lying,
Half-senseless, on the hearth;
And never turn . . . though I . . . though I . . .
But he had gone, long, long before I tumbled.
He kissed me . . . ere he went;
He always kisses . . .

Ay, and his babe,
He kissed the babe and took it in his arms·;
For he's the best of fathers;
He loves his babe . . . he's never harsh with it.
I thought of that, while I lay, listening
For his return . . .
 SUSAN. For his return? You thought he'd come again?
 HETTY. I don't know what I'm saying!
How could he come, when he's been long at work?
And knowing nothing . . .
 SUSAN. Still . . .
 HETTY. You don't believe me, mother?
 SUSAN. I scarce know what to think.
 HETTY. When did I ever lie to you,
That you should doubt . . .
 SUSAN. Nay; you've been always truthful;
But Phillip . . .
 HETTY. Can you think he'd go,
And slam the door behind him,
And leave me, lying helpless . . .
But you . . .
Why do you look at me like that;
What can I say . . .
 SUSAN. Say nothing, daughter.
 HETTY. You don't believe me, mother?
 SUSAN. I know that Phillip's hot, at times;
And you would screen him.
 HETTY. Nay! there's naught to screen.
'Twas I that . . . Nay!
And, if he's hot, at times,
You know he's much to try him;
The racket that he works in, all day long,
Would wear the best of tempers.
Why, mother, who should know as well as you
How soon a riveter is done?
The hammers break a man, before his time;
And father was a shattered man at forty;
And Phillip's thirty-five;
And if he's failed a bit . . .
And, sometimes, overhasty,
Well, I am hasty, too;
You know my temper; no one knows it better.
 SUSAN. But, such a wound! And then to leave . . .
 HETTY. You do not dare to look me in the eyes,

And say you think he struck . . .
 SUSAN. There's some one at the door; I'll open it.

 [*She goes to the door, and throws it open.* JOHN RID-
  DLE *steps in, but hesitates on the threshold withou[t]
  speaking.*]

 SUSAN. Why, John, you here?
Are you not working, then?
 JOHN. Ay, . . . I am working, Susan.
I've only left the Yard . . . I've come . . .
 HETTY. Oh, tell me what has happened!
Why don't you speak!
Will you stand there, all day, and never speak . . .
 JOHN. I've that to say which is not spoken easily,
Nor easy hearing for a wife.
 HETTY. Speak out! Speak out!
You know that I'm no coward.
Speak! Where is Phillip? Speak!
 JOHN. They're bringing him along.
 SUSAN. Ah, God!
 HETTY. They're bringing him . . . And I . . . I lay
  and listened . . .
 SUSAN. How did it happen?
 JOHN. How? I scarcely know,
Though I was face to face with him;
For he and I were hammer-mates.
We sat astride the beam;
And I was chaffing him;
But, he was dazed, and silent;
And, when the red-hot rivet was thrust up,
He never struck at it;
He must have lost his nerve;
And so, I took his turn;
And still he did not strike,
But, looked at it, bewildered;
And, all at once, cried out:
" It bleeds! It bleeds!"
And then, his fingers slackened on the hammer,
Which clattered to the bottom of the ship:
And then, he swayed,
And tumbled after it . . .
I tried to clutch . . .
 SUSAN. And nothing broke his fall?

JOHN.   We found him in a heap.

SUSAN.   Dead?

JOHN.   At the point of death:
He scarcely breathed a moment;
But, as I bent down over him,
I heard him whisper . . .

HETTY.   Spare me what he said!
I dare not hear it . . .

JOHN.   I'd not hurt . . .

HETTY.   Nay! Nay! speak out.
I am no coward . . . I . . .
Tell all, tell all.

JOHN.   There is not much to tell.
He whispered: " Lass, forgive me."
Then, he died.

HETTY.   Forgive you, lad!
There's nothing to forgive.
'Twas I who angered you; my foolish tongue . . .
It's I who need . . .
But, I . . . I'm dazed;
And don't know what I'm saying . . .
Nay! Nay! you did not hear aright!
He needed no forgiveness.
Why should he beg forgiveness,
Of me, his wife . . . and he, the best of husbands . . .
And I . . . I lay, and listened for his footstep . . .
If he'd but turned!
There's nothing to forgive . . .
'Twas I . . . and now,
Where shall I seek forgiveness!

SUSAN.   I hear steps coming up the court.

JOHN [*starting forward, and catching* HETTY, *as she swoons*].   Nay, steady, lass!

HETTY.   He's coming back.

SUMMER-DAWN

Persons:

LABAN CARPENTER, *a hind.*
BETTY CARPENTER, *his wife.*

Scene: LABAN CARPENTER'S *cottage, before dawn.* LABAN *still lies in bed, dozing; but his wife is already dressed; and is setting the kettle on a newly-lit fire. In the bed, beside* LABAN, *is a six-months old baby; and, in another bed, are five children, all under the age of seven; the boys sleeping at one end, the girls, at the other.*

    BETTY.   Come, lad, get up, or we'll be late.
    LABAN.   So soon, lass! What o'clock is it?
    BETTY.   It's getting on for three.
The fire is kindling famously:
I'll have the kettle boiling in a twinkling.
We'll have a sup of tea, before we start,
To keep the bitter chill out.
It's raw work, turning out these dewy mornings.
    LABAN.   It seems but half-an-hour ago,
Since I lay down in bed.
    BETTY.   Nay, Laban, it was half-past ten,
At most, when you turned in.
You'd scarcely got your trousers off,
Before you dropt asleep;
And, you were snoring, like a pig,
Until I turned you off your back.
'Twas nigh eleven, when I got to bed.
    LABAN.   I can't tell how you manage.
A man must have his sleep out,
If he's to do his day's work:
But, women, somehow, seem . . .
    BETTY.   Come, lad, don't lie there, talking:
But, stir yourself . . .
    LABAN.   My back is nearly broken.
    BETTY.   Ay, some folk's backs are broken easily.

LABAN. You call it easily!
It's easy, hoeing turnips, every night,
Until it is too dark to see our feet;
And then, to start again, at dawn:
And, Summer-nights so short!
        BETTY. If Summer-nights were longer,
Your children would go shoeless through the Winter.
        LABAN. And still, it's heavy on a man,
As well as all his day's work.
        BETTY. Have I no day's work, too?
Your day's work will not keep you, housed and fed —
You, and your wife, and children.
And if your father'd talked like that,
Lad, where would you be now?
He can have been no lie-abed:
He'd not a lazy bone in all his body.
You've heard him boast, a hundred times:
" Though I have had bad seasons,
I've not done far amiss:
Since I have reared eleven men and women."
Ay! and your mother, crippled with rheumatics,
For more than half her lifetime:
And only him to do the housework;
And see to all the lot of you,
And keep you decent, single-handed,
Until the girls were old enough,
As well as all his day's work.
You talk of day's work!
Why, I've heard him tell,
How, once, to save the corn,
He worked a week, without a wink of sleep:
All day, at his own job in Stobshill mine:
And, all night, helping in the harvest-field.
        LABAN. And then, he slept . . .
        BETTY. He slept his fill:
But, not till all was harvested.
He saved the corn.
        LABAN. Ay: somehow, fathers . . .
        BETTY. You're a father, too:
And should think shame to lie and grumble there;
And only be too glad that we are able
To earn a little extra in the Summer,
To tide us over Winter.
        LABAN. True, wife, true:

And yet, it's hard that, in an honest day's work,
A strong man cannot earn enough
To keep his wife and family.
  BETTY. Twelve shillings won't go far,
With rents so high,
And food, and clothes, and firing.
But I have naught to grumble at:
I only have six babes to feed:
My mother had thirteen;
And ten of us were born,
After my father lost his sight,
While blasting in the quarry.
And she'd three babes-in-arms, at once —
The twins, and Dick.
I've heard her say that, ere the boy was born,
While she lay sick in bed, and near her time,
Her two, poor helpless babies at the bed-foot,
Sat up, with big eyes, watching her,
As good as gold;
And she, poor woman, wondering,
How ever she would nurse the three, at once.
I cannot think how she got through, at all:
But, when I used to ask her, she would answer:
"Ay! looking back, you wonder how you managed;
But, at the time, each single thing you do for them
Makes you yourself so happy,
That you think nothing of it."
And mother had the truth of things.
And we're quite rich to her —
She'd hoe, a summer's day, for sixpence:
And spent her life's best years in picking stones.
She only had one holiday,
That ever I heard tell of:
And that, when she'd been married fourteen years.
She went to see her cousin at the Stell:
And rode both ways in Farmer Thomson's pig-cart;
And, ever afterwards, she said;
She couldn't tell why folks liked holidays,
Or why they need go seeking happiness,
While they had homes to work in;
And that, for her part, she found little pleasure
In sitting still all day,
In other people's houses, with cold legs,
And idle, folded hands,

When there was darning to be done at home,
And one's own hearth to sit by;
Though there was little sitting down for her,
At any time at all.
She couldn't rest;
Up first, and last to bed,
I never saw her quiet, till the end.
She always hoped that death would find her working,
Her wish was granted her . . .
Death found her at the job she liked the best . . .
The clothes she washed that week were left for me to
        iron . . .
Ay, mother knew what hardship was;
And laboured, day and night, to rear her children.
    LABAN. It's ever children, children!
A woman slaves her very life away
To rear her children;
And they grow up and slave their lives away
To rear their children.
We little thought, lass, when we married!
Do you remember the fine Summer-nights,
When first we walked together?
Ah, those were happy times!
We little thought . . .
    BETTY. You little thought;
I knew.
Yes; those were happy times;
No girl was ever happier than I was,
When first I walked with you in Malden Meadows:
But I am happy now, for all the difference.
Life was not over easy, even then:
They worked me sorely at the farm,
Though I was but a child.
On Monday mornings, we were up at one,
To get the washing through,
Before the day's work started.
I wasn't fifteen then; but I remember
The coastguards whistling to us,
As they passed the lighted window,
On the cold, black Winter-mornings.
And often, I'd been working many hours,
Before you turned out with your team.
I used to think that you went bravely, Laban,
Behind your dappled horses.

LABAN. Ay! then I little knew —
I little knew that life was labour, labour,
And labour till the end.
I thought that there'd be ease, somewhere. [*Rises and be-
        gins to dress.*]
    BETTY. If men will marry, and have children,
They must not look for ease.
Yet, husband, you'd not be a boy again,
Unwedded . . .
    LABAN. Nay! I couldn't do without you.
    BETTY. But, you've too many children?
Too many hungry mouths to fill,
Too many little feet to keep in leather!
And can you look upon them, sleeping there,
(My father ne'er set eyes on me, poor fellow!)
And talk like that?
And is it Tommy you would be without?
You've had him longest; and perhaps you're tired . . .
    LABAN. Nay, wife: he was the first;
And you were such a girl — just seventeen!
And I, but two years older.
Do you remember, lass, how proud . . .
    BETTY. Or is it Nell, who brings your bait to you?
    LABAN. She grows more like her mother every day.
    BETTY. It must be Robin, then,
That all the neighbours say takes after you.
    LABAN. He's got my temper, sure enough,
The little Turk!
    BETTY. Or Kit and Kate the twins?
They're surely twice too much for you.
    LABAN. Folk say that never such a pair
Was seen in all the countryside.
    BETTY. There's just the baby left.
Poor little mite, so you're the one too many!
    LABAN. Come, Betty, come!
Enough of teasing!
You know that I was only talking;
I'm ready, now, for work.
    BETTY. The kettle's boiling. [*She makes the tea, and
        fills two mugs.*]
Drink it up;
'Twill help to keep the chill out.
    LABAN. Ay; but it's dank work, hoeing swedes at dawn.
    BETTY. The sun will soon be up.

LABAN.   The sun gets up a deal too soon for me.
BETTY.   Nay; never rail against the sun.
I'd sooner, lad, be shut away from you,
Than from the sunshine, any day.
I'll never hear a word against the sun.

> [*They take up their hoes from behind the door, give a
> last look at their sleeping children, and go out
> together into the dawn.*]

HOLIDAY

Persons:

EVA SPARK, *a widow.*
NELLY SPARK, ⎱ *her daughters.*
POLLY SPARK, ⎰
DANIEL WEBB, *a navvy.*

Scene: A room in tenements: evening. NELLY SPARK *lies unconscious on the bed with her eyes open and her hands moving in a regular succession of mechanical motions. Her mother sits by the bed sewing.* POLLY SPARK *stands near the window looking out into the dingy court.*

    EVA.   Her hands are never quiet.
    POLLY.   She's tending the machine;
And slipping in the brush-backs
As we do all day long.
Day after day, and every day,
Year in, year out, year in, year out,
Save Sunday and the holiday . . .
To think to-day's a holiday —
And what a holiday for her!
    EVA.   She cannot rest a moment.
Her hands are working, working . . .
It must be weary work, at best;
But now . . .
    POLLY.   And yet we do it,
Year in, year out, year in, year out,
Until it drives us dizzy,
And we, maybe, slip in a hand as she did —
Six holes it drills —
And then they call it carelessness!
    EVA.   Ay! that began the trouble —
Her poor hand!
It gives me quite a turn to think of it.
She's never been herself since.
It's hard she cannot rest.

POLLY.   To think to-day's a holiday!
And last year she was dancing . . .
EVA.   She's ever been a dancer,
From a baby:
Ay! even as a child-in-arms,
I could not keep her quiet,
If she but heard an organ;
And though 'twas half a street away,
'Twould take me all my time to hold her
From tumbling off my lap.
'Twas in her blood;
I danced before I married —
Though afterwards, God knows,
I'd little list for dancing —
And, in my day,
While I'd the heart for it,
I danced among the best.
When first your father saw me,
I was dancing.
POLLY.   Last year, she danced the live-long day
She danced us all out easily,
Although the sun was blazing;
And we were fit to drop.
She would have danced herself to death;
But, some one stopped the music —
I think 'twas Daniel —
Even he was done,
Though he's not beaten easily.
EVA.   He'd scarcely go to-day.
He said, he could not go without her.
I told him that 'twas worse than useless
For him to sit here, watching her.
I think he only went, at last,
Because he could not bear to see her hands.
It's bad enough for me . . .
I could not have him, too . . .
I cannot help but watch . . .
Her poor, poor hands!
They're never still a moment.
All night, I watched them working.
POLLY.   And, last year, she was dancing —
Was dancing in the sun!
And there was none could dance with her —
Not one!

I never knew where she could pick the steps up:
There seemed to be no end to them,
As though she made them up as she went on.
They came to her, I fancy,
As trudging comes to us.
    EVA.   Ay! she'd a dancing heart.
    POLLY.   You scarcely saw her feet move,
Because they went so quickly:
It dazzled me to watch them.
And, as she danced so madly,
She waved a branch of hawthorn
That Daniel plucked for her.
    EVA.   That night when she came home
Her arms were full of blossom.
The room was white for days:
She'd scarcely left a pot or pan
For me to cook a meal in:
And, yet, I dared not toss it out.
The scent was nigh too much for me:
A hawthorn grew beside the door at home;
And, in the drenching rain,
It used to smell so fresh and sweet.
'Twill be there still . . . but I . . .
And she was born about the blossom-time;
For I remember how I lay,
And dreamt that I could smell the hawthorn,
Though we had left the country then,
And I was far from any blowing thing.
And I can smell it now,
Though I've not seen a growing thorn for years.
    POLLY.   The smell of hawthorn, and the heat,
Together, turned me faint.
She did not seem to mind it;
But, danced, till I was dizzy —
Quite dizzy, watching her:
And, when I called to stop her,
She only laughed, and answered:
That she could dance for ever —
For ever in the sunshine,
Until she dropt down dead.
Then Daniel stopped the music,
Suddenly . . .
Her feet stopt with it:
And, she nearly tumbled:

But, Daniel caught her in his arms:
And she was dazed and quiet:
And scarcely spoke a word,
Till we were home in bed,
And I had blown the light out.
I did not take much notice at the time:
For I was half-asleep:
Yet, I remember every word,
As though she said them over, lying there:
" At least, I've danced a day away!
To-morrow, we'll be working —
To-morrow, and to-morrow,
Till we're dead.
And yet, to-day,
The job was nearly done:
If they'd not stopt the music,
I might have finished, dancing! "
    Eva.   Her hands are never quiet:
They're always working, working . . .
They move so quickly,
I can scarcely follow . . .
    Polly.   She always worked like that:
Indeed, the only wonder is
She'd never slipt her hand before.
She worked as madly as she danced:
And she danced madly.
    Eva.   Ay . . . she'll dance no more.
Poor Daniel, I'd no heart to tell him,
That there . . . that there's no hope for her.
He never asked me what the doctor said:
I think he knew, somehow.
He'd scarcely go:
But, he . . . he could not bear to see . . .
I cannot bear to watch them;
Yet, cannot keep my eyes off:
They're always working, working —
Poor broken hands!
And, once, they'd beat to music, on my breast,
When she was but a baby in my lap.
Would God, that time had never passed . . .
    Polly.   To think they'll all be dancing.
While she . . . she's lying . . .
    Eva.   Daniel went, poor lad;
But, he was loth to go;

And there'll be little dancing,
For him, to-day,
And many days to come.
He'll not stay late:
I looked for him, ere now.
    POLLY.   Ay! we are only " hands."
And, in the end . . .
I wonder if I'll lie like that, one day,
With useless fingers working . . .
God spare me!
But I think there's little chance.
I never worked, or danced, as she did.
She danced, and danced . . .
    EVA.   I smell the hawthorn now, as strongly
As we could smell it, after rain . . .
    POLLY.   There's some one on the stairs:
I think it's Dan.

> [*The door opens, gently; and* DANIEL WEBB *enters,
> quietly, carrying a branch of hawthorn.*]

    DANIEL.   How's Nelly, now?
I've brought some bloom for her.
I thought she might . . .
Last year, she liked the hawthorn:
A year to-day, she danced beneath the blossom . . .
I could not stay,
And see them jigging . . .
And yet I cannot bear to watch . . .
    EVA [*turning suddenly*].   Her hands have stopt!
She's quiet now . . .
Ah, God!
She's getting up!
She'll fall . . .

> [*They all rush towards* NELLY, *as she rises from the
> bed; but, something in her eyes stays them half-
> way; and they stand, spell-bound, watching her,
> as she steps to the floor; and moves towards*
> DANIEL, *stretching out her hand for the haw-
> thorn, which he gives to her without a word.
> Holding the branch over her head, she begins
> to dance slowly; her feet gradually moving more
> rapidly.*]

NELLY. Faster . . . faster . . . fast . . .
Who's stopt the music?

> [*She pauses; stands a moment, dazed; then drops to
> the floor in a heap.*]

EVA [*running towards her*]. Ah, God!
She's done!
She does not breathe . . .

> [*They bend over her; and* DANIEL *picks up the dropt
> branch.*]

DANIEL. It's fallen, now —
The bloom . . .
I thought she might . . .
Last year . . .
And now!
I brought the bloom . . .
EVA. Her hands stopt working,
When she smelt it.
It set her dancing . . . dancing to her death.
DANIEL. Oh, Christ!
What have I done!
Nelly!
I brought the bloom . . .
POLLY. She's had her wish.

1908–9.

WOMENKIND

(1909)

TO
STEPHEN AND
LOUISE WISE

WOMENKIND

Persons:

EZRA BARRASFORD, *an old blind shepherd.*
ELIZA BARRASFORD, *his wife.*
JIM BARRASFORD, *their youngest son.*
PHŒBE BARRASFORD, *Jim's bride.*
JUDITH ELLERSHAW.

*Scene: The living-room at Krindlesyke, a lonely cottage on the
fells. EZRA, blind, feeble-minded, and decrepit, sits in an
armchair near the open door. ELIZA BARRASFORD is busy
near the hearth.*

  ELIZA [*glancing at the clock*]. It's nearly three.
They'll not be long in being here.
  EZRA. What's that?
  ELIZA. You're growing duller, every day.
I say they'll not be long now.
  EZRA. Who'll not be long?
  ELIZA. Jim and his bride, of course.
  EZRA. His bride?
  ELIZA. Why, man alive, you never mean to tell me
That you've forgotten Jim's away to wed!
You're not so dull as that.
  EZRA. We cannot all be needles.
I'm dull, at times . . .
Since blindness overtook me.
While yet I had my eyesight,
No chap was cuter in the countryside.
My wits just failed me, once . . .
The day I married . . .
And Jim's away to wed, is he?
I thought he'd gone for turnips.
He might, at least, have told his dad . . .
Though, now I come to think of it,
I do remember hearing something . . .
It's Judith Ellershaw that he's to marry.

201

ELIZA.   No! No! You're dull, indeed!
It's Phœbe Martin Jim's to marry.
      EZRA.   Who's Phœbe Martin?
I know naught of her.
      ELIZA.   And I know little, either.
She's only been here, once . . .
And now, she'll be here, always.
I'll find it strange, at first,
To have another woman in the house.
But, I must needs get used to it.
Your mother, doubtless, found it strange
To have me here, at first . . .
And it's been long enough in coming.
Perhaps, that makes it harder.
But, since your mother died,
And she, poor soul, she didn't last too long
After you brought me home with you . . .
She didn't live to see a grandchild . . .
I wonder, now, if she . . .
And yet, I spared her all I could . . .
Ay! that was it, for certain!
Poor soul, she could not bear to see
Another woman do her work;
And so, she pined and wasted.
If only I had known!
Since she was carried out,
There's scarce a woman crossed the threshold.
No other woman's slept the night
At Krindlesyke for forty years . . .
Just forty years with none but menfolk!
A queer life, when you think of it.
Well, well, they've kept me busy, doing for them.
And there's few left now,
Only you and Jim . . .
And now, Jim's bride . . .
Another woman comes . . .
And I must share with her.
I dare say that we'll manage well enough:
She seemed a decent lass,
When she was here, that once . . .
Though, there was something in her eyes
I couldn't quite make out.
She hardly seemed Jim's sort, somehow.
I wondered at the time . . .

But, who can ever tell why women marry?
Still, Jim will have his hands full,
Unless she's used to menfolk.
I never saw her like . . .
She'll take her own way through the world,
Or I am sore mistaken:
Though, she seemed fond enough of Jim.
He's handsome . . . yet . . .
It's hard to say why such a girl as she . . .
    EZRA. Tut! tut! girls take their chance.
And Jim takes after me, they say.
If he were only half as handsome
As I was at his age . . .
You know yourself . . .
You did not need much coaxing.
    ELIZA. Well . . . doubtless, she knows best . . .
And you can never tell . . .
    EZRA. Where does she hail from?
    ELIZA. Somewhere Bentdale way.
Jim met her at the Fair, a year ago.
    EZRA. I met you at the Fair.
    ELIZA. Ay, fairs have much to answer for . . .
But, she is not my sort.
And yet, she's taken Jim . . .
    EZRA. I thought 'twas Judith Ellershaw.
    ELIZA. No! No! I'm glad that it's not Judith.
Jim fancied her, at one time;
But Jim's had many fancies.
He never knew his mind.
    EZRA. Ay, Jim is gay, is gay!
And I was gay, when I was young.
And Jim . . .
    ELIZA. Ay: Jim's his father's son.
'Twas well that went no further:
For Judith flitted one fine night . . .
'Twas whispered that her father'd turned her out.
He's never spoken of her since,
Or so his neighbours say . . .
And no one's heard a word of her.
I never liked the lass . . .
She'd big cow-eyes . . .
There's little good in that sort:
And Jim's well quit of her.
He'll never hear of her again.

That sort . . .

EZRA.　I liked the wench.

ELIZA.　Ay! you're Jim's father.
It's well he's settling down, at last.
He's wild, like all the others . . .
Sometimes I've feared he'd follow them . . .
Six sons, and only one at home,
And he the youngest of the bunch,
To do his parents credit!
The others all . . .
But, now Jim's married, he may settle down.
If you'd not married young,
God knows where you'd have been to-day.

EZRA.　God knows where you'd have been,
If we'd not met, that Fair day!
I'd spent the last Fair with another girl —
A giggling, red-haired wench —
And we were pledged to meet again.
And I was waiting for her, when I saw you.
But, she was late . . .
And you were young and bonnie . . .
Ay, you were young and pink . . .
There's little pink about you now, I'm doubting.

ELIZA.　Nay! forty years of Krindlesyke, and all . . .

EZRA.　If she'd turned up in time, young Carroty,
You'd never have clapped eyes on Krindlesyke:
This countryside and you would still be strangers.

ELIZA.　If she'd turned up . . .
She'd lived at Krindlesyke, instead of me.
This forty year . . . and I . . . I might . . .
But, what's to be, will be:
And we must take our luck.

EZRA.　I'm not so sure that she'd have seen it either:
Though she was merry, she'd big rabbit-teeth
That might be ill to live with . . .
Though they'd have mattered little, now
Since I am blind . . .
And she was always merry . . .
While you . . . but you were young . . .

ELIZA.　And foolish!

EZRA.　Not so foolish . . .
For I was handsome then.

ELIZA.　Ay: you were handsome, sure enough:
And I believed my eyes, in those days,

And other people's tongues.
There's something in a young girl seems to fight
Against her better sense,
And gives her up, in spite of her.
Yes, I was young!
And just as foolish then as you were handsome.

    EZRA.   Well, fools, or not, we had our time of it:
And you could laugh in those days . . .
And did not giggle like the red-haired wench.
Your voice was like a bird's . . .
But, you laugh little, now . . .
And Lord! your voice . . .
Well, still it's like a bird's, maybe,
For there be birds, and birds —
There's curlew, and there's corncrake.
But then, 'twas soft and sweet.
Do you remember how, nigh all day long,
We sat together on the roundabout?
I must have spent a fortune . . .
Besides the sixpence that I dropped . . .
For we rode round and round,
And round and round again:
And music playing all the while.
We sat together in a golden carriage;
And you were young and bonnie:
And when, at night, 'twas lighted up,
And all the gold, aglitter,
And we were rushing round and round,
The music and the dazzle . . .

    ELIZA.   Ay! that was it, the music and the dazzle . . .
The music and the dazzle, and the rushing . . .
Maybe, 'twas in a roundabout
That Jim won Phœbe Martin.

    EZRA.   And you were young . . .

    ELIZA.   And I was young.

    EZRA.   Ay, you were young and bonnie:
And then, when you were dizzy . . .

    ELIZA.   Yes, I was dizzy . . .

    EZRA.   You snuggled up against me . . .
I held you in my arms . . .
And warm against me . . .
And round we went . . .
With music playing . . .
And gold, aglitter . . .

The music and the dazzle . . .
  ELIZA. And there's been little dazzle, since, or music.
  EZRA. Ay: I was gay, when I was young,
Gay, till I brought you home.
  ELIZA. You brought me home?
You brought me from my home.
If I'd but known before I crossed the threshold,
If I'd but known . . .
But what's to be, will be.
And now, another bride is coming home,
Is coming home to Krindlesyke . . .
God help the lass, if she . . .
But they will soon be here.
Their train was due at Mallerford at three.
The walk should take them scarce an hour,
Though they be bride and bridegroom.
  EZRA. I wish that Jim had married Judith.
I liked the lass.
  ELIZA. You liked . . .
But, come, I'll shift your chair outside,
Where you can feel the sunshine;
And listen to the curlew;
And be the first to welcome Jim and Phœbe.
  EZRA. Wife, are the curlews calling?
  ELIZA. Ay: they've been calling all day long,
As they were calling on the day,
The day I came to Krindlesyke.
  EZRA. I've never caught a note.
I'm getting old,
And deaf, as well as blind.
I used to like to hear the curlew,
At mating-time, when I was young and gay.
And they were whistling all about me
That night, when I came home . . .
The music and the dazzle in my head,
And you and all . . .
And yet I heard them whistling . . .
But I was young and gay!
And you were plump and pink . . .
And I could see and hear . . .
And now!
  ELIZA. And now, it's Jim and Phœbe —
The music and the dazzle in their heads —
And they'll be here in no time.

EZRA. I wish he'd married Judith.

[EZRA *rises, and* ELIZA *carries out his chair, and he hobbles after her. She soon returns, and begins to sweep up the hearth, and then puts some cakes into the oven to keep hot. Presently, a step is heard on the threshold, and* JUDITH ELLER-SHAW *stands in the doorway, a baby in her arms.* ELIZA *does not see her, for a moment, then looks up, and recognises her with a start.*]

ELIZA. You, Judith Ellershaw!
I thought 'twas Jim . . .
    JUDITH. You thought 'twas Jim?
    ELIZA. Ay; Jim and . . . [*breaks off*].
Where've you sprung from, Judith?
It's long since you've shown face in these parts.
I thought we'd seen the last of you.
I little dreamt . . .
And, least of all, to-day!
    JUDITH. To-day? And should I be more welcome
On any other day?
    ELIZA. Welcome? I hardly know.
Your sort is never overwelcome
To decent folk . . .
    JUDITH. I know that well.
That's why I've kept away so long.
    ELIZA. You've kept away?
But you were little here, at any time.
I doubt if your foot soiled the doorstep
A dozen times, in all your life.
And then, to come to-day, of all days —
When Jim . . . [*breaks off suddenly*].
    JUDITH. When Jim?
    ELIZA. But, don't stand there . . .
You're looking pale and tired . . .
It's heavy, walking with a baby.
Come in, and rest a moment, if you're **weary.**
You cannot stay here long:
For I'm expecting . . . company.
And you, I think, will not be over eager . . .
    JUDITH. I'm tired enough, God knows!
We'll not stay long to shame you;
And you can send us packing,
Before your company arrives.

[*She comes in, and seats herself near the door. ELIZA busies herself in laying the table for tea, and there is silence for a while.*]

JUDITH.   And so, Jim's gone to fetch the company?
ELIZA.   Ay: Jim has gone . . .

[*She breaks off suddenly, and says no more for a while. Presently, she goes to the oven, and takes out a piece of cake, and butters it, and hands it to JUDITH.*]

ELIZA.   Perhaps, you're hungry, and could take a bit.
JUDITH.   Ay; but I'm famished . . . Cake!
We're grand to-day, indeed!
It's almost like a wedding.
ELIZA.   A wedding, woman!
Cannot folk have cake,
But you must talk of weddings?
And you of all . . .
JUDITH.   I meant no harm.
I thought, perhaps, that Jim . . .
But, doubtless, he was married long ago?

[*Her baby begins to whimper, and she tries to hush it in an absent manner.*]

Hush! hush! my lass.
You must not cry,
And shame the ears of decent folk.
ELIZA.   Why, that's no way to soothe it!
Come, give the child to me:
I'll show you how to handle babies.
JUDITH.   And you would nurse my child!
ELIZA [*taking it in her arms*].   A babe's a babe . . .
Ay, even though its mother . . .

[*She breaks off suddenly, and stands gazing before her, holding the baby against her bosom.*]

JUDITH.   Why don't you finish, woman?
You were saying . . .
" Ay, even though its mother . . ."
ELIZA [*slowly, gazing before her in a dazed manner*].
Nay, lass; it's ill work, calling names.

Poor babe, poor babe!
It's strange . . . but, as you snuggled to my breast,
I thought, a moment, it was Jim
I held within my arms again.
I must be growing old and foolish
To have such fancies . . . still . . .
   JUDITH.   You thought that it was Jim,
This bastard . . .
    ELIZA.   Shame upon you, woman,
To call your own child such!
Poor innocent . . . and yet . . .
O Jim! O Jim!
   JUDITH.   Why do you call on Jim?
He hasn't come yet?
But I must go, before . . . [*rising*]
Give me the child.
    ELIZA [*facing her, and withholding the baby*].   Nay!
       not until I know the father's name.
   JUDITH.   The father's name?
What right have you to ask?
    ELIZA.   I hardly know . . . and yet . . .
   JUDITH.   Give me the child.
You'll never have the name from my lips.
    ELIZA.   O Jim! O Jim [*giving back the child*].
Go, daughter, go, before . . .
Oh, why'd you ever come,
To-day, of all days!
   JUDITH.   To-day? Why not to-day
As well as any other?
Come, woman, I'd know that before I go.
I've half a mind to stay till Jim . . .
    ELIZA.   Nay, daughter, nay!
You said that you would go;
You know, you said . . .
   JUDITH [*sitting down again*].   Perhaps, I've changed
      my mind.
I liked the cake; and, maybe, if I stay,
There'll be some more of it.
It isn't every day . . .
    ELIZA.   Judith, you know!
   JUDITH.   Nay; I know nothing —
Only what you tell me.
    ELIZA.   Then I will tell you everything.
You'll never have the heart to stay . . .

The heart to stay, and shame us,
When you know all.
    JUDITH.   When I know all?
    ELIZA.   Lass, when you talked of weddings,
You'd hit upon the truth:
And Jim brings home his bride, to-day.
    JUDITH.   And Jim brings home his bride . . .
    ELIZA.   Ay, lass; you would not stay . . .
    JUDITH.   And Jim brings home his bride . . .
    ELIZA.   They'll soon be here . . .
I looked for them, ere now.
But, you've still time . . .
    JUDITH.   The bride comes home:
And you and I must take the road,
My bonnie babe, my little lass,
Lest she should blush to see us.
We're not a sight for decent folk,
My little lass, my bonnie babe,
And we must go . . .
The bride comes home to-day . . .
We're no fit sight for fair young brides,
Nor yet for gallant bridegrooms.
If we should meet them on the road,
You must not cry to him . . .
I must not lift my eyes to his . . .
We're naught to him, the gallant bridegroom.
And she might hear your cry . . .
The bonnie bride . . .
Her eyes might meet my eyes . . .
Your cry might tell her heart too much:
My eyes might show her heart too much . . .
Some bush must hide our shame, till they are by,
The bonnie bride and bridegroom,
If we should meet them on the road,
Their road, and ours . . . the road's the same,
Though we be travelling different ways.
The bride comes home, the bride comes home, to-day . . .
And you and I must take the road.
    ELIZA.   Ay, lass; there's nothing else for it.
    JUDITH.   There's nothing else?
    ELIZA.   Nay, lass! How could you stay now?
They'll soon be here . . .
But, you'll not meet them, if you go . . .
    JUDITH.   Go . . . where?

ELIZA. And how should I know where you're bound
for?
I thought you might be making home.
JUDITH. Home . . . home . . . and where's my
home —
Ay! and my child's home, if it be not here?
ELIZA. Here, daughter! You'd not stay . . .
JUDITH. Why not . . . have I no right? . . .
ELIZA. If you'll not go for my sake,
Go, for Jim's.
If you were ever fond of him,
You would not have him shamed.
JUDITH. And, think you, woman, I'd be here,
If I had not been fond . . .
And yet why should I spare him?
He's spared me little.
ELIZA. But, think of her, his bride,
And her home-coming!
JUDITH. Ay . . . I'll go.
God help her, that she never suffer,
As I have suffered for your son.
Jim! Jim!
ELIZA. You lose but little, daughter.
I know, too well, how little,
For I've lived forty years at Krindlesyke.
JUDITH. Maybe, you never loved . . .
And you don't know the road . . .
The road I've come,
The road that I must go . . .
You've never tramped it . . .
God send it stretch not forty years!
ELIZA. I've come that forty years.
We're out upon the same road, daughter,
The bride, and you, and I . . .
And she has still the stoniest bit to travel.
We've known the worst . . .
And you've your little lass.
Thank God, it's not a son . . .
If I had only had one daughter . . .
JUDITH. You'll have a daughter, now.
But I must go, before she comes.
The bride comes home . . .
Jim brings a daughter home for you.

[*As she speaks, a step is heard, and* EZRA BARRAS
FORD *appears in the doorway. Turning to go*
JUDITH *meets him. She tries to pass him, but
he clutches her arm, and she stands as if dazed
while his fingers grope over her.*]

EZRA.   So, Jim's got back?
I never heard you come, lad.
But, I am growing deaf.
As deaf as a stone-wall.
I couldn't hear the curlew, not a note;
I used to like to hear them . . .
And now, I'll never hear them, any more.
But, I forget . . .
You're welcome home . . .
Is this the bonnie bride?
You're welcome home to Krindlesyke. [*feeling her face*]
Why, wife, it's Judith, after all!
I knew 'twas she that was to be Jim's bride.
You said 'twas some one else . . .
I can't remember . . . some outlandish name.
But, I was right, you see.
Though I be dull, at times,
And deafer than an adder,
I'm not so dull as some folks think.
There's others growing old, as well as I . . .
You're welcome . . .

[*His hand, travelling down* JUDITH's *shoulder*
touches the child.]

Ah, a baby!
Jim's child!   Jim's child!
Come, let me take it, daughter.
I've never had a grandchild in my arms,
Though I've had many sons.
They've all been wild, but Jim:
And Jim's the last one left.
Come, I'll not let it fall:
I've always had a way with babies,
With babies, and with women.

[*He snatches the child from* JUDITH, *before she real-*
ises what he is after, and hobbles away with it t

*the settle beside the fire. Before she can move
to follow him, footsteps are heard on the threshold.*]

ELIZA. Ah, God, they're at the door!

[*As she speaks,* JIM BARRASFORD *and* PHŒBE, *his
bride, enter, talking and laughing.* JUDITH
ELLERSHAW *shrinks into the shadow behind the
door, while they come between her and the high-
backed settle on which* EZRA *is sitting, with the
child, out of sight.* ELIZA *stands dazed, in the
middle of the room.*]

JIM. Well . . . so that's over!
And we're home, at last!
I hope the tea is ready.
I'm almost famished, mother —
As hungry as a hawk.
I've hardly had a bite, to-day:
And getting married's hungry work,
As Phœbe knows . . .
But, you've stopped laughing, now, lass . . .
And you look scared . . .
There's nothing here to scare you.
Have you no word of welcome, mother,
That you stand like a stock, and gaping —
And gaping like a foundered ewe?
I'll have you give my bride the greeting
That's due to her, my bride . . .
Poor lass, she's all atremble . . .
But, we'll soon see who's mistress!
  ELIZA [*coming forward*]. You're welcome, daughter.
May you . . .
  EZRA [*crooning, unseen, to the baby*]. " Sing to your
      mammy!
Sing to your daddy! "
  JIM. What ails the old fool now?
You must not heed him, Phœbe.
He's simple; there's no harm in him.

[*Going towards the settle.*]

Come, dad, and stir your stumps . . .

Why, mother, what is this!
Whose brat . . .
   Ezra.   Whose brat! Whose brat!
And who should know but he!
He's gay . . . he's gay!
He asks whose brat!
Maybe, you came too soon, my little lass:
But, he's a funny daddy,
To ask whose brat! [*crooning*].
" Sing to your mammy . . ."

> [Judith Ellershaw *steps forward to take the chil*
> *from* Ezra.]

   Jim. You! Judith Ellershaw!
Why, lass . . .

> [*He moves to meet her, but stops in confusion.* N
> *one speaks, as* Judith *takes the child, and wrap*
> *it in her shawl. She is moving towards th*
> *door, when* Phœbe *steps before her, and shut*
> *it, then turns and faces* Judith.]

   Phœbe.   You shall not go.
   Judith.   And who are you to stay me?
   Phœbe.   I . . . I'm Jim's bride.
   Judith.   And what should Jim's bride have to say t
     me?
Come, let me pass.
   Phœbe.   You shall not go.
   Judith.   Nay, woman, let me by!
You do not know me for the thing I am.
If you but guessed, you'd fling the door wide open;
And draw your skirts about you,
Lest any rag of mine should smirch them.
I'm not fit company for fair young brides.
I never should have come 'mid decent folk.
You little know . . .
   Phœbe.   I heard your name just now . . .
And I have heard that name before.
   Judith.   You've heard my name before!
I wonder . . . but you heard no good of it,
Whoever spoke . . .
   Phœbe.   I heard it from the lips

That uttered it just now.

    JUDITH. From Jim!

Well . . . Jim knows what I am.

I wonder that he lets you talk with me.

Come, woman, I must go.

    PHŒBE. Not till I know the name of your child's
        father.

    JUDITH. Nay! you've no right to ask it.

    PHŒBE. Maybe . . . and yet, you shall not cross
        that step,

Until you tell . . .

    JUDITH. Come, woman, don't be foolish.

    PHŒBE. You say that I've no right.

Pray God, you speak the truth.

Yet, there may be no woman in the world

Who has a better right.

    JUDITH. Why, lass: you'd surely never heed

An old man's witless babble!

A poor, old crazy . . .

    PHŒBE [*still facing* JUDITH]. If I've no right, you
        will not have the heart

To keep the name from me.

But set my mind at ease.

    JUDITH. I will not have the heart!

If it will set your mind at ease,

I'll speak my shame . . .

I'll speak my shame right out . . .

I'll speak my shame right out before you all.

    JIM. But, lass . . .

    JUDITH. I would not have a bride unhappy,

Upon her wedding-day.

The father of my child was William Burn . . .

A stranger to these parts . . .

Now . . . let me pass.

    [*She tries to slip by, but* PHŒBE *does not make way
        for her.*]

    JIM. Ay, Phœbe: let her go:

Don't be too hard on her:

She's told you what you asked . . .

Though, why . . . unless . . .

Yet, I don't blame the lass.

She should know best.

PHŒBE [*to* JUDITH, *looking her straight in the eyes*]
    You lie!
JUDITH. I lie?
PHŒBE. To-day, I wedded your child's father.
ELIZA. O God!
JIM. Come, lass, I say . . .
JUDITH. No! woman, no!
I spoke the truth.
Have I not shamed myself enough, already,
That you must call me liar?
[*To* ELIZA.] Speak out, speak out, and tell . . .
At least, you know me well enough
To tell her I'm no liar.
Speak out, if you're not tongue-tied:
And tell her all you know . . .
How I'm a byeword among honest women,
And yet, no liar . . . Speak!
You'd tongue enough a while ago:
And have you none to answer your son's wife;
And save your son from slander?
    ELIZA [*hesitatingly*]. I never knew the lass to lie.

> [*While they have been talking,* EZRA *has risen from
> the settle, unnoticed, and has hobbled round t*
> *where* PHŒBE *and* JUDITH *are standing. H*
> *suddenly touches* PHŒBE'S *arm.*]

EZRA. Give me the babe again . . .
Nay! this is not the lass . . .
I want Jim's bride,
The mother of his daughter.
Come, Judith, lass, where are you?
I want to nurse my grandchild,
The little lass, Jim's little lass.

> [*While he is speaking,* JUDITH *tries to slip pas*
> PHŒBE, *but* EZRA *clutches hold of her, an*
> PHŒBE *sets her back against the door.* ELIZ*
> *goes up to* EZRA *and takes him by the arm*
> *and leads him, mutteringly, back to the settle.*]

ELIZA. Come, Ezra, hold your foolish tongue.
You don't know what you're saying . . .
JIM. If he don't hold his tongue, I'll . . .

JUDITH [*to* PHŒBE]. And will you weigh an old
    man's witlessness
Against my word?
O woman, pay no heed to idle tongues,
If you would keep your happiness!
    PHŒBE [*looking her in the face*]. But, even while the
    tongue is lying,
The eyes speak out the truth.
    JUDITH. The eyes!
Then, you will pay no heed to me;
But let a dothering old man
Destroy your life with idle chatter.
You know my worth!
Yet, if you care for Jim,
You'll trust his word.
If Jim denies the child,
Then, you'll believe . . .
You would not doubt your husband's word,
And on your wedding-day . . .
Small wonder you doubt mine:
You've got good reason . . .
But, Jim's not my sort: he's an honest lad:
And he'll speak true . . .
If Jim denies the child . . .
    PHŒBE. If Jim can look me in the eyes . . .
    JUDITH. Speak, Jim, and set her mind at ease.
Don't spare me, Jim; but tell her all:
For she's your wife; and has a right to know
The child's no child of yours.

                  [JIM *stands, hesitating.*]

Come, lad, speak out!
And don't stand gaping there.
You know, as well as I, the child . . .
Speak! speak!
Have you no tongue?

                  [*He still hesitates.*]

Don't think of me . . .
You've naught to fear from me.
Tell all you know of me right out . . .
No word of yours can hurt me . . .

I'm shameless, now . . .
You know, my father turned me out . . .

[JIM *still hesitates.*

Speak, lad! Your wife is waiting.
If you don't tell the truth, and quickly,
You'll have a merry life of it, I'll warrant!
I would not be in your shoes . . .
See, how she's badgered me:
And all because . . .
Come, be a man! and speak!
      JIM.   The brat's no child of mine . . .
Phœbe, I swear . . .

       [*He stops in confusion, and drops his eyes. Afte*
        a pause, PHŒBE *turns from him and lays on*
        hand on the latch and the other on JUDITH'
        arm.]

      PHŒBE [*to* JUDITH].   Come, lass, it's time that w
         were getting home.
      JUDITH [*starting back*].   That we?
      PHŒBE.   Unless you wish to stay?
      JUDITH.   I stay? . . . You mean . . .
O God, what have I done!
That I had never crossed this door!
      ELIZA [*to* PHŒBE].   You're never going, woman!
You're his wife . . .
You cannot leave him . . .
      JIM.   Leave! Leave me! She's mad!
I never heard . . . and on my wedding-day!
But, I'm your husband:
And I bid you bide.
      PHŒBE.   Oh, Jim, if you had only told the truth . .
I might . . .
God knows . . .
For I was fond . . .
      JIM.   Ay! now, you're talking sense.
It's well to let a woman know who's master.
And what's the odds, lass, even if the brat . . .
      PHŒBE [*to* JUDITH].   Come, Judith, are you ready
It's time that we were getting home.
      JUDITH.   Home? I've no home . . .

I've long been homeless.

PHŒBE. That much he told me of you:
He spoke the truth, so far.
Thank God, he could not rob me of my home!
My mother will be glad to have me back:
And she will welcome you,
If only for your baby's sake.
She's just a child, to children.
We're poor; and labour hard for all we have.
There's but two rooms:
So we must lie together,
Unless you are too proud . . .
Nay, lass: I see you'll come with me:
And we will live, and work, and tend the child,
As sisters, we who care . . .
Come, Judith!

[*She flings the door wide, and goes out, without looking back.* JIM *steps forward to stay her, but halts in the doorway, and stands staring after her.*]

JIM. Nay, lass! I bid you stay . . .
I bid . . . I bid . . .
The blasted wench! She's gone!

[*He stands speechless, but at last turns to* JUDITH, *who is still gazing after* PHŒBE *with an unrealising stare.*]

Well . . . you will not forsake me, Judith?
Old friends are best . . .
And I . . . I always liked you.
And so, this is my baby!
Who'd have thought . . .

[JUDITH *starts, clutches her baby to her breast, and slips past him.*]

JUDITH [*calling*]. I'm coming, Phœbe . . .
Coming home with you . . .

[JIM *stands in the doorway, staring after her dumbfounded, till they are both out of sight, when he turns and slams the door to.*]

JIM.   I've done with women;
They're a faithless lot.
EZRA.   Ay: womenkind are all the same:
I've ever found them faithless.
But, where's your baby, Jim,
Your little lass?
JIM.   They've taken even her from me.

[ELIZA, *who has been filling the teapot, takes* EZR*
by the arm, and leads him to a seat at the table.*

ELIZA.   Come, husband, take your tea, before it's cold
And you, too, son.
Ay: we're a faithless lot.

(1909)

FIRES

(1910–1911)

Snug in my easy chair,
I stirred the fire to flame.
Fantastically fair,
The flickering fancies came,
Born of heart's desire:
Amber woodland streaming;
Topaz islands dreaming;
Sunset-cities gleaming,
Spire on burning spire;
Ruddy-windowed taverns;
Sunshine-spilling wines;
Crystal-lighted caverns
Of Golconda's mines;
Summers, unreturning;
Passion's crater yearning;
Troy, the ever-burning;
Shelley's lustral pyre;
Dragon-eyes, unsleeping;
Witches' cauldrons leaping;
Golden galleys sweeping
Out from sea-walled Tyre:
Fancies, fugitive and fair,
Flashed with singing through the air;
Till, dazzled by the drowsy glare,
I shut my eyes to heat and light;
And saw, in sudden night,
Crouched in the dripping dark,
With steaming shoulders stark,
The man who hews the coal to feed my fire.

FIRES

THE STONE

" And will you cut a stone for him,
To set above his head?
And will you cut a stone for him —
A stone for him? " she said.

Three days before, a splintered rock
Had struck her lover dead —
Had struck him in the quarry dead,
Where, careless of the warning call,
He loitered, while the shot was fired —
A lively stripling, brave and tall,
And sure of all his heart desired . . .
A flash, a shock,
A rumbling fall . . .
And, broken 'neath the broken rock,
A lifeless heap, with face of clay,
And still as any stone he lay,
With eyes that saw the end of all.

I went to break the news to her:
And I could hear my own heart beat
With dread of what my lips might say;
But some poor fool had sped before;
And, flinging wide her father's door,
Had blurted out the news to her,
Had struck her lover dead for her,
Had struck the girl's heart dead in her,
Had struck life, lifeless, at a word,
And dropped it at her feet:
Then hurried on his witless way,
Scarce knowing she had heard.

And when I came, she stood alone —
A woman, turned to stone:

And, though no word at all she said,
I knew that all was known.

Because her heart was dead,
She did not sigh nor moan.
His mother wept:
She could not weep.
Her lover slept:
She could not sleep.
Three days, three nights,
She did not stir:
Three days, three nights,
Were one to her,
Who never closed her eyes
From sunset to sunrise,
From dawn to evenfall —
Her tearless, staring eyes,
That, seeing naught, saw all.

The fourth night when I came from work,
I found her at my door.
" And will you cut a stone for him? "
She said: and spoke no more:
But followed me, as I went in,
And sank upon a chair;
And fixed her grey eyes on my face,
With still, unseeing stare.
And, as she waited patiently,
I could not bear to feel
Those still, grey eyes that followed me,
Those eyes that plucked the heart from me,
Those eyes that sucked the breath from me
And curdled the warm blood in me,
Those eyes that cut me to the bone,
And pierced my marrow like cold steel.

And so I rose, and sought a stone;
And cut it, smooth and square:
And, as I worked, she sat and watched,
Beside me, in her chair.
Night after night, by candlelight,
I cut her lover's name:
Night after night, so still and white,
And like a ghost she came;

And sat beside me, in her chair,
And watched with eyes aflame.

She eyed each stroke,
And hardly stirred:
She never spoke
A single word:
And not a sound or murmur broke
The quiet, save the mallet-stroke.

With still eyes ever on my hands,
With eyes that seemed to burn my hands,
My wincing, overwearied hands,
She watched, with bloodless lips apart,
And silent, indrawn breath:
And every stroke my chisel cut,
Death cut still deeper in her heart:
The two of us were chiselling,
Together, I and death.

And when at length the job was done,
And I had laid the mallet by,
As if, at last, her peace were won,
She breathed his name; and, with a sigh,
Passed slowly through the open door:
And never crossed my threshold more.

Next night I laboured late, alone,
To cut her name upon the stone.

THE WIFE

That night she dreamt that he had died,
As they were sleeping, side by side:
And she awakened in affright,
To think of him, so cold and white:
And, when she turned her eyes to him,
The tears of dream had made them dim;
And, for a while, she could not see
That he was sleeping quietly.
But, as she saw him lying there,
The moonlight on his curly hair,
With happy face and even breath,
Although she thought no more of death;
And it was very good to rest
Her trembling hand on his calm breast,
And feel the warm and breathing life;
And know that she was still his wife;
Yet, in his bosom's easy stir,
She felt a something trouble her;
And wept again, she knew not why;
And thought it would be good to die —
To sink into the deep, sweet rest,
Her hand upon his quiet breast.

She slept: and when she woke again,
A bird was at the window-pane,
A wild-eyed bird, with wings of white
That fluttered in the cold moonlight,
As though for very fear of night;
And flapped the pane, as if afraid:
Yet, not a sound the white wings made.
Her eyes met those beseeching eyes;
And then she felt she needs must rise,
To let the poor, wild creature in
To find the rest it sought to win.
She rose and set the casement wide,
And caught the murmur of the tide;
And saw, afar, the mounded graves

About the church beside the waves —
The huddled headstones gleaming white
And ghostly in the cold moonlight.

The bird flew straightway to the bed;
And hovered o'er the husband's head,
And circled thrice above his head,
Three times above his dreaming head:
And, as she watched it flying round,
She wondered that it made no sound;
And while she wondered, it was gone:
And cold and white the moonlight shone
Upon her husband, sleeping there;
And turned to silver his gold hair;
And paled like death his ruddy face.
Then, creeping back into her place,
She lay beside him in the bed:
But, if she closed her eyes, with dread
She saw that wild bird's eyes that burned
Through her shut eyelids, though she turned
Her blessings over in her heart,
That peace might come: and with a start,
If she but drowsed, or dreamt of rest,
She felt that wild beak in her breast.
So, wearying for the time to rise,
She watched, till dawn was in the skies.

Her husband woke: but not a word
She told him of the strange, white bird:
But, as at breakfast-time, she took
The pan of porridge from the crook,
And all was ready to begin,
A neighbour gossip hurried in,
And told the news, that Phœbe Wright
Had died in childbirth in the night.
The husband neither spoke, nor stirred,
But sat as one who, having heard,
May never hearken to a word
From any living lips again;
And, heedless of the tongues of men,
Hears, in a silence, dread and deep,
The dead folk talking in their sleep.
His porridge stood till it was cold:
And as he sat, his face grew old;

And all his yellow hair turned white,
As it had looked to her last night,
When it was drenched with cold moonlight.
And she knew all: yet never said
A word to him about the dead;
Or pestered him to take his meat:
But, sitting silent in her seat,
She left him quiet with his heart
To thoughts in which she had no part
Until he rose to go about
His daily work; and staggered out.
And all that day, her eyes were dim
That she had borne no child to him.

Days passed: and then, one evening late,
As she came by the churchyard-gate,
She saw him, near the new-made grave:
And with a lifted head and brave,
She hurried home, lest he should know
That she had looked upon his woe.
And when they sat beside the fire,
Although it seemed he could not tire
Of gazing on the glowing coal,
And though a fire was in her soul;
She sat beside him with a smile,
Lest he should look on her, the while,
And wonder what could make her sad
When all the world but him was glad.
But, not a word to her he said:
And silently they went to bed.

She never closed her eyes that night:
And she was stirring, ere the light;
And while her husband lay at rest,
She left his side, and quickly dressed;
And stole downstairs, as though in fear
That he should chance to wake, and hear.
And still the stars were burning bright,
As she passed out into the night;
And all the dewy air was sweet
With flowers that grew about her feet,
Where he, for her, when they were wed,
Had digged and sown a wallflower-bed:
And on the rich, deep, mellow scent
A gust of memories came and went,

As, dreaming of those old glad hours,
She stooped to pluck a bunch of flowers,
To lay upon the flowerless grave
That held his heart beside the wave.
Though, like a troop of ghosts in white,
The headstones watched in cold starlight,
As, by the dead girl's grave she knelt,
No fear in her full heart she felt:
But hurried home, when she had laid
Her offering on the turf, afraid
That he should wake, and find her gone:
And still the stars in heaven shone,
When into bed again she crept,
And lay beside him, while he slept.
And when day came, upon his hair,
The warm light fell: and young and fair,
He looked again to her kind eyes
That watched him till 'twas time to rise.

And, every day, as he went by
The churchyard-gate with downcast eye,
He saw fresh blooms upon the grave
That held his heart beside the wave:
And, wondering, he was glad to find
That any living soul was kind
To that dead girl who died the death
Of shame for his sake: and the breath
Of those fresh flowers to him was sweet,
As he trudged home with laggard feet,
Still wondering who could be her friend.

He never knew, until the end,
When, in the churchyard by the wave,
He stood beside another grave:
And, as the priest's last words were said,
He turned, and lifting up his head,
He saw the bunch of flowers was dead
Upon the dead girl's grave; and felt
The truth shoot through his heart, and melt
The frost of icy bitterness,
And flood his heart with warm distress:
And, kneeling by his dead wife's grave,
To her, at last, her hour he gave.

That night she dreamt he, too, had died,
And they were sleeping, side by side.

THE MACHINE

Since Thursday he'd been working overtime,
With only three short hours for food and sleep,
When no sleep came, because of the dull beat
Of his fagged brain; and he could scarcely eat.
And now, on Saturday, when he was free,
And all his fellows hurried home to tea,
He was so dazed that he could hardly keep
His hands from going through the pantomime
Of keeping-even sheets in his machine —
The sleek machine that, day and night,
Fed with paper, virgin white,
Through those glaring, flaring hours
In the incandescent light,
Printed children's picture-books —
Red and yellow, blue and green,
With sunny fields and running brooks,
Ships at sea, and golden sands,
Queer white towns in Eastern lands,
Tossing palms on coral strands —
Until at times the clank and whirr and click,
And shimmer of white paper turned him sick;
And though at first the colours made him glad,
They soon were dancing in his brain like mad;
And kept on flaring through his burning head:
Now, in a flash, the workshop, flaming red;
Now blazing green; now staring blue;
And then the yellow glow too well he knew:
Until the sleek machine, with roar and glare,
Began to take him in a dazzling snare;
When, fascinated, with a senseless stare,
It drew him slowly towards it, till his hair
Was caught betwixt the rollers; but his hand,
Almost before his brain could understand,
Had clutched the lever; and the wheels were stopped
Just in the nick of time; though now he dropped,
Half-senseless on the littered workshop floor:
And he'd lain dazed a minute there or more,
When his machine-girl helped him to a seat.
But soon again he was upon his feet,
And tending that unsatisfied machine;

And printing pictures, red and blue and green,
Until again the green and blue and red
Went jigging in a riot through his head;
And, wildest of the raging rout,
The blinding, screeching, racking yellow —
A crazy devil of a fellow —
O'er all the others seemed to shout.
For hands must not be idle when the year
Is getting through, and Christmas drawing near,
With piles on piles of picture-books to print
For people who spend money without stint:
And, while they're paying down their liberal gold,
Guess little what is bought, and what is sold.

But he, at last, was free till Monday, free
To sleep, to eat, to dream, to sulk, to walk,
To laugh, to sing, to whistle, or to talk . . .
If only, through his brain, unceasingly,
The wheels would not keep whirring, while the smell —
The oily smell of thick and sticky glaze
Clung to his nostrils, till 'twas hard to tell
If he were really out in the fresh air;
And still before his eyes, the blind, white glare,
And then the colours dancing in his head,
A maddening maze of yellow, blue and red.
So, on he wandered in a kind of daze,
Too racked with sleeplessness to think of bed
Save as a hell, where you must toss and toss,
With colours shooting in insane criss-cross
Before wide, prickling, gritty, sleepless eyes.

But, as he walked along the darkening street
Too tired to rest, and far too spent to eat,
The swish and patter of the passing feet,
The living, human murmur, and keen cries,
The deep, cool shadows of the coming night,
About quick-kindling jets of clustered light;
And the fresh breathing of the rain-washed air,
Brought something of sweet healing to his mind;
And, though he trailed along as if half-blind,
Yet often on the pavement he would stop
To gaze at goods displayed within a shop;
And wonder, in a dull and lifeless way,
What they had cost, and who'd the price to pay.

But those two kinds of shop which, as a boy,
Had been to him a never-failing joy,
The bookshop and the fruitshop, he passed by,
As if their colours seared his wincing eye;
For still he feared the yellow, blue and red
Would start that devils' dancing in his head.
And soon, through throngs of people almost gay
To be let loose from work, he pushed his way;
And ripples of their careless laughter stole
Like waves of cooling waters through his soul,
While sometimes he would lift his aching eyes,
And see a child's face, flushed with proud surprise,
As, gripping both its parents' hands quite tight,
It found itself in fairylands of light,
Walking with grown-up people through the night:
Then, turning, with a shudder he would see
Poor painted faces, leering frightfully,
And so drop back from heaven again to hell.

And then, somehow, though how he scarce could tell,
He found that he was walking through the throng,
Quite happy, with a young girl at his side —
A young girl apple-cheeked and eager-eyed;
And her frank, friendly chatter seemed a song
To him, who ne'er till now had heard life sing.
And youth within him kindled quick and strong,
As he drank in that careless chattering.
She told him how just lately she had come
From some far Northern Isle to earn her bread;
And in a stuffy office all day long,
In shiny ledgers, with a splitting head,
She added dazzling figures till they danced,
And tied themselves in wriggling knots, and pranced,
And scrambled helter-skelter o'er the page:
And though it seemed already quite an age
Since she had left her home, from end to end
Of this big town she had not any friend:
At times she almost dreaded she'd go dumb,
With not a soul to speak to; for, at home
In her own Island, she knew every one . . .
No strangers there! save when the tinkers came,
With pots and pans a-glinting in the sun —
You saw the tin far off, like glancing flame,
As all about the Island they would roam. . . .

Then, of themselves at home, there were six brothers,
Five sisters, with herself, besides the others —
Two homeless babes, whom, having last their mothers,
Her mother'd taken in among her own . . .
And she in all her life had hardly known
Her mother with no baby at her breast . . .
She'd always sing to hush them all to sleep;
And sang, too, for the dancing, sang to keep
The feet in time and tune; and still sang best,
Clean best of all the singers of the Isle.
And as she talked of home, he saw her smile,
With happy, far-off gaze; and then as though
In wonder how she'd come to chatter so
To this pale, grave-eyed boy, she paused, half shy;
And then she laughed, with laughter clear and true;
And looked into his eyes; and he laughed too,
And they were happy, hardly knowing why.

And now he told her of his life, and how
He too had been nigh friendless, until now.
And soon he talked to her about his work;
But when he spoke of it, as with a jerk,
The light dropped from his eyes. He seemed to slip
Once more in the machine's relentless grip;
And hear again the clank and whirr and click;
And see the dancing colours and the glare;
Until his dizzy brain again turned sick:
And seeing him look round with vacant air,
Fierce pity cut her to the very quick;
And as her eyes with keen distress were filled,
She touched his hand; and soon her kind touch stilled
The agony: and so, to bring him ease,
She told more of that Isle in Northern seas,
Where she was born, and of the folks at home:
And how, all night, you heard the wash of foam . . .
Sometimes, on stormy nights, against the pane
The sousing spray would rattle just like rain;
And oft the high-tides scoured the threshold clean . . .

And as she talked, he saw the sea-light glint
In her dark eyes: and then the sleek machine
Lost hold on him at last; and ceased to print:
And in his eyes there sprang a kindred light,
As, hand in hand, they wandered through the night.

THE LODESTAR

From hag to hag, o'er miles of quaking moss,
Benighted, in an unknown countryside,
Among gaunt hills, the stars my only guide;
Bewildered by peat-waters, black and deep,
Wherein the mocking stars swam; spent for sleep;
O'er-wearied by long trudging; at a loss
Which way to turn for shelter from the night;
I struggled on, until, my head grown light
From utter weariness, I almost sank
To rest among the tussocks, soft and dank,
Drowsing, half-dazed, and murmuring it were best
To stray no further, but to lie at rest,
Beneath the cold, white stars, for evermore:
When, suddenly, I came across
A runnel oozing from the moss;
And knew that, if I followed where it led,
'Twould bring me to a valley, in the end,
Where there'd be houses, and, perhaps, a bed.

And so the little runnel was my friend;
And as I walked beside its path, at first
It kept a friendly silence: then it burst
Into a friendly singing, as it rambled,
Among big boulders, down a craggy steep,
'Mid bracken, nigh breast-deep,
Through which I scrambled,
Half-blind and numb for sleep,
Until it seemed that I could strive no more:
When, startled by a startled sheep,
Looking down, I saw a track —
A stony trackway, dimly white,
Disappearing in the night,
Across a waste of heather, burnt and black.
And so, I took it, mumbling o'er and o'er,
In witlessness of weariness,
And featherheaded foolishness:
A track must lead, at some time, to a door.

And, trudging to this senseless tune,
That kept on drumming in my head,
I followed where the pathway led;
But, all too soon,
It left the ling, and nigh was lost
Among the bent that glimmered grey
About my sore-bewildered way:
But when, at length, it crossed
A brawling burn, I saw, afar,
A cottage window light —
A star, but no cold, heavenly star —
A warm red star of welcome in the night.

Far off it burned upon the black hillside,
Sole star of earth in all that waste so wide —
A little human lantern in the night,
Yet more to me than all the bright
Unfriendly stars of heaven, so cold and white.

And as it dimly shone,
Though towards it I could only go
With stumbling step and slow,
It quickened in my heart a kindred glow;
And seemed to draw me on
That last rough mile or so,
Now seen, now hidden, when the track
Dipped down into a slack,
And all the earth again was black:
And from the unseen fern,
Grey ghost of all bewildered things,
An owl brushed by me on unrustling wings,
And gave me quite a turn,
And sent a shiver through my hair.

Then, again, more fair
Flashed the friendly light,
Beckoning through the night,
A golden, glowing square,
Growing big and clearer,
As I drew slowly nearer,
With eager, stumbling feet;
And snuffed the homely reek of peat:
And saw, above me, lone and high,
A cottage, dark against the sky —
A candle shining on the window-sill.

With thankful heart, I climbed the hill;
And stood, at last, before
The dark and unknown door,
Wondering if food and shelter lay behind,
And what the welcome I should find,
Whether kindly, or unkind:
But I had scarcely knocked, to learn my fate,
When the latch lifted, and the door şwung wide
On creaking hinges; and I saw, inside,
A frail old woman, very worn and white,
Her body all a-tremble in the light,
Who gazed with strange, still eyes into the night,
As though she did not see me, but looked straight
Beyond me, to some unforgotten past:
And I was startled when she said at last,
With strange, still voice: "You're welcome, though
      you're late."

And then an old man, nodding in a chair
Beside the fire, awoke with sleepy stare,
And rose in haste, and led her to a seat
Beside the cosy hearth of glowing peat;
And muttered to me, as he took her hand:
"It's queer, it's queer, that she, to-night, should stand,
Who has not stood alone for fifteen year.
Though I heard nothing, she was quick to hear.
I must have dozed; but she has been awake,
And listening for your footstep since daybreak:
For she was certain you would come to-day;
Ay, she was sure, for all that I could say:
Talk as I might, she would not go to bed,
Till you should come. Your supper has been spread
This long while: you'll be ready for your meat."
With that he beckoned me to take a seat
Before the table, lifting from the crook
The singing kettle; while, with far-off look,
As though she neither saw nor heard,
His wife sat gazing at the glowing peat.

So, wondering sorely, I sat down to eat;
And yet she neither spoke, nor stirred;
But in her high-backed chair sat bolt-upright,
With still grey eyes; and tumbled hair, as white
As fairy-cotton, straggling o'er her brow,

And hung in wisps about her wasted cheek.
But when I'd finished, and drew near the fire,
She suddenly turned round to speak,
Her old eyes kindling with a tense desire.
Her words came tremblingly: " You'll tell me now
What news you bring of him, my son? "   Amazed,
I met that searching and love-famished look:
And then the old man, seeing I was dazed,
Made shift to swing aside the kettle-crook;
And muttered in my ear:
" John Netherton, his name ": and as I gazed
Into the peat that broke in clear blue flame,
Remembrance flashed upon me with the name
And I slipped back in memory twenty year —
Back to the fo'c'sle of a villainous boat;
And once again in that hot hell I lay,
Watching the smoky lantern duck and sway,
As though in steamy stench it kept afloat . . .
The fiery fangs of fever at my throat;
And my poor broken arm, ill-set,
A bar of white-hot iron at my side:
And, as I lay, with staring eyes pricked wide,
Throughout eternities of agony,
I saw a big, black shadow stoop o'er me;
And felt a cool hand touch my brow, and wet
My cracking lips: and sank in healing sleep:
And when I rose from that unfathomed deep,
I saw the youngest of that rascal crew
Beside my bunk; and heard his name; and knew
'Twas he who'd brought me ease: but soon, ashore,
We parted; and I never saw him more;
Though, some while after, in another place,
I heard he'd perished in a drunken brawl . . .

And now the old man touched me, to recall
My wandering thoughts; and breathed again the name:
And I looked up into the mother's face
That burned before me with grey eyes aflame.
And so I told her how I'd met her son;
And of the kindly things that he had done.
And as I spoke her quivering spirit drank
The news that it had thirsted for so long;
And for a flashing moment gay and strong
Life flamed in her old eyes, then slowly sank.

"And he was happy when you saw him last?"
She asked: and I was glad to answer, "Yes."
Then all sat dreaming without stir or sound,
As gradually she sank into the past,
With eyes that looked beyond all happiness,
Beyond all earthly trouble and distress,
Into some other world than ours. The thread
That long had held the straining life earthbound
Was loosed at last: her eyes grew dark: her head
Drooped slowly on her breast; and she was dead.

The old man at her side spoke not a word,
As we arose, and bore her to the bed;
And laid her on the clean, white quilt at rest
With calm hands folded on her quiet breast.
And, hour by hour, he hardly even stirred,
Crouching beside me in the ingle-seat;
And staring, staring at the still red glow:
But, only when the fire was burning low,
He rose to bring fresh peat;
And muttered with dull voice and slow:
"This fire has ne'er burned out through all these years —
Not since the hearthstone first was set —
And that is nigh two hundred year ago.
My father's father built this house; and I . . .
I thought my son . . ." and then he gave a sigh;
And as he stooped, his wizened cheek was wet
With slowly-trickling tears.
And now he hearkened, while an owl's keen cry
Sang through the silence, as it fluttered nigh
The cottage-window, dazzled by the light,
Then back, with fainter hootings, into night.

But when the fresh peats broke into a blaze,
He watched it with a steady, dry-eyed gaze;
And spoke once more: "And he, dead, too!
You did not tell her; but I knew . . . I knew!"

And now came all the tale of their distress:
Their only son, in wanton waywardness,
Had left them, nearly thirty year ago;
And they had never had a word from him
In all that time . . . the reckless blow
Of his unkindness struck his mother low . . .

Her hair, as ruddy as the fern
In late September by a moorland burn,
Had shrivelled rimy-white
In one short summer's night:
And they had looked, and looked for his return . . .
His mother set for him at every meal,
And kept his bed well-aired . . . the knife and fork
I'd used were John's . . . but, as all hope grew dim,
She sickened, dwindling feebler every day:
Though, when it seemed that she must pass away,
She grew more confident that, ere she passed,
A stranger would bring news to her, at last,
Of her lost son. " And when I woke in bed
Beside her, as the dawn was burning red,
She turned to me, with sleepless eyes, and said:
' The news will come, to-day.' "

He spoke no more: and silent in my seat,
With burning eyes upon the burning peat,
I pondered on this strangest of strange things
That had befallen in my vagrant life:
And how, at last, my idle wanderings
Had brought me to this old man and his wife.
And as I brooded o'er the blaze,
I thought with awe of that steadfast desire
Which, unto me unknown,
Had drawn me through long years, by such strange ways,
From that dark fo'c'sle to this cottage-fire.

And now, at last, quite spent, I dropped asleep;
And slumbered long and deep:
And when I waked, the peats were smouldering white
Upon the white hearthstone:
And over heath and bent dawn kindled bright
Beyond dark ridges in a rosy fleece:
While from the little window morning light
Fell on her face, made holy with the peace
That passeth understanding; and was shed
In tender beams upon the low-bowed head
Of that old man, forlorn beside the bed.

THE SHOP

Tin-tinkle-tinkle-tinkle, went the bell,
As I pushed in; and, once again, the smell
Of groceries, and news-sheets freshly printed,
That always greeted me when I looked in
To buy my evening-paper: but, to-night,
I wondered not to see the well-known face,
With kind, brown eyes, and ever-friendly smile,
Behind the counter; and to find the place
Deserted at this hour, and not a light
In either window.   Waiting there a while,
Though wondering at what change these changes hinted,
I yet was grateful for the quiet gloom —
Lit only by a gleam from the back-room,
And, here and there, a glint of glass and tin —
So pleasant, after all the flare and din
And hubbub of the foundry: and my eyes,
Still tingling from the smoke, were glad to rest
Upon the ordered shelves, so neatly dressed
That, even in the dusk, they seemed to tell
No little of the hand that kept them clean,
And of the head that sorted things so well
That naught of waste or worry could be seen,
And kept all sweet with ever-fresh supplies.
And as I thought upon her quiet way,
Wondering what could have got her, that she'd left
The shop, unlit, untended, and bereft
Of her kind presence, overhead I heard
A tiptoe creak, as though somebody stirred,
With careful step, across the upper floor:
Then all was silent, till the back-room door
Swung open; and her husband hurried in.
He feared he'd kept me, waiting in the dark;
And he was sorry: but his wife who served
The customers at night-time usually —
While he made up the ledger after tea,
Was busy, when I . . . Well, to tell the truth,
They were in trouble, for their little son
Had come in ill from school . . . the doctor said

Pneumonia . . . they'd been putting him to bed:
Perhaps I'd heard them, moving overhead,
For boards would creak, and creak, for all your care.
They hoped the best; for he was young; and youth
Could come through much; and all that could be done
Would be . . . then he stood, listening, quite unnerved,
As though he heard a footstep on the stair,
Though I heard nothing: but at my remark
About the fog and sleet, he turned,
And answered quickly, as there burned
In his brown eyes an eager flame:
The raw and damp were much to blame:
If but his son might breathe West-country air!
A certain Cornish village he could name
Was just the place; if they could send him there,
And only for a week, he'd come back stronger . . .
And then, again, he listened: and I took
My paper, and went, afraid to keep him longer;
And left him standing with that haggard look.

Next night, as I pushed in, there was no tinkle:
And, glancing up, I saw the bell was gone;
Although, in either window, the gas shone;
And I was greeted by a cheery twinkle
Of burnished tins and bottles from the shelves:
And now, I saw the father busy there
Behind the counter, cutting with a string
A bar of soap up for a customer,
With weary eyes, and jerky, harassed air,
As if his mind were hardly on the task:
And when 'twas done, and parcelled up for her,
And she had gone, he turned to me, and said:
He thought that folks might cut their soap themselves . . .
'Twas nothing much . . . but any little thing,
At such a time . . . And, having little doubt
The boy was worse, I did not like to ask;
So picked my paper up, and hurried out.

And, all next day, amid the glare and clang
And clatter of the workshop, his words rang;
And kept on ringing, in my head a-ring;
But any little thing . . . at such a time . . .
And kept on chiming to the anvils' chime:
But any little thing . . . at such a time . . .

And they were hissed and sputtered in the sizzle
Of water on hot iron: little thing . . .
At such a time: and, when I left, at last,
The smoke and steam; and walked through the cold drizzle
The lumbering of the 'buses as they passed
Seemed full of it; and to the passing feet,
The words kept patter, patter, with dull beat.

I almost feared to turn into their street,
Lest I should find the blinds down in the shop:
And, more than once, I'd half-a-mind to stop,
And buy my paper from the yelling boys,
Who darted all about with such a noise
That I half-wondered, in a foolish way,
How they could shriek so, knowing that the sound
Must worry children, lying ill in bed . . .
Then, thinking even they must earn their bread,
As I earned mine, and scarce as noisily!
I wandered on; and very soon I found
I'd followed where my thoughts had been all day,
And stood before the shop, relieved to see
The gases burning, and no window-blind
Of blank foreboding.   With an easier mind,
I entered slowly; and was glad to find
The father by the counter, 'waiting me,
With paper ready and a cheery face.
Yes! yes! the boy was better . . . took the turn,
Last night, just after I had left the place.
He feared that he'd been short and cross last night . . .
But, when a little child was suffering,
It worried you . . . and any little thing,
At such a moment, made you cut up rough:
Though, now that he was going on all right . . .
Well, he'd have patience, now, to be polite!
And, soon as ever he was well enough,
The boy should go to Cornwall for a change —
Should go to his own home; for he, himself,
Was Cornish, born and bred, his wife as well:
And still his parents lived in the old place —
A little place, as snug as snug could be . . .
Where apple-blossom dipped into the sea . . .
Perhaps, to strangers' ears, that sounded strange —
But not to any Cornishman who knew
How sea and land ran up into each other;

And how, all round each wide, blue estuary,
The flowers were blooming to the waters' edge:
You'd come on blue-bells like a sea of blue . . .
But they would not be out for some while yet . . .
'Twould be primroses, blowing everywhere,
Primroses, and primroses, and primroses . . .
You'd never half-know what primroses were,
Unless you'd seen them growing in the West;
But, having seen, would never more forget.
Why, every bank and every lane and hedge
Was just one blaze of yellow; and the smell,
When the sun shone upon them, after wet . . .
And his eyes sparkled, as he turned to sell
A penny loaf and half-an-ounce of tea
To a poor child, who waited patiently,
With hacking cough that tore her hollow chest:
And, as she went out, clutching tight the change,
He muttered to himself: "It's strange, it's strange
That little ones should suffer so." . . . The light
Had left his eyes: but when he turned to me,
I saw a flame leap in them, hot and bright.
I'd like to take them all, he said, to-night!

And, in the workshop, all through the next day,
The anvils had another tune to play . . .
Primroses, and primroses, and primroses:
The bellows puffing out: It's strange, it's strange
That little ones should suffer so . . .
And now, my hammer, at a blow:
I'd like to take them all, to-night!
And in the clouds of steam and white-hot glow
I seemed to see primroses everywhere,
Primroses, and primroses, and primroses.

And each night after that I heard the boy
Was mending quickly; and would soon be well:
Till one night I was startled by the bell —
Tin-tinkle-tinkle-tinkle, loud and clear;
And tried to hush it, lest the lad should hear.
But, when the father saw me clutch the thing,
He said the boy had missed it yesterday;
And wondered why he could not hear it ring;
And wanted it; and had to have his way.
And then, with brown eyes burning with deep joy,

He told me, that his son was going West —
Was going home . . . the doctor thought, next week,
He'd be quite well enough: the way was long;
But trains were quick; and he would soon be there:
And on the journey he'd have every care,
His mother being with him . . . it was best,
That she should go: for he would find it strange,
The little chap, at first . . . she needed change . . .
And, when they'd had a whiff of Western air!
'Twould cost a deal; and there was naught to spare:
But, what was money, if you hadn't health:
And, what more could you buy, if you'd the wealth . . .
Yes! 'twould be lonely for himself, and rough;
Though, on the whole, he'd manage well enough:
He'd have a lot to do: and there was naught
Like work to keep folk cheerful: when the hand
Was busy, you had little time for thought;
And thinking was the mischief . . . and 'twas grand
To know that they'd be happy. Then the bell
Went tinkle-tinkle; and he turned to sell.

One night he greeted me with face that shone,
Although the eyes were wistful; they were gone —
Had gone this morning, he was glad to say:
And, though 'twas sore work, setting them away,
Still, 'twas the best for them . . . and they would be
Already in the cottage by the sea . . .
He spoke no more of them; but turned his head;
And said he wondered if the price of bread . . .
And, as I went again into the night,
I saw his eyes were glistening in the light.

And, two nights after that, he'd got a letter:
And all was well: the boy was keeping better;
And was as happy as a child could be,
All day with the primroses and the sea,
And pigs! Of all the wonders of the West,
His mother wrote, he liked the pigs the best.
And now the father laughed until the tears
Were in his eyes, and chuckled: Ay! he knew!
Had he not been a boy there once, himself?
He'd liked pigs, too, when he was his son's years.
And then, he reached a half-loaf from the shelf;
And twisted up a farthing's worth of tea,

And farthing's worth of sugar, for the child,
The same poor child who waited patiently,
Still shaken by a hacking, racking cough.

And all next day the anvils rang with jigs:
The bellows roared and rumbled with loud laughter,
Until it seemed the workshop had gone wild,
And it would echo, echo, ever after
The tune the hammers tinkled on and off,
A silly tune of primroses and pigs . . .
Of all the wonders of the West
He liked the pigs, he liked the pigs the best!

Next night, as I went in, I caught
A strange, fresh smell.   The postman had just brought
A precious box from Cornwall, and the shop
Was lit with primroses, that lay atop
A Cornish pasty, and a pot of cream:
And as, with gentle hands, the father lifted
The flowers his little son had plucked for him,
He stood a moment in a far-off dream,
As though in glad remembrances he drifted
On Western seas: and, as his eyes grew dim,
He stooped, and buried them in deep, sweet bloom:
Till, hearing once again the poor child's cough,
He served her hurriedly, and sent her off,
Quite happily, with thin hands filled with flowers.
And as I followed to the street, the gloom
Was starred with primroses; and many hours
The strange, shy flickering surprise
Of that child's keen, enchanted eyes
Lit up my heart, and brightened my dull room.

Then, many nights the foundry kept me late
With overtime; and I was much too tired
To go round by the shop; but made for bed
As straight as I could go: until one night
We'd left off earlier, though 'twas after eight,
I thought I'd like some news about the boy
I found the shop untended; and the bell
Tin-tinkle-tinkle-tinkled all in vain.
And then I saw, through the half-curtained pane,
The back-room was a very blaze of joy:
And knew the mother and son had come safe back.

And as I slipped away, now all was well,
I heard the boy shriek out, in shrill delight:
" And, father, all the little pigs were black! "

FLANNAN ISLE

"Though three men dwell on Flannan Isle
To keep the lamp alight,
As we steered under the lee, we caught
No glimmer through the night."

A passing ship at dawn had brought
The news; and quickly we set sail,
To find out what strange thing might ail
The keepers of the deep-sea light.

The Winter day broke blue and bright,
With glancing sun and glancing spray,
While o'er the swell our boat made way,
As gallant as a gull in flight.

But as we neared the lonely Isle,
And looked up at the naked height,
And saw the lighthouse towering white,
With blinded lantern, that all night
Had never shot a spark
Of comfort through the dark,
So ghostly in the cold sunlight
It seemed, that we were struck the while
With wonder all too dread for words.

And as into the tiny creek
We stole beneath the hanging crag,
We saw three queer, black, ugly birds —
Too big, by far, in my belief,
For cormorant or shag —
Like seamen sitting bolt-upright
Upon a half-tide reef:
But, as we neared, they plunged from sight,
Without a sound, or spurt of white.

And still too mazed to speak,
We landed; and made fast the boat;

And climbed the track in single file,
Each wishing he were safe afloat,
On any sea, however far,
So it be far from Flannan Isle:
And still we seemed to climb, and climb,
As though we'd lost all count of time,
And so must climb for evermore.
Yet, all too soon, we reached the door —
The black, sun-blistered lighthouse-door,
That gaped for us ajar.

As, on the threshold, for a spell,
We paused, we seemed to breathe the smell
Of limewash and of tar,
Familiar as our daily breath,
As though 'twere some strange scent of death:
And so, yet wondering, side by side,
We stood a moment, still tongue-tied:
And each with black foreboding eyed
The door, ere we should fling it wide,
To leave the sunlight for the gloom:
Till, plucking courage up, at last,
Hard on each other's heels we passed,
Into the living-room.

Yet, as we crowded through the door,
We only saw a table, spread
For dinner, meat and cheese and bread;
But, all untouched; and no one there:
As though, when they sat down to eat,
Ere they could even taste,
Alarm had come; and they in haste
Had risen and left the bread and meat:
For at the table-head a chair
Lay tumbled on the floor.

We listened; but we only heard
The feeble cheeping of a bird
That starved upon its perch:
And, listening still, without a word,
We set about our hopeless search.

We hunted high, we hunted low;
And soon ransacked the empty house;

Then o'er the Island, to and fro,
We ranged, to listen and to look
In every cranny, cleft or nook
That might have hid a bird or mouse:
But, though we searched from shore to shore,
We found no sign in any place:
And soon again stood face to face
Before the gaping door:
And stole into the room once more
As frightened children steal.

Ay: though we hunted high and low,
And hunted everywhere,
Of the three men's fate we found no trace
Of any kind in any place,
But a door ajar, and an untouched meal,
And an overtoppled chair.

And as we listened in the gloom
Of that forsaken living-room —
A chill clutch on our breath —
We thought how ill-chance came to all
Who kept the Flannan Light:
And how the rock had been the death
Of many a likely lad:
How six had come to a sudden end,
And three had gone stark mad:
And one whom we'd all known as friend
Had leapt from the lantern one still night,
And fallen dead by the lighthouse wall:
And long we thought
On the three we sought,
And of what might yet befall.

Like curs a glance has brought to heel,
We listened, flinching there:
And looked, and looked, on the untouched meal,
And the overtoppled chair.

We seemed to stand for an endless while,
Though still no word was said,
Three men alive on Flannan Isle,
Who thought on three men dead.

THE BROTHERS

All morning they had quarrelled, as they worked,
A little off their fellows, in the pit:
Dick growled at Robert; Robert said Dick shirked:
And when the roof, dropt more than they had reckoned,
Began to crack and split,
Though both rushed like a shot to set
The pit-props in their places,
Each said the other was to blame,
When, all secure, with flushed and grimy faces,
They faced each other for a second.
All morning they had quarrelled: yet,
Neither had breathed her name.

Again they turned to work:
And in the dusty murk
Of that black gallery
Which ran out three miles underneath the sea,
There was no sound at all,
Save whispering creak of roof and wall,
And crack of coal, and tap of pick,
And now and then a rattling fall:
While Robert worked on steadily, but Dick,
In fits and starts, with teeth clenched tight,
And dark eyes flashing in his lamp's dull light.

And when he paused, nigh spent, to wipe the sweat
From off his dripping brow: and Robert turned
To fling some idle jibe at him, the spark
Of anger, smouldering in him, flared and burned —
Though all his body quivered, wringing-wet —
Till that black hole
To him blazed red,
As if the very coal
Had kindled underfoot and overhead:
Then, gripping tight his pick,
He rushed upon his brother:
But Robert, turning quick,
Leapt up, and now they faced each other.

They faced each other: Dick with arm upraised,
In act to strike, and murder in his eyes . . .
When, suddenly, with noise of thunder,
The earth shook round them, rumbling o'er and under;
And Dick saw Robert, lying at his feet:
As, close behind, the gallery crashed in:
And almost at his heel, earth gaped asunder.
By black disaster dazed,
His wrath died; and he dropped the pick;
And staggered, dizzily and terror-sick.
But when the dust and din
Had settled to a stillness, dread as death,
And he once more could draw his breath,
He gave a little joyful shout
To find the lamps had not gone out.

And on his knees he fell
Beside his brother, buried in black dust:
And, full of tense misgiving,
He lifted him, and thrust
A knee beneath his head; and cleared
The dust from mouth and nose: but could not tell
Awhile if he were dead or living.
Too fearful to know what he feared,
He fumbled at the open shirt,
And felt till he could feel the heart,
Still beating with a feeble beat:
And then he saw the closed lids part,
And saw the nostrils quiver;
And knew his brother lived, though sorely hurt.

Again he staggered to his feet,
And fetched his water-can, and wet
The ashy lips, and bathed the brow,
Until his brother sat up with a shiver,
And gazed before him with a senseless stare
And dull eyes strangely set.
Too well Dick knew that now
They must not linger there,
Cut off from all their mates, to be o'ertaken
In less than no time by the deadly damp:
So, picking up his lamp,
He made his brother rise;
Then took him by the arm,

And shook him, till he'd shaken
An inkling of the danger and alarm
Into those dull, still eyes:
Then dragged him, and half-carried him, in haste,
To reach the airway, where 'twould still be sweet
When all the gallery was foul with gas:
But, soon as they had reached it, they were faced
By a big fall of roof they could not pass;
And found themselves cut off from all retreat,
On every hand, by that black shining wall;
With naught to do but sit and wait
Till rescue came, if rescue came at all,
And did not come too late.

And, in the fresher airway, light came back
To Robert's eyes, although he never spoke:
And not a sound the deathly quiet broke,
As they sat staring at that wall of black —
As, in the glimmer of the dusky lamp,
They sat and wondered, wondered if the damp —
The stealthy after-damp that creeping, creeping,
Takes strong lads by the throat, and drops them sleeping,
To wake no more for any woman's weeping —
Would steal upon them, ere the rescue came. . . .
And if the rescuers would find them sitting,
Would find them sitting cold . . .
Then, as they sat and wondered, like a flame
One thought burned up both hearts:
Still, neither breathed her name.

And now their thoughts dropped back into the pit,
And through the league-long gallery went flitting
With speed no fall could hold:
They wondered how their mates had fared:
If they'd been struck stone-dead,
Or if they shared
Like fate with them, or reached the shaft,
Unhurt, and only scared,
Before disaster overtook them:
And then, although their courage ne'er forsook them,
They wondered once again if they must sit
Awaiting death . . . but knowing well
That even for a while to dwell
On such like thoughts will drive a strong man daft:

They shook themselves until their thoughts ran free
Along the drift, and clambered in the cage;
And in a trice were shooting up the shaft:
But when their thoughts had come to the pithead,
And found the fearful people gathered there,
Beneath the noonday sun,
Bright-eyed with terror, blinded by despair,
Dick rose, and with his chalk wrote on the wall,
This message for their folk:
" We can't get any further, 12, noonday "—
And signed both names; and, when he'd done,
Though neither of them spoke,
They both seemed easier in a way,
Now that they'd left a word,
Though nothing but a scrawl.

And silent still they sat,
And never stirred:
And Dick's thoughts dwelt on this and that:
How, far above their heads, upon the sea
The sun was shining merrily,
And in its golden glancing
The windy waves were dancing:
And how he'd slipt that morning on his way:
And how on Friday, when he drew his pay,
He'd buy a blanket for his whippet, Nell;
He felt dead certain she would win the race,
On Saturday . . . though you could never tell,
There were such odds against her . . . but his face
Lit up as though, even now, he saw her run,
A little slip of lightning, in the sun:
While Robert's thoughts were ever on the match
His team was booked to play on Saturday;
He placed the field, and settled who should play
In Will Burn's stead; for Will he had a doubt
Was scarcely up to form, although . . .

Just then, the lamp went slowly out.

Still, neither stirred,
Nor spoke a word;
Though either's breath came quickly, with a catch.

And now again one thought

Set both their hearts afire
In one fierce flame
Of quick desire:
Though neither breathed her name.

Then Dick stretched out his hand; and caught
His brother's arm; and whispered in his ear:
" Bob, lad, there's naught to fear . . .
And, when we're out, lad, you and she shall wed."

Bob gripped Dick's hand; and then no more was said,
As, slowly, all about them rose
The deadly after-damp; but close
They sat together, hand in hand.
Then their minds wandered; and Dick seemed to stand
And shout till he was hoarse
To speed his winning whippet down the course . . .
And Robert, with the ball
Secure within his oxter charged ahead
Straight for the goal, and none could hold,
Though many tried a fall.

Then dreaming they were lucky boys in bed
Once more, and lying snugly by each other:
Dick, with his arms clasped tight about his brother,
Whispered with failing breath
Into the ear of death:
" Come, Robert, cuddle closer, lad, it's cold."

THE BLIND ROWER

And since he rowed his father home,
His hand has never touched an oar.
All day he wanders on the shore,
And hearkens to the swishing foam.
Though blind from birth, he still could row
As well as any lad with sight;
And knew strange things that none may know
Save those who live without the light.

When they put out that Summer eve
To sink the lobster-pots at sea,
The sun was crimson in the sky;
And not a breath was in the sky,
The brooding, thunder-laden sky,
That, heavily and wearily,
Weighed down upon the waveless sea
That scarcely seemed to heave.

The pots were safely sunk; and then
The father gave the word for home:
He took the tiller in his hand,
And, in his heart already home,
He brought her nose round towards the land,
To steer her straight for home.

He never spoke,
Nor stirred again:
A sudden stroke,
And he lay dead,
With staring eyes, and lips of lead.

The son rowed on, and nothing feared:
And sometimes, merrily,
He lifted up his voice, and sang,
Both high and low,
And loud and sweet:
For he was ever gay at sea,

And ever glad to row,
And rowed as only blind men row:
And little did the blind lad know
That death was at his feet:
For still he thought his father steered;
Nor knew that he was all alone
With death upon the open sea.
So merrily, he rowed, and sang:
And, strangely on the silence rang
That lonely melody,
As, through the livid, brooding gloam,
By rock and reef, he rowed for home —
The blind man rowed the dead man home.

But, as they neared the shore,
He rested on his oar:
And, wondering that his father kept
So very quiet in the stern,
He laughed, and asked him if he slept;
And vowed he heard him snore just now.
Though, when his father spoke no word,
A sudden fear upon him came:
And, crying on his father's name,
With flinching heart, he heard
The water lapping on the shore;
And all his blood ran cold, to feel
The shingle grate beneath the keel:
And stretching over towards the stern,
His knuckle touched the dead man's brow.

But help was near at hand;
And safe he came to land:
Though none has ever known
How he rowed in, alone,
And never touched a reef.
Some say they saw the dead man steer —
The dead man steer the blind man home —
Though, when they found him dead,
His hand was cold as lead.

So, ever restless, to and fro,
In every sort of weather,
The blind lad wanders on the shore,
And hearkens to the foam.

His hand has never touched an oar,
Since they came home together —
The blind, who rowed his father home —
The dead, who steered his blind son home.

THE FLUTE

"Good-night!" he sang out cheerily:
"Good-night!" and yet again: "Good-night!"

And I was gay that night to be
Once more in my clean countryside,
Among the windy hills and wide.
Six days of city slush and mud,
Of hooting horn, and spattering wheel,
Made me rejoice again to feel
The tingling frost that fires the blood,
And sets life burning keen and bright;
And down the ringing road to stride
The eager swinging stride that braces
The straining thews from hip to heel:
To breathe again the wind that sweeps
Across the grassy, Northern steeps,
From crystal deeps and starry spaces.

And I was glad again to hear
The old man's greeting of good cheer:
For every night for many a year
At that same corner we had met,
Summer and Winter, dry and wet:
And though I never once had heard
The old man speak another word,
His cheery greeting at the bend
Seemed like the welcome of a friend.

But, as we neared to-night, somehow,
I felt that he would stop and speak —
Though he went by: and when I turned,
I saw him standing in the road,
And looking back, with hand to brow,
As if to shade old eyes, grown weak
Awaiting the long sleep they'd earned:
Though, as again towards him I strode,
A friendly light within them burned.

And then, as I drew nigh, he spoke
With shaking head, and voice that broke:
" I've missed you these last nights," he said:
" And I have not so many now
That I can miss friends easily : . .
Ay: friends grow scarce, as you grow old:
And roads are rough: and winds are cold:
And when you feel you're losing hold,
Life does not go too merrily."
And then he stood with nodding head,
And spoke no more.   And so I told
How I had been, six days and nights,
Exiled from pleasant sounds and sights.
And now, as though my voice had stirred
His heart to speech, he told right out,
With quickening eye and quavering word,
The things I care to hear about,
The little things that make up life:
How he'd been lonesome, since his wife
Had died, some thirty year ago:
And how he trudged three mile or so
To reach the farmstead where he worked,
And three mile back to his own door . . .
For he dwelt outby on the moor:
And every day the distance irked
More sorely still his poor, old bones;
And all the road seemed strewn with stones
To trip you up, when you were old —
When you were old, and friends were few:
How, since the farmstead had been sold,
The master and the men were new,
All save himself; and they were young;
And Mistress had a raspy tongue:
So, often, he would hardly speak
A friendly word from week to week
With any soul.   Old friends had died,
Or else had quit the countryside:
And since his wife was taken, he
Had lived alone, this thirty year:
And there were few who cared to hear
An old man's jabber . . . and too long
He'd kept me, standing in the cold,
With his long tongue, and such a song
About himself!   And I would be . . .

I put my arm through his; and turned
To go upon his way with him:
And once again that warm light burned
In those old eyes, so weak and dim:
While, with thin, piping voice, he told
How much it meant to him each night
To change a kindly word with me:
To think that he'd at least one friend
Who'd maybe miss him, in the end.

Then, as we walked, he said no more:
And, silent, in the starry light,
Across the wide, sweet-smelling bent,
Between the grass and stars we went
In quiet, friendly company:
And, all the way, we only heard
A chirrup where some partridge stirred,
And ran before us through the grass,
To hide his head till we should pass.

At length we reached the cottage-door:
But when I stopped, and turned to go,
His words came falteringly and slow:
If I would step inside, and rest,
I'd be right welcome: not a guest
Had crossed his threshold, thirty year . . .
He'd naught but bread and cheese and beer
To offer me . . . but, I'd know best . . .

He spoke with hand upon the latch;
And when I answered, opened wide
The cottage-door, and stepped inside;
And, as I followed, struck a match,
And lit a tallow-dip: and stirred
The banked-up peats into a glow:
And then with shuffling step and slow
He moved about: and soon had set
Two mugs of beer, and bread and cheese:
And while we made a meal off these,
The old man never spoke a word;
But, brooding in the ingle-seat,
With eyes upon the kindling peat,
He seemed a while to quite forget
He was not sitting by himself

To-night, like any other night;
When, as in the dim candle-light
I glanced around me, with surprise
I saw upon the rafter-shelf
A flute, nigh hidden in the shade.

And when I asked him if he played,
The light came back into his eyes:
Ay, ay, he sometimes piped a bit,
But not so often since she died.
And then, as though old memories lit
His poor, old heart, and made it glad,
He told how he, when quite a lad,
Had taught himself: and they would play
On penny whistles all the day —
He and the miller's son, beside
The millpool, chirping all they knew,
Till they could whistle clean and true:
And how, when old enough to earn,
They both saved up to buy a flute;
And they had played it, turn for turn:
But Jake was dead, this long while back . . .
Ah! if I'd only heard him toot,
I'd know what music meant.   Ay, ay . . .
He'd play me something, by-and-bye;
Though he was naught to Jake . . . and now
His breath was scant, and fingering slack . . .
He used to play to her at night
The melodies that she liked best,
While she worked on: she'd never rest
By daylight, or by candle-light . . .
And then, with hand upon his brow,
He brooded, quiet in his chair,
With eyes upon the red peat-glare;
Until, at length, he roused himself,
And reached the flute down from the shelf;
And, carrying it outside the door,
I saw him take a can, and pour
Fresh water through the instrument,
To make it sweet of tone, he said.
Then in his seat, so old and bent,
With kindling eyes and swaying head,
He played the airs he used to play
To please his wife, before she died.

And as I watched his body sway
In time and tune, from side to side —
So happy, just to play, and please
With old familiar melodies —
His eyes grew brighter and more bright,
As though they saw some well-loved sight:
And, following his happy gaze,
I turned, and saw, without amaze,
A woman standing, young and fair,
With hazel eyes, and thick brown hair
Brushed smoothly backward from the brow,
Beside the table that but now,
Save for the empty mugs, was bare.
Upon it she had spread a sheet,
And stood there, ironing a shirt,
Her husband's, as he played to her
Her favourite tunes, so old and sweet.
I watched her move with soundless stir;
Then stand with listening eyes, and hold
The iron near her glowing cheek,
Lest it, too hot, should do some hurt,
And she, so careful not to burn
The well-darned shirt, so worn and old.
Then, something seemed to make me turn
To look on the old man again:
And, as I looked, the playing stopped;
And now I saw that he had dropped
Into his brooding mood once more,
With eyes again grown dull and weak.
He seemed the oldest of old men
Who grope through life with sight worn dim:
And, even as I looked at him,
Too full of tender awe to speak,
I knew once more the board was bare,
With no young woman standing there
With hazel eyes and thick, brown hair.

And so, at last, I rose, and took
His hand: and as he clasped mine tight,
I saw again that friendly look
Fill his old weary eyes with light,
And wish me, without words, good-night.
And in my heart, that look glowed bright
Till I reached home across the moor.

And, at the corner of the lane,
Next night, I heard the old voice cry
In greeting, as I struggled by,
Head-down against the wind and rain.
And so each night, until one day,
His master chanced across my way:
But, when I spoke of him, he said:
Did I not know the man was dead,
And had been dead a week or so?
One morn he'd not turned up to work;
And never having known him shirk;
And hearing that he lived alone;
He thought it best himself to go
And see what ailed: and coming there,
He found the old man in his chair,
Stone-dead beside the cold hearthstone.
It must be full a week, or more . . .
Ay, just two weeks, come Saturday,
He'd found him; but he must have died
O'ernight — (the night I heard him play!)
And they had found, dropt by his side,
A broken flute upon the floor.

Yet, every night, his greeting still
At that same corner of the hill,
Summer and Winter, wet or dry,
'Neath cloud, or moon, or cold starlight,
Is waiting there to welcome me:
And ever as I hurry by,
The old voice sings out cheerily:
" Good-night! " and yet again, " Good-night! "

THE CRANE

The biggest crane on earth, it lifts
Two hundred ton more easily
Than I can lift my heavy head:
And when it swings, the whole world shifts,
Or so, at least, it seems to me,
As, day and night, adream I lie
Upon my crippled back in bed,
And watch it up against the sky.

My mother, hunching in her chair,
Day-long, and stitching trousers there —
At three-and-three the dozen pair . . .
She'd sit all night, and stitch for me,
Her son, if I could only wear . . .
She never lifts her eyes to see
The big crane swinging through the air.

But though she has no time to talk,
She always cleans the window-pane,
That I may see it clear and plain:
And as I watch it move, I walk
Who never walked in all my days . . .
And often, as I dream agaze,
I'm up and out: and it is I
Who swing the crane across the sky.

Right up above the wharf I stand,
And touch a lever with my hand,
To lift a bunch of girders high,
A truck of coal, a field of grain
In sacks, a bundle of big trees,
Or beasts, too frightened in my grip
To wonder at their skiey trip:
And then I let the long arm dip
Without a hitch, without a slip,
To set them safely in the ship
That waits to take them overseas.

My mother little dreams it's I,
Up there, as tiny as a fly,
Who stand above the biggest crane,
And swing the ship-loads through the sky;
While she sits, hunching in her chair,
Day-long, and stitching trousers there —
At three-and-three the dozen pair.

And sometimes when it turns me dizzy,
I lie and watch her, ever busy;
And wonder at a lot of things
I never speak to her about:
I wonder why she never sings
Like other people on the stair . . .
And why, whenever she goes out
Upon a windy day, the air
Makes her sad eyes so strangely bright . . .
And if the colour of her hair
Was brown like mine, or always white . . .
And why, when through the noise of feet
Of people passing in the street,
She hears a dog yelp or sheep bleat,
She always starts up in her chair,
And looks before her with strange stare,
Yet seeing nothing anywhere:
Though right before her, through the sky,
The biggest crane goes swinging by.

But it's a lucky day and rare
When she's the time to talk with me . . .
Though, only yesterday, when night
Shut out, at last, the crane from sight . . .
She, in her bed, and thinking I
Was sleeping — though I watch the sky,
At times, till it is morning-light,
And ships are waiting to unload —
I heard her murmur drowsily:
" The pit-pat-pattering of feet,
All night, along the moonlit road . . .
A yelp, a whistle, and a bleat . . .
The bracken's deep and soft and dry . . .
And safe and snug, and no one near . . .
The little burn sings low and sweet,
The little burn sings shrill and clear . . .

And loud all night the cock-grouse talks . . .
There's naught in heaven or earth to fear . . .
The pit-pat-pattering of feet . . .
A yelp, a whistle, and a bleat . . ."
And then she started up in bed:
I felt her staring, as she said:
" I wonder if he ever hears
The pit-pat-pattering of sheep,
Or smells the broken bracken stalks . . .
While she is lying sound-asleep
Beside him . . . after all these years —
Just nineteen years, this very night —
Remembering? . . . and now, his son,
A man . . . and never stood upright! "

And then I heard a sound of tears;
But dared not speak, or let her know
I'd caught a single whisper, though
I wondered long what she had done
That she should fear the pattering feet:
And when those queer words in the night
Had fretted me half-dead with fright,
And set my throbbing head abeat . . .
Out of the darkness, suddenly,
The crane's long arm swung over me,
Among the stars, high overhead . . .
And then it dipped, and clutched my bed:
And I had not a breath to cry,
Before it swung me through the sky,
Above the sleeping city high,
Where blinding stars went blazing by . . .

My mother, hunching in her chair,
Day-long, and stitching trousers there,
At three-and-three the dozen pair,
With quiet eyes and smooth white hair . . .
You'd little think a yelp or bleat
Could start her; or that she was weeping
So sorely, when she thought me sleeping.
She never tells me why she fears
The pit-pat-pattering of feet
All night along the moonlit road . . .
Or what's the wrong that she has done . . .
I wonder if 't would bring her tears,

If she could know that I, her son —
A man, who never stood upright,
But all the livelong day must lie,
And watch beyond the window-pane
The swaying of the biggest crane —
That I, within its clutch, last night,
Went whirling through the starry sky.

THE LIGHTHOUSE

Just as my watch was done, the fog had lifted;
And we could see the flashing of our light;
And see, once more, the reef beyond the Head,
O'er which, six days and nights, the mist had drifted —
Six days and nights in thick white mist had drifted,
Until it seemed all time to mist had drifted,
And day and night were but one blind white night.

But on the seventh midnight the wind shifted:
And I was glad to tumble into bed,
Thankful to hear no more the blaring horn,
That ceaselessly had sounded, night and morn,
With moaning echoes through the mist, to warn
The blind, bewildered ships at sea:
Yet, though as tired as any dog,
I lay awhile, and seemed to feel
Fog lying on my eyes still heavily;
And still, the horn unceasingly
Sang through my head, till gradually
Through night's strange stillness, over me
Sweet sleep began to steal,
Sleep, blind and thick and fleecy as the fog.
For all I knew, I might have slept
A moment, or eternity;
When, startled by a crash,
I waked to find I'd leapt
Upright on the floor:
And stood there, listening to the smash
Of falling glass . . . and then a thud
Of something heavy tumbling
Into the next room . . .
A pad of naked feet . . .
A moan . . . a sound of stumbling . . .
A heavier thud . . . and then no more.
And I stood shivering in the gloom,
With creeping flesh, and tingling blood,
Until I gave myself a shake

To bring my wits more wide awake;
And lit a lantern, and flung wide the door.
Half-dazed, and dazzled by the light,
At first it seemed I'd only find
A broken pane, a flapping blind:
But when I raised the lantern o'er my head,
I saw a naked boy upon the bed,
Who crouched and shuddered on the folded sheet;
And, on his face, before my feet,
A naked man, who lay as if quite dead,
Though on his broken knuckles blood was red:
And all my wits awakened at the sight.

I set the lantern down; and took the child,
Who looked at me, with piteous eyes and wild;
And chafed his chill, wet body, till it glowed;
And forcing spirit 'twixt his chattering teeth,
I tucked him snugly in beneath
The blankets, and soon left him warmly stowed:
And stooped to tend the man, who lay
Still senseless on the floor.
I turned him off his face;
And laid him on the other bed;
And washed and staunched his wound.
And yet for all that I could do,
I could not bring him to,
Or see a trace
Of life returning to that heavy head.

It seemed he'd swooned,
When through the window he'd made way,
Just having strength to lay
The boy in safety. Still as death,
He lay, without a breath:
And seeing I could do no more
To help him in the fight for life;
I turned again to tend the lad;
And, as I looked on him, was glad
To find him sleeping quietly.

So, fetching fuel, I lit a fire:
And quickly had as big a blaze
As any housewife could desire:
Then 'twixt the beds I set a chair,

That I might watch until they stirred:
And as I saw them lying there —
The sleeping boy, and him who lay
In that strange stiller sleep, 'twas plain
That they were son and father, now
I'd time to look, and wonder how,
In such a desperate plight,
Without a stitch or rag,
They'd taken refuge from the night.
And, as I wondered drowsily,
It seemed yet queerer and more queer;
For round the Head the rocks are sheer,
With scarce a foothold for a bird;
And it seemed quite beyond belief
That any wrecked upon the reef,
Could swim ashore, and scale the crag,
By daylight, let alone by night.

But they who live beside the sea
Know naught's too wonderful to be:
And as I sat, and heard
The quiet breathing of the child,
Great weariness came over me;
And, in a kind of daze,
I watched the blaze,
With nodding head:
And must have slept, for, presently,
I found the man was sitting up in bed:
And talking to himself, with wide, unseeing eyes.
At first, I hardly made out what he said:
But soon his voice, so hoarse and wild,
Grew calm: and, straining, I could hear
The broken words that came with many sighs.

" Yes, lad: she's going: but there's naught to fear:
For I can swim: and tow you in the belt.
Come, let's join hands together; and leap clear . . .
Ay, son: it's dark and cold . . . but you have felt
The cold and dark before . . .
And you should scorn . . .
And we must be near shore . . .
For hark, the horn!
Think of your mother, and your home, and leap . . .
She thinks of us, lad, waking or asleep . . .

You would not leave her lonely?
Nay! . . . then . . . go! . . .
Well done, lad! . . . Nay! I'm here . . .
Ay, son, it's cold: but you're too big to fear.
Now then, you're snug: I've got you safe in tow:
The worst is over: and we've only
To make for land . . . we've naught . . . to do . . .
        but steer . . .
But steer . . . but steer . . ."

He paused; and sank down in the bed, quite done:
And lay a moment silent, while his son
Still slumbered in the other bed,
And on his quiet face the firelight shone.
Then, once again, the father raised his head,
And rambled on . . .
" Say, lad, what cheer?
I thought you'd dropped asleep: but you're all right.
We'll rest a moment . . . I'm quite out of breath . . .
It's further than . . . Nay, son! there's naught to fear . . .
The land must be quite near . . .
The horn is loud enough!
Ay, lad, it's cold:
But, you're too old
To cry for cold.
Now . . . keep . . . tight hold:
And we'll be off again.
I've got my breath . . ."

He sank, once more, as still as death,
With hands that clutched the counterpane:
But still the boy was sleeping quietly.
And then, the father sat up suddenly:
And cried: " See! See!
The land! the land!
It's near . . . I touch it with my hand."
And now, " Oh God! " he moaned.
Small wonder, when he saw what lay before —
The black, unbroken crags, so grim and high,
That must have seemed to him to soar
Sheer from the sea's edge to the sky.
But soon he plucked up heart, once more:
" We're safe, lad — safe ashore!
A narrow ledge, but land, firm land.

We'll soon be high and dry.
Nay, son: we can't stay here:
The waves would have us back;
Or we should perish of the cold.
Come, lad: there's naught to fear . . .
You must be brave and bold.
Perhaps, we'll strike a track.
Ay, son: it's steep, and black,
And slimy to the hold:
But we must climb, and see! the mist is gone.
The stars are shining clear . . .
Think, son, your mother's at the top;
And you'll be up in no time.   See, that star,
The brightest star that ever shone,
Just think it's she who watches you;
And knows that you'll be brave and true.
Come, lad: we may not stop . . .
Or, else, the cold . . .
Give me your hand . . .
Your foot there, now . . . just room to stand.
It cannot be so far . . .
We'll soon be up . . . this work should make us warm.
Thank God, it's not a storm,
Or we should scarce . . . your foot, here, firm . . .
Nay, lad! you must not squirm.
Come, be a man: you shall not fall:
I'll hold you tight.
There: now, you are my own son, after all!
Your mother, lad,
Her star burns bright . . .
And we're already half-way up the height . . .
Your mother will be glad,
Ay, she'll be glad to hear
Of her brave boy who had no fear.

Your foot . . . your hand . . . 'twas but a bird
You startled out of bed:
'Twould think it queer
To wake up, suddenly, and see your head!
And when you stirred . . .
Nay! steady, lad!
Or you will send your dad . . .
Your hand . . . your foot . . . we'll rest upon this
     ledge . . .

Why, son, we're at the top! I feel the edge,
And grass, soft, dewy grass!
Let go, one moment; and I'll draw you up . . .
Now, lad! . . . Thank God! that's past . . .
And you are safe, at last:
You're safe, you're safe . . . and now my precious lass
Will see her son, her little son, again.

I never thought to reach the top, to-night.
God! What a height!
Nay! but you must not look: 'twould turn your head.
And we must not stand shivering here . . .
And see . . . a flashing light . . .
It's sweeping towards us: and now you stand bright . . .
Ah, your poor, bleeding hands and feet!
My little son, my sweet!
There's nothing more to fear.
A lighthouse, lad! And we must make for it.
You're tired; I'll carry you a bit.
Nay, son: 'twill warm me up . . .
And there will be a fire and bed;
And even perhaps a cup
Of something hot to drink,
And something good to eat.
And think, son, only think,
Your home . . . and mother . . . once again."

Once more, the weary head
Sank back upon the bed:
And for a while he hardly stirred;
But only muttered, now and then,
A broken word,
As though to cheer
His son, who still slept quietly,
Upon the other side of me.

And then, my blood ran cold to hear
A sudden cry of fear:
" My son! My son!
Ah, God, he's done!
I thought I'd laid him on the bed . . .
I've laid him on white mist, instead:
He's fallen sheer . . ."
Then, I sprang up; and cried: " Your son is here!

And taking up the sleeping boy,
I bore him to his father's arms:
And as he nestled to his breast,
Kind life came back to those wild eyes,
And filled them with deep joy:
And free of all alarms,
The son and father lay
Together, in sweet rest,
While through the window stole the strange, clear light
    of day.

THE MONEY

They found her cold upon the bed.
The cause of death, the doctor said,
Was nothing save the lack of bread.

Her clothes were but a sorry rag
That barely hid the nakedness
Of her poor body's piteous wreck:
Yet, when they stripped her of her dress,
They found she was not penniless;
For, in a little silken bag,
Tied with red ribbon round her neck,
Was four-pound-seventeen-and-five.

" It seems a strange and shameful thing
That she should starve herself to death,
While she'd the means to keep alive.
Why, such a sum would keep the breath
Within her body till she'd found
A livelihood; and it would bring . . .
But there is very little doubt
She'd set her heart upon a grand
And foolish funeral — for the pride
Of poor folk, who can understand! —
And so, because she was too proud
To meet death penniless, she died."

And talking, talking, they trooped out:
And, as they went, I turned about
To look upon her in her shroud;
And saw again the quiet face
That filled with light that shameful place,
Touched with the tender, youthful grace
Death brings the broken and outworn
To comfort kind hearts left to mourn.

And as I stood, the sum they'd found
Rang with a queer, familiar ring

Of some uncouth, uncanny sound
Heard in dark ages underground;
And " four-pound-seventeen-and-five "
Through all my body seemed to sing,
Without recalling anything
To help me, strive as I might strive.

But, as I stumbled down the stairs
Into the alley's gloom and stench —
A whiff of burning oil
That took me unawares —
And I knew all there was to tell.
And though the rain in torrents fell,
I walked on, heedless, through the drench . . .
And all the while, I seemed to sit
Upon a tub in Lansel pit;
And in the candle-light to see
John Askerton, a " deputy,"
Who paused awhile to talk with me,
His kind face glistening black with toil.

" 'Twas here I found him dead, beside
His engine.   All the other men
Were up — for things were slack just then —
And I'd one foot upon the cage;
When, all at once, I caught the smell
Of burning.   Even as I turned
To see what it could be that burned,
The seam behind was choked with stife.
And so I dropped on hands and knees,
And crawled along the gallery,
Beneath the smoke, that I might see
What ailed: and as I crept, half-blind,
With smarting eyes, and breath awheeze,
I scarcely knew what I should find.
At times, I thought I'd never know . . .
And 'twas already quite an age
Since I set out . . . I felt as though
I had been crawling all my life
Beneath the stifling cloud of smoke
That clung about me fit to choke:
And when, at last, I'd struggled here,
'Twas long ere I could see things clear . . .
That he was lying here . . . and he

Was dead . . . and burning like a tree . . .
A tree-trunk soaked in oil . . . No doubt,
The engine had caught fire, somehow;
And when he tried to put it out,
His greasy clothes had caught . . . and now!
As fine a lad as you could see . . .
And such a lad for singing . . . I
Had heard him when I worked hard by;
And often quiet I would sit
To hear him, singing in the pit,
As though his heart knew naught of it
And life was nothing but a song.

" He'd not been working with us long:
And little of his ways I knew:
But when I'd got him up, at last,
And he was lying in the shed,
The sweet song silent in his breast,
And there was nothing more to do;
The notion came into my head
That he had always been well-dressed;
And seemed a neat and thrifty lad . . .
And lived in lodgings . . . so, maybe,
Would carry on him all he had.
So, back into the cage I stepped:
And when it reached the bottom, crept
Along the gallery again;
And in the dust where he had lain,
I rummaged, until I found all
That from his burning pockets fell.
And when it seemed there was no more,
I thought how, happy and alive,
And recking naught what might befall,
He, too, for all that I could tell,
Just where I stood, had reckoned o'er
That four-pound-seventeen-and-five.

" Ay, like enough . . . for soon we heard
That in a week he'd looked to wed.
He'd meant to give the girl that night
The money to buy furniture.
She came, and watched till morning-light
Beside the body in the shed:
Then rose: and took, without a word,

The money he had left for her."

*   *   *   *

Then, as I wandered through the rain,
I seemed to stand in awe again
Beside that lonely garret-bed.
And it was good to think the dead
Had known the wealth she would not spend
To keep a little while alive —
His four-pound-seventeen-and-five —
Would buy her houseroom in the end.

THE SNOW

Just as the school came out,
The first white flakes were drifting round about:
And all the children shouted with delight
To see such flakes, so big, so white,
Tumbling from a cloud so black,
And whirling helter-skelter
Across the windy moor:
And as they saw the light flakes race,
Started off in headlong chase,
Swooping on them with a shout,
When they seemed to drop for shelter
Underneath the dry-stone wall.

And then the master, at the schoolhouse door,
Called out to them to hurry home, before
The storm should come on worse: and watched till all
Had started off by road or moorland track:
When, turning to his wife, he said
It looked like dirty weather overhead:
He thought 'twould be a heavy fall,
And threatened for a roughish night;
But they would all reach home in broad daylight.
'Twas early yet; he'd let the school out soon,
As it had looked so lowering since forenoon,
And many had a goodish step to go:
And it was but ill-travelling in the snow.
Then by the fire he settled down to read;
And to the weather paid no further heed.

And on their road home, full three miles away,
John, and his little sister, Janey, started;
And at the setting out, were happy-hearted
To be let loose into a world so gay,
With jolly winds and frisking flakes at play
That flicked your cheek, and whistled in your **teeth:**
And now hard on each other's heels they darted
To catch a flake that floated like a feather,

Then dropt to nestle in a clump of heather;
And often tumbled both together
Into a deep delicious bed
Of brown and springy heath.
But when the sky grew blacker overhead,
As if it were the coming on of night,
And every little hill, well-known to sight,
Looked big and strange in its new fleece of white;
And as yet faster and more thickly
The big flakes fell,
To John the thought came that it might be well
To hurry home; so, striding on before,
He set a steady face across the moor;
And called to Janey she must come more quickly.

The wind soon dropped: and fine and dry the snow
Came whispering down about them, as they trudged:
And when they'd travelled for a mile or so,
They found it ankle-deep: for here the storm
Had started long before it reached the school:
And as he felt the dry flakes tingling warm
Upon his cheek, and set him all aglow,
John in his manly pride, a little grudged
That now and then he had to wait awhile
For Janey, lagging like a little fool:
But when they'd covered near another mile
Through that bewildering white without a sound,
Save rustling, rustling, rustling all around,
And all his well-known world, so queer and dim,
He waited until she caught up to him;
And felt quite glad that he was not alone.

And when they reached the low, half-buried stone
That marked where some old shepherd had been found,
Lost in the snow in seeking his lost sheep,
One wild March night, full forty years ago,
He wished, and wished, that they were safe and sound
In their own house: and as the snow got deeper,
And every little bank seemed strangely steeper,
He thought, and thought of that lost sleeper,
And saw him lying in the snow;
Till every fleecy clump of heath
Seemed to shroud a man beneath;
And now his blood went hot and cold

Through very fear of that dread sight;
And then he felt that, in sheer fright,
He must take to his heels in flight,
He cared not whither, so that it might be
Where there were no more bundles, cold and white,
Like sheeted bodies, plain to see.
And, all on edge, he turned to chide
His sister, dragging at his side:
But when he found that she was crying,
Because her feet and hands were cold,
He quite forgot to scold:
And spoke kind words of cheer to her:
And saw no more dead shepherds lying
In any snowy clump of heather.
So, hand in hand, they trudged together,
Through that strange world of drifting gloam,
Sharp-set and longing sore for home.

And John remembered how that morning
When they set out, the sky was blue —
Clean, cloudless blue; and gave no warning;
And how through air as clear as glass,
The far-off hills he knew
Looked strangely near, and glittered brightly;
Each sprig of heath and blade of grass
In the cold wind blowing lightly,
Each clump of green and crimson moss
Sparkling in the wintry sun.

But now as they toiled home, across
These unfamiliar fells, nigh done,
The wind again began to blow;
And thicker, thicker fell the snow:
Till Janey sank, too numb to stir:
When John stooped down, and lifted her,
To carry her upon his back.
And then his head began to tire:
And soon he seemed to lose the track . . .
And now the world was all afire . . .
Now dazzling white, now dazzling black . . .
And then, through some strange land of light,
Where clouds of butterflies all white,
Fluttered and flickered all about,
Dancing ever in and out,

He wandered, blinded by white wings,
That rustled, rustled in his ears
With cold, uncanny whisperings . . .
And then it seemed his bones must crack
With that dead weight upon his back . . .
When, on his cheek, he felt warm tears,
And a cold tangle of wet hair;
And knew 'twas Janey weeping there:
And, taking heart, he stumbled on,
While in his breast the hearthlight shone:
And it was all of his desire
To sit once more before the fire;
And feel the friendly glowing heat.
But as he strove with fumbling feet,
It seemed that he would never find
Again that cheery hearth and kind;
But wander ever, bent and blind,
Beneath his burden through the night
Of dreadful, spangly, whispering white.

The wind rose; and the dry snow drifted
In little eddies round the track:
And when, at last, the dark cloud rifted,
He saw a strange lough, lying cold and black,
'Mid unknown, ghostly hills; and knew
That they were lost: and once again,
The snow closed in: and swept from view
The dead black water and strange fells.
But still he struggled on: and then,
When he seemed climbing up an endless steep,
And ever slipping, sliding back,
With ankles aching like to crack,
And only longed for sleep;
He heard a tinkling sound of bells,
That kept on ringing, ringing, ringing,
Until his dizzy head was singing;
And he could think of nothing else:
And then it seemed the weight was lifted
From off his back; and on the ground
His sister stood, while, all around
Were giants clad in coats of wool,
With big, curled horns, and queer black faces,
Who bobbed and curtsied in their places,
With blazing eyes and strange grimaces;

But never made a sound;
Then nearly shook themselves to pieces,
Shedding round a smell of warm, wet fleeces:
Then one it seemed as if he knew,
Looking like the old lame ewe,
Began to bite his coat, and pull
Till he could hardly stand: its eyes
Glowing to a monstrous size,
Till they were like a lantern light
Burning brightly through the night . . .
When some one stooped from out the sky,
To rescue him; and set him high:
And he was riding, snug and warm,
In some king's chariot through the storm,
Without a sound of wheel or hoof —
In some king's chariot, filled with straw,
And he would nevermore be cold . . .

And then with wondering eyes he saw
Deep caverns of pure burning gold;
And knew himself in fairyland:
But when he stretched an eager hand
To touch the glowing walls, he felt
A queer warm puff, as though of fire . . .
And suddenly he smelt
The reek of peat; and looking higher,
He saw the old, black porridge-kettle
Hanging from the cavern roof,
Hanging on its own black crook:
And he was lying on the settle,
While by his side,   *all about*
With tender look,
His mother knelt;
And he had only one desire
In all the world; and t'was to fling
His arms about her neck, and hide
His happy tears upon her breast.
And as to her he closely pressed,
He heard his merry father sing:
"There was a silly sleepyhead,
Who thought he'd like to go to bed:
So in a stell he went to sleep,
And snored among the other sheep."
And then his mother gently said:

"Nay, father: do not tease him now:
He's quite worn out: and needs a deal
Of quiet sleep: and, after all,
He brought his sister safe from school."
And now he felt her warm tears fall
Upon his cheek: and thrilled to feel
His father's hand on his hot brow,
And hear him say: "The lad's no fool."

RED FOX

I hated him . . . his beard was red . . .
Red fox, red thief! . . . Ah, God, that she —
She with the proud and lifted head
That never stooped to glance at me —
So fair and fancy-free, should wed
A slinking dog-fox such as he!

Was it last night I hated him?
Last night?   It seems an age ago . . .
At whiles, my mind comes over dim
As if God's breath . . . yet, ever slow
And dull, too dull she . . . limb from limb
Last night I could have torn him, so!

My lonely bed was fire and ice.
I could not sleep.   I could not lie.
I shut my hot eyes once or twice . . .
And saw a red fox slinking by . . .
A red dog-fox that turned back thrice
To mock me with a merry eye.

And so I rose to pace the floor . . .
And ere I knew, my clothes were on . . .
And as I stood outside the door,
Cold in the Summer moonlight shone
The gleaming barrel . . . and no more
I feared the fox, for fear was gone.

" The best of friends," I said, " must part . . ."
" The best of friends must part," I said:
And like the creaking of a cart
The words went wheeling through my head.
" The best of friends . . ." and, in my heart,
Red fox, already lying dead!

I took the trackway through the wood.
Red fox had sought a woodland den,

When she . . . when she . . . but, 'twas not good
To think too much on her just then . . .
The woman must beware, who stood
Between two stark and fearless men.

The pathway took a sudden turn . . .
And in a trice my steps were stayed.
Before me, in the moonlit fern,
A young dog-fox and vixen played
With their red cubs beside the burn . . .
And I stood trembling and afraid.

They frolicked in the warm moonlight —
A scuffling heap of heads and heels . . .
A rascal rush . . . a playful bite . . .
A scuttling brush, and frightened squeals . . .
A flash of teeth . . . a show of fight . . .
Then lively as a bunch of eels

Once more they gambolled in the brake,
And tumbled headlong in the stream,
Then scrambled gasping out to shake
Their sleek, wet, furry coats agleam.
I watched them, fearful and awake . . .
I watched them, hateless and adream.

The dog-fox gave a bark, and then
All ran to him: and, full of pride,
He took the trackway up the glen,
His family trotting by his side:
The young cubs nosing for the den,
With trailing brushes, sleepy-eyed.

And then it seems I must have slept —
Dropt dead asleep . . . dropt dead outworn.
I wakened, as the first gleam crept
Among the fern, and it was morn . . .
God's eye about their home had kept
Good watch, the night her son was born.

THE OVENS

He trailed along the cinder-track
Beside the sleek canal, whose black
Cold, slinking waters shivered back
Each frosty spark of starry light;
And each star pricked, an icy pin,
Through his old jacket worn and thin:
The raw wind rasped his shrinking skin
As if stark naked to its bite;
Yet, cutting through him like a knife,
It would not cut the thread of life;
But only turned his feet to stones
With red-hot soles, that weighed like lead
In his old broken boots.   His head,
Sunk low upon his sunken chest,
Was but a burning, icy ache
That strained a skull which would not break
To let him tumble down to rest.
He felt the cold stars in his bones:
And only wished that he were dead,
With no curst searching wind to shred
The very flesh from off his bones —
No wind to whistle through his bones,
His naked, icy, burning bones:
When, looking up, he saw, ahead,
The far coke-ovens' glowing light
That burnt a red hole in the night.
And but to snooze beside that fire
Was all the heaven of his desire . . .
To tread no more this cursed track
Of crunching cinders, through a black
And blasted world of cinder-heaps,
Beside a sleek canal that creeps
Like crawling ice through every bone,
Beneath the cruel stars, alone
With this hell-raking wind that sets
The cold teeth rattling castanets . . .
Yea, heaven, indeed, that core of red

In night's black heart that seemed quite dead.
Though still far off, the crimson glow
Through his chilled veins began to flow,
And fill his shrivelled heart with heat;
And as he dragged his senseless feet,
That lagged as though to hold him back
In cold, eternal hell of black,
With heaven before him, blazing red,
The set eyes staring in his head
Were held by spell of fire quite blind
To that black world that fell behind,
A cindery wilderness of death;
As he drew slowly near and nearer,
And saw the ovens glowing clearer —
Low-domed and humming hives of heat —
And felt the blast of burning breath
That quivered from each white-hot brick:
Till, blinded by the blaze, and sick
He dropped into a welcome seat
Of warm white ashes, sinking low
To soak his body in the glow
That shot him through with prickling pain,
An eager agony of fire,
Delicious after the cold ache,
And scorched his tingling, frosted skin.
Then gradually the anguish passed;
And blissfully he lay, at last,
Without an unfulfilled desire,
His grateful body drinking in
Warm, blessed, snug forgetfulness.
And yet with staring eyes awake,
As though no drench of heat could slake
His thirst for fire, he watched a red
Hot eye that burned within a chink
Between the bricks: while overhead
The quivering stream of hot, gold air
Surged up to quench the cold starlight.
His brain, too numbed and dull to think
Throughout the day, in that fierce glare
Awoke, at last, with startled stare
Of pitiless, insistent sight
That stript the stark, mean, bitter strife
Of his poor, broken, wasted life,
Crippled from birth, and struggling on,

The last, least shred of hope long gone,
To some unknown, black, bitter end.
But, even as he looked, his brain
Sank back to sightless sloth again;
Then, all at once, he seemed to choke;
And knew it was the stealthy stife
And deadly fume of burning coke
That filled his lungs, and seemed to soak
Through every pore, until the blood
Grew thick and heavy in his veins,
And he could scarcely draw a breath.
He lay, and murmured drowsily,
With closing eyes: " If this be death,
It's snug and easy . . . let it come . . .
For life is cold and hard . . . the flood
Is rising with the heavy rains
That pour and pour . . . that damned old drum,
Why ever can't they let it be . . .
Beat-beating, beating, beating, beat . . ."
Then, suddenly, he sat upright,
For, close behind him in the night,
He heard a breathing loud and deep,
And caught a whiff of burning leather.
He shook himself alive, and turned;
And on a heap of ashes white,
O'ercome by the full blast of heat,
Where fieriest the dread blaze burned,
He saw a young girl stretched in sleep.
He sat awhile with heavy gaze
Fixed on her in a dull amaze,
Until he saw her scorched boots smoking:
Then, whispering huskily: " She's dying,
While I look on and watch her choking!"
He roused, and pulled himself together:
And rose, and went where she was lying:
And, bending o'er the senseless lass,
In his weak arms he lifted her;
And bore her out beyond the glare,
Beyond the stealthy, stifling gas,
Into the fresh and eager air:
And laid her gently on the ground
Beneath the cold and starry sky;
And did his best to bring her round;
Though still, for all that he could try,

She seemed, with each deep-labouring breath
Just brought up on the brink of death.
He sought, and found an icy pool,
Though he had but a cap to fill,
And bathed her hands and face, until
The troubled breath was quieter,
And her flushed forehead felt quite cool:
And then he saw an eyelid stir;
And shivering she sat up at last,
And looked about her sullenly.
" I'm cold . . . I'm mortal cold," she said:
" What call had you to waken me?
I was so warm and happy, dead . . .
And still those staring stars!" Her head
Dropt in her hands: and thick and fast
The tears came with a heavy sobbing.
He stood quite helpless while she cried;
And watched her shaken bosom throbbing
With passionate, wild, weak distress,
Till it was spent. And then she dried
Her eyes upon her singed black dress;
Looked up, and saw him standing there,
Wondering, and more than half-afraid.
But now the nipping, hungry air
Took hold of her, and struck fear dead.
She only felt the starving sting
That must, at any price, be stayed;
And cried out: " I am famishing!"
Then from his pocket he took bread
That he had been too weak and sick
To eat o'ernight: and eager-eyed,
She took it timidly; and said:
" I have not tasted food two days."
And as he waited by her side,
He watched her with a quiet gaze;
And saw her munch the broken crust
So gladly, seated in the dust
Of that black desert's bitter night,
Beneath the freezing stars, so white
And hunger-pinched: and at the sight
Keen pity touched him to the quick;
Although he never said a word,
Till she had finished every crumb.
And then he led her to a seat

A little closer to the heat,
But well beyond the deadly stife.
And in the ashes, side by side,
They sat together, dazed and dumb,
With eyes upon the ovens' glare,
Each looking nakedly on life.
And then, at length, she sighed, and stirred,
Still staring deep and dreamy-eyed
Into the whitening, steady glow.
With jerky, broken words and slow,
And biting at her finger-ends,
She talked at last: and spoke out all
Quite open-heartedly, as though
There were not any stranger there —
The fire and he, both bosom-friends.
She'd left her home three months ago —
She, country-born and country-bred,
Had got the notion in her head
That she'd like city-service best . . .
And so no country place could please . . .
And she had worried without rest
Until, at last, she got her ends;
And, wiser than her folk and friends,
She left her home among the trees . . .
The trees grew thick for miles about
Her father's house . . . the forest spread
As far as ever you could see . . .
And it was green, in Summer, green . . .
Since she had left her home, she'd seen
No greenness could compare with it . . .
And everything was fresh and clean,
And not all smutched and smirched with smoke . . .
They burned no sooty coal and coke,
But only wood-logs, ash and oak . . .
And by the fire at night they'd sit . . .
Ah! wouldn't it be rare and good
To smell the sappy, sizzling wood,
Once more; and listen to the stream
That runs just by the garden-gate . . .
And often, in a Winter spate,
She'd wakened from a troubled dream,
And lain in bed, and heard it roar;
And quaked to hear it, as a child . . .
It seemed so angry, and so wild —

Just mad to sweep the house away!
And now, it was three months or more
Since she had heard it, on the day . . .
The day she left . . . and Michael stood . . .
He was a woodman, too, and he
Worked with her father in the wood . . .
And wanted her, she knew . . . but she
Was proud, and thought herself too good
To marry any country lad . . .
'Twas queer to think she'd once been proud —
And such a little while ago —
A beggar, wolfing crusts! . . . The pride
That made her quit her countryside
Soon left her stranded in the crowd . . .
And precious little pride she had
To keep her warm these freezing days
Since she had fled the city-ways
To walk back home . . . ay! home again:
For, in the town, she'd tried in vain,
For honest work to earn her bread . . .
At one place, they'd nigh slaved her dead,
And starved her, too; and, when she left,
Had cheated her of half her wage:
But she'd no means to stop the theft . . .
And she'd had no more work to do . . .
Two months since, now . . . it seemed an age!
How she had lived, she scarcely knew . . .
And still, poor fool, too proud to write
To home for help, until, at length,
She'd not a penny for a bite,
Or pride enough to clothe her back . . .
So she was tramping home, too poor
To pay the train-fare . . . she'd the strength,
If she'd the food . . . but that hard track,
And that cold, cruel, bitter night
Had taken all the heart from her . . .
If Michael knew, she felt quite sure . . .
For she would rather drop stone-dead
Than live as some . . . if she had cared
To feed upon the devil's bread,
She could have earned it easily . . .
She'd pride enough to starve instead,
Ay, starve, than fare as some girls fared . . .
But that was all behind . . . and she

Was going home . . . and yet, maybe,
If they'd a home like hers, they, too,
Would be too proud . . . she only knew
The thought of home had kept her straight,
And saved her ere it was too late.
She'd soon be home again . . .

                  And now
She sat with hand upon her brow;
And did not speak again nor stir.

And as he heard her words, his gaze
Still set upon the steady glare,
His thoughts turned back to city-ways:
And he remembered common sights
That he had seen in city nights:
And, once again, in early June,
He wandered through the midnight street;
And heard those ever-pacing feet
Of young girls, children yet in years,
With gaudy ribbons in their hair,
And shameless fevered eyes astare,
And slack lips set in brazen leers,
Who walked the pavements of despair,
Beneath the fair full Summer moon . . .
Shadowed by worn-out, wizened hags,
With claw-hands clutching filthy rags
About old bosoms, shrunk and thin,
And mouths aleer without a tooth,
Who dogged them, cursing their sleek youth
That filched their custom and their bread . . .
Then, in a reek of hot gas light,
He stood where, through the Summer night,
Half-dozing in the stifling air,
The greasy landlord, fat with sin,
Sat, lolling in his easy chair,
Just half-way up the brothel stair,
To tax the earnings they brought in,
And hearken for the policeman's tread . . .

Then, shuddering back from that foul place
And turning from the ovens' glare,
He looked into her dreaming face;
And saw green, sunlit woodlands there,
And waters flashing in between
Low-drooping boughs of Summer green.

And as he looked, still in a dream
She murmured: " Michael would, she knew . . .
Though she'd been foolish . . . he was true,
As true as steel, and fond of her . . .
And then she sat with eyes agleam
In dreaming silence, till the stir
Of cold dawn shivered through the air:
When, twisting up her tumbled hair,
She rose, and said, she must be gone.
Though she'd still far to go, the day
Would see her well upon her way . . .
And she had best be jogging on,
While she'd the strength . . . and so, " Good-bye."

And as, beneath the paling sky,
He trudged again the cinder-track
That stretched before him, dead and black,
He muttered: " It's a chance the light
Has found me living still . . . and she —
She, too . . . and Michael . . . and through me!
God knows whom I may wake to-night."

THE DANCING SEAL

When we were building Skua Light —
The first men who had lived a night
Upon that deep-sea Isle —
As soon as chisel touched the stone,
The friendly seals would come ashore;
And sit and watch us all the while,
As though they'd not seen men before;
And so, poor beasts, had never known
Men had the heart to do them harm.
They'd little cause to feel alarm
With us, for we were glad to find
Some friendliness in that strange sea;
Only too pleased to let them be
And sit as long as they'd a mind
To watch us: for their eyes were kind
Like women's eyes, it seemed to me.
So, hour on hour, they sat: I think
They liked to hear the chisels' clink:
And when the boy sang loud and clear,
They scrambled closer in to hear;
And if he whistled sweet and shrill,
The queer beasts shuffled nearer still:
But every sleek and sheeny skin
Was mad to hear his violin.

When, work all over for the day,
He'd take his fiddle down and play
His merry tunes beside the sea,
Their eyes grew brighter and more bright,
And burned and twinkled merrily:
And as I watched them one still night,
And saw their eager sparkling eyes,
I felt those lively seals would rise
Some shiny night ere he could know,
And dance about him, heel and toe,
Unto the fiddle's heady tune.

And at the rising of the moon,
Half-daft, I took my stand before
A young seal lying on the shore;
And called on her to dance with me.
And it seemed hardly strange when she
Stood up before me suddenly,
And shed her black and sheeny skin;
And smiled, all eager to begin . . .
And I was dancing, heel and toe,
With a young maiden white as snow,
Unto a crazy violin.

We danced beneath the dancing moon
All night, beside the dancing sea,
With tripping toes and skipping heels:
And all about us friendly seals
Like Christian folk were dancing reels
Unto the fiddle's endless tune
That kept on spinning merrily
As though it never meant to stop.
And never once the snow-white maid
A moment stayed
To take a breath,
Though I was fit to drop:
And while those wild eyes challenged me,
I knew as well as well could be
I must keep step with that young girl,
Though we should dance to death.

Then with a skirl
The fiddle broke:
The moon went out:
The sea stopped dead:
And, in a twinkling, all the rout
Of dancing folk had fled . . .
And in the chill bleak dawn I woke
Upon the naked rock, alone.

They've brought me far from Skua Isle . . .
I laugh to think they do not know
That as, all day, I chip the stone,
Among my fellows here inland,
I smell the sea-wrack on the shore . . .
And see her snowy-tossing hand,

And meet again her merry smile . . .
And dream I'm dancing all the while,
I'm dancing ever, heel and toe,
With a seal-maiden, white as snow,
On that moonshiny Island-strand,
For ever and for evermore.

THE SLAG

Among bleak hills of mounded slag they walked,
'Neath sullen evening skies that seemed to sag
O'er-burdened by the belching smoke, and lie
Upon their aching foreheads, dense and dank,
Till both felt youth within them fail and flag —
Even as the flame which shot a fiery rag
A fluttering moment through the murky sky
Above the black blast-furnaces, then sank
Again beneath the iron bell close-bound —
And it was all that they could do to drag
Themselves along, 'neath that dead-weight of smoke,
Over the cinder-blasted, barren ground.
Though fitfully and fretfully she talked,
He never turned his eyes to her, or spoke:
And as he slouched with her along the track
That skirted a stupendous, lowering mound,
With listless eyes, and o'er-strained sinews slack,
She bit a petted, puckered lip, and frowned
To think she ever should be walking out
With this tongue-tied, slow-witted, hulking lout,
As cold and dull and lifeless as the slag.

On edge, and over-wrought by the crampt day
Of crouched, close stitching at her dull machine,
It seemed to her a girl of seventeen
Should have, at least, an hour of careless talking —
Should have, at least, an hour of life, out walking
Beside a lover, mettlesome and gay —
Not through her too short freedom doomed to lag
Beside a sparkless giant, glum and grim,
Till all her eager youth should waste away.
Yet, even as she looked askance at him —
Well-knit, big-thewed, broad-chested, steady-eyed —
She dimly knew of depths she could not sound
In this strong lover, silent at her side:
And, once again, her heart was touched with pride
To think that he was hers, this strapping lad —

300

Black-haired, close-cropt, clean-skinned, and neatly
    clad . . .
His crimson neckerchief, so smartly tied —
And hers alone, and more than all she had
In all the world to her . . . and yet, so grave!
If he would only show that he was glad
To be with her — a gleam, a spark of fire,
A spurt of flame to shoot into the night,
A moment through the murky heavens to wave
An eager beacon of enkindling light
In answer to her young heart's quick desire!

Yet, though he walked with dreaming eyes agaze,
As, deep within a mound of slag, a core
Of unseen fire may smoulder many days,
Till suddenly the whole heap glow ablaze,
That seemed, but now, dead cinder, grey and cold,
Life smouldered in his heart.   The fire he fed
Day-long in the tall furnace just ahead
From that frail gallery slung against the sky
Had burned through all his being, till the ore
Glowed in him.   Though no surface-stream of gold,
Quick-molten slag of speech was his to spill
Unceasingly, the burning metal still
Seethed in him, from the broken furnace-side
To burst at any moment in a tide
Of white-hot molten iron o'er the mould . . .

But still he spoke no word as they strolled on
Into the early-gathering Winter night:
And, as she watched the leaping furnace-light,
She had no thought of smouldering fires unseen . . .
The daylong clattering whirr of her machine
Hummed in her ears again — the straining thread
And stabbing needle starting through her head —
Until the last dull gleam of day was gone. . . .

When, all at once, upon the right,
A crackling crash, a blinding flare . . .
A shower of cinders through the air . . .
A grind of blocks of slag aslide . . .
And, far above them, in the night,
The looming heap had opened wide
About a fiery, gaping pit . . .

And, startled and aghast at it,
With clasping hands they stood astare,
And gazed upon the awful glare:
And, as she felt him clutch her hand,
She seemed to know her heart's desire,
For evermore with him to stand
In that enkindling blaze of fire . . .
When, suddenly, he left her side;
And started scrambling up the heap:
And looking up, with stifled cry,
She saw, against the glowing sky,
Almost upon the pit's red brink,
A little lad, stock-still with fright
Before the blazing pit of dread
Agape before him in the night,
Where, playing castles on the height
Since noon, he'd fallen, spent, asleep
And dreaming he was home in bed . . .

With brain afire, too strained to think,
She watched her lover climb and leap
From jag to jag
Of broken slag . . .
And still he only seemed to creep . . .
She felt that he would never reach
That little lad, though he should climb
Until the very end of time . . .
And, as she looked, the burning breach
Gaped suddenly more wide . . .
The slag again began to slide
And crash into the pit,
Until the dazed lad's feet
Stood on the edge of it.
She saw him reel and fall . . .
And thought him done for . . . then
Her lover, brave and tall,
Against the glare and heat,
A very fire-bright god of men!
He stooped . . . and now she knew the lad
Was safe with Robert, after all.

And while she watched, a throng of folk
Attracted by the crash and flare,
Had gathered round, though no one spoke;

But all stood terror-stricken there,
With lifted eyes and indrawn breath,
Until the lad was snatched from death
Upon the very pit's edge, when,
As Robert picked him up, and turned,
A sigh ran through the crowd; and fear
Gave place to joy, as cheer on cheer
Sang through the kindled air . . .

But still she never uttered word,
As though she neither saw nor heard;
Till as, at last, her lad drew near,
She saw him bend with tender care
Over the sobbing child who lay
Safe in his arms, and hug him tight
Against his breast — his brow alight
With eager, loving eyes that burned
In his transfigured face aflame . . .
And even when the parents came
It almost seemed that he was loth
To yield them up their little son;
As though the lad were his by right
Of rescue, from the pit's edge won.

Then, as his eyes met hers, she felt
An answering thrill of tenderness
Run, quickening, through her breast; and both
Stood quivering there, with envious eyes,
And stricken with a strange distress,
As quickly homeward through the night
The happy parents bore their boy . . .

And then, about her reeling bright,
The whole night seemed to her to melt
In one fierce, fiery flood of joy.

DEVIL'S EDGE

All night I lay on Devil's Edge,
Along an overhanging ledge
Between the sky and sea:
And as I rested 'waiting sleep,
The windless sky and soundless deep
In one dim, blue infinity
Of starry peace encompassed me.

And I remembered, drowsily,
How 'mid the hills last night I'd lain
Beside a singing moorland burn;
And waked at dawn, to feel the rain
Fall on my face, as on the fern
That drooped about my heather-bed:
And how by noon the wind had blown
The last grey shred from out the sky,
And blew my homespun jacket dry,
As I stood on the topmost stone
That crowns the cairn on Hawkshaw Head,
And caught a gleam of far-off sea;
And heard the wind sing in the bent
Like those far waters calling me:
When, my heart answering to the call,
I followed down the seaward stream,
By silent pool and singing fall;
Till with a quiet, keen content,
I watched the sun, a crimson ball,
Shoot through grey seas a fiery gleam,
Then sink in opal deeps from sight.

And with the coming on of night,
The wind had dropped: and as I lay,
Retracing all the happy day,
And gazing long and dreamily
Across the dim, unsounding sea,
Over the far horizon came
A sudden sail of amber flame;

And soon the new moon rode on high
Through cloudless deeps of crystal sky.

Too holy seemed the night for sleep:
And yet I must have slept, it seems;
For, suddenly, I woke to hear
A strange voice singing, shrill and clear,
Down in a gully black and deep
That cleft the beetling crag in twain.
It seemed the very voice of dreams
That drive hag-ridden souls in fear
Through echoing, unearthly vales,
To plunge in black, slow-crawling streams,
Seeking to drown that cry, in vain . . .
Or some sea creature's voice that wails
Through blind, white banks of fog unlifting
To God-forgotten sailors drifting
Rudderless to death . . .
And as I heard,
Though no wind stirred,
An icy breath
Was in my hair . . .
And clutched my heart with cold despair.
But, as the wild song died away,
There came a faltering break
That shivered to a sobbing fall;
And seemed half-human, after all . . .

And yet, what foot could find a track
In that deep gully, sheer and black . . .
And singing wildly in the night!
So, wondering, I lay awake,
Until the coming of the light
Brought day's familiar presence back.

Down by the harbour-mouth that day,
A fisher told the tale to me.
Three months before, while out at sea,
Young Philip Burn was lost, though how,
None knew, and none would ever know.
The boat becalmed at noonday lay . . .
And not a ripple on the sea . . .
And Philip standing in the bow,
When his six comrades went below

To sleep away an hour or so,
Dog-tired with working day and night,
While he kept watch . . . and not a sound
They heard, until at set of sun
They woke; and coming up, they found
The deck was empty, Philip gone . . .
Yet not another boat in sight . . .
And not a ripple on the sea.
How he had vanished, none could tell.
They only knew the lad was dead
They'd left but now, alive and well . . .
And he, poor fellow, newly-wed . . .
And when they broke the news to her,
She spoke no word to any one:
But sat all day, and would not stir —
Just staring, staring in the fire,
With eyes that never seemed to tire;
Until, at last, the day was done,
And darkness came; when she would rise,
And seek the door with queer, wild eyes;
And wander singing all the night
Unearthly songs beside the sea:
But always the first blink of light
Would find her back at her own door.

'Twas Winter when I came once more
To that old village by the shore:
And as, at night, I climbed the street,
I heard a singing, low and sweet,
Within a cottage near at hand:
And I was glad awhile to stand
And listen by the glowing pane:
And as I hearkened, that sweet strain
Brought back the night when I had lain
Awake on Devil's Edge . . .
And now I knew the voice again,
So different, free of pain and fear —
Its terror turned to tenderness —
And yet the same voice none the less,
Though singing now so true and clear:
And drawing nigh the window-ledge,
I watched the mother sing to rest
The baby snuggling to her breast.

THE LILAC TREE

" I planted her the lilac tree
Upon our wedding day:
But when the time of blossom came,
With her dead babe she lay . . .
And as I stood beside the bed,
The scent of lilac filled the room:
And always when I smell the bloom,
I think upon the dead."

He spoke: and, speaking, sauntered on,
The young girl by his side:
And then they talked no more of death,
But only of the happy things
That burst their buds, and spread their wings,
And break in song at Whitsuntide,
That burst to bloom at Whitsuntide,
And bring the summer in a breath.

And as they talked, the young girl's life
Broke into bloom and song;
And, one with all the happy things
That burst their buds, and spread their wings,
Her very blood was singing,
And at her pulses ringing;
Life tingled through her, sweet and strong,
From secret sources springing:
And, all at once, a quickening strife
Of hopes and fears was in her heart,
Where only wondering joy had been;
And, kindling with a sudden light,
Her eyes had sight
Of things unseen:
And, in a flash, a woman grown,
With pangs of knowledge, fierce and keen,
She knew strange things unknown.

A year went by: at Whitsuntide,
He brought her home, a bride.

He planted her no lilac tree
Upon their wedding day:
And strange distress came over her,
As on the bed she lay:
For as he stood beside the bed,
The scent of lilac filled the room.
Her heart knew well he smelt the bloom,
And thought upon the dead.
Yet, she was glad to be his wife:
And when the blossom-time was past,
Her days no more were overcast;
And deep she drank of life:
And, thronged with happy household cares,
Her busy days went pleasantly:
Her foot was light upon the stairs;
And every room rang merrily,
And merrily, and merrily,
With song and mirth, for unto her
His heart seemed hers, and hers alone:
Until new dreams began to stir
Her wondering breast with bliss unknown
Of some new miracle to be:
And, though she moved more quietly,
And seldom sang, yet, happily,
From happy dawn to happy night
The mother's eyes shone bright.

But as her time drew near,
Her heart was filled with fear:
And when the lilac burst to bloom,
And brought the Summer in a breath,
A presence seemed to fill the room,
And fill her heart with death:
And as her husband lay asleep,
Beside her, on the bed,
Into her breast the thought would creep
That he was dreaming of the dead.
And all the mother's heart in her
Was mad with mother-jealousy
Of that sweet scented lilac tree;
And, blind with savage ecstasy,
Night after night she lay,
Until the blink of day,
With staring eyes and wild,

Half-crazy, lest the lilac tree
Should come betwixt him and his child.
By day, her mother-tenderness
Was turned to brooding bitterness,
Whene'er she looked upon the bloom:
And, if she slept at all at night,
Her heart would waken in affright
To smell the lilac in the gloom:
And when it rained, it seemed to her,
The fresh keen scent was bitterer:
Though when the blaze of morning came,
And flooded all the room,
The perfume burnt her heart like flame.

As, in the dark,
One night she lay,
A dark thought shot
Through her hot heart:
And, from a spark
Of smouldering wrong,
Hate burst to fire.
Now, quaking cold,
Now, quivering hot,
With breath indrawn,
Through time untold,
She 'waited dawn
That lagged too long
For her desire.

And when, at last, at break of day,
Her husband rose, and went his way
About his daily toil,
She, too, arose, and dressed,
With frenzy in her breast;
And stole downstairs, and took a spade,
And digged about the lilac roots,
And laid them bare of soil:
Then, with a jagged blade,
She hacked and slashed the naked roots —
She hacked and slashed with frantic hand,
Until the lilac scarce might stand;
And then again the soil she laid
About the bleeding roots —
(It seemed to her, the sap ran red

About the writing roots!)
But now her heart was eased of strife,
Since she had sapped the lilac's life;
And, frenzy-spent, she dropped the knife:
Then dizzily she crept to bed,
And lay all day as one nigh dead.

That night a sudden storm awoke,
And struck the slumbering earth to life:
And as the heavens in thunder broke,
She lay exulting in the strife
Of flash and peal,
And gust and rain;
For now, she thought: the lightning-stroke
Will lay the lilac low;
And he need never know
How I . . . and then, again,
Her heart went cold with dread,
As she remembered that the knife
Still lay beneath the lilac tree . . .
A blinding flash,
A lull, a crash,
A rattling peal . . .
And suddenly,
She felt her senses reel:
And, crying out: "The knife! The knife!"
Her pangs were on her . . .

                                        Dawn was red,
When she awoke upon the bed
To life — and knew her babe was dead.
She rose: and cried out fearfully:
"The lilac tree! The lilac tree!"
Then fell back in a swoon.

But, when she waked again at noon,
And looked upon her sleeping child;
And laid her hand upon its head,
No more the mother's heart was wild,
For hate and fear were dead;
And all her brooding bitterness
Broke into tears of tenderness.

And not a word the father said
About the lilac, lying dead.

A week went by, and Whitsuntide
Came round: and as she lay,
And looked upon the newborn day,
Her husband, lying by her side,
Spoke to her very tenderly:
" Wife, 'tis again our wedding day,
And we will plant a lilac tree
In memory of the babe that died."

They planted a white lilac tree
Upon their wedding day:
And, when the time of blossom came,
With kindly hearts they lay.
The sunlight streamed upon the bed:
The scent of lilac filled the room:
And, as they smelt the breathing bloom,
They thought upon the dead.

THE OLD MAN

The boat put in at dead of night;
And when I reached the house, 'twas sleeping dark.
I knew my gentlest tap would be a spark
To set my home alight:
My mother ever listening in her sleep
For my returning step, would leap
Awake with welcome; and my father's eyes
Would twinkle merrily to greet me;
And my young sister would run down to meet me
With sleepy sweet surprise.

And yet, awhile I lingered
Upon the threshold, listening;
And watched the cold stars glistening,
And seemed to hear the deep
Calm breathing of the house asleep —
In easy sleep, so deep, I almost feared to break it
And, even as I fingered
The knocker, loth to wake it,
Like some uncanny inkling
Of news from otherwhere,
I felt a cold breath in my hair,
As though, with chin upon my shoulder,
One waited hard, upon my heel,
With pricking eyes of steel,
Though well I knew that not a soul was there.

Until, at last, grown bolder,
I rapped; and in a twinkling,
The house was all afire
With welcome in the night:
First, in my mother's room, a light;
And then, her foot upon the stair;
A bolt shot back; a candle's flare;
A happy cry; and to her breast
She hugged her heart's desire,
And hushed her fears to rest.

Then, shivering in the keen night air,
My sleepy sister laughing came;
And drew us in: and stirred to flame
The smouldering kitchen-fire; and set
The kettle on the kindling red:
And as I watched the homely blaze,
And thought of wandering days
With sharp regret,
I missed my father: then I heard
How he was still a-bed;
And had been ailing, for a day or so;
But now was waking, if I'd go . . .
My foot already on the stair,
In answer to my mother's word
I turned; and saw in dull amaze,
Behind her, as she stood all unaware,
An old man sitting in my father's chair.

A strange old man . . . yet, as I looked at him,
Before my eyes a dim
Remembrance seemed to swim
Of some old man, who'd lurked about the boat,
While we were still at sea;
And who had crouched beside me, at the oar,
As we had rowed ashore;
Though, at the time, I'd taken little note,
I felt I'd seen that strange old man before:
But how he'd come to follow me,
Unknown . . .
And to be sitting there . . .
Then I recalled the cold breath in my hair,
When I had stood, alone,
Before the bolted door.

And now my mother, wondering sore
To see me stare and stare,
So strangely, at an empty chair,
Turned, too; and saw the old man there.

And as she turned, he slowly raised
His drooping head,
And looked upon her with her husband's eyes.
She stood, a moment, dazed
And watched him slowly rise,

As though to come to her:
Then, with a cry, she sped
Upstairs, ere I could stir.

Still dazed, I let her go, alone:
I heard her footsteps overhead:
I heard her drop beside the bed,
With low forsaken moan.

Yet, I could only stare and stare
Upon my father's empty chair.

THE HARE

My hands were hot upon a hare,
Half-strangled, struggling in a snare —
My knuckles at her warm wind-pipe —
When suddenly, her eyes shot back,
Big, fearful, staggering and black:
And, ere I knew, my grip was slack;
And I was clutching empty air,
Half-mad, half-glad at my lost luck . . .
When I awoke beside the stack.

'Twas just the minute when the snipe,
As though clock-wakened on the stroke
An hour ere dawn, dart in and out
Mist-wreaths in every syke asoak,
And flutter wheeling round about,
And drumming out the Summer night.
I lay star-gazing yet a bit;
Then, chilly-skinned, I sat upright,
To shrug the shivers from my back;
And drawing out a straw to suck,
My teeth nipped through it at a bite . . .
The liveliest lad is out of pluck
An hour ere dawn — a tame cock-sparrow —
When cold stars shiver through his marrow,
And wet mist soaks his mother-wit.

But as the snipe dropped, one by one,
And one by one the stars blinked out,
I knew 'twould only need the sun
To send the shudders right about:
And, as the clear East faded white,
I watched and wearied for the sun —
The jolly, welcome, friendly sun —
The sleepy sluggard of a sun
That still kept snoozing out of sight,
Though well he knew the night was done . . .
And, after all, he caught me dozing,
And leapt up, laughing, in the sky
Just as my lazy eyes were closing:

And it was good as gold to lie
Full-length among the straw, and feel
The day wax warmer every minute,
As, glowing glad, from head to heel,
I soaked and rolled rejoicing in it . . .
When from the corner of my eye,
Upon a heathery knowe hard-by,
With long lugs cocked, and eyes astare,
Yet all serene, I saw a hare.

Upon my belly in the straw
I lay, and watched her sleek her fur,
As, daintily, with well-licked paw,
She washed her face and neck and ears:
Then, clean and comely in the sun,
She kicked her heels up, full of fun,
As if she did not care a pin
Though she should jump out of her skin,
And leapt and lolloped, free of fears,
Until my heart frisked round with her.

" And yet, if I but lift my head,
You'll scamper off, young Puss," I said.
" Still, I can't lie, and watch you play,
Upon my belly half-the-day.
The Lord alone knows where I'm going:
But I had best be getting there.
Last night I loosed you from the snare —
Asleep, or waking, who's for knowing —
So I shall thank you now for showing
Which art to take to bring me where
My luck awaits me.   When you're ready
To start, I'll follow on your track.
Though slow of foot, I'm sure and steady . . ."
She pricked her ears, then set them back;
And like a shot was out of sight:
And, with a happy heart and light,
As quickly I was on my feet;
And following the way she went,
Keen as a lurcher on the scent,
Across the heather and the bent,
Across the quaking moss and peat.
Of course, I lost her soon enough,
For moorland tracks are steep and rough;
And hares are made of nimbler stuff

Than any lad of seventeen,
However lanky-legged and tough,
However, kestrel-eyed and keen:
And I'd at last to stop and eat
The little bit of bread and meat
Left in my pocket overnight.
So, in a hollow, snug and green,
I sat beside a burn, and dipped
The dry bread in an icy pool;
And munched a breakfast fresh and cool . . .
And then sat gaping like a fool . . .
For, right before my very eyes,
With lugs acock, and eyes astare,
I saw again the selfsame hare.

So up I jumped, and off she slipped:
And I kept sight of her until
I stumbled in a hole, and tripped;
And came a heavy, headlong spill:
And she, ere I'd the wit to rise,
Was o'er the hill, and out of sight:
And sore and shaken with the tumbling,
And sicker at my foot for stumbling,
I cursed my luck, and went on, grumbling,
The way her flying heels had fled.

The sky was cloudless overhead;
And just alive with larks asinging:
And, in a twinkling, I was swinging
Across the windy hills, lighthearted.
A kestrel at my footstep started,
Just pouncing on a frightened mouse,
And hung o'erhead with wings a-hover:
Through rustling heath an adder darted:
A hundred rabbits bobbed to cover:
A weasel, sleek and rusty-red,
Popped out of sight as quick as winking:
I saw a grizzled vixen slinking
Behind a clucking brood of grouse
That rose and cackled at my coming:
And all about my way were flying
The peewit, with their slow wings creaking:
And little grey snipe darted, drumming:
And now and then a golden plover
Or redshank piped with reedy whistle.

But never shaken bent or thistle
Betrayed the quarry I was seeking
And not an instant, anywhere
Did I clap eyes upon a hare.

So, travelling still, the twilight caught me:
And as I stumbled on, I muttered:
" A deal of luck the hare has brought me!
The wind and I must spend together
A hungry night among the heather.
If I'd her here . . ."   And as I uttered,
I tripped, and heard a frightened squeal;
And dropped my hands in time to feel
The hare just bolting 'twixt my feet.
She slipped my clutch: and I stood there
And cursed that devil-littered hare,
That left me stranded in the dark
In that wide waste of quaggy peat
Beneath black night without a spark:
When, looking up, I saw a flare
Upon a far-off hill, and said:
" By God, the heather is afire!
It's mischief at this time of year . . ."
And then, as one bright flame shot higher,
And booths and vans stood out quite clear;
My wits came back into my head:
And I remembered Brough Hill Fair.
And, as I stumbled towards the glare,
I knew the sudden kindling meant
The Fair was over for the day,
And all the cattle-folk away;
And gipsy-folk and tinkers now
Were lighting supper-fires without
Each caravan and booth and tent.
And as I climbed the stiff hill-brow,
I quite forgot my lucky hare.
I'd something else to think about:
For well I knew there's broken meat
For empty bellies after fair-time;
And looked to have a royal rare time
With something rich and prime to eat:
And then to lie and toast my feet
All night beside the biggest fire.

But even as I neared the first,

A pleasant whiff of stewing burst
From out a smoking pot a-bubble:
And as I stopped behind the folk
Who sprawled around, and watched it seething
A woman heard my eager breathing,
And, turning, caught my hungry eye:
And called out to me: " Draw in nigher,
Unless you find it too much trouble;
Or you've a nose for better fare,
And go to supper with the Squire . . .
You've got the hungry parson's air! "
And all looked up, and took the joke,
As I dropped gladly to the ground
Among them, where they all lay gazing
Upon the bubbling and the blazing.
My eyes were dazzled by the fire
At first; and then I glanced around;
And, in those swarthy, fire-lit faces —
Though drowsing in the glare and heat
And snuffing the warm savour in,
Dead-certain of their fill of meat —
I felt the bit between the teeth,
The flying heels, the broken traces,
And heard the highroad ring beneath
The trampling hoofs: and knew them kin.

Then for the first time, standing there
Behind the woman who had hailed me,
I saw a girl with eyes astare
That looked in terror o'er my head:
And, all at once, my courage failed me . . .
For now again, and sore adread,
My hands were hot upon a hare,
That struggled, strangling in the snare . . .
Then once more as the girl stood clear,
Before me — quaking cold with fear
I saw the hare look from her eyes . . .

And when, at last, I turned to see
What held her scared, I saw a man —
A fat man with dull eyes aleer —
Within the shadow of the van:
And I was on the point to rise
To send him spinning 'mid the wheels,

And twist his neck between his heels,
And stop his leering grin with mud . . .
And would have done it in a tick . . .
When, suddenly, alive with fright,
She started, with red, parted lips,
As though she guessed we'd come to grips,
And turned her black eyes full on me . . .
And as I looked into their light,
My heart forgot the lust of fight,
And something shot me to the quick,
And ran like wildfire through my blood
And tingled to my finger-tips . . .
And in a dazzling flash, I knew
I'd never been alive before . . .
And she was mine for evermore.

While all the others slept asnore
In caravan and tent that night,
I lay alone beside the fire;
And stared into its blazing core,
With eyes that would not shut or tire,
Because the best of all was true,
And they looked still into the light
Of her eyes, burning ever bright.
Within the brightest coal for me . . .
Once more, I saw her, as she started,
And glanced at me with red lips parted:
And, as she looked, the frightened hare
Had fled her eyes; and, merrily,
She smiled, with fine teeth flashing white,
As though she, too, were happy-hearted . . .
Then she had trembled suddenly,
And dropped her eyes, as that fat man
Stepped from the shadow of the van,
And joined the circle, as the pot
Was lifted off, and, piping-hot,
The supper steamed in wooden bowls.
Yet, she had scarcely touched a bite:
And never raised her eyes all night
To mine again: but on the coals,
As I sat staring, she had stared —
The black curls, shining round her head
From under the red kerchief, tied
So nattily beneath her chin —

And she had stolen off to bed
Quite early, looking dazed and scared.
Then, all agape and sleepy-eyed,
Ere long the others had turned in:
And I was rid of that fat man,
Who slouched away to his own van.

And now before her van I lay,
With sleepless eyes, awaiting day:
And as I gazed upon the glare,
I heard, behind, a gentle stir:
And turning round, I looked on her
Where she stood on the little stair
Outside the van, with listening air —
And in her eyes, the hunted hare . . .
And then I saw her slip away,
A bundle underneath her arm,
Without a single glance at me.
I lay a moment wondering,
My heart a-thump like anything,
Then, fearing she should come to harm,
I rose, and followed speedily
Where she had vanished in the night.
And as she heard my step behind,
She started, and stopt dead with fright:
Then blundered on as if struck blind:
And now as I caught up with her,
Just as she took the moorland track,
I saw the hare's eyes, big and black . . .
She made as though she'd double back . . .
But when she looked into my eyes,
She stood quite still and did not stir . . .
And picking up her fallen pack,
I tucked it 'neath my arm; and she
Just took her luck quite quietly,
As she must take what chance might come,
And would not have it otherwise,
And walked into the night with me,
Without a word across the fells.

And all about us, through the night,
The mists were stealing, cold and white,
Down every rushy syke or slack:
But soon the moon swung into sight;
And as we went, my heart was light

And singing like a burn in flood:
And in my ears were tinkling bells:
My body was a rattled drum:
And fifes were shrilling through my blood
That summer night, to think that she
Was walking through the world with me.
But when the air with dawn was chill,
As we were travelling down a hill,
She broke her silence with low sobbing:
And told her tale, her bosom throbbing
As though her very heart were shaken
With fear she'd yet be overtaken . . .
She'd always lived in caravans —
Her father's, gay as any man's,
Grass-green, picked out with red and yellow
And glittering brave with burnished brass
That sparkled in the sun like flame,
And window curtains, white as snow . . .
But they had died, ten years ago,
Her parents both, when fever came . . .
And they were buried, side by side,
Somewhere beneath the wayside grass . . .
In times of sickness they kept wide
Of towns and busybodies, so
No parson's or policeman's tricks
Should bother them when in a fix . . .
Her father never could abide
A black coat or a blue, poor man . . .
And so Long Dick, a kindly fellow,
When you could keep him from the can,
And Meg, his easy-going wife,
Had taken her into their van;
And kept her since her parents died . . .
And she had lived a happy life,
Until Fat Pete's young wife was taken . . .
But, ever since, he'd pestered her . . .
And she dared scarcely breathe or stir,
Lest she should see his eyes aleer . . .
And many a night she'd lain and shaken,
And very nearly died of fear —
Though safe enough within the van
With Mother Meg and her good-man —
For, since Fat Pete was Long Dick's friend,
And they were thick and sweet as honey,

And Dick owed Pete a pot of money,
She knew too well how it must end . . .
And she would rather lie stone dead
Beneath the wayside grass than wed
With leering Pete, and live the life,
And die the death, of his first wife . . .
And so, last night, clean-daft with dread,
She'd bundled up a pack and fled . . .

When all the sobbing tale was out,
She dried her eyes, and looked about,
As though she'd left all fear behind,
And out of sight were out of mind.
Then, when the dawn was burning red,
" I'm hungry as a hawk! " she said:
And from the bundle took out bread.
And at the happy end of night
We sat together by a burn,
And ate a thick slice, turn by turn,
And laughed and kissed between each bite.

Then, up again, and on our way
We went; and tramped the livelong day
The moorland trackways, steep and rough,
Though there was little fear enough
That they would follow on our flight.

And then again a shiny night
Among the honey-scented heather,
We wandered in the moonblaze bright,
Together through a land of light,
A lad and lass alone with life.
And merrily we laughed together,
When, starting up from sleep, we heard
The cock-grouse talking to his wife . . .
And " Old Fat Pete " she called the bird.

Six months and more have cantered by:
And, Winter past, we're out again —
We've left the fat and weatherwise
To keep their coops and reeking sties,
And eat their fill of oven-pies,
While we win free and out again
To take potluck beneath the sky

With sun and moon and wind and rain.
Six happy months . . . and yet, at night,
I've often wakened in affright,
And looked upon her lying there,
Beside me sleeping quietly,
Adread that when she waked, I'd see
The hunted hare within her eyes.

And, only last night, as I slept
Beneath the shelter of a stack . . .
My hands were hot upon a hare,
Half-strangled, struggling in the snare,
When, suddenly, her eyes shot back,
Big, fearful, staggering and black;
And ere I knew, my grip was slack,
And I was clutching empty air . . .
Bolt-upright from my sleep I leapt . . .
Her place was empty in the straw . . .
And then, with quaking heart, I saw
That she was standing in the night,
A leveret cuddled to her breast . . .

I spoke no word: but, as the light
Through banks of Eastern cloud was breaking
She turned, and saw that I was waking:
And told me how she could not rest;
And, rising in the night, she'd found
This baby-hare crouched on the ground
And she had nursed it quite a while:
But, now, she'd better let it go . . .
Its mother would be fretting so . . .
A mother's heart . . .
                              I saw her smile,
And look at me with tender eyes:
And as I looked into their light,
My foolish, fearful heart grew wise . . .
And now, I knew that never there
I'd see again the startled hare,
Or need to dread the dreams of night.

1910–1911.

THOROUGHFARES

(1908–1914)

THOROUGHFARES

SOLWAY FORD

He greets you with a smile from friendly eyes;
But never speaks, nor rises from his bed:
Beneath the green night of the sea he lies,
The whole world's waters weighing on his head.

The empty wain made slowly over the sand;
And he, with hands in pockets by the side
Was trudging, deep in dream, the while he scanned
With blue, unseeing eyes the far-off tide:
When, stumbling in a hole, with startled neigh,
His young horse reared; and, snatching at the rein,
He slipped: the wheels crushed on him as he lay;
Then, tilting over him, the lumbering wain
Turned turtle as the plunging beast broke free,
And made for home: and pinioned and half-dead
He lay, and listened to the far-off sea;
And seemed to hear it surging overhead
Already: though 'twas full an hour or more
Until high-tide, when Solway's shining flood
Should sweep the shallow firth from shore to shore.
He felt a salty tingle in his blood;
And seemed to stifle, drowning. Then again,
He knew that he must lie a lingering while
Before the sea might close above his pain,
Although the advancing waves had scarce a mile
To travel, creeping nearer, inch by inch,
With little runs and sallies over the sand.
Cooped in the dark, he felt his body flinch
From each cold wave as it drew nearer hand.
He saw the froth of each oncoming crest;
And felt the tugging of the ebb and flow,
And waves already breaking over his breast;
Though still far-off they murmured, faint and low;

Yet, creeping nearer, inch by inch; and now
He felt the cold drench of the drowning wave,
And the salt cold of death on lips and brow;
And sank, and sank . . . while still, as in a grave,
In the close dark beneath the crushing cart,
He lay, and listened to the far-off sea.
Wave after wave was knocking at his heart,
And swishing, swishing, swishing ceaselessly
About the wain — cool waves that never reached
His cracking lips, to slake his hell-hot thirst . . .
Shrill in his ear a startled barn-owl screeched . . .
He smelt the smell of oil-cake . . . when there burst,
Through the big barn's wide-open door, the sea —
The whole sea sweeping on him with a roar . . .
He clutched a falling rafter, dizzily . . .
Then sank through drowning deeps, to rise no more.

Down, ever down, a hundred years he sank
Through cold green death, ten thousand fathom deep.
His fiery lips deep draughts of cold sea drank
That filled his body with strange icy sleep,
Until he felt no longer that numb ache,
The dead-weight lifted from his legs at last:
And yet, he gazed with wondering eyes awake
Up the green glassy gloom through which he passed:
And saw, far overhead, the keels of ships
Grow small and smaller, dwindling out of sight;
And watched the bubbles rising from his lips;
And silver salmon swimming in green night;
And queer big, golden bream with scarlet fins
And emerald eyes and fiery-flashing tails;
Enormous eels with purple-spotted skins;
And mammoth unknown fish with sapphire scales
That bore down on him with red jaws agape,
Like yawning furnaces of blinding heat;
And when it seemed to him as though escape
From those hell-mouths were hopeless, his bare feet
Touched bottom: and he lay down in his place
Among the dreamless legion of the drowned,
The calm of deeps unsounded on his face,
And calm within his heart; while all around
Upon the midmost ocean's crystal floor
The naked bodies of dead seamen lay,

Dropped, sheer and clean, from hubbub, brawl and roar,
To peace, too deep for any tide to sway.

The little waves were lapping round the cart
Already, when they rescued him from death.
Life cannot touch the quiet of his heart
To joy or sorrow, as, with easy breath,
And smiling lips upon his back he lies,
And never speaks, nor rises from his bed ;
Gazing through those green glooms with happy eyes,
While gold and sapphire fish swim overhead.

A CATCH FOR SINGING

Said the Old Young Man to the Young Old Man:
" Alack, and well a-day! "
Said the Young Old Man to the Old Young Man:
" The cherry-tree's in flourish! "

Said the Old Young Man to the Young Old Man:
" The world is growing grey."
Said the Young Old Man to the Old Young Man:
" The cherry-tree's in flourish! "

Said the Old Young Man to the Young Old Man:
" Both flower and fruit decay."
Said the Young Old Man to the Old Young Man:
" The cherry-tree's in flourish! "

Said the Old Young Man to the Young Old Man:
" Alack, and well-a-day!
The world is growing grey:
And flower and fruit decay.
Beware Old Man, beware Old Man!
For the end of life is nearing;
And the grave yawns by the way . . ."

Said the Young Old Man to the Old Young Man:
" I'm a trifle hard of hearing;
And can't catch a word you say . . .
But the cherry-tree's in flourish! "

GERANIUMS

Stuck in a bottle on the window-sill,
In the cold gaslight burning gaily red
Against the luminous blue of London night,
These flowers are mine: while somewhere out of sight
In some black-throated alley's stench and heat,
Oblivious of the racket of the street,
A poor old weary woman lies in bed.

Broken with lust and, drink, blear-eyed and ill,
Her battered bonnet nodding on her head,
From a dark door she clutched my sleeve and said:
" I've sold no bunch to-day, nor touched a bite . . .
Son, buy six-penn'orth; and 'twill mean a bed."

So, blazing gaily red
Against the luminous deeps
Of starless London night,
They burn for my delight:
While somewhere, snug in bed,
A worn old woman sleeps.

And yet to-morrow will these blooms be dead
With all their lively beauty; and to-morrow
May end the light lusts and the heavy sorrow
Of that old body with the nodding head.
The last oath muttered, the last pint drained deep,
She'll sink, as Cleopatra sank, to sleep;
Nor need to barter blossoms for a bed.

THE WHISPERERS

As beneath the moon I walked,
Dog-at-heel my shadow stalked,
Keeping ghostly company:
And as we went gallantly
Down the fell-road, dusty-white,
Round us in the windy night
Bracken, rushes, bent and heather
Whispered ceaselessly together:
" Would he ever journey more,
Ever stride so carelessly,
If he knew what lies before,
And could see what we can see? "

As I listened, cold with dread,
Every hair upon my head
Strained to hear them talk of me,
Whispering, whispering ceaselessly:
" Folly's fool the man must be,
Surely, since, though where he goes
He knows not, his shadow knows:
And his secret shadow never
Utters warning words, or ever
Seeks to save him from his fate,
Reckless, blindfold, and unknown,
Till death tells him all, too late,
And his shadow walks alone."

MABEL

When Nigger Dick and Hell-for-Women slouched
Into the taproom of the " Duck and De'il,"
The three Dalmatian pups slunk in at heel
And down among the slushy saw-dust crouched;
But Mabel would not leave the windy street
For any gaudy tavern's reek and heat —
Not she! for Mabel was no spotted dog
To crawl among the steaming muddy feet
Beneath a bench, and slumber like a log.

And so she set her hoofs, and stayed outside,
Though Hell-for-Women pushed the swing-door wide,
And " Mabel, darling! Mabel, darling! " cried,
And Nigger Dick thrust out his head and cursed
Until his tongue burned with so hot a thirst,
He turned and swore that he'd not split his throat
To save the soul of any giddy goat.

And then they left her, stubborn, wild and white,
Snuffing the wet air of the windy night:
And as she stood beneath a cold blue star
That pierced the narrow strip of midnight sky
Between the sleeping houses black and high,
The glare and glitter of the reeking bar,
And all the filth and squalor of the street
Were blotted out . . .
              And she was lost between
The beetling crags of some deep, dark ravine
In Andalusian solitudes of stone,
A trembling, young, bewildered nanny-goat
Within the cold blue heart of night alone . . .
Until her ears pricked, tingling to a bleat,
As, far above her, on a naked scar,
The dews of morning dripping from his beard,
Rejoicing in his strength the herd-king reared,
Shaking the darkness from his shaggy coat.

THE VIXEN

The vixen made for Deadman's Flow,
Where not a mare but mine could go;
And three hounds only splashed across
The quaking hags of mile-wide moss;
Only three of the deadbeat pack
Scrambled out by Lone Maid's Slack,
Bolter, Tough, and Ne'er-Die-Nell:
But as they broke across the fell
The tongue they gave was good to hear,
Lively music, clean and clear,
Such as only light-coats make,
Hot-trod through the girth-deep brake.

The vixen, draggled and nigh-spent,
Twisted through the rimy bent
Towards the Christhope Crags. I thought
Every earth stopt — winded — caught .. . .
She's a mask and brush! When white
A squall of snow swept all from sight;
And hoodman-blind, Lightfoot and I
Battled with the roaring sky.

When southerly the snow had swept,
Light broke, as the vixen crept
Slinking up the stony brae.
On a jutting scar she lay,
Panting, lathered, while she eyed
The hounds that took the stiff brae-side
With yelping music, mad to kill.

Then vixen, hounds and craggy hill
Were smothered in a blinding swirl:
And when it passed, there stood a girl
Where the vixen late had lain,
Smiling down, as I drew rein,
Baffled; and the hounds, deadbeat,
Fawning at the young girl's feet,

Whimpered, cowed, where her red hair,
Streaming to her ankles bare,
Turned as white among the heather
As the vixen's brush's feather.

Flinching on my flinching mare,
I watched her, gaping and astare,
As she smiled with red lips wide,
White fangs curving either side
Of her lolling tongue . . . My thrapple
Felt fear's fang: I strove, agrapple,
Reeling . . . and again blind snow
Closed like night.
                    No man may know
How Lightfoot won through Deadman's Flow
And naught I knew till, in the glow
Of home's wide door, my wife's kind face
Smiled welcome. And for me the chase,
The last chase, ended. Though the pack
Through the blizzard struggled back,
Gone were Bolter, Tough and Nell,
Where, the vixen's self can tell!
Long we sought them, high and low,
By Christhope Crag and Deadman's Flow,
By slack and syke and hag: and found
Never bone nor hair of hound.

THE LODGING HOUSE

When up the fretful, creaking stair,
From floor to floor
I creep
On tiptoe, lest I wake from their first beauty-sleep
The unknown lodgers lying, layer on layer,
In the packed house from roof to basement
Behind each landing's unseen door;
The well-known steps are strangely steep,
And the old stairway seems to soar,
For my amazement
Hung in air,
Flight on flight
Through pitchy night,
Evermore and evermore.
And when at last I stand outside
My garret-door I hardly dare
To open it,
Lest, when I fling it wide,
With candle lit
And reading in my only chair,
I find myself already there . . .

And so must crawl back down the sheer black pit
Of hell's own stair,
Past lodgers sleeping layer on layer,
To seek a home I know not where.

THE ICE

Her day out from the workhouse-ward, she stands,
A grey-haired woman, decent and precise,
With prim black bonnet and neat paisley shawl,
Among the other children by the stall;
And with grave relish eats a penny ice.

To wizened toothless gums, with quaking hands
She holds it, shuddering with delicious cold;
Nor heeds the jeering laughter of young men —
The happiest, in her innocence, of all:
For, while their insolent youth must soon grow old,
She, who's been old, is now a child again.

WOOLGATHERING

Youth that goes woolgathering,
Mooning and stargazing,
Always finding everything
Full of fresh amazing,
Best will meet the moment's need
When the dream brings forth the deed.

He who keeps through all his days
Open eyes of wonder
Is the lord of skiey ways,
And the earth thereunder:
For the heart to do and sing
Comes of youth's woolgathering.

THE TRAM

Humming and creaking, the car down the street
Lumbered and lurched through thunderous gloam
Bearing us, spent and dumb with the heat,
From office and counter and factory home:

Sallow-faced clerks, genteel in black;
Girls from the laundries, draggled and dank;
Ruddy-faced labourers slouching slack;
A broken actor, grizzled and lank;

A mother with querulous babe on her lap;
A schoolboy whistling under his breath;
An old man crouched in a dreamless nap;
A widow with eyes on the eyes of death;

A priest; a sailor with deepsea gaze;
A soldier in scarlet with waxed moustache;
A drunken trollop in velvet and lace;
All silent in that tense dusk . . . when a flash

Of lightning shivered the sultry gloom:
With shattering brattle the whole sky fell
About us, and rapt to a dazzling doom
We glided on in a timeless spell,

Unscathed through deluge and flying fire
In a magical chariot of streaming glass,
Cut off from our kind and the world's desire,
Made one by the awe that had come to pass.

ON THE EMBANKMENT

Down on the sunlit ebb, with the wind in her sails, and
    free
Of cable and anchor, she swept rejoicing to seek the sea.

And my eyes and my heart swept out with her,
When at my elbow I felt a stir;
And glancing down, I saw a lad —
A shambling lad with shifty air,
Weak-chested, stunted and ill-clad,
Who watched her with unseeing stare.

Dull, watery grey eyes he had
Blinking beneath the slouching cap
That hid the low-browed, close-cropped head:
And as I turned to him he said
With hopeless hangdog air:
" Just out of gaol three days ago;
And I'll be back before I know:
For nothing else is left a chap
When once he's been inside . . . and so . . ."
Then dumb he stood with sightless stare
Set on the sunlit, windy sail of the far-off boat that free
Of cable and anchor still swept on rejoicing to seek the
    sea.

My heart is a sunlit, windy sail:
My heart is a hopeless lad in gaol.

THE DANCERS

'Neath a thorn as white as snow,
High above the peacock sea,
Hither, thither, to and fro,
Merrily the grey rats go:
To the song of ebb and flow
Moving as to melody.

Over gnarled roots, high and low,
Twisting, frisking fearlessly,
Six young hearts that needs must know,
When the ragged thorn's in blow,
Spring, and Spring's desire, and so
Dance, above the dancing sea.

THE WIND

To the lean, clean land, to the last cold height,
You shall come with a whickering breath,
From the depths of despair or the depths of delight,
Stript stark to the wind of death.

And whether you're sinless, or whether you've sinned,
It's useless to whimper and whine;
For the lean, clean blade of the cut-throat wind
Will slit your weasand, and mine.

THE VINDICTIVE STAIRCASE
OR
THE REWARD OF INDUSTRY

In a doomed and empty house in Houndsditch
All night long I lie awake and listen,
While all night the ghost of Mrs. Murphy
Tiptoes up and down the wheezy staircase,
Sweeling ghostly grease of quaking candles.

Mrs. Murphy, timidest of spectres,
You who were the cheeriest of charers,
With the heart of innocence and only
Torn between a zest for priests and porter,
Mrs. Murphy of the ample bosom,—
Suckler of a score or so of children
("Children? Bless you! Why, I've buried six, Sir.")
Who in forty years wore out three husbands
And one everlasting, shameless bonnet
Which I've little doubt was coffined with you —
Mrs. Murphy, wherefor do you wander,
Sweeling ghostly grease of quaking candles,
Up and down the stairs you scrubbed so sorely,
Scrubbed till they were naked, dank, and aching?

Now that you are dead, is this their vengeance?
Recollecting all you made them suffer
With your bristled brush and soapy water
When you scrubbed them naked, dank and aching,
Have they power to hold your ghostly footsteps
Chained as to an everlasting treadmill?

Mrs. Murphy, think you 'twould appease them
If I rose now in my shivering nightshirt,
Rose and told them how you, too, had suffered —
You, their seeming tyrant, but their bondslave —
Toiling uncomplaining in their service,
Till your knuckles and your knees were knotted

343

Into writhing fires of red rheumatics,
And how, in the end, 'twas they who killed you?

Even should their knots still harden to you,
Bow your one and all-enduring bonnet
Till your ear is level with my keyhole,
While I whisper ghostly consolation:
Know this house is marked out for the spoiler,
Doomed to fall to Hobnails with his pickaxe;
And its crazy staircase chopped to firewood,
Splintered, bundled, burned to smoke and ashes,
Soon shall perish, scattered to the fourwinds.
Then, God rest your spirit, Mrs. Murphy!

Yet, who knows! A staircase . . . Mrs. Murphy,
God forbid that you be doomed to tiptoe
Through eternity, a timid spectre,
Sweeling ghostly grease of quaking candles,
Up and down the spectre of a staircase,
While all night I lie awake and listen
In a damned and ghostly house in Houndsditch!

RAGAMUFFINS

Few folk like the wind's way;
Fewer folk like mine,—
Folk who rise at nine,
Who live to drudge and dine,
Who never see the starry light,
And sleep in the same bed each night
Under the same roof;
When the rascal wind and I
Happen to be gadding by,
Gentlefolk, so fat and fine
Beg to hold aloof,
Leaving us to starlit beds, and husks amid the swine.

Few folk like the wind's song,
And fewer folk like mine,—
Folk who trudge the trodden way,
Who keep the track and never stray,
Who think the sun's for making hay,—
Folk who cannot dance or play,
Faultless folk and fine.
Yet, the wind and I are gay,
In our ragamuffin way,
Singing, storm or shine.

THE ALARUM

Stark to the skin, I crawled a knife-edged blade
Of melting ice above the pit of Hell,
Flame-licked and scorched; yet strangely undismayed,
Till on my ears a dizzy clamour fell,
And dropt me sheer . . . and, wakening in my bed,
I saw the sky, beyond the chimneys red
And heard the crazy clanging of a bell.

IN A RESTAURANT

He wears a red rose in his buttonhole,
A city-clerk on Sunday dining out:
And as the music surges over the din
The heady quavering of the violin
Sings through his blood, and puts old cares to rout,
And tingles, quickening, through his shrunken soul,

Till he forgets his ledgers, and the prim
Black, crabbèd figures, and the qualmy smell
Of ink and musty leather and leadglaze,
As, in eternities of Summer days,
He dives through shivering waves, or rides the swell
On rose-red seas of melody aswim.

THE GREETING

"What fettle, mate?" to me he said
As he went by
With lifted head
And laughing eye,
Where, black against the dawning red,
The pit-heaps cut the sky:
"What fettle, mate?"

"What fettle, mate?" to him I said,
As he went by
With shrouded head
And darkened eye,
Borne homeward by his marrows, dead
Beneath the noonday sky:
"What fettle, mate?"

WHEELS

To safety of the curb he thrust the crone:
When a shaft took him in the back, and prone
He tumbled heavily, but all unheard
Amid the scurry of wheels that crashed and whirred
About his senseless head — his helmet crushed
Like crumpled paper by a car that rushed
Upon him unaware. And as he lay
He heard again the wheels he'd heard all day
About him on point-duty . . . only now
Each red-hot wheel ran searing over his brow —
A sizzling star with hub and spokes and tyre
One monstrous Catherine-wheel of sparkling fire
Whirring down windy tunnels of the night . . .
That Catherine-wheel, somehow it will not light —
Fixed to the broken paling; and the pin
Pricks the boy's finger as he jabs it in:
He sucks the salty blood — the spiteful thing
Fires, whizzing, sputtering sparks: he feels them sting
His wincing cheek; and, on the damp night-air,
The stench of burnt saltpetre and singed hair . . .
While still he lies and listens without fear
To the loud traffic rumbling in his ear —
Wheels rumbling in his ear, and through his brain
For evermore, a never-ending train
Of scarlet postal-vans that whirl one red
Perpetual hot procession through his head —
His head that's just a clanking, clattering mill
Of grinding wheels . . . and down an endless hill
After his hoop he runs, a little lad,
Barefooted 'neath the stars, in nightshirt clad —
And stumbles into bed, the stars all gone
Though in his head the hoop keeps running on
And on and on: his head grown big and wide
Holds all the windy night and stars inside . . .
And still within a hair's breadth of his ear
The crunch and gride of wheels rings sharp and clear —
Huge lumbering wagons, crusted axle-deep

With country marl, their drivers half-asleep
Against green toppling mounds of cabbages
Still crisp with dewy airs, or stacks of cheese
Smelling of Arcady, till all the sky
In clouds of cheese and cabbages rolls by —
Great golden cheeses wheeling through the night,
And giant cabbages of emerald light
That tumble after, scattering crystal drops . . .
While in his ear the grinding never stops —
Wheels grinding asphalt . . . then a high-piled wain
Of mignonette in boxes . . . and again,
A baby at his father's cottage-door
He toddles, treading on his pinafore,
And tumbles headlong in a bed of bloom,
Half-smothered in the deep, sweet honeyed gloom
Of crushed, wet blossom, and the hum of bees —
Big bumble-bees that buzz through flowery trees —
Grows furious . . . changing to a roar of wheels
And honk of hooting horns: and now he feels
That all the cars in London filled with light
Are bearing down upon him through the night,
As out of hall and theatre there pour
White-shouldered women, ever more and more,
Bright-eyed, with flashing teeth, borne in a throng
Of purring, glittering cars, ten thousand strong:
Each drowsy dame, and eager chattering lass
Laughing unheard within her box of glass . . .
And then great darkness, and a clanging bell —
Clanging beneath the hollow dome of hell
Aglow like burnished copper; and a roar
Of wheels and wheels and wheels for evermore,
As engine after engine crashes by
With clank and rattle under that red sky
Dropping a trail of burning coals behind,
That scorch his eyeballs till he lies half-blind,
Smouldering to cinder in a vasty night
Of wheeling worlds and stars in whirring flight,
And suns that blaze in thunderous fury on
For ever and for ever, yet are gone
Ere he can gasp to see them . . . head to heels
Slung round a monstrous red-hot hub, that wheels
Across infinity, with spokes of fire
That dwindle slowly till the shrinking tyre
Is clamped like aching ice about his head . . .

He smells clean acid smells: and safe in bed
He wakens in a lime-washed ward, to hear
Somebody moaning almost in his ear,
And knows that it's himself that moans: and then,
Battling his way back to the world of men,
He sees with leaden eyelids opening wide,
His young wife gravely knitting by his side.

PROMETHEUS

All day beneath the bleak, indifferent skies,
Broken and blind, a shivering bag of bones,
He trudges over icy paving stones,
And " Matches! Matches! Matches! Matches! "
    cries.

And now beneath the dismal, dripping night
And shadowed by a deeper night, he stands:
And yet he holds within his palsied hands
Quick fire enough to set his world alight.

NIGHT

Suddenly kindling the skylight's pitchy square,
The eyes of a cat, sinister, glassy and green,
Caught by a trick of the light in a senseless stare . . .
And the powers of the older night, abhorrent, obscene,
Each from his den of darkness and loathly lair,
Slink to my bedside, and gibber and mow, and fill
My heart with the Fear of the Fen and the Dread of the Hill
And the Terror that stalks by night through the Wood of Doom.
And things that are headless and nameless throng the room:
The cold webbed fingers of witches are in my hair:
The clammy lips of the warlock are clenched to mine:
The Eel of the bottomless pit of Deadman's Bog
Slithers an icy spiral about my spine:
A corpse-clutch freezes my midriff, the foul reek of Fog . . .

When my hand is licked by the warm wet tongue of my dog;
The eyes blink out; and Horror slinks back to her den;
And I breathe again.

ON HAMPSTEAD HEATH

Against the green flame of the hawthorn-tree,
His scarlet tunic burns;
And livelier than the green sap's mantling glee
The Spring fire tingles through him headily
As quivering he turns

And stammers out the old amazing tale
Of youth and April weather;
While she, with half-breathed jests that, sobbing, fail,
Sits, tight-lipped, quaking, eager-eyed and pale,
Beneath her purple feather.

A VISION IN A TEA-SHOP

His hair lit up the tea-shop like a fire,
The naked flame of youth made manifest —
Young hunger's unappeasable desire
Devouring cakes and cream with eager zest:

While cheek by jowl, an old man, bald and blind
And peaked and withered as a waning moon,
With toothless, mumbling gums, and wandering mind
Supped barley-water from a tremulous spoon.

I turned a moment: and the man was gone:
And as I looked upon the red-haired boy,
About him in a blinding glory shone
The sons of morning singing together for joy.

LINES

Addressed to the Spectre of an Elderly Gentleman, recently demised, Whom the Author had once observed performing a Benevolent Office in the Vicinity of Holborn, W. C.

I saw you, seated on a horse's head,
While the blaspheming carter cut the traces,
Obese, white-waistcoated, and newly fed,
Through bland, indifferent monocle surveying
The gaping circle of indifferent faces.

And now, the news has come that you are dead,
I see you, while they cut the tangled traces,
On your own hearse's fallen horse's head,
Through bland, indifferent monocle surveying
The unseeing circle of funereal faces.

THE DREADNOUGHT

Breasting the tide of the traffic, the " Dreadnought " comes,
Be-ribboned and gay, the first of the holiday brakes,
Brimful of broken old women, a parish's mothers,
Bearing them out for the day from grey alleys and slums —
A day in the forest of Epping grown green for their sakes.

Listless and stolid they crouch, everlastingly tired,
Mere bundles of patience outworn, half-deaf and half-blind,
Save only one apple-cheeked grannie, more brisk than the others,
Who, remembering, with youth in her eyes and the old dreams
     desired,
Sits kissing her hand to the drivers who follow behind.

SIGHT

By the lamplit stall I loitered, feasting my eyes
On colours ripe and rich for the heart's desire —
Tomatoes, redder than Krakatoa's fire,
Oranges like old sunsets over Tyre,
And apples golden-green as the glades of Paradise.

And as I lingered, lost in divine delight,
My heart thanked God for the goodly gift of sight
And all youth's lively senses keen and quick . . .
When suddenly, behind me in the night,
I heard the tapping of a blind man's stick.

THE GORSE

In dream, again within the clean, cold hell
Of glazed and aching silence he was trapped;
And, closing in, the blank walls of his cell
Crushed stifling on him . . . when the bracken snapped,
Caught in his clutching fingers: and he lay
Awake upon his back among the fern,
With free eyes travelling the wide blue day
Unhindered, unremembering; while a burn
Tinkled and gurgled somewhere out of sight,
Unheard of him, till, suddenly aware
Of its cold music, shivering in the light,
He raised himself; and with far-ranging stare
Looked all about him: and, with dazed eyes wide
Saw, still as in a numb, unreal dream,
Black figures scouring a far hill-side,
With now and then a sunlit rifle's gleam;
And knew the hunt was hot upon his track:
Yet hardly seemed to mind, somehow, just then . . .
But kept on wondering why they looked so black
On that hot hillside, all those little men
Who scurried round like beetles — twelve, all told . . .
He counted them twice over; and began
A third time reckoning them, but could not hold
His starved wits to the business, while they ran
So brokenly, and always stuck at " five " . . .
And " One, two, three, four, five " a dozen times
He muttered . . . " Can you catch a fish alive? "
Sang mocking echoes of old nursery-rhymes
Through the strained, tingling hollow of his head.
And now almost remembering, he was stirred
To pity them; and wondered if they'd fed
Since he had, or if, ever since they'd heard
Two nights ago the sudden signal-gun
That raised alarm of his escape, they, too,
Had fasted in the wilderness, and run
With nothing but the thirsty wind to chew,
And nothing in their bellies but a fill
Of cold peat-water, till their heads were light . . .

The crackling of a rifle on the hill
Rang in his ears; and stung to headlong flight,
He started to his feet; and through the brake
He plunged in panic, heedless of the sun
That burned his cropped head to a red-hot ache
Still racked with crackling echoes of the gun.

Then suddenly the sun-enkindled fire
Of gorse upon the moor-top caught his eye;
And that gold glow held all his heart's desire,
As, like a witless, flame-bewildered fly,
He blundered towards the league-wide yellow blaze,
And tumbled headlong on the spikes of bloom;
And rising, bruised and bleeding and adaze,
Struggled through clutching spines: the dense sweet
        fume
Of nutty, acrid scent like poison stealing
Through his hot blood: the bristling yellow glare
Spiking his eyes with fire, till he went reeling,
Stifling and blinded, on — and did not care
Though he were taken — wandering round and round,
" Jerusalem the Golden " quavering shrill,
Changing his tune to " Tommy Tiddler's Ground ":
Till, just a lost child on that dazzling hill,
Bewildered in a glittering golden maze
Of stinging scented fire, he dropped, quite done,
A shrivelling wisp within a world ablaze
Beneath a blinding sky, one blaze of sun.

1908–14.

BORDERLANDS

(1912–1914)

BORDERLANDS

THE QUEEN'S CRAGS

Scene: The Queen's Crags, a fantastic group of rocks and boulders on the fells. MICHAEL CROZIER, *a young hind, lies in the evening glow at the foot of the tallest crag, with a faraway look in his eyes. Presently* GEORGE DODD, *an old hind, enters and stops on seeing* MICHAEL.

GEORGE.   Of all the lazy louts!
It's here, then, that you moon away the evenings,
Stretched like a collie, basking in the sun,
Your noble self for company!
At your age, Michael, lad,
I'd have thought shame to find myself alone,
A night like this:
And such a lass as Peggie, lonesome, too.
I wasted little time, when I was young;
And lost no Summer evenings by myself.
I always was a lad among the lasses,
And not a moony, moping gowk like you.
No sooner was I through,
Than I was washed and out.
Sunlight, moonlight, starlight, dark,
I never missed the screeching of the owls,
Nor listened to it lonesome.
But you, I've never seen you with a lass:
Though Peggie Haliburton, she . . .
Lad, take your pleasure, while you're young,
And Summer nights be fine.
Though youth and Summer nights seem long —
Long enough to last for ever,
For ever and a day,
Before you've looked about a bit,
Old age and Winter are upon you.
To-day you're lithe and lusty,
And to-morrow,

363

A grizzled, pithless, aching bag-of-bones.
And Peggie Haliburton, too,
The lass was made for love and Summer nights:
Yet she's out walking with herself,
And no one by to see her but the peewits,
Or, maybe, a cock grouse or so:
A bonnie young thing wasting.

[*He pauses, looking at* MICHAEL, *who pays little heed,
but still lies with a far-away look in his eyes.*]

But, maybe, Michael, you're like me,
And cannot 'bide red hair?
I never liked a red-haired wench,
If there were any other by.
Red . . . it's the colour of the fox and kestrel,
And stoat and weasel, and such thieves and vermin.
And, as for stock, if I could have my way,
I shouldn't have a red beast on the farm.
I'd never let a chestnut stallion whinny
Within a mile of Skarlindyke.
I'd sell all chestnut colts and fillies:
The red bull, too, should go:
And no red heifer should come nigh the byres.
I'd have all black, coal-black:
Black stallions and black mares:
Black bulls, black stirks and heifers:
All black, save tups and ewes:
I'm somehow not so partial to black sheep.
But, in this world, we cannot all be farmers,
And lords of all creation.
Still, even hinds may have their fancies:
And you and I, lad, cannot 'bide red hair:
And so, red Peggy walks alone.
Ay! and it seems that hinds can hold their tongues,
At least, the youngsters can;
For my old tongue keeps wagging,
And wags to little purpose seemingly.
It must have lost its sting;
Or, Peggy's not in favour.

[*A pause.*]

Well, Mister Mum, you've chosen a snug corner
To stretch your lazy bones in.

[Sitting down by MICHAEL, *with his back against the
    rock.]*

I think I'll bear you company awhile,
If you can call a hedgehog company,
Tight-curled, and prickles bristling!
Still, though you mayn't be over-lively,
You're livelier than Myself.
I find him but glum company —
A grumpy, sulky beggar,
Who keeps on telling me I'm getting old,
And 'minding me of happiness gone by.
Myself and I were never fellows:
But ill-yoked at the best of times,
We seldom pulled together:
And, Lord! the times that we've upset the cart!
So you must serve to keep the peace between us,
By listening to my chatter.
I'm always happiest, talking,
For then I needn't listen to Myself.
Though I, when I was your age, Michael,
I should have scorned an old man's company,
While any lass . . .
And on Midsummer Eve!

*[He pauses again: then resumes, pointing to a pillared
    rock, standing apart from the others.]*

So, yon's the tooth, chipped out of the Queen's comb,
When Arthur pitched a rock at her,
While she was combing out her yellow hair,
And he, at his own Crags, a mile away!
It must have been a spanker of a comb,
To bear so brave a tooth!
I wonder what she'd said, to make him pitch it . . .
Though likely she'd said nothing,
But just sat combing out her yellow hair,
And combing, combing, combing.
A woman with a devil in her tongue,
When she plays mum, is far more aggravating.
Sometimes, when Susan sits and combs her hair,
At night, like Arthur's Queen,
And combs, and combs,
Till I'm half-mad with watching from the bed,

I only stop Myself,—
The surly chap who wants the light out,—
Just in the nick of time
To loose the pillow from his clutch.
King Arthur must have been a handsome lad,
To chuck a pebble that size near a mile.
But, there were giants in those days:
And he . . .

    MICHAEL. A lie!

    GEORGE. A lie? Of course, it's all a lie:
But it's a brave lie, Michael!
I doubt if there were ever King or Queen,
In these outlandish parts.

    MICHAEL. There was a Queen,
Though she was not a giant.
She was no bigger than . . .
Than you, or me . . .
Or Peggy . . . she was nearer Peggy's height.

    GEORGE. You seem to know a deal about her, Michael.
Just Peggy's height?
And red-haired, too, I'll warrant?
You've found your tongue:
And got it pat:
And all the gospel truth!
But, how d'you come by so much truth, I wonder?
Scarcely by honest means, I doubt.
And how d'you know . . .

    MICHAEL. Because I've seen her.

    GEORGE. Who?

    MICHAEL. The Queen.

    GEORGE. You've seen the Queen?
Well, that's a brave one, Michael!
Myself can sometimes tell a little one;
But he was ever but a craven liar.
His were but cheepy bantams, barely hatched:
While yours, why, it's a strutting cock, and crowing,
Comb pricked, and hackles quivering!
There's nothing like a big, bold, brazen lie
To warm the blood . . .

    MICHAEL. I'm telling truth.
I've seen her twice.

    GEORGE. Nay! stop, before you spoil it all.
A lie, blown out too big, will burst.

    MICHAEL. It is no lie . . .

I saw the Queen, herself.
    GEORGE. You saw her . . . where?
    MICHAEL. I saw her here.
    GEORGE. Here? In the Crags?
I trust she's not here now:
And listening down behind the rock.
Lord! if she'd heard Myself about the combing!
But Queens should be above eavesdropping;
And know the luck of listeners.
Though, how d'you know her, lad, for Arthur's Queen?
Did she sing out:
" Hi! lad, I'm Arthur's Queen! "
    MICHAEL. She wore a crown . . .
A golden crown . . .
    GEORGE. I saw a Queen once, with a golden crown;
And sitting on a golden throne,
Set high upon a monster golden ball,
Drawn in a golden chariot through the streets
By four-and-twenty little piebald ponies,
At Hexham, on a fairday, long ago . . .
Ay, long ago, in my young days,
When circuses were circuses.
They made a brave procession through the town,
To draw the folk in after them . . .
Though outside shows are usually the bravest . . .
But, not that time . . .
She was a Queen, a black-eyed, gypsy Queen . . .
Black eyes that sparked . . .
And tilted chin . . .
You never saw . . .
    MICHAEL. Mine was no circus-queen.
I saw her first, when I was but a boy,
Six years ago, to-day . . . Midsummer Eve . . .
I'd spent the whole day, playing round the Crags
At Kings and castles,
Crowning or killing,
Or conquering myself,
Or putting black-faced bands
Of robber-sheep to rout;
Or seeking to take, unawares,
Some traitor stoat or weasel
That spied on my dominions.
When, ere I knew,
The sky was black,

And broke in flame,
And burst in thunder . . .
And rain, such rain . . .
Lightning, flash on flash . . .
Thunder, brattle after brattle . . .
Rain and rain . . .
You never saw such rain —
One pelting, crashing, teeming, drenching downpour.
Soaked to the skin, in no time,
And scared out of my senses,
I crept into a hole among the rocks,
A hole I'd never spied before,
No bigger than a fox's earth.
I had to wriggle on my belly,
To squeeze myself in, head-first;
And half-expecting, every moment,
To feel a vixen's teeth,
Though more I feared the lightning at my heels.
When, all at once, my arms were free:
And, lifting up my head, I found
I'd almost crawled into a chamber,
A big square chamber in the rock,
That I had ne'er heard tell of —
Four blue and shiny walls, that soared
Sheer to the sky — a still and starry sky,
Though, in the world without, black storm was raging.
But, I'd no eyes for stars,
Nor even wits to wonder at the quiet.
My eyes were on the Queen,
Who sat beside a hearth of burning peats,
Right in the middle of the chamber,
A golden crown upon her golden head;
And she was spinning golden wool,
That flickered in the firelight,
Until it seemed that she was spinning flame,
Or her own fire-bright hair.
    GEORGE. Red hair! And she'd red hair . . .
Then, you had only snoozed;
And dreamt of Peggy.
I saw my queen by daylight.
    MICHAEL. Peggy!
I tell you, 'twas the Queen.
I saw her, plainly as I see yon rabbit;
She wore a furry cloak of weasel skins,

Or something like,
Though round the neck 'twas white —
White as yon rabbit's scut . . .
For it was mortal cold in that stone chamber.
 GEORGE. Was anybody with her?
 MICHAEL. I only saw the Queen,
And her, but for a moment.
She lifted up her eyes;
And I was frightened . . .
And wriggled backwards like an adder,
Till I was in the storm again.
And then, I scuttled home —
A rabbit to its warren —
Across the splashy heather:
The lightning, playing round my heels,
The thunder, rattling round my head,
Though it was not the lightning or the thunder
That scared me now . . .
I'd not a thought for them . . .
My heart was flying from that quiet chamber
That stone-cold chamber, roofed with quiet stars . . .
And from the eyes . . .
The eyes I had not seen.
 GEORGE. And where's this stony chamber, then?
 MICHAEL. I never found the way to it again,
Though I've ransacked the Crags for it,
Since I grew big, and bolder.
 GEORGE. A vixen in her den,
For she'd be red enough.
Yet, you'd have felt her teeth for certain!
It must have been a dream.
 MICHAEL. I might have thought so, too,
Had I not seen the Queen, again.
 GEORGE. Again?
I saw my Queen, again, too.
But what was your Queen's name?
 MICHAEL. Queen Guinevere.
 GEORGE. Mine had a braver name.
They called her, Donna Bella di Braganza,
Castilian Queen of the Equestrian World.
I spelled it out upon the rainbow bills
The clown, who wagged the tail of the procession,
Was scattering from his donkey-cart.
I saw my Queen again . . .

My gipsy Queen!
My black-haired, black-eyed gipsy . . .
You, and your red-haired Queens!
I'd give a world of red-haired Guineveres,
To see those gipsy eyes again . . .
I smell the sawdust now . . . and oranges . . .
'Twas in the tent . . .
She'd doffed her robes and crown . . .
I knew her by the flashing of her eyes,
Tripping nimbly into the ring,
So brave in yellow silk, skin-fitting silk,
Yellow as dandelions,
And sprinkled all with spangles;
And yellow ribbons in her hair,
Her jet-black hair that hung about her shoulders.
I see her tripping now into the ring,
With flashing eyes and teeth,
Clean-limbed, and mettlesome as the coal-black mare,
Coal-black from mane to fetlocks,
That pawed and champed to greet her . . .
And there's naught bonnier than a bonnie mare . . .
She clapped its glossy neck:
It nuzzled her:
Then ere I knew,
She'd lighted on its flanks,
Nimble and springy as a thistle-down:
And they were racing round the ring together,
She, standing tip-toe,
And with ne'er a rein,
A straw between her teeth,
Her flashing teeth . . .
And tilted chin . . .
And flashing eyes . . .
Her beautiful long hair, as black and silky,
As black and silky as the mare's long mane,
Was streaming out behind . . .
And ribbons streaming . . .
Spangles sparkling . . .
Sawdust flying,
Whips, a-cracking . . .
Music, playing . . .
And now, she sprang
Through flaming hoops,
And my heart, through the fire with her,

And lighted on the steamy flanks:
And on, and on,
And round, and round the ring,
Till I was dazzled dizzy,
And out of breath, but watching her.
And what, with crack of whips . . .
Thudding thresh of hoofs . . .
Smell of spirting sawdust . . .
Crash of drums and trumpets . . .
Flaming hoops of fire . . .
Flying hair . . .
Yellow ribbons . . .
Flashing teeth . . .
And flashing eyes . . .
My blood was mad, was mad for her,
I wanted to be flying round,
For ever flying round with her,
For ever, and for ever . . .
I wanted her
As I have never wanted woman,
Before or since . . .

[*A pause.*]

And yet, I've little doubt
That she'd have been a poor hand with the porridge,
And poorer at the milking,
Though she could manage horses;
And, maybe, 'twas as well
That I walked home that night with Susan.
Within nine months, we'd wedded.
There's naught amiss with Susan's porridge,
And she could milk a stone.
She's been a good and careful wife enough.
She never spares herself . . . nor me.
Though, I dare say, I'm even more a trial
To her, than to myself.
And, though I'm often harking back,
And sometimes hanker . . .
Somehow, I cannot see the Donna Bella,
In yellow skin-tights, cleaning out the byre!
And yet!
    MICHAEL.   I saw Queen Guinevere, again,
Three years ago, upon Midsummer Eve.

She sat upon a little hill, and sang:
And combed her long red hair, beside the lough —
Just sitting like a leveret in the sun
To sleek its fur —
And all about her, grey snipe darted, drumming.
She combed her long red hair
That tumbled down her shoulders,
Her long hair, red as bracken,
As bracken in October;
And with a gleam of wind in it,
A light of running water.
Her crown was in the heather, at her feet:
And, now and then, a snipe would perch upon it;
And with his long neb preen his gleaming feathers,
As if to mock the Queen,
Queen Guinevere, a-combing her long hair
That tumbled over a gown of blue . . .
As blue and shimmery as a mallard's neck . . .
And with a light of running water:
And, as she sang, 'twas like the curlew calling,
And rippled through my heart like curlew calling,
Like curlew calling in the month of April,
And with a clear cool noise of running water.

I dropped upon my belly in the bracken:
And lay and watched her, combing her red hair:
And hearkened to her singing . . .
And I was sorry, when she'd done, at last,
And took her long red hair, and twisted it,
And fixed it with a golden pin.
Though she'd but little need of crown,
Whose hair was golden crown enough,
She stooped to take her gold crown from the heather,
And set it on her brow:
Then stood upright,
Stood like a birch-tree in the wind,
A silver birch-tree in the sunset wind
That ripples through its leaves like running water;
The little snipe about her drumming . . .
And then, I looked into her eyes,
Looked into golden pools,
Pools, golden 'neath October bracken . . .
And into the heart of fire . . .

                                        [*A pause.*]

A shrew's cold muzzle touched my hand,
Among the bracken, startling me . . .
And she was gone . . .
    GEORGE [*after a pause*]. And so, the leveret bolted!
You never saw her more?
So all tales end . . .
At least the true tales told by life itself.
Though I . . . I saw my Queen again . . .
Yet . . . with a difference . . .
'Twas at the next fair after I was married.
I thought I'd like a glimpse of her once more:
Though I had much ado, persuading Susan:
She'd never been inside a circus;
And thought it sorry waste of silver.
But, once inside the tent,
She liked it well enough:
And gaped and grinned her money's worth.
And I . . . I sat, and waited,
And waited for my gipsy . . .
And snuffed the smell of sawdust:
While Susan giggled at the clown —
A yellow-legged old corncrake —
And nudged me with her elbow;
And asked me if I'd ever heard the like.
But, I'd no ears nor eyes
For any save my gipsy . . .
And she . . . she never came.
Another woman rode the coal-black mare —
A red-haired jumping-jenny —
And there was cracking whips . . .
And sawdust flying . . .
Drums and trumpets . . .
Flaming hoops . . .
And all the razzle-dazzle . . .
But not my black-eyed gipsy.
And I sat, waiting still, when all was over,
Until the tent was empty . . .
Sat waiting for the Donna Bella . . .
Till Susan tugged me by the jacket,
And asked if I'd sit gaping there all night.
She got me out, at last.
And then . . . I met her . . .
Met her, face to face,
My gipsy Queen!

But, oh! . . . how changed . . .
Except her eyes . . .
I knew her by her eyes:
For they still flashed and sparkled,
Though she was bent and hunched,
And hobbled with a crutch.
She'd had a tumble, since I'd seen her flying
Around the ring, as light as thistle-down.
She clutched me with a skinny hand,
Wanting to tell my fortune:
But Susan wouldn't let her:
She said, a married man had got his fortune;
So needn't waste his earnings.
The gipsy bit the straw between her teeth,
Her flashing teeth;
And, tilting her proud chin,
She laughed at that, with merry eyes
Twinkling 'neath her yellow kerchief —
Dandelion yellow —
Bound about her jet-black hair,
The hair that I'd seen flying free . . .
And when she laughed,
And looked into my eyes . . .
The heather was afire . . .
I could have caught her to me,
There and then . . .
Whipped her up, and run with her
To the world's end, and over . . .
But, Susan . . . dragging on my arm . . .
Ay! broken as she was,
And hunched and hobbling,
I would have wedded her outright,
Had it not been for Susan . . .
I lost her in the crowd . . .
And never saw her more . . .

[*Pause.*]

And so, went home to decent porridge:
And 'twas as well, maybe.
A man must have his meat, if he's to work,
And victuals count for much.
And Susan's ever been a careful wife,
And had no easy time of it.

[*Pause.*]

But, love's a queer thing, Michael.
It comes to you . . . like that! [*striking his hands together*].
I've known a man walk seven miles each night
To see a woman's shadow on the blind.
And, in the end,
It's one, and one alone, that holds you,
Be't Donna Bella, Guinevere, or Peggy.

[*Pause.*]

But you . . . you never saw your carroty Queen,
Combing her long red hair again, I'll warrant.
    MICHAEL [*slowly, as in a trance*]. I saw her once, upon
        Midsummer Eve,
Six years ago . . .
I saw her, twice, upon Midsummer Eve,
Three years ago . . .
I'll see her thrice . . .
    GEORGE. And, it's Midsummer Eve!
    MICHAEL [*listening*]. And nigh the hour . . .
And hark, the snipe a-drumming!
    GEORGE. You cannot think . . .
It's all a pack of lies . . .
Or else, you're daft, clean daft!
Your eyes are queer and wild. . . .
You do not see her now?
No! No! I thought not!
It's all stuff and nonsense,
Your silly tale about a red-haired Queen,
Who's been dead dust a thousand years, or more.
    MICHAEL [*leaping to his feet*]. She's coming . . . com-
        ing now . . .
    GEORGE [*leaping up, too, and gripping* MICHAEL'S *arm*].
        No! No!
You're crazy, surely . . .
Yet . . . queer things happen on the fells, at times . . .
And on Midsummer Eve . . .
    MICHAEL [*listening more intently*]. She's drawing
        slowly nearer . . .
I hear her silks a-rustling through the grass . . .
    GEORGE [*listening*]. I seem to hear . . .
What are you gaping at?
    MICHAEL [*looking up*]. The Queen! The Queen!

[*They both stand, spellbound, gazing at a woman*

*standing on the crest of a boulder, burning like a
golden flame in the last rays of the setting sun.
Presently, looking down, and seeing them, she
laughs.*]

GEORGE [*shaking himself, while* MICHAEL *still stands,
    spellbound*].   It's Peggy Haliburton, after all!
[*To* PEGGY.]   Why, Michael said: 'twas Arthur's Queen.
He called her some outlandish name;
And said, she'd long red foxy hair,
And eyes like pools;
And sang just like the curlew.
But he'll be telling you himself:
For, all along, I knew 'twas you he meant.
Men's tongues wag madly on Midsummer Eve:
And I've been talking, too,
A pack of nonsense,
As Michael, here, could tell you,
If he'd not too much sense to heed
An old man's witless blathering.
Well, I had best be going;
And getting home to Susan.
She doesn't hold with owls, and such like.

1912.

BLOODYBUSH EDGE

*Bloodybush Edge is a remote spot on the borderline between Eng-
land and Scotland, marked by a dumpy obelisk, on which is
inscribed an old scale of tolls. A rough sandy road runs down
across the dark moors, into England on the one hand, and into
Scotland on the other. It is a fine, starry night in early September.* DAFT DICK, *a fantastic figure, in appearance half-
gamekeeper, half-tramp (dressed as he is in cast-off clothes of
country-gentlemen) swings up the road from the Scottish side,
singing.*

> " Now Liddisdale has ridden a raid ;
> But I wat they better hae stayed at hame ;
> For Michael o' Winfield, he lies dead ;
> And Jock o' the Side is prisoner ta'en."

[*He stands for a moment, looking across the fells, which are
very dark, in spite of the starry sky; then flings himself
down in the heather, with his back to the obelisk, and
lights his pipe. Presently, he sees a dark figure, stumbling with uncertain steps across the boggy moor; and
watches it keenly as it approaches, until it reaches the
road, when he sees that it is a strange man, evidently a
tramp.*]

TRAMP.   A track, at last, thank God !
DICK.   Ay, there be whiles
When beaten tracks are welcome.
TRAMP.   Who the . . . Oh !
I didn't count on having company
Again in this world ; and when I heard a voice
I thought it must be another ghost.   It's queer
Hearing a voice bleat when you haven't heard
A mortal voice for ages.   I've not changed
A word with a soul since noon ; and when you spoke
It gave me quite a turn.   A feather, Lord !
But it wouldn't take the shadow of a feather
To knock me over.   I'm in such a stickle,

Dead-beat, and fit to drop.   To drop!   I've dropped
A hundred times already, humpty-dumpty!
Why, I've been tumbling in and out black holes,
Since sunset, on that god-forsaken moor,
Half-crazed with fear of . . . Ah, you've got a light:
And I've been tramping all the livelong day
With a pipeful of comfort in my waistcoat-pocket;
And would have swopt the frizzling sun itself;
For a match to kindle it.   Thanks, mate, that's better.
And now, what was it you were saying, Old Cock,
When I mistook you then for Hamlet's father?
Lord! if you'd seen him at the " Elephant,"
In queer, blue sheeny armour, you'd have shivered.
" I am thy father's spirit," he says, like that,
Down in his boots.   But you were saying ——

    DICK.   There are times
When beaten tracks are welcome.

    TRAMP.   True for you:
And truer by a score of bumps, for me.
My neck's been broken half-a-dozen times:
My body's just an aching bag of bones.
I'm one big bruise from top to toe, as though
I'd played in the Cup Final, as the ball.
And mud, I'm mud to the eyes, and over, carrying
Half of the country that I've passed through on me.
My best suit, too!   And I was always faddy
About my clothes.   My mother used to call me
Finicky Fred.   If she could see me now!
I couldn't count the times that I've pitched headlong
Into black bog.

    DICK.   Ay, there are clarty bits
In Foulmire Moss.   But what set you stravaging
Among the peat-hags at this time of night?
Unless you know the tracks by heart. . . .

    TRAMP.   I know
The Old Kent Road by heart.

    DICK.   The Old Kent Road?

    TRAMP.   London, S. E.   You've heard of London, likely?

    DICK.   Ay!   Ay!   I've heard. . . .

    TRAMP.   Well, mate, I've walked from London.

    DICK.   You've walked from London, here?

    TRAMP.   Well, not to-day.
It must be nigh three hundred mile, I reckon.
Just five weeks, yesterday, since I set out:

But, as you say, I've walked from London, here:
Though where " here " is the devil only knows!
What is " here " called, if it has any name
But Back o' Beyond, or World's End, eh?
  DICK.   You're sitting
On Bloodybush Edge this moment.
  TRAMP.   To think of that!
Bloodybush Edge! And that's what I have come to;
While all my friends, the men and women I know,
Are strolling up and down the Old Kent Road,
Chattering and laughing by the lighted stalls
And the barrows of bananas and oranges;
Or sitting snugly in bars; and here am I,
On Bloodybush Edge, talking to Hamlet's father.
  DICK. My name's Dick Dodd.
  TRAMP.   Well, no offence, Old Cock!
And Hamlet's father was a gentleman,
A king of ghosts; and Lord! but he could groan.
My name's . . . Jack Smith: and Jack would give a sovereign,
A sovereign down, if he could borrow it,
And drinks all around, and here's to you, and you!
Just to be sitting in The Seven Stars,
And listening to the jabber, just to snuff
A whiff of the smoke and spirit. Seven Stars!
I'm lodging under stars enough to-night:
Seven times seven hundred. . . .
  DICK.   Often I have tried
To count them, lying here upon my back:
But they're too many for me. Just when you think
You've reckoned all between two sprigs of heather,
One tumbles from its place, or else a hundred
Spring out of nowhere. If you only stare
Hard at the darkest patch, for long enough
You'll see that it's all alive with little stars;
And there isn't any dark at all.
  TRAMP.   No dark!
If you'd been tumbling into those black holes,
You'd not think overmuch of these same stars.
I couldn't see my hand before me. Stars!
Give me the lamps along the Old Kent Road:
And I'm content to leave the stars to you.
They're well enough: but hung a trifle high
For walking with clean boots. Now a lamp or so . . .
  DICK. If it's so fine and brave, the Old Kent Road,

How is it you came to leave it?
   TRAMP.   I'd my reasons.
   DICK.   Reasons! Queer reasons surely to set you trapesing
Over Foulmire in the dark: though I could travel
The fells from here to Cheviot, blindfold. Ay!
And never come a cropper.
   TRAMP.   'Twas my luck,
My lovely luck, and naught to do with reasons —
My gaudy luck, and the devilish dust and heat,
And hell's own thirst that drove me; and too snug
A bed among the heather. Oversleeping,
That's always played the mischief with me. Once
I slept till three in the morning, and . . .
   DICK.   Till three?
You're an early bird, if you call that oversleeping.
Folk hereabouts are mostly astir by three:
But, city-folk, I thought. . . .
   TRAMP.   I'm on the night-shift.
I sleep by day, for the most part, like a cat.
That's why, though dog-tired now, I couldn't sleep
A wink though you paid me gold down.
   DICK.   Night-shift, you!
And what may your job be? Cat's night-shift, likely,
As well as day's sleep!
   TRAMP.   Now, look here, Old Cock,
There's just one little thing that we could teach you
Down London way. Why, even babes in London
Know better than to ask too many questions.
You ask no questions, and you'll hear no lies,
Is the first lesson that's hammered into them.
No London gentleman asks questions. Lord!
If you went " What's-your-job? "-ing down our way
You'd soon be smelling some one's fist, I reckon;
Or tripping over somebody in the dark
Upon the stairs: and with a broken neck,
Be left, still asking questions in your coffin,
Till the worms had satisfied you. Not that I
Have anything to hide, myself. I'm only
Advising you for your own good. But, Old Chap,
We were talking of something else . . . that hell-hot road,
I'd pegged along it through the blazing dust
From Bellingham, till I could peg no more;
My mouth was just a limekiln; and each foot
One bleeding blister. A kipper on the grid,

That's what I was on the road.   And the heather looked
So cool and cosy, I left the road for a bit;
And coming on a patch of wet green moss,
I took my boots off; and it was so champion
To feel cold water squelching between my toes,
I paddled on like a child, till I came to a clump
Of heather in full bloom, just reeking honey;
And curled up in it, and dropt sound asleep;
And, when I wakened, it was dark, pitch-dark,
For all your stars.   The sky was light enough,
Had I been travelling that way.   But, for the road,
I hadn't a notion of its whereabouts.
A blessed babe-in-the-woods I was, clean lost,
And fit to cry for my mammy.   Babes-in-the-wood!
But there were two of them, for company,
And only one of me, by my lone self.
However, I said to myself: You've got to spend
A night in the heather.   Well, you've known worse beds,
And worse bed-fellows than a sheep or so —
Trying to make believe I wasn't frightened.
And then, somehow, I couldn't, God knows why!
But I was scared: the loneliness, and all;
The quietness, and the queer creepy noises;
And something that I couldn't put a name to,
A kind of feeling in my marrow bones,
As though the great black hills against the sky
Had come alive about me in the night;
And they were watching me; as though I stood
Naked, in a big room, with blind men sitting,
Unseen, all round me, in the quiet darkness,
That was not dark to them.   And all the stars
Were eyeing me; and whisperings in the heather
Were like cold water trickling down my spine:
And when I heard a cough. . . .
    DICK.   A coughing sheep.
    TRAMP.   Maybe: but 'twas a coughing ghost to me.
I've never yet set eyes on a ghost, unless . . . [*looking askance at*
      DICK]
Though I've often felt them near me.   Once, when I . . .
But, Lord, I'm talking, talking . . .
    DICK.   I've seen ghosts,
A hundred times.   The ghost of reivers ride
The fells at night; and you'd have ghosts in plenty
About you, lad, though you were blind to them.

But, why d'you fear them?   There's no harm in ghosts.
Even should they ride over you, it's only
Like a cold wind blowing through you.   The other night,
As I came down by Girsonsfield, the ghost
Of Parcy Reed, with neither hands nor feet,
Rode clean through me; the false Halls, and the Croziers
Hard on his heels, though I kept clear of them;
And often I've heard him, cracking his hunting-crop,
On a winter's night, when the winds were in full cry;
And heard the yelp of the pack, and the horn's halloo,
Over the howl of the storm, or caught at dawn
A glimpse of the tails of his green hunting-jacket.
Whenever you shudder, or break in a cold sweat,
Not knowing why, folk say that some one's stepping
Over your grave; but that's all stuff and nonsense.
It's only some poor ghost that's walking through you.
        TRAMP.   Well, ghosts or sheep, I'd had my fill of them;
Went all to pieces, took to my heels and ran;
And hadn't run three yards, when I pitched headlong.
That was the first.   Since then, I've felt the bottom
Of every hole, five hundred to my reckoning,
From there to here.
        DICK.   You've covered some rough ground.
But you have doubled back upon your tracks
If you were making North.
        TRAMP.   Ay: I was making
For Scotland.   I'd a notion . . .
        DICK.   Scotland lies
Under your left heel, though your right's in England.
        TRAMP.   To think of that!   Well, I can't feel much difference
Twixt one and the other.   Perhaps, if I'd my boots off . . .
But, Hamlet's father, isn't it a king's bed
We're lying on, and sprawling over two countries!
And yet, I'd rather be in Millicent Place,
London, S. E., and sleeping three in a bed.
This room's too big for me, too wide and windy;
The bed, too broad, and not what I call snug:
The ceiling, far too high, and full of eyes.
I hate the loneliness.   I like to feel
There are houses, packed with people, all about me
For miles on miles: I'm fond of company;
I'm only really happy in a throng,
Crowds jostling thick and hot about me.   Here
I feel, somehow, as if I were walking naked

Among the hills, the last man left alive.
I haven't so much as set eyes on a house,
Not since I left that blistering road.
    DICK.   The nearest
Is three miles off, or more.
    TRAMP.   Well, country-people
Should be good neighbours, and quiet; but, for me,
I'd rather be packed like herrings in a barrel.
I hate the loneliness: it makes me think . . .
I'm fond of company; too fond at times.
If I hadn't been so fond of company
A while back, I'd have hardly been lying now
On Bloodybush Edge, talking of ghosts at midnight,
When I might be . . . but it won't bear thinking on.
Yet, even with you beside me, Bloodybush Edge
Is a size too big in beds — leaves too much room
For ghosts, to suit my fancy. Three in a bed,
And you sleep sound.
    DICK.   And why should you fear ghosts,
When, one fine night, you'll be a ghost yourself?
How soon, who knows! Why, even at this moment,
If you had broken your neck among the moss-hags
You'd be your own ghost sitting there, not you.
If you hadn't been so muddy, and so frightened . . .
Nay! but I've seen too many ghosts in my time
For you to take me in. Ghosts often lean
Over me, when I'm fishing in the moonlight.
They're keen, are ghosts. I sometimes feel their breath
Upon my neck, when I am guddling trout;
Or the clutch of their clammy fingers on my wrist
When I am spearing salmon, lest I should miss.
And always at the burning of the water
You'll see them lurking in the shadows, beyond
The flare and the smoke of the torches, in the night,
Eager as boys to join in the sport; and at times,
When they have pressed too near, and a torch has flared,
I've seen the live flame running through their bodies.
But oftenest they appear to me when alone
I'm fishing like a heron; and last night
As I stooped over Deadwater, I felt . . .
    TRAMP. And you're an honest man to be asking questions
Of gentlemen on tour! So, you're a poacher,
A common poacher: though it must be rare sport,
I've often fancied . . .

DICK.   To creep up to a pool
Where a big bull-trout lies beneath a boulder
With nose against the stream, his tail scarce flicking;
To creep up quiet and without a shadow,
And lie upon your belly in the gravel;
And slide your hands as noiseless as an otter
Into the water, icy-cold and aching,
And tickle, tickle, till you have him fuddled;
Then lift him, cold and slithery, from the burn,
A quivering bit of silver in the moonlight . . .
    TRAMP.   Ay, that must be rare sport; but, for myself,
I'd rather manage without the help of ghosts.
Once, I remember, I was bending down —
'Twas in an empty house . . . I'd cut my thumb,
The window jamming somehow, a nasty cut:
The mark's still there . . . (not that! nay, that's the place
I was bitten by a friend) and as I fumbled
With a damned tricky lock, some Yankee patent,
I felt a ghost was standing close behind me,
And dared not stir, nor squint over my shoulder:
But crouched there, moving neither hand nor foot,
Till I was just a solid ache of terror,
And could have squealed aloud with the numb cramp,
And pins and needles in my arms and legs.
And then at last, when I was almost dropping,
I lost my head, took to my heels, and bolted
Headfirst down stairs, and through the broken window,
Leaving my kit and the swag, without a thought:
And never coming to my senses, till
I saw a bullseye glimmering down the lane.
And then I found my brow was bleeding, too —
At first I thought 'twas sweat — a three-inch cut,
Clean to the bone.   I had to have it stitched.
I told the doctor that I'd put my head
Through a window in the dark, but not a word
About my body following it.   The doctor,
He was a gentleman, and asked no questions.
A civil chap: he'd stitched my scalp before
Once, when the heel of a lady's slipper . . .
    DICK.   So you
Are a common poacher, too; although you take
Only dead silver and gold.   Still it must be
A risky business, burgling, when the folk . . .

TRAMP. Risk! ay, there's risk! That's where the fun comes
   in;
To steal into a house, with people sleeping
So warm and snug and innocent overhead;
To hear them snoring as you pass their doors
With all they're dreaming of stowed in your pockets;
To tiptoe from the attic to the basement,
With a chance that you may find on any landing
A door flung open, and a man to tackle.
It's only empty houses I'm afraid of.
I've more than once looked up a pistol's snout,
And never turned a hair . . . though once I heard
A telephone-bell ring in an empty house —
And I can hear the damned thing tinkling yet . . .
I'm all in a cold sweat just thinking of it.
It tinkled, tinkled . . . Risk! Why man alive,
Life's all a risky business, till you're dead.
There's no risk then . . . unless . . . I never feared
A living man, sleeping or waking, yet.
But ghosts, well, ghosts are different somehow. There's
A world of difference between men and ghosts.
Let's think no more of ghosts — but lighted streets,
And crowds, and women; though it's my belief
There's not a woman in all this country-side.
   DICK. There's womenfolk, and plenty. And they are kind,
The womenfolk, to me. Daft Dick is ever
A favourite with the womenfolk. His belly
Would oft go empty, were it not for them.
   TRAMP. You call those women, gawky, rawboned creatures,
Thin-lipped, hard-jawed, cold-eyed! I like fat women.
If you could walk just now down the Old Kent Road,
And see the plump young girls in furs and feathers,
With saucy black eyes, sparkling in the gaslight;
And looking at you, munching oranges,
Or whispering to each other with shrill giggles
As you go by, and nudging one another;
Or standing with a soldier eating winkles,
Grimacing with the vinegar and pepper,
Then laughing so merrily you almost wish
You were a red-coat, too! And the fat old mothers,
Too old for feathers and follies, with their tight
Nigh-bursting bodices, and their double chins,
They're homely, motherly and comfortable,

And do a man's eyes good.   There's not a sight
In all the world that's half as rare to see
As a fat old wife with jellied eels and porter.
Ay, women should be plump . . . though Ellen Ann
Was neither old nor fat, when she and I
Were walking out together, and she'd red hair,
As red as blazes, and a peaked white face.
But 'twas her eyes, her eyes that always laughed,
And the merry way she had with her . . . But, Lord,
I'm talking!   Only mention petticoats,
And I'm the boy to talk till doomsday.   Women!
If it hadn't been for a petticoat, this moment
I might be drinking my own health in the bar
Of The Seven Stars or The World Turned Upside Down,
Instead of . . . Well, Old Cock, it's good to have
Someone to talk to, after such a day.
You cannot get much further with a sheep;
And I met none but sheep, and they all scuttled,
Not even stopping to pass the time of day,
And the birds, well, they'd enough to say, and more,
When I was running away from myself in the dark,
With their " Go back!   Go back! "
    DICK.   You'd scared the grouse.
They talk like Christians.   Often in the dawn . . .
    TRAMP.   Bloodybush Edge!   But why the Bloodybush?
I see no bush . . .
    DICK.   Some fight in the old days, likely,
In the days when men were men . . .
    TRAMP.   I little thought,
When I set out from London on my travels,
That I was making straight for Bloodybush Edge.
I had my reasons, but, reason or none, it's certain
That I'd have turned up here, some day or other:
For I must travel.   I've the itching foot.
I talk of London, when I'm well out of it
By a hundred miles or so; but, when I'm in it,
There always comes a time when I couldn't stay
A moment longer, not for love or money:
Though in the end it always has me back.
I cannot rest.   There's something in my bones —
They'll need to screw the lid down with brass screws
To keep them in my coffin.   When I'm dead,
If I don't walk, I'll be surprised, I . . . Lord,
We're on to ghosts again!   But I'm the sort

That's always hankering to be elsewhere,
Wherever I am. Some men can stick to a job
As though they liked it. I'm not made that way.
I couldn't heave the same pick two days running.
I've tried it: and I know. I must have change.
It's in my blood. And work, why work's for fools.

 DICK. Ay, fools indeed: and yet they seem content.
Content! why my old uncle, Richard Dodd,
He worked till he was naught but skin and bone,
And rheumatism: and when the doctor told him:
"You must give up. It's no use; you're past work."
"Past work," he says, "past work, like an old horse:
"They shoot old nags, when they are past their work.
"Doctor," he says, "I'll give you five pound down
"To take that gun, and shoot me like a nag."
The doctor only laughed, and answered, "Nay.
"An old nag's carcase is worth money, Richard:
"But yours, why, who'd give anything for yours!"
They call me daft — Daft Dick. It pleases them.
But I have never been daft enough to work.
I never did a hand's turn in my life:
And won't, while there are trout-streams left, and women.
And I am a traveller, too, I cannot rest.
The wind's in my bones, I think, and like the wind,
I'm here, to-night; to-morrow, Lord knows where!

 TRAMP. London, perhaps, or well upon the road there,
Since I'm on Bloodybush Edge.

 DICK.   Nay, never London.
I cannot thole the towns. They stifle me.
I spent a black day in Newcastle, once.
Never again! I cannot abide the crowds.
I must be by myself. I must have air:
I must have room to breathe, and elbow-room,
Wide spaces round me, winds and running water.
I know the singing-note of every burn
Twixt here and High Cup Nick, by Appleby.
And birds and beasts, I must have them about me —
Rabbits and hares, weasels and stoats and adders,
Plover and grouse, partridge and snipe and curlew,
Red-shank and heron. I think that towns would choke me;
And I'd go blind shut in by the tall houses,
With never a far sight to stretch my eyes.
I must have hills, and hills beyond. And beds —
I never held with beds and stuffiness.

I'm seldom at my ease beneath a roof:
The rafters all seem crushing on my head,
A dead weight. Though I sleep in barns in Winter,
I'm never at home except beneath the stars.
I've seen enough of towns; and as for the women,
Fat blowsy sluts and slatterns . . .
    TRAMP.   Easy, Old Cock!
" What's one man's meat . . ." as the saying is; and so,
Each man to his own world, and his own women.

> [*They sit for awhile smoking in silence. Then* DAFT DICK
> *begins singing softly to himself again.*]

DICK [*singing*].   " Their horses were the wrong way shod,
And Hobbie has mounted his grey sae fine,
Wat on his old horse, Jock on his bay;
And on they rode for the waters of Tyne.

" And when they came to Chollerton Ford,
They lighted down by the light o' the moon;
And a tree they cut with nogs on each side,
To climb up the wa' of Newcastle toun."

    TRAMP.   What's that you're singing, matey?
    DICK.   " Jock o' the Side."
A ballad of the days when men were men,
And sheep were sheep, and not all mixter-maxter.
Thon were brave days, or brave nights, rather, thon!
Brave nights, when Liddisdale was Liddisdale,
And Tynedale, Tynedale, not all hand-in-glove,
And hanky-panky, and naught but market-haggling
Twixt men whose fathers' swords were the bargainers!
That was a man's work, riding out, hot-trod,
Over the hills to lift a herd of cattle,
And leave behind a blazing byre, or to steal
Your neighbour's sheep, while he lay drunk and snoring —
A man's work, ever bringing a man's wages,
The fight to the death, or life won at the sword's point.
God! those were nights: the heather and sky alow
With the light of burning peel-towers, and the wind
Ringing with slogans, as the dalesmen met,
Over the singing of the swords:
" An Armstrong! An Armstrong! "
" A Milburne! A Milburne! "

" An Elliott!   An Elliott! "
" A Robson!   A Robson! "
" A Charlton!   A Charlton! "
" A Fenwick!   A Fenwick! "
" Fy, Tynedale, to it! "
" Jethert's here!   Jethert's here! "
" Tarset and Tarretburn!
" Hardy and heatherbred!
" Yet!   Yet! "
Man, did you ever hear the story told
Of Barty Milburne, Barty of the Comb,
Down Tarset way? and how he waked one morning
To find that overnight some Scottish reiver
Had lifted the pick of his flock: and how hot-foot
He was up the Blackburn, summoning Corbet Jock:
And how the two set out to track the thieves
By Emblehope, Berrymoor Edge and Blackman's Law,
By Blakehope Nick, and under Oh Me Edge,
And over Girdle Fell to Chattlehope Spout,
And so to Carter Bar; but lost the trail
Somewhere about the Reidswire: and how, being loth
To go home empty-handed, they just lifted
The best sheep grazing on the Scottish side,
As fair exchange: and turned their faces home.
By this, snow had set in: and 'twas sore work
Driving the wethers against it over the fell;
When, finding they were followed in their turn
By the laird of Leatham and his son, they laughed,
And waited for the Scots by Chattlehope Spout
Above Catcleugh: and in the snow they fought,
Till Corbet Jock and one of the Scots were killed,
And Barty himself sore wounded in the thigh;
When the other Scot, thinking him good as dead,
Sprang on him, as he stooped, with a whickering laugh:
And Barty, with one clean, back-handed blow,
Struck off his head, and, as they tell the tale,
" Garred it spang like an onion along the heather."
Then, picking up the body of Corbet Jock,
He slung it over his shoulder; and carried his mate,
With wounded thigh and driving the wethers before him,
Through blinding snow, across the boggy fells
To the Blackburn, though his boot was filled with blood.
Or the other tale, how one of the Robson lads
Stole a Scot's ewes: and when he'd got them home,

And had mixed them with his own, found out, too late,
They'd got the scab: and how he went straight back
With a stout hempen rope to the Scot's house
And hanged him from his own rooftree by the neck
Till he was dead, to teach the rascal a lesson,
Or so he said, that when a gentleman called
For sheep the next time, he'd think twice about it
Before he tried to palm off scabbit ewes.
Poachers and housebreakers and bargainers!
Those men were men: and lived and died like men;
Taking their own road — asking no man's leave;
Doing and speaking outright, hot and clean,
The thing that burned in them, and paying the price.
And those same gawky, rawboned women mothered
Such sons as these; and still do, nowadays —
For hunting foxes, and for market-haggling!
You fear no living man!   A glinting bullseye
Down a dark lane would not have set them scuttling.
They didn't dread the mosshags in the dark.
And seemingly they'd little fear of ghosts,
Being themselves so free in making ghosts.
Ghosts! why the night is all alive with ghosts,
Ghosts of dead raiders, and dead cattle-lifters;
Poor, headless ghosts; and ghosts with broken necks . . .
See that chap, yonder, with the bleeding thigh,
On a grey gelding, making for Hurklewinter —
A horse-thief, sure . . . And the ghostly stallions whinney
As the ghostly reivers drive their flocks and herds . . .
[*Listening.*]   They are quiet now: but I've often heard the patter
Of sheep, or the trot-trot of the frightened stirks
Down this same road . . .
      TRAMP.   Stop man!   You'll drive me crazy!
Let's talk no more of ghosts!   I want to sleep:
I'm dog-tired . . . but I'll never sleep to-night.
What's that . . . I thought I heard . . . I'm all a-tremble.
My very blood stops, listening, in my veins.
I'm all to fiddlestrings . . . Let's talk of London,
And lights, and crowds, and women.   Once I met
A chap in the bar of The World Turned Upside Down,
With three blue snakes tattooed around his wrist:
A joker, he was; and what he didn't know
Of women the world over you could shove
Between the nail and the quick, and never feel it —
He told me that in Valparaiso once

A half-breed wench that he . . . but, Lord, what's that!

[*A low distant sound of trotting drawing quickly nearer.*]

I thought I heard . . . Do you hear nothing?

DICK.   Naught.

TRAMP.   I'm all on edge: I could have sworn I heard —
Where was I? Well, as I was saying . . . God!
Can you hear nothing now? Trot-trot! Trot-trot!
I must be going crazy, or you're stone deaf.

DICK.   Nay, I'm none deaf.

TRAMP.   It's coming nearer, nearer . . .
Trot-trot! trot-trot! Man, tell me that you hear it,
For God's sake, or I'll go mad!

DICK.   No two men ever
May hear or see them, together, at one time.

TRAMP.   Hear what? See what? Speak, man, if you've a
    tongue!

DICK.   The ghostly stirks.

TRAMP.   The ghostly stirks! Trot-trot!
Trot-trot! They're almost on us. Look you! there!
Along the road there, black against the sky.
They're charging down with eyes ablaze . . . O Christ . . .

> [*He takes to his heels, running lamely down the road on the
> Scottish side, as a herd of frightened young stirks gallops
> down the road from the English side. They pass DICK,
> who watches them, placidly smoking, until they are by
> when, taking his pipe from his mouth, he gives a blood-
> curdling whoop, which sends them scampering more
> wildly after the tramp. Presently the cattle-drover,
> panting and limping half-a-mile behind his herd, comes
> down the road. Seeing DICK, he stops.*]

DROVER.   Have any beasts come by? Lord, what a dance
They've led me, since we quitted Bellingham!
I've chased them over half the countryside!

DICK.   Ay: they were making straight for Dinlabyre.

DROVER.   Then I can rest. They cannot go far wrong now.
We're for Saughtree; and I'm fair hattered, and they
Can't have the spunk left in them to stray far.
They'll be all right.

DICK.   Ay! and your brother's with them.

DROVER.   Brother? I have no brother . . .

DICK. Well, he and you
Are as like as peas — a pair of gallows-birds.
And he was driving them, and walloping them . . .

DROVER [*starting to run*]. Good God! Just wait till I catch
up with him!

DICK [*calling after him*]. It will take you all your time and
more, to catch him.

[*To himself.*] Now, I can sleep in peace, without bed-fellows.
Two in a bed is one too many for me —
And such a clatter-jaw!

1913.

HOOPS

Scene: The big tent-stable of a travelling circus. On the ground near the entrance, GENTLEMAN JOHN, *stable-man and general odd-job man, lies smoking beside* MERRY ANDREW, *the clown.* GENTLEMAN JOHN *is a little hunched man with a sensitive face and dreamy eyes.* MERRY ANDREW, *who is resting between the afternoon and evening performances, with his clown's hat lying beside him, wears a crimson wig, and a baggy suit of orange-coloured cotton, patterned with purple cats. His face is chalked dead white and painted with a set grin, so that it is impossible to see what manner of man he is. In the background are camels and elephants feeding, dimly visible in the steamy dusk of the tent.*

GENTLEMAN JOHN. And then consider camels: only think
Of camels long enough, and you'd go mad —
With all their humps and lumps, their knobbly knees,
Splay feet and straddle legs, their sagging necks,
Flat flanks, and scraggy tails, and monstrous teeth.
I've not forgotten the first fiend I met,
'Twas in a lane in Smyrna, just a ditch
Between the shuttered houses, and so narrow
The brute's bulk blocked the road; the huge, green stack
Of dewy fodder that it slouched beneath
Brushing the yellow walls on either hand,
And shutting out the strip of burning blue:
And I'd to face that vicious, bobbing head
With evil eyes, slack lips, and nightmare teeth,
And duck beneath the snaky, squirming neck,
Pranked with its silly string of bright blue beads,
That seemed to wriggle every way at once,
As though it were a hydra. Allah's beard!
But I was scared and nearly turned and ran:
I felt that muzzle take me by the scruff
And heard those murderous teeth crunching my spine,
Before I stooped — though I dodged safely under.
I've always been afraid of ugliness.
I'm such a toad myself, I hate all toads;

And the camel is the ugliest toad of all
To my mind: and it's just my devil's luck
I've come to this — to be a camel's lackey,
To fetch and carry for original sin,
For sure enough, the camel's old evil incarnate.
Blue beads and amulets to ward off evil!
No eye's more evil than a camel's eye.
The elephant is quite a comely brute,
Compared with Satan camel,— trunk and all,
His floppy ears and his impertinent tail.
He's stolid, but, at least, a gentleman.
It doesn't hurt my pride to valet him,
And bring his shaving-water.   He's a lord.
Only the bluest blood that has come down
Through generations from the mastodon
Could carry off that tail with dignity,
That tail and trunk.   He cannot look absurd
For all the monkey tricks you put him through,
Your paper hoops and popguns.   He just makes
His masters look ridiculous, when his pomp's
Butchered to make a bumpkins' holiday.
He's dignity itself, and proper pride,
That stands serenely in a circus-world
Of mountebanks and monkeys.   He has weight
Behind him: æons of primeval power
Have shaped that pillared bulk; and he stands sure,
Solid, substantial on the world's foundations.
And he has form, form that's too big a thing
To be called beauty.   Once long since, I thought
To be a poet, and shape words, and mould   .
A poem like an elephant, huge, sublime,
To front oblivion: and because I failed
And all my rhymes were gawky, shambling camels,
Or else obscene, blue-buttocked apes, I'm doomed
To fetch and carry for the things I've made,
Till one of them crunches my back-bone with his teeth,
Or knocks my wind out with a forthright kick
Clean in the midriff; crumpling up in death
The hunched and stunted body that was me,
John, the apostle of the Perfect Form!
Jerusalem!   I'm talking, like a book,
As you would say: and a bad book at that,
A maundering, kiss-mammy book — The Hunchback's End,
Or The Camel-Keeper's Reward — would be its title.

I froth and bubble like a new-broached cask.
No wonder you look glum for all your grin.
What makes you mope?   You've naught to growse about.
You've got no hump.   Your body's brave and straight —
So shapely even that you can afford
To trick it in fantastic shapelessness,
Knowing that there's a clean-limbed man beneath
Preposterous pantaloons and purple cats.
I would have been a poet, if I could:
But better than shaping poems, 'twould have been
To have had a comely body and clean limbs
Obedient to my bidding.
    MERRY ANDREW.   I missed a hoop
This afternoon.
    GENTLEMAN JOHN.   You missed a hoop?   You mean . . .
    MERRY ANDREW.   That I am done, used up, scrapped, on the
      shelf,
Out of the running,— only that, no more.
    GENTLEMAN JOHN.   Well, I've been missing hoops my whole
      life long;
Though, when I come to think of it, perhaps
There's little consolation to be chewed
From crumbs that I can offer.
    MERRY ANDREW.   I've not missed
A hoop since I was six.   I'm forty-two.
This is the first time that my body's failed me:
But 'twill not be the last.   And . . .
    GENTLEMAN JOHN.   Such is life!
You're going to say.   You see I've got it pat,
Your jaded wheeze.   Lord, what a wit I'd make
If I'd a set grin painted on my face.
And such is life, I'd say a hundred times,
And each time set the world aroar afresh
At my original humour.   Missed a hoop!
Why, man alive, you've naught to grumble at.
I've boggled every hoop since I was six.
I'm fifty-five; and I've run round a ring
Would make this potty circus seem a pinhole.
I wasn't born to sawdust.   I'd the world
For circus . . .
    MERRY ANDREW.   It's no time for crowing now.
I know a gentleman, and take on trust
The silver spoon and all.   My teeth were cut
Upon a horseshoe: and I wasn't born

To purple and fine linen — but to sawdust,
To sawdust, as you say — brought up on sawdust.
I've had to make my daily bread of sawdust:
Ay, and my children's — children's, that's the rub,
As Shakespeare says . . .

GENTLEMAN JOHN.   Ah, there you go again!
What a rare wit to set the ring aroar —
As Shakespeare says! Crowing? A gentleman?
Man, didn't you say you'd never missed a hoop?
It's only gentlemen who miss no hoops,
Clean-livers, easy lords of life who take
Each obstacle at a leap, who never fail.
You are the gentleman.

MERRY ANDREW.   Now don't you try
Being funny at my expense; or you'll soon find
I'm not quite done for yet — not quite snuffed out.
There's still a spark of life. You may have words:
But I've a fist will be a match for them.
Words slaver feebly from a broken jaw.
I've always lived straight, as a man must do
In my profession, if he'd keep in fettle:
But I'm no gentleman, for I fail to see
There's any sport in baiting a poor man
Because he's losing grip at forty-two,
And sees his livelihood slipping from his grasp —
Ay, and his children's bread.

GENTLEMAN JOHN.   Why, man alive,
Who's baiting you? This winded, broken cur,
That limps through life, to bait a bull like you!
You don't want pity, man? The beaten bull,
Even when the dogs are tearing at his gullet,
Turns no eye up for pity. I, myself,
Crippled and hunched and twisted as I am,
Would make a brave fend to stand up to you
Until you swallowed your words, if you should slobber
Your pity over me. A bull! Nay, man,
You're nothing but a bear with a sore head.
A bee has stung you — you who've lived on honey.
Sawdust, forsooth! You've had the sweet of life:
You've munched the honeycomb till . . .

MERRY ANDREW.   Ay: talk's cheap.
But you've no children. You don't understand.

GENTLEMAN JOHN. I have no children: I don't understand!

MERRY ANDREW. It's children make the difference.

GENTLEMAN JOHN.   Man alive —
Alive and kicking, though you're shamming dead —
You've hit the truth at last.   It's that, just that,
Makes all the difference.   If you hadn't children,
I'd find it in my heart to pity you,
Granted you'd let me.   I don't understand!
I've seen you stripped.   I've seen your children stripped.
You've never seen me naked; but you can guess
The misstitched, gnarled, and crooked thing I am.
Now, do you understand?   I may have words:
But you; man, do you never burn with pride
That you've begotten those six limber bodies,
Firm flesh, and supple sinew, and lithe limb —
Six nimble lads, each like young Absalom,
With red blood running lively in his veins,
Bone of your bone, your very flesh and blood?
It's you don't understand: God, what I'd give
This moment to be you, just as you are,
Preposterous pantaloons, and purple cats,
And painted leer, and crimson curls, and all,
To be you now, with only one missed hoop,
If I'd six clean-limbed children of my loins,
Born of the ecstasy of life within me,
To keep it quick and valiant in the ring
When I . . . but I . . . Man, man, you've missed a hoop:
But they'll take every hoop like blooded colts:
And 'twill be you in them that leaps through life,
And in their children, and their children's children.
God! doesn't it make you hold your breath to think
There'll always be an Andrew in the ring,
The very spit and image of you stripped,
While life's old circus lasts?   And I . . . at least,
There is no twisted thing of my begetting
To keep my shame alive: and that's the most
That I've to pride myself upon.   But, God,
I'm proud, ay, proud as Lucifer, of that.
Think what it means, with all the urge and sting,
When such a lust of life runs in the veins.
You, with your six sons, and your one missed hoop,
Put that thought in your pipe and smoke it.   Well,
And how d'you like the flavour?   Something bitter?
And burns the tongue a trifle?   That's the brand
That I must smoke while I've the breath to puff.

                                              [*Pause.*]

I've always worshipped the body, all my life —
The body, quick with the perfect health which is beauty,
Lively, lissom, alert, and taking its way
Through the world with the easy gait of the early gods.
The only moments I've lived my life to the full
And that live again in remembrance unfaded are those
When I've seen life compact in some perfect body,
The living God made manifest in man:
A diver in the Mediterranean, resting,
With sleeked black hair, and glistening salt-tanned skin,
Gripping the quivering gunwale with tense hands,
His torso lifted out of the peacock sea,
Like Neptune, carved in amber, come to life:
A stark Egyptian on the Nile's edge poised
Like a bronze Osiris against the lush, rank green:
A fisherman dancing reels, on New Year's Eve,
In a hall of shadowy rafters and flickering lights,
At St. Abbs on the Berwickshire coast, to the skirl of the pipes,
The lift of the wave in his heels, the sea in his veins:
A Cherokee Indian, as though he were one with his horse,
His coppery shoulders agleam, his feathers aflame
With the last of the sun, descending a gulch in Nebraska:
A brawny Cleveland puddler, stripped to the loins,
On the cauldron's brink, stirring the molten iron
In the white-hot glow, a man of white-hot metal:
A Cornish ploughboy driving an easy share
Through the grey, light soil of a headland, against a sea
Of sapphire, gay in his new white corduroys,
Blue-eyed, dark-haired and whistling a careless tune:
Jack Johnson, stripped for the ring, in his swarthy pride
Of sleek and rippling muscle . . .

   MERRY ANDREW.   ·   Jack's the boy!
Ay, he's the proper figure of a man:
But he'll grow fat and flabby and scant of breath.
He'll miss his hoop some day.

   GENTLEMAN JOHN.   But what are words
To shape the joy of form?   The Greeks did best
To cut in marble or to cast in bronze
Their ecstasy of living.   I remember
A marvellous Hermes that I saw in Athens,
Fished from the very bottom of the deep
Where he had lain, two thousand years or more,
Wrecked with a galley-full of Roman pirates,
Among the white bones of his plunderers

Whose flesh had fed the fishes as they sank,—
Serene in cold imperishable beauty,
Biding his time, till he should rise again,
Exultant from the wave, for all men's worship,
The morning-spring of life, the youth of the world,
Shaped in sea-coloured bronze for everlasting.
Ay, the Greeks knew; but men have forgotten now.
Not easily do we meet beauty walking
The world to-day in all the body's pride.
That's why I'm here — a stable-boy to camels —
For in the circus-ring there's more delight
Of seemly bodies, goodly in sheer health,
Bodies trained and tuned to the perfect pitch,
Eager, blithe, debonaire, from head to heel
Aglow and alive in every pulse, than elsewhere
In this machine-ridden land of grimy, glum,
Round-shouldered, coughing mechanics.   Once I lived
In London, in a slum called Paradise,
Sickened to see the greasy pavements crawling
With puny, flabby babies, thick as maggots.
Poor brats! I'd soon go mad, if I'd to live
In London, with its stunted men and women
But little better to look on than myself.

Yet, there's an island where the men keep fit —
St. Kilda's, a stark fastness of high crag:
They must keep fit or famish; their main food
The Solan goose; and it's a chancy job
To climb down a sheer face of slippery granite
And drop a noose over the sentinel bird
Ere he can squawk to rouse the sleeping flock.
They must keep fit — their bodies taut and trim —
To have the nerve: and they're like tempered steel,
Suppled and fined.   But even they've grown slacker
Through traffic with the mainland, in these days.
A hundred years ago, the custom held
That none should take a wife till he had stood,
His left heel on the dizziest point of crag,
His right leg and both arms, stretched in mid air,
Above the sea: three hundred feet to drop
To death, if he should fail — a Spartan test.
But any man who could have failed, would scarce
Have earned his livelihood, or his children's bread
On that bleak rock.

MERRY ANDREW [*drowsily*].   Ay, children — that's it, children!

GENTLEMAN JOHN.   St. Kilda's children had a chance, at least,
With none begotten idly of weakling fathers.
A Spartan test for fatherhood!   Should they miss
Their hoop, 'twas death, and childless.   You have still
Six lives to take unending hoops for you,
And you yourself are not done yet . . .

MERRY ANDREW [*more drowsily*].   Not yet:
And there's much comfort in the thought of children.
They're bonnie boys enough; and should do well,
If I can but keep going a little while,
A little longer till . . .

GENTLEMAN JOHN.   Six strapping sons!
And I have naught but camels.

[*Pause.*]

Yet, I've seen
A vision in this stable that puts to shame
Each ecstasy of mortal flesh and blood
That's been my eyes' delight.   I never breathed
A word of it to man or woman yet:
I couldn't whisper it now to you, if you looked
Like any human thing this side of death.
'Twas on the night I stumbled on the circus.
I'd wandered all day, lost among the fells,
Over snow-smothered hills, through blinding blizzard,
Whipped by a wind that seemed to strip and skin me,
Till I was one numb ache of sodden ice.
Quite done, and drunk with cold, I'd soon have dropped
Dead in a ditch; when suddenly a lantern
Dazzled my eyes.   I smelt a queer warm smell;
And felt a hot puff in my face; and blundered
Out of the flurry of snow and raking wind
Dizzily into a glowing Arabian night
Of elephants and camels having supper.
I thought that I'd gone mad, stark, staring mad:
But I was much too sleepy to mind just then —
Dropped dead asleep upon a truss of hay;
And lay, a log, till — well, I cannot tell
How long I lay unconscious.   I but know
I slept, and wakened: and that 'twas no dream.
I heard a rustle in the hay beside me;
And opening sleepy eyes, scarce marvelling,
I saw her, standing naked in the lamplight,

Beneath the huge tent's cavernous canopy,
Against the throng of elephants and camels
That champed unwondering in the golden dusk,
Moon-white Diana, mettled Artemis —
Her body, quick and tense as her own bow-string —
Her spirit, an arrow barbed and strung for flight —
White snow-flakes melting on her night-black hair,
And on her glistening breasts and supple thighs:
Her red lips parted, her keen eyes alive
With fierce, far-ranging hungers of the chase
Over the hills of morn . . .

                  The lantern guttered:
And I was left alone in the outer darkness
Among the champing elephants and camels.
And I'll be a camel-keeper to the end:
Though never again my eyes . . .

                                    [Pause.]

                        So, you can sleep,
You merry Andrew, for all you missed your hoop.
It's just as well, perhaps.   Now I can hold
My secret to the end.   Ah, here they come!

   *[Six lads, between the ages of three and twelve, clad in pink
tights covered with silver spangles, tumble into the tent.]*

THE ELDEST BOY.   Daddy, the bell's rung, and . . .
GENTLEMAN JOHN.   He's snoozing sound.
[To the youngest boy.]   You just creep quietly, and take tight
    hold
Of the crimson curls, and tug, and you will hear
The purple pussies all caterwaul at once.

1914.

BATTLE

(1914–1915)

BATTLE

BEFORE ACTION

I sit beside the brazier's glow,
And, drowsing in the heat,
I dream of daffodils that blow
And lambs that frisk and bleat —

Black lambs that frolic in the snow
Among the daffodils,
In a far orchard that I know
Beneath the Malvern hills.

Next year the daffodils will blow,
And lambs will frisk and bleat;
But I'll not feel the brazier's glow,
Nor any cold or heat.

BREAKFAST

We ate our breakfast lying on our backs,
Because the shells were screeching overhead.
I bet a rasher to a loaf of bread
That Hull United would beat Halifax
When Jimmy Stainthorpe played full-back instead
Of Billy Bradford.   Ginger raised his head
And cursed, and took the bet; and dropt back dead.
We ate our breakfast lying on our backs,
Because the shells were screeching overhead.

THE BAYONET

This bloody steel
Has killed a man.
I heard him squeal
As on I ran.

He watched me come
With wagging head.
I pressed it home,
And he was dead.

Though clean and clear
I've wiped the steel,
I still can hear
That dying squeal.

THE QUESTION

I wonder if the old cow died or not.
Gey bad she was the night I left, and sick.
Dick reckoned she would mend.   He knows a lot —
At least he fancies so himself, does Dick.

Dick knows a lot.   But maybe I did wrong
To leave the cow to him, and come away.
Over and over like a silly song
These words keep bumming in my head all day.

And all I think of, as I face the foe
And take my lucky chance of being shot,
Is this — that if I'm hit, I'll never know
Till Doomsday if the old cow died or not.

THE RETURN

He went, and he was gay to go;
And I smiled on him as he went.
My son —'twas well he couldn't know
My darkest dread, nor what it meant —

Just what it meant to smile and smile
And let my son go cheerily —
My son . . . and wondering all the while
What stranger would come back to me.

SALVAGE

So suddenly her life
Had crashed about that grey old country wife,
Naked she stood, and gazed
Bewildered, while her home about her blazed,
New-widowed, and bereft
Of her five sons, she clung to what was left,
Still hugging all she'd got —
A toy gun and a copper coffee-pot.

DEAF

This day last year I heard the curlew calling
By Hallypike
And the clear tinkle of hill-waters falling
Down slack and syke.

But now I cannot hear the shrapnel's screaming,
The screech of shells:
And if again I see the blue lough gleaming
Among the fells

Unheard of me will be the curlew's calling
By Hallypike
And the clear tinkle of hill-waters falling
Down slack and syke.

MAD

Neck-deep in mud,
He mowed and raved —
He who had braved
The field of blood —

And as a lad
Just out of school
Yelled: " April fool! "
And laughed like mad.

RAINING

The night I left my father said:
"You'll go and do some stupid thing.
You've no more sense in that fat head
Than Silly Billy Witterling.

"Not sense to come in when it rains —
Not sense enough for that, you've got.
You'll get a bullet through your brains,
Before you know, as like as not."

And now I'm lying in the trench
And shells and bullets through the night
Are raining in a steady drench,
I'm thinking the old man was right.

SPORT

And such a morning for cubbing —
The dew so thick on the grass!
Two hares are lolloping just out of range
Scattering the dew as they pass.

A covey of partridge whirrs overhead
Scatheless, and gets clean away;
For it's other and crueller, craftier game
We're out for and after to-day!

THE FEAR

I do not fear to die
'Neath the open sky,
To meet death in the fight
Face to face, upright.

But when at last we creep
Into a hole to sleep,
I tremble, cold with dread,
Lest I wake up dead.

How come?

415

IN THE AMBULANCE

" Two rows of cabbages,
Two of curly-greens,
Two rows of early peas,
Two of kidney-beans."

That's what he is muttering,
Making such a song,
Keeping other chaps awake,
The whole night long.

Both his legs are shot away,
And his head is light;
So he keeps on muttering
All the blessed night.

" Two rows of cabbages,
Two of curly-greens,
Two rows of early peas,
Two of kidney-beans."

HILL-BORN

I sometimes wonder if it's really true
I ever knew
Another life
Than this unending strife
With unseen enemies in lowland mud,
And wonder if my blood
Thrilled ever to the tune
Of clean winds blowing through an April noon
Mile after sunny mile
On the green ridges of the Windy Gile.

THE FATHER

That was his sort.
It didn't matter
What we were at
But he must chatter
Of this and that
His little son
Had said and done:
Till, as he told
The fiftieth time
Without a change
How three-year-old
Prattled a rhyme,
They got the range
And cut him short.

THE REEK

To-night they're sitting by the peat
Talking of me, I know —
Grandfather in the ingle-seat,
Mother and Meg and Joe.

I feel a sudden puff of heat
That sets my ears aglow,
And smell the reek of burning peat
Across the Belgian snow.

NIGHTMARE

They gave him a shilling,
They gave him a gun,
And so he's gone killing
The Germans, my son.

I dream of that shilling —
I dream of that gun —
And it's they that are killing
The boy who's my son.

COMRADES

As I was marching in Flanders
A ghost kept step with me —
Kept step with me and chuckled
And muttered ceaselessly:

"Once I too marched in Flanders,
The very spit of you,
And just a hundred years since,
To fall at Waterloo.

"They buried me in Flanders
Upon the field of blood,
And long I've lain forgotten
Deep in the Flemish mud.

"But now you march in Flanders,
The very spit of me;
To the ending of the day's march
I'll bear you company."

THE LARK

A lull in the racket and brattle,
And a lark soars into the light —
And its song seems the voice of the light
Quelling the voices of night
And the shattering fury of battle.

But again the fury of battle
Breaks out, and he drops from the height —
Dead as a stone from the height —
Drops dead, and the voice of the light
Is drowned in the shattering brattle.

THE VOW

Does he ever remember,
The lad that I knew,
That night in September
He vowed to be true—

Does he hear my heart crying
And fighting for breath
In the land where he's lying
As quiet as death?

MANGEL-WURZELS

Last year I was hoeing,
Hoeing mangel-wurzels,
Hoeing mangel-wurzels all day in the sun,
Hoeing for the squire
Down in Gloucestershire
Willy-nilly till the sweaty job was done.

Now I'm in the 'wurzels,
In the mangel-wurzels,
All day in the 'wurzels 'neath the Belgian sun.
But among this little lot
It's a different job I've got —
For you don't hoe mangel-wurzels with a gun.

HIS FATHER

I quite forgot to put the spigot in.
It's just come over me. . . . And it is queer
To think he'll not care if we lose or win
And yet be jumping-mad about that beer.

I left it running full.   He must have said
A thing or two.   I'd give my stripes to hear
What he will say if I'm reported dead
Before he gets me told about that beer!

HIT

Out of the sparkling sea
I drew my tingling body clear, and lay
On a low ledge the livelong summer day,
Basking, and watching lazily
White sails in Falmouth Bay.

My body seemed to burn
Salt in the sun that drenched it through and through
Till every particle glowed clean and new
And slowly seemed to turn
To lucent amber in a world of blue. . . . .

I felt a sudden wrench —
A trickle of warm blood —
And found that I was sprawling in the mud
Among the dead men in the trench.

BACK

They ask me where I've been,
And what I've done and seen.
But what can I reply
Who know it wasn't I,
But someone just like me,
Who went across the sea
And with my head and hands
Killed men in foreign lands. . . . .
Though I must bear the blame
Because he bore my name.

HIS MATE

" Hi-diddle-diddle
The cat and the fiddle " . . .

I raised my head,
And saw him seated on a heap of dead,
Yelling the nursery-tune,
Grimacing at the moon. . . .

" And the cow jumped over the moon.
The little dog laughed to see such sport
And the dish ran away with the spoon."

And, as he stopt to snigger,
I struggled to my knees and pulled the trigger.

THE DANCERS

All day beneath the hurtling shells
Before my burning eyes
Hover the dainty demoiselles —
The peacock dragon-flies.

Unceasingly they dart and glance
Above the stagnant stream —
And I am fighting here in France
As in a senseless dream —

A dream of shattering black shells
That hurtle overhead,
And dainty dancing demoiselles
Above the dreamless dead.

THE JOKE

He'd even have his joke
While we were sitting tight,
And so he needs must poke
His silly head in sight
To whisper some new jest
Chortling, but as he spoke
A rifle cracked. . . .
And now God knows when I shall hear the rest!

CHERRIES

A handful of cherries
She gave me in passing,
The wizened old woman,
And wished me good luck —

And again I was dreaming,
A boy in the sunshine,
And life but an orchard
Of cherries to pluck.

THE HOUSEWIFE

She must go back, she said,
Because she'd not had time to make the bed.
We'd hurried her away
So roughly . . . and, for all that we could say,
She broke from us, and passed
Into the night, shells falling thick and fast.

VICTORY

I watched it oozing quietly
Out of the gaping gash.
The lads thrust on to victory
With lunge and curse and crash.

Half-dazed, that uproar seemed to me
Like some old battle-sound
Heard long ago, as quietly
His blood soaked in the ground.

The lads thrust on to victory
With lunge and crash and shout.
I lay and watched, as quietly
His life was running out.

THE MESSAGES

" I cannot quite remember. . . . There were five
Dropt dead beside me in the trench — and three
Whispered their dying messages to me. . . ."

Back from the trenches, more dead than alive,
Stone-deaf and dazed, and with a broken knee,
He hobbled slowly, muttering vacantly:

" I cannot quite remember. . . . There were five
Dropt dead beside me in the trench, and three
Whispered their dying messages to me. . . .

" Their friends are waiting, wondering how they thrive —
Waiting a word in silence patiently. . . .
But what they said, or who their friends may be

" I cannot quite remember. . . . There were five
Dropt dead beside me in the trench,— and three
Whispered their dying messages to me. . . ."

THE QUIET

I could not understand the sudden quiet —
The sudden darkness — in the crash of fight,
The din and glare of day quenched in a twinkling
In utter starless night.

I lay an age and idly gazed at nothing,
Half-puzzled that I could not lift my head;
And then I knew somehow that I was lying
Among the other dead.

FRIENDS

(1915–1916)

He's gone.
I do not understand.
I only know
That as he turned to go
And waved his hand
In his young eyes a sudden glory shone:
And I was dazzled by a sunset glow,
And he was gone.

23d April, 1915.

FRIENDS

RUPERT BROOKE

I

Your face was lifted to the golden sky
Ablaze beyond the black roofs of the square
As flame on flame leapt, flourishing in air
Its tumult of red stars exultantly
To the cold constellations dim and high:
And as we neared the roaring ruddy flare
Kindled to gold your throat and brow and hair
Until you burned, a flame of ecstasy.

The golden head goes down into the night
Quenched in cold gloom — and yet again you stand
Beside me now with lifted face alight,
As, flame to flame, and fire to fire you burn. . . .
Then, recollecting, laughingly you turn,
And look into my eyes and take my hand.

II

Once in my garret — you being far away
Tramping the hills and breathing upland air,
Or so I fancied — brooding in my chair,
I watched the London sunshine feeble and grey
Dapple my desk, too tired to labour more,
When, looking up, I saw you standing there
Although I'd caught no footstep on the stair,
Like sudden April at my open door.

Though now beyond earth's farthest hills you fare,
Song-crowned, immortal, sometimes it seems to me
That, if I listen very quietly.
Perhaps I'll hear a light foot on the stair

And see you, standing with your angel air,
Fresh from the uplands of eternity.

III

Your eyes rejoiced in colour's ecstasy,
Fulfilling even their uttermost desire,
When, over a great sunlit field afire
With windy poppies streaming like a sea
Of scarlet flame that flaunted riotously
Among green orchards of that western shire,
You gazed as though your heart could never tir
Of life's red flood in summer revelry.

And as I watched you, little thought had I
How soon beneath the dim low-drifting sky
Your soul should wander down the darkling way,
With eyes that peer a little wistfully,
Half-glad, half-sad, remembering, as they see
Lethean poppies, shrivelling ashen grey.

IV

October chestnuts showered their perishing gold
Over us as beside the stream we lay
In the Old Vicarage garden that blue day,
Talking of verse and all the manifold
Delights a little net of words may hold,
While in the sunlight water-voles at play
Dived under a trailing crimson bramble-spray,
And walnuts thudded ripe on soft black mould.

Your soul goes down unto a darker stream
Alone, O friend, yet even in death's deep night
Your eyes may grow accustomed to the dark,
And Styx for you may have the ripple and gleam
Of your familiar river, and Charon's bark
Tarry by that old garden of your delight.

WILLIAM DENIS BROWNE

(Gallipoli, 11th June, 1915)

Night after night we two together heard
The music of the Ring,
The inmost silence of our being stirred
By voice and string.

Though I to-night in silence sit, and you,
In stranger silence, sleep,
Eternal music stirs and thrills anew
The severing deep.

TENANTS

Suddenly, out of dark and leafy ways,
We came upon the little house asleep
In cold blind stillness, shadowless and deep,
In the white magic of the full moon-blaze:
Strangers without the gate, we stood agaze,
Fearful to break that quiet, and to creep
Into the house that had been ours to keep
Through a long year of happy nights and days.

So unfamiliar in the white moon-gleam,
So old and ghostly like a house of dream
It seemed, that over us there stole the dread
That even as we watched it, side by side,
The ghosts of lovers, who had lived and died
Within its walls, were sleeping in our bed.

SEA-CHANGE

Wind-flicked and ruddy her young body glowed
In sunny shallows, splashing them to spray:
But when on rippled silver sand she lay,
And over her the little green waves flowed,
Coldly translucent and moon-coloured showed
Her frail young beauty, as if rapt away
From all the light and laughter of the day
To some twilit, forlorn sea-god's abode.

Again into the sun with happy cry
She leapt alive and sparkling from the sea,
Sprinkling white spray against the hot blue sky,
A laughing girl . . . and yet, I see her lie
Under a deeper tide eternally
In cold moon-coloured immortality.

GOLD

All day the mallet thudded, far below
My garret, in an old ramshackle shed
Where ceaselessly, with stiffly nodding head
And rigid motions ever to and fro
A figure like a puppet in a show
Before the window moved till day was dead,
Beating out gold to earn his daily bread,
Beating out thin fine gold-leaf blow on blow.

And I within my garret all day long
To that unceasing thudding tuned my song,
Beating out golden words in tune and time
To that dull thudding, rhyme on golden rhyme.
But in my dreams all night in that dark shed
With aching arms I beat fine gold for bread

THE OLD BED

Streaming beneath the eaves, the sunset light
Turns the white walls and ceiling to pure gold,
And gold, the quilt and pillows on the old
Fourposter bed — all day a cold drift-white —
As if, in a gold casket glistering bright,
The gleam of winter sunshine sought to hold
The sleeping child safe from the dark and cold
And creeping shadows of the coming night.

Slowly it fades: and stealing through the gloom
Home-coming shadows throng the quiet room,
Grey ghosts that move unrustling, without breath,
To their familiar rest, and closer creep
About the little dreamless child asleep
Upon the bed of bridal, birth and death.

TREES

(To Lascelles Abercrombie)

The flames half lit the cavernous mystery
Of the over-arching elm that loomed profound
And mountainous above us, from the ground
Soaring to midnight stars majestically,
As, under the shelter of that ageless tree
In a rapt dreaming circle we lay around
The crackling faggots, listening to the sound
Of old words moving in new harmony.

And as you read, before our wondering eyes
Arose another tree of mighty girth —
Crested with stars though rooted in the earth,
Its heavy-foliaged branches, lit with gleams
Of ruddy firelight and the light of dreams —
Soaring immortal to eternal skies.

OBLIVION

Near the great pyramid, unshadowed, white,
With apex piercing the white noon-day blaze,
Swathed in white robes beneath the blinding rays
Lie sleeping Bedouins drenched in white-hot light.
About them, searing to the tingling sight,
Swims the white dazzle of the desert ways
Where the sense shudders, witless and adaze,
In a white void with neither depth nor height.

Within the black core of the pyramid
Beneath the weight of sunless centuries
Lapt in dead night King Cheops lies asleep:
Yet in the darkness of his chamber hid
He knows no black oblivion more deep
Than that blind white oblivion of noon skies.

COLOUR

A blue-black Nubian plucking oranges
At Jaffa by a sea of malachite
In red tarboosh, green sash, and flowing white
Burnous — among the shadowy memories
That haunt me yet by these bleak Northern seas
He lives for ever in my eyes' delight,
Bizarre, superb in young immortal might —
A god of old barbaric mysteries.

Maybe he lived a life of lies and lust:
Maybe his bones are now but scattered dust:
Yet, for a moment he was life supreme
Exultant and unchallenged: and my rhyme
Would set him safely out of reach of time
In that old heaven where things are what they seem.

RETREAT

Broken, bewildered by the long retreat
Across the stifling leagues of Southern plain,
Across the scorching leagues of trampled grain,
Half-stunned, half-blinded by the trudge of feet
And dusty smother of the August heat,
He dreamt of flowers in an English lane,
Of hedgerow flowers glistening after rain —
All-heal and willowherb and meadowsweet.

All-heal and willowherb and meadowsweet —
The innocent names kept up a cool refrain,
All-heal and willowherb and meadowsweet,
Chiming and tinkling through his aching brain
Until he babbled as a child again —
" All-heal and willowherb and meadowsweet."

NIGHT

Vesuvius, purple under purple skies
Beyond the purple, still, unrippling sea;
Sheer amber lightning, streaming ceaselessly
From heaven to earth, dazzling bewildered eyes
With all the terror of beauty: thus day dies
That dawned in blue, unclouded innocency;
And thus we look our last on Italy
That soon, obscured by night, behind us lies.

And night descends on us, tempestuous night,
Night, torn with terror, as we sail the deep;
And like a cataract down a mountain-steep
Pours, loud with thunder, that red perilous fire. . . .
Yet shall the dawn, O land of our desire,
Show thee again, re-orient, crowned with light!

THE ORPHANS

At five o'clock one April morn
I met them making tracks,
Young Benjamin and Abel Horn,
With bundles on their backs.

Young Benjamin is seventy-five,
Young Abel, seventy-seven —
The oldest innocents alive
Beneath that April heaven.

I asked them why they trudged about
With crabby looks and sour —
"And does your mother know you're out
At this unearthly hour?"

They stopped: and scowling up at me
Each shook a grizzled head,
And swore; and then spat bitterly,
As with one voice they said:

"Homeless, about the country-side
We never thought to roam;
But mother, she has gone and died,
And broken up the home."

?

Mooning in the moonlight
I met a mottled pig,
Grubbing mast and acorn,
On the Gallows Rigg.

" Tell, oh tell me truly,
While I wander blind,
Do your peepy pig's eyes
Really see the wind —

" See the great wind flowing
Darkling and agleam
Through the fields of heaven
In a crystal stream?

" Do the singing eddies
Break on bough and twig
Into silvery sparkles
For your eyes, O pig?

" Do celestial surges
Sweep across the night
Like a sea of glory
In your blessed sight?

" Tell, oh tell me truly! "
But the mottled pig
Grubbing mast and acorns,
Did not care a fig.

THE PESSIMIST

His body bulged with puppies — little eyes
Peeped out of every pocket, black and bright;
And with as innocent, round-eyed surprise
He watched the glittering traffic of the night.

"What this world's coming to I cannot tell,"
He muttered, as I passed him, with a whine —
"Things surely must be making slap for hell,
When no one wants these little dogs of mine."

THE SWEET-TOOTH

Taking a turn after tea
Through orchards of Mirabelea
Where clusters of yellow and red
Dangled and glowed overhead,
Who should I see
But old Timothy,
Hale and hearty as hearty could be —
Timothy under a crab-apple tree.

His blue eyes twinkling at me,
Munching and crunching with glee
And wagging his wicked old head,
" I've still got a sweet-tooth," he said,
" A hundred and three
Come January,
I've one tooth left in my head," said he —
Timothy under the crab-apple tree.

GIRL'S SONG

I saw three black pigs riding
In a blue and yellow cart —
Three black pigs riding to the fair
Behind the old grey dappled mare —
But it wasn't black pigs riding
In a gay and gaudy cart
That sent me into hiding
With a flutter in my heart.

I heard the cart returning,
The jolting jingling cart —
Returning empty from the fair
Behind the old jog-trotting mare —
But it wasn't the returning
Of a clattering, empty cart
That sent the hot blood burning
And throbbing through my heart.

THE ICE-CART

Perched on my city office-stool,
I watched with envy, while a cool
And lucky carter handled ice. . . .
And I was wandering in a trice,
Far from the grey and grimy heat
Of that intolerable street,
O'er sapphire berg and emerald floe,
Beneath the still, cold ruby glow
Of everlasting Polar night,
Bewildered by the queer half-light,
Until I stumbled, unawares,
Upon a creek where big white bears
Plunged headlong down with flourished heels
And floundered after shining seals
Through shivering seas of blinding blue.
And as I watched them, ere I knew,
I'd stripped, and I was swimming, too,
Among the seal-pack, young and hale,
And thrusting on with threshing tail,
With twist and twirl and sudden leap
Through crackling ice and salty deep —
Diving and doubling with my kind,
Until, at last, we left behind
Those big, white, blundering bulks of death,
And lay, at length, with panting breath
Upon a far untravelled floe,
Beneath a gentle drift of snow —
Snow drifting gently, fine and white,
Out of the endless Polar night,
Falling and falling evermore
Upon that far untravelled shore,
Till I was buried fathoms deep
Beneath that cold white drifting sleep —
Sleep drifting deep,
Deep drifting sleep. . . .

The carter cracked a sudden whip:
I clutched my stool with startled grip,
Awakening to the grimy heat
Of that intolerable street.

TO E. M.

(In memory of R. B.)

The night we saw the stacks of timber blaze
To terrible golden fury, young and strong
He watched between us with dream-dazzled gaze
Aflame, and burning like a god of song,
As we together stood against the throng
Drawn from the midnight of the city ways.

To-night the world about us is ablaze
And he is dead, is dead. . . . Yet, young and strong
He watches with us still with deathless gaze
Aflame, and burning like a god of song,
As we together stand against the throng
Drawn from the bottomless midnight of hell's ways.

10th June, 1915.

MARRIAGE

Going my way of old
Contented more or less
I dreamt not life could hold
Such happiness.

I dreamt not that love's way
Could keep the golden height
Day after happy day,
Night after night.

ROSES

Red roses floating in a crystal bowl
You bring, O love; and in your eyes I see,
Blossom on blossom, your warm love of me
Burning within the crystal of your soul —
Red roses floating in a crystal bowl.

FOR G.

All night under the moon
Plovers are flying
Over the dreaming meadows of silvery light,
Over the meadows of June
Flying and crying —
Wandering voices of love in the hush of the night.

All night under the moon,
Love, though we're lying
Quietly under the thatch, in silvery light
Over the meadows of June
Together we're flying —
Rapturous voices of love in the hush of the night.

HOME

I

RETURN

Under the brown bird-haunted eaves of thatch
The hollyhocks in crimson glory burned
Against black timbers and old rosy brick,
And over the green door in clusters thick
Hung tangled passion-flowers, when we returned
To our own threshold: and with hand on latch
We stood a moment in the sunset gleam
And looked upon our home as in a dream.

Rapt in a golden glow of still delight
Together on the threshold in the sun
We stood rejoicing that we two had won
To this deep golden peace ere day was done,
That over gloomy plain and storm-swept height
We two, O love, had won to home ere night.

II

CANDLE-LIGHT

Where through the open window I could see
The supper-table in the golden light
Of tall white candles — brasses glinting bright
On the black gleaming board, and crockery,
Coloured like gardens of old Araby —
In your blue gown against the walls of white
You stood adream, and in the starry night
I felt strange loneliness steal over me.

You stood with eyes upon the candle flame
That kindled your thick hair to burnished gold,
As in a golden spell that seemed to hold
My heart's love rapt from me for evermore. . . .

And then you stirred, and opening the door,
Into the starry night you breathed my name.

III
FIRELIGHT

Against the curtained casement wind and sleet
Rattle and thresh, while snug by our own fire
In dear companionship that naught may tire
We sit,— you listening, sewing in your seat,
Half-dreaming in the glow of light and heat,
I reading some old tale of love's desire
That swept on gold wings to disaster dire
Then sprang re-orient from black defeat.

I close the book, and louder yet the storm
Threshes without.   Your busy hands are still;
And on your face and hair the light is warm,
As we sit gazing on the coals' red gleam
In a gold glow of happiness, and dream
Diviner dreams the years shall yet fulfil.

IV
MIDNIGHT

Between the midnight pillars of black elms
The old moon hangs, a thin, cold, amber flame
Over low ghostly mist: a lone snipe wheels
Through shadowy moonshine, droning: and there steals
Into my heart a fear without a name
Out of primæval night's resurgent realms,
Unearthly terror, chilling me with dread
As I lie waking wide-eyed on the bed.

And then you turn towards me in your sleep
Murmuring, and with a sigh of deep content
You nestle to my breast; and over me
Steals the warm peace of you; and, all fear spent,
I hold you to me sleeping quietly,
Till I, too, sink in slumber sound and deep.

LIVELIHOOD

(1914–1916)

TO

AUDREY

Audrey, these men and women I have known
I have brought together in a book for you,
So that my child some day when she is grown
May know the friendly folk her father knew.

Wondering how fathers can be so absurd,
Perhaps you'll take it idly from the shelves,
And, reading, hear, as once I overheard,
These men and women talking to themselves.

And so find out how they faced life and earned,
As you one day must earn, a livelihood,
And how, in spite of everything, they learned
To take their luck through life and find it good.

And, maybe, as you share each hope and fear
And all the secrets that they never told,
For their sake you'll forgive your father, dear,
Almost, for being so absurd and old.

And may it somewhat help to make amends
To think that, in their sorrow and their mirth,
Such men and women were your father's friends
In old incredible days before your birth.

The Old Nail-shop.   1916.

LIVELIHOOD

THE OLD NAIL-SHOP

I dreamt of wings,— and waked to hear
Through the low-sloping ceiling clear
The nesting starlings flutter and scratch
Among the rafters of the thatch,
Not twenty inches from my head;
And lay, half-dreaming in my bed,
Watching the far elms — bolt-upright
Black towers of silence in a night
Of stars, between the window-sill
And the low-hung eaves, square-framed, until
I drowsed, and must have slept a wink . . .
And wakened to a ceaseless clink
Of hammers ringing on the air . . .
And, somehow, only half-aware,
I'd risen and crept down the stair,
Bewildered by strange smoky gloom,
Until I'd reached the living-room
That once had been a nail-shop shed.
And where my hearth had blazed, instead
I saw the nail-forge glowing red;
And, through the stife and smoky glare,
Three dreaming women standing there
With hammers beating red-hot wire
On tinkling anvils, by the fire,
To ten-a-penny nails; and heard —
Though none looked up or breathed a word —
The song each heart sang to the tune
Of hammers, through a summer's noon,
When they had wrought in that red glow,
Alive, a hundred years ago —
The song of girl and wife and crone,
Sung in the heart of each alone . . .

The dim-eyed crone with nodding head —
" He's dead; and I'll, too, soon be dead."

The grave-eyed mother, gaunt with need —
" Another little mouth to feed! "

The black-eyed girl, with eyes alight —
" I'll wear the yellow beads to-night."

THE SHAFT

He must have lost his way, somehow. 'Twould seem
He'd taken the wrong turning, back a bit,
After his lamp . . . or was it all a dream
That he'd nigh reached the cage — his new lamp lit
And swinging in his hand, and whistling, glad
To think the shift was over — when he'd tripped
And stumbled, like the daft, club-footed lad
His mother called him; and his lamp had slipped
And smashed to smithereens; and left him there
In pitchy dark, half-stunned, and with barked shins?
He'd cursed his luck; although he didn't care,
Not overmuch: you suffered for your sins:
And, anyway, he must be nigh the shaft;
And he could fumble his way out somehow,
If he were last, and none came by. 'Twas daft
To do a trick like thon.
                                          And even now
His mother would be waiting. How she'd laugh
To hear about it! She was always game
For fun, she was, and such a one for chaff —
A fellow had no chance. But 'twas the same
With women always: you could never tell
What they'd be at, or after saying next:
They'd such queer, tricky tongues; and it was well
For men to let them talk when they were vexed —
Although, his mother, she was seldom cross.
But she'd be wondering, now, ay, that she would —
Hands folded in her apron, at a loss
To know what kept him, even now she stood,
Biting her lips, he'd warrant. She aye bit
Her lips till they were white when things went wrong.
She'd never liked his taking to the pit,
After his father'd. . . . Ay, and what a song
She'd make . . . and supper cold! It must be late.
The last on the last shift! After to-day
The pit was being laid idle! Jack, his mate,
Had left him, tidying — hurrying away

To back . . . And no night-shift . . .

                                     If that cursed lamp
Had not gone out. . . . But that was hours ago —
How many hours he couldn't tell.   The cramp
Was in his thighs.   And what could a lad know
Who'd crawled for hours upon his hands and knees
Through miles on miles of hot, black, dripping night
Of low-roofed, unfamiliar galleries?
He'd give a hundred pound to stand upright
And stretch his legs a moment: but, somehow,
He'd never reached a refuge, though he'd felt
The walls on either hand.   He'd bumped his brow
Till he was dizzy.   And the heat would melt
The marrow in his bones.   And yet he'd gone
A dozen miles at least, and hadn't found
Even a crossway.   On and on and on
He'd crawled, and crawled; and never caught a sound
Save water dripping, dripping, or the creak
Of settling coal.   If he could only hear
His own voice even; but he dared not speak
Above a whisper . . .
                         There was naught to fear;
And he was not afraid of aught, not he!
He would come on a shaft, before he knew.
He couldn't miss.   The longest gallery
Must end somewhere or other; though 'twas true
He hadn't guessed the drift could be so long.

If he had not come straight . . . If he had turned,
Unknowing, in the dark . . . If he'd gone wrong
Once, then why not a dozen times!   It burned
His very heart to tinder, just to think
That he, maybe, was crawling round and round
And round and round, and hadn't caught a blink
Of light at all, or hadn't heard a sound. . . .
'Twas queer, gey queer . . .
                      Or was he going daft,
And only dreaming he was underground
In some black pit of hell, without a shaft —
Just one long gallery that wound and wound,
Where he must crawl forever with the drip
Of lukewarm water drumming on his back . . .

'Twas nightmare, surely, had him in its grip.

His head was like to split, his spine to crack . . .
If he could only call, his mother'd come
And shake him; and he'd find himself in bed . . .
She'd joke his fright away . . . But he was dumb,
And couldn't shout to save himself . . . His head
Seemed full of water, dripping, dripping, dripping . . .
And he, somehow, inside it — huge and dark
His own skull soared above him . . . He kept slipping,
And clutching at the crumbling walls . . . A spark
Flared suddenly; and to a blood-red blaze
His head was bursting; and the pain would break . . .

'Twas solid coal he'd run against, adaze —
Coal, sure enough. And he was broad awake,
And crawling still through that unending drift
Of some old working, long disused. He'd known
That there were such. If he could only lift
His head a moment; but the roof of stone
Crushed low upon him. A gey narrow seam
He must be in,— and bad to work: no doubt
That's why 'twas given up. He'd like to scream,
His cut knees hurt so sorely; but a shout
Might bring the crumbling roof down on his head,
And squash him flat.
                    If he could only creep
Between the cool white sheets of his own bed,
And turn towards the wall, and sleep, and sleep —
And dream, maybe, of pigeons soaring high,
Turning and tumbling in the morning light,
With wings ashimmer in a cloudless sky.
He'd give the world to see a bonnie flight
Of his own pigeons rise with flapping wings,
Soaring and sweeping almost out of sight,
Till he was dizzy, watching the mad things
Tossing and tumbling at that dazzling height.
Ay, and his homers, too — if they'd come in,
He hoped his mother'd fed them. They would be
Fair famished after such a flight, and thin.
But she would feed them, sure enough; for she
Liked pigeons, too — would stand there at the door
With arms akimbo, staring at the blue,
Her black eyes shining as she watched them soar,
Without a word, till they were out of view.
And how she laughed to hear them scold and pout,

Ruffle and fuss — like menfolk, she would say:
Nobody knowing what 'twas all about,
And least of all themselves.   That was her way,
To joke and laugh the tantrums out of him.
He'd tie his neckerchief before the glass;
And she'd call him her pigeon, Peter Prim,
Preening himself, she'd say, to meet his lass —
Though he'd no lass, not he!   A scarf well tied,
No gaudy colours, just a red or yellow,
Was what he fancied.   What harm if he tried
To keep himself respectable!   A fellow —
Though womenfolk might laugh and laugh . . .

                                              And now

He wondered if he'd hear her laugh again
With hands on hips and sparkling eyes.   His brow
Seemed clampt with red-hot iron bands; and pain
Shot red-hot needles through his legs — his back,
A raw and aching spine that bore the strain
Of all the earth above him: the dead black
Unending clammy night blinding his brain
To a black blankness shot with scarlet streaks
Of searing lightning; and he scarcely knew
If he'd been crawling hours, or days, or weeks . . .
And now the lightning glimmered faintly blue,
And gradually the blackness paled to grey:
And somewhere, far ahead, he caught the gleam
Of light, daylight, the very light of day,
Day, dazzling day!

                          Thank God, it was no dream.
He felt a cooler air upon his face;
And scrambling madly for some moments more,
Though centuries it seemed, he reached the place
Where through the chinks of the old crumbling door
Of a disused upcast-shaft, grey ghostly light
Strained feebly, though it seemed the sun's own blaze
To eyes so long accustomed to the night
And peering blindly through that pitchy maze.

The door dropped from its hinges — and upright
He stood, at last, bewildered and adaze,
In a strange dazzling world of flowering white.
Plumed snowy fronds and delicate downy sprays,
Fantastic as the feathery work of frost,
Drooped round him from the wet walls of the shaft —

A monstrous growth of mould, huge mould.   And lost
In wonder he stood gaping; and then laughed
To see that living beauty — quietly
He laughed to see it: and awhile forgot
All danger.   He would tell his mother: she
Would scarce know whether to believe or not,—
But laugh to hear how, when he came on it,
It dazzled him.   If she could only see
That fluffy white — come on it from the pit,
Snow-white as fantails' feathers, suddenly
As he had, she'd laugh too: she . . .

                      Icy cold
Shot shuddering through him, as he stept beneath
A trickle.   He looked up.   That monstrous mould
Frightened him; and he stood with chattering teeth,
Seeming to feel it growing over him
Already, shutting out the fleck of sky
That up the slimy shaft gleamed far and dim.
'Twould flourish on his bones when he should lie
Forgotten in the shaft.   Its clammy breath
Was choking him already.   He would die,
And no one know how he'd come by his death . . .
Dank, cold mould growing slowly.   By and by
'Twould cover him; and not a soul to tell . . .

With a wild cry he tried to scramble out,
Clutching the wall . . . Mould covered him . . . He fell,
As, close at hand, there came an answering shout.

IN THE ORCHESTRA

He'd played each night for months; and never heard
A single tinkly tune, or caught a word
Of all the silly songs and sillier jests;
And he'd seen nothing, even in the rests,
Of that huge audience piled from floor to ceiling
Whose stacked white faces sent his dazed wits reeling . . .
He'd been too happy; and had other things
To think of while he scraped his fiddle-strings . . .

But now, he'd nothing left to think about —
Nothing he dared to think of . . .

                         In and out
The hollow fiddle of his head the notes
Jingled and jangled; and the raucous throats
Of every star rasped jibes into his ear,—
Each separate syllable, precise and clear,
As though 'twere life or death if he should miss
A single cackle, crow or quack, or hiss
Of cockadoodling fools . . .

                     A week ago
He'd sat beside her bed; and heard her low
Dear voice talk softly of her hopes and fears —
Their hopes and fears; and every afternoon
He'd watched her lying there . . .

                       A fat buffoon
In crimson trousers prancing, strut and cluck —
Cackling: " A fellow never knows his luck.
He never knows his luck.   He never knows
His luck." . . . And in and out the old gag goes
Of either ear, and in and out again,
Playing at " You-can't-catch-me " through his brain —
" 'Er knows his luck." . . .

                   How well they thought they knew
Their luck, and such a short while since, they two
Together.   Life was lucky; and 'twas good
Then, to be fiddling for a livelihood —
His livelihood and hers . . .

476

                                        A woman sang
With grinning teeth.   The whole house rocked and rang.
In the whole house there was no empty place:
And there were grinning teeth in every face
Of all those faces, grinning, tier on tier,
From orchestra to ceiling chandelier
That caught in every prism a grinning light,
As from the little black box up a height
The changing limelight streamed down on the stage.
And he was filled with reasonless, dull rage
To see those grinning teeth, those grinning rows;
And wondered if those lips would never close,
But gape for ever through an endless night,
Grinning and mowing in the green limelight.

And now they seemed to grin in mockery
Of him; and then, as he turned suddenly
To face them, flaming, it was his own face
That mowed and grinned at him from every place —
Grimacing on him with the set, white grin
Of his own misery through that dazzling din . . .
Yet, all the while he hadn't raised his head,
But fiddled, fiddled for his daily bread,
His livelihood — no longer hers . . .
                                        And now
He heard no more the racket and the row,
Nor saw the aching, glittering glare, nor smelt
The smother of hot breaths and smoke — but felt
A wet wind on his face . . .
                                        He sails again
Home with her up the river in the rain —
Leaving the grey domes and grey colonnades
Of Greenwich in their wake as daylight fades —
By huge dark cavernous wharves with flaring lights,
Warehouses built for some mad London night's
Fantastic entertainment,— grimmer far
Than Bagdad dreamt of — monstrous and bizarre,
They loom against the night; and seem to hold
Preposterous secrets horrible and old,
Behind black doors and windows.
                                        Yet even they
Make magic with more mystery the way,
As, hand in hand, they sail through the blue gloam
Up the old river of enchantment, home . . .

He heard strange, strangled voices — he, alone
Once more,— like voices through the telephone,
Thin and unreal, inarticulate
Twanging and clucking at terrific rate —
Pattering, pattering . . .
                            And again aware
He grew of all the racket and the glare,
Aware again of the antic strut and cluck —
And there was poor old " Never-know-his-luck "
Doing another turn — yet, not a smile,
Although he'd changed his trousers and his style.
The same old trousers and the same old wheeze
Was what the audience liked.   He tried to please,
And knew he failed: and suddenly turned old
Before those circling faces glum and cold —
A fat old man with cracked voice piping thin,
Trying to make those wooden faces grin,
With frantic kicks and desperate wagging head,
To win the applause that meant his daily bread —
Gagging and prancing for a livelihood,
His daily bread . . .
                        God! how he understood!
He'd fiddled for their livelihood — for her,
And for the one who never came . . .
                                        A stir
Upon the stage; and now another turn —
The old star guttered out, too old to burn.
And he remembered she had liked the chap
When she'd been there that night.   He'd seen her clap
Laughing so merrily.   She liked it all —
The razzle-dazzle of the music-hall —
And laughing faces . . . said she liked to see
Hardworking people laughing heartily
After the day's work.   She liked everything —
His playing, even!   Snap . . . another string —
The third!
            And she'd been happy in that place,
Seeing a friendly face in every face.
That was her way — the whole world was her friend.
And she'd been happy, happy to the end,
As happy as the day was long . . .
                                    And he
Fiddled on, dreaming of her quietly.

THE SWING

'Twas jolly, swinging through the air,
With young Dick Garland sitting there
Tugging the rope with might and main,
His round face flushed, his arms astrain,
His laughing blue eyes shining bright,
As they went swinging through the light —
As they went swinging, ever higher
Until it seemed that they came nigher
At every swing to the blue sky —
Until it seemed that by-and-by
The boat would suddenly swing through
That sunny dazzle of clear blue —
And they, together . . .
      Yesterday
She'd hardly thought she'd get away:
The mistress was that cross, and she
Had only told her after tea
That ere she left she must set to
And turn the parlour out.   She knew,
Ay, well enough, that it meant more
Than two hours' work.   And so at four
She'd risen that morn; and done it all
Before her mistress went to call
And batter at her bedroom door
At six to rouse her.   Such a floor,
So hard to sweep; and all that brass
To polish!   Any other lass
But her would have thrown up the place,
And told the mistress to her face . . .

But how could she!   Her money meant
So much to them at home.   'Twas spent
So quickly, though so hard to earn.
She'd got to keep her place, and learn
To hold her tongue.   Though it was hard,
The little house in Skinner's Yard
Must be kept going.   She would rob
The bairns if she should lose her job,

And they'd go hungry . . .
      Since the night
They'd brought home father, cold and white,
Upon a stretcher, mother and she
Had had to struggle ceaselessly
To keep a home together at all.
'Twas lucky she was big and tall
And such a strong lass for fifteen.
She couldn't think where they'd have been
If she'd not earned enough to feed
And help to keep the bairns from need —
Those five young hungry mouths . . .
       And she

For one long day beside the sea
Was having a rare holiday . . .

'Twas queer that Dick should want to pay
So much good money, hardly earned,
To bring her with him . . .
      How it burned,
That blazing sun in the blue sky!
And it was good to swing so high —
So high into the burning blue,
Until it seemed they'd swing right through . . .

And good just to be sitting there
And watching Dick with tumbled hair
And his red necktie floating free
Against the blue of sky and sea,
As up and down and up and down
Beyond the low roofs of the town
They swung and swung . . .
      And he was glad
To pay for her, the foolish lad,
And happy to be swinging there
With her, and rushing through the air,
So high into the burning blue
It seemed that they would swing right through . . .

'Twas well that she had caught the train,
She'd had to run with might and main
To catch it: and Dick waiting there
With tickets ready . . .
      How his hair

Shone in the sunshine, and the light
Made his blue, laughing eyes so bright
Whenever he looked up at her . . .

She'd like to sit, and never stir
Again out of that easy seat —
With no more mats to shake and beat
And no more floors to sweep, no stairs
To scrub, and no more heavy chairs
To move — for she was sleepy now . . .
Dick's hair had fallen over his brow
Into his eyes. He shook them free,
And laughed to her. 'Twas queer that he
Should think it worth his while to pay,
And give her such a holiday . . .
But she was sleepy now. 'Twas rare,
As they were rushing through the air
To see Dick's blue eyes shining bright
As they went swinging through the light,
As they went swinging ever higher
Until it seemed that they came nigher
At every swing to that blue sky —
Until it seemed that by-and-by
Their boat would suddenly swing through
That sunny dazzle of clear blue . . .

If she could swing for evermore
With Dick above that golden shore,
With no more parlour-floors to sweep —
If she could only swing and sleep . . .
And wake to see Dick's eyes burn bright,
To see them laughing with delight
As suddenly they swung right through
That sunny dazzle of clear blue —
And they two, sailing on together
For ever through that shining weather!

THE DROVE-ROAD

'Twas going to snow —'twas snowing!   Curse his luck!
And fifteen mile to travel — here was he
With nothing but an empty pipe to suck,
And half a flask of rum — but that would be
More welcome later on.   He'd had a drink
Before he left; and that would keep him warm
A tidy while: and 'twould be good to think
He'd something to fall back on, if the storm
Should come to much.   You never knew with snow.
A sup of rain he didn't mind at all,
But snow was different with so far to go —
Full fifteen mile, and not a house of call.
Ay, snow was quite another story, quite —
Snow on these fell-tops with a north-east wind
Behind it, blowing steadily with a bite
That made you feel that you were stark and skinned.

And these poor beasts — and they just off the boat
A day or so, and hardly used to land —
Still dizzy with the sea, their wits afloat.
When they first reached the dock, they scarce could stand,
They'd been so joggled.   It's gey bad to cross,
After a long day's jolting in the train
Thon Irish Channel, always pitch and toss —
And heads or tails, not much for them to gain!
And then the market, and the throng and noise
Of yapping dogs; and they stung mad with fear,
Welted with switches by those senseless boys —
He'd like to dust their jackets!   But 'twas queer,
A beast's life, when you came to think of it
From start to finish — queerer, ay, a lot
Than any man's, and chancier a good bit.
With his ash-sapling at their heels they'd got
To travel before night those fifteen miles
Of hard fell-road, against the driving snow,
Half-blinded, on and on.   He thought at whiles
'Twas just as well for them they couldn't know . . .

Though, as for that, 'twas little that he knew
Himself what was in store for him.   He took
Things as they came.   'Twas all a man could do;
And he'd kept going, somehow, by hook or crook.
And here was he, with fifteen mile of fell,
And snow, and . . . God, but it was blowing stiff!
And no tobacco.   Blest if he could tell
Where he had lost it — but, for half a whiff
He'd swop the very jacket off his back —
Not that he'd miss the cobweb of old shreds
That held the holes together.

                    Thon Cheap-Jack
Who'd sold it him had said it was Lord Ted's,
And London cut.   But Teddy had grown fat
Since he'd been made an alderman . . . His bid?
And did the gentleman not want a hat
To go with it, a topper?   If he did,
Here was the very . . .

                Hell, but it was cold:
And driving dark it was — nigh dark as night.
He'd almost think he must be getting old,
To feel the wind so.   And long out of sight
The beasts had trotted.   Well, what odds!   The way
Ran straight for ten miles on, and they'd go straight.
They'd never heed a by-road.   Many a day
He'd had to trudge on, trusting them to fate,
And always found them safe.   They scamper fast,
But in the end a man could walk them down.
They're showy trotters; but they cannot last.
He'd race the fastest beast for half-a-crown
On a day's journey.   Beasts were never made
For steady travelling; drive them twenty mile,
And they were done; while he was not afraid
To tackle twice that distance with a smile.

But not a day like this!   He'd never felt
A wind with such an edge.   'Twas like the blade
Of the rasper in the pocket of his belt
He kept for easy shaving.   In his trade
You'd oft to make your toilet under a dyke —
And he was always one for a clean chin,
And carried soap.

               He'd never felt the like —
That wind, it cut clean through him to the skin.

He might be mother-naked, walking bare,
For all the use his clothes were, with the snow
Half-blinding him, and clagging to his hair,
And trickling down his spine.   He'd like to know
What was the sense of pegging steadily,
Chilled to the marrow, after a daft herd
Of draggled beasts he couldn't even see!

But that was him all over!   Just a word,
A nod, a wink, the price of half-and-half —
And he'd be setting out for God-knows-where,
With no more notion than a yearling calf
Where he would find himself when he got there.
And he'd been travelling hard on sixty year
The same old road, the same old giddy gait;
And he'd be walking, for a pint of beer,
Into his coffin, one day, soon or late —
But not with such a tempest in his teeth,
Half-blinded and half-dothered, that he hoped!
He'd met a sight of weather on the heath,
But this beat all.
                        'Twas worse than when he'd groped
His way that evening down the Mallerstang —
Thon was a blizzard, thon — and he was done,
And almost dropping when he came a bang
Against a house — slap-bang, and like to stun! —
Though that just saved his senses — and right there
He saw a lighted window he'd not seen,
Although he'd nearly staggered through its glare
Into a goodwife's kitchen, where she'd been
Baking hot griddlecakes upon the peat.
And he could taste them now, and feel the glow
Of steady, aching, tingly, drowsy heat,
As he sat there and let the caking snow
Melt off his boots, staining the sanded floor.
And that brown jug she took down from the shelf —
And every time he'd finished, fetching more,
And piping: " Now reach up, and help yourself! "
She was a wonder, thon, the gay old wife —
But no such luck this journey.   Things like that
Could hardly happen every day of life,
Or no one would be dying, but the fat
And oily undertakers, starved to death
For want of custom . . . Hell! but he would soon

Be giving them a job . . . It caught your breath,
That throttling wind.   And it was not yet noon;
And he'd be travelling through it until dark.
Dark!   'Twas already dark, and might be night
For all that he could see . . .

                And not a spark
Of comfort for him!   Just to strike a light,
And press the kindling shag down in the bowl,
Keeping the flame well-shielded by his hand,
And puff, and puff!   He'd give his very soul
For half-a-pipe.   He couldn't understand
How he had come to lose it.   He'd the rum —
Ay, that was safe enough: but it would keep
Awhile, you never knew what chance might come
In such a storm . . .

             If he could only sleep . . .
If he could only sleep . . . That rustling sound
Of drifting snow, it made him sleepy-like —
Drowsy and dizzy, dithering round and round . . .
If he could only curl up under a dyke,
And sleep and sleep . . . It dazzled him, that white,
Drifting and drifting, round and round and round . . .
Just half-a-moment's snooze . . . He'd be all right.
It made his head quite dizzy, that dry sound
Of rustling snow.   It made his head go round —
That rustling in his ears . . . and drifting, drifting . . .
If he could only sleep . . . he would sleep sound . . .
God, he was nearly gone!

              The storm was lifting;
And he'd run into something soft and warm —
Slap into his own beasts, and never knew.
Huddled they were, bamboozled by the storm —
And little wonder either, when it blew
A blasted blizzard.   Still, they'd got to go.
They couldn't stand there snoozing until night.

But they were sniffing something in the snow.
'Twas that had stopped them, something big and white —
A bundle — nay, a woman . . . and she slept.
But it was death to sleep.

            He'd nearly dropt
Asleep himself.   'Twas well that he had kept
That rum; and lucky that the beasts had stopt.
Ay, it was well that he had kept the rum.

He liked his drink: but he had never cared
For soaking by himself, and sitting mum.
Even the best rum tasted better, shared.

THE ROCKLIGHT

Ay, he must keep his mind clear — must not think
Of those two lying dead, or he'd go mad.
The glitter on the lenses made him blink;
The brass glared speckless: work was all he had
To keep his mind clear.   He must keep it clear
And free of fancies, now that there was none,
None left but him to light the lantern — near
On fourteen hours yet till that blazing sun
Should drop into that quiet oily sea,
And he must light . . . though it was not his turn:
'Twas Jacob's,— Jacob, lying quietly
Upon his bed . . . And yet the light would burn
And flash across the darkness just as though
Nothing had happened, white and innocent,
As if Jake's hand had lit it.   None would know,
No seaman steering by it, what it meant
To him, since he'd seen Jacob . . .

                                    But that way
Lay madness.   He, at least, must keep his wits;
Or there'd be none to tell why those two lay . . .
He must keep working, or he'd go to bits.

Ere sunset, he must wind the lantern up.
He'd like to wind it now — but 'twould go round,
And he'd be fancying . . . Neither bite nor sup
He'd touched this morning; and the clicking sound
Would set his light head fancying . . . Jacob wound
So madly that last time, before . . . But he,
He mustn't think of Jacob.   He was bound,
In duty bound, to keep his own wits free
And clear of fancies.

                        He would think of home.
That thought would keep him whole, when all else failed —
The green door; and the doorstep, white as foam;
The window that blazed bright the night he sailed
Out of the moonlit harbour,— clean and gay
'Twould shine this morning in the sun, with white

487

Dimity curtains, and a grand display
Of red geraniums, glowing in the light.
He always liked geraniums: such a red —
It put a heart in you.   His mother, too,
She liked . . .

           And she'd be lying still in bed,
And never dreaming!   If she only knew!
But he, . . . he mustn't think of them just now —
Must keep off fancies . . .

              She'd be lying there,
Sleeping so quietly — her smooth white brow
So calm beneath the wisps of silver hair
Slipped out beneath her mutch-frills.   She had pride
In those fine caps, and ironed them herself.
The very morning that his father'd died,
Drowned in the harbour, turning to the shelf,
She took her iron down, without a word,
And ironed, with her husband lying dead . . .
As they were lying now . . . He never heard
Her speak, or saw her look towards the bed.
She ironed, ironed.   He had thought it queer —
The little shivering lad perched in his chair,
And hungry — though he dared not speak for fear
His father'd wake, and with wet streaming hair
Would rise up from the bed . . .

             He'd thought it strange
Then, but he understood now, understood.
You'd got to work, or let your fancies range;
And fancies played the devil when they could.
They got the upper hand, if you loosed grip
A moment.   Iron frills, or polish brass
To keep a hold upon yourself, not slip
As Jacob slipt . . .

           A very burning-glass
Those lenses were.   He'd have to drop off soon,
And find another job to fill the morn,
And keep him going through the afternoon —
And it was not yet five! . . .

           Ay, he was born
In the very bed where still his mother slept,
And where his father'd lain — a cupboard bed
Let in the wall, more like a bunk, and kept
Decent with curtains drawn from foot to head
By day, though why — but 'twas the women's way:

They always liked things tidy.   They were right —
Better to keep things tidy through the day,
Or there would be the devil's mess by night.
He liked things shipshape, too, himself.   He took
After his mother in more ways than one.
He'd say this for her — she could never brook
A sloven; and she'd made a tidy son.

'Twas well for him that he was tidy, now
That he was left; or how'd he ever keep
His thoughts in hand . . . The Lord alone knew how
He'd keep them tidy, till . . .
                  Yet, she could sleep:
And he was glad, ay, glad that she slept sound.
It did him good, to think of her so still.
It kept his thoughts from running round and round
Like Jacob in the lighted lantern, till . . .
God! They were breaking loose! He must keep hold . . .

On one side, " Albert Edward, Prince of Wales,"
Framed in cut cork, painted to look like gold —
On the other a red frigate, with white sails
Bellying, and a blue pennon fluttering free,
Upon a sea dead calm.   He couldn't think,
As a wee lad, how ever this could be.
And when he'd asked, his father with a wink
Had only answered laughing: Little chaps
Might think they knew a lot, and had sharp eyes.
But only pigs could see the wind.   Perhaps
The painter'd no pig by him to advise.

That was his father's way: he'd always jest,
And chuckle in his beard, with eyes half-shut
And twinkling . . . Strange to think of them at rest
And lightless, those blue eyes, beneath that cut
Where the jagged rock had gashed his brow — the day
His wife kept ironing those snowy frills,
To keep herself from thinking how he lay,
And wouldn't jest again.   It's that that kills —
The thinking over . . .
               Jacob jested, too:
He'd always some new game, was full of chaff.
The very morn before the lantern drew . . .
Yesterday morn that was, he heard him laugh . . .

Yesterday morn! And was it just last night
He'd wakened, startled; and run out, to find
Jacob within the lantern, round the light
Fluttering like a moth, naked and blind
And laughing . . . Peter staring, turned to stone . . .
The struggle . . . Peter killed . . .
                        And he must keep
His mind clear at all costs, himself, alone
On that grey naked rock of the great deep,
Full forty mile from shore — where there were men
Alive and breathing at this moment — ay,
Men deep in easy slumber even then,
Who yet would waken and look on the sky.

He must keep his mind clear, to light the lamp
Ere sunset: ay, and clear the long night through
To tell how they had died. He mustn't scamp
The truth — and yet 'twas little that he knew . . .
What had come over Jacob in the night
To send him mad and stripping himself bare . . .
And how he'd ever climbed into the light —
And it revolving . . . and the heat and glare!
No wonder he'd gone blind — the lenses burning
And blazing round him; and in each he'd see
A little naked self . . . and turning, turning,
Till, blinded, scorched, and laughing crazily,
He'd dropped: and Peter . . . Peter might have known
The truth, if he had lived to tell the tale —
But Peter'd tripped . . . and he was left alone . . .

Just thirty hours till he should see the sail
Bringing them food and letters — food for them;
Letters from home for them . . . and here was he
Shuddering like a boat from stern to stem
When a wave takes it broadside suddenly.
He must keep his mind clear . . .
                        His mother lay
Peacefully slumbering. And she, poor soul,
Had kept her mind clear, ironing that day —
Had kept her wits about her, sound and whole —
And for his sake. Ay, where would he have been,
If she had let her fancies have their way
That morning, having seen what she had seen!
He'd thought it queer . . . But it was no child's play

Keeping the upper hand of your own wits.
He knew that now. If only for her sake.
He mustn't let his fancies champ their bits
Until they foamed . . . He must jam on the brake
Or he . . .
                He must think how his mother slept;
How soon she would be getting out of bed;
Would dress; and breakfast by the window, kept
So lively with geraniums blazing red;
Would open the green door, and wash the stone,
Foam-white enough already: then, maybe,
She'd take her iron down, and, all alone,
Would iron, iron, iron steadily —
Keeping her fancies quiet, till he came . . .

To-morrow, he'd be home: he'd see the white
Welcoming threshold, and the window's flame,
And her grave eyes kindling with kindly light.

THE PLOUGH

He sniffed the clean and eager smell
Of crushed wild garlic, as he thrust
Beneath the sallows: and a spell
He stood there munching a thick crust —
The fresh tang giving keener zest
To bread and cheese; and watched a pair
Of wagtails preening wing and breast,
Then running — flirting tails in air,
And pied plumes sleeked to silky sheen —
Chasing each other in and out
The wet wild garlic's white and green.

And then remembering, with a shout,
And rattle whirring, he ran back
Again into the Fair Maid's Mead,
To scare the rascal thieves and black
That flocked from far and near to feed
Upon the sprouting grain. As one
They rose with clapping rustling wings —
Rooks, starlings, pigeons, in the sun
Circling about him in wide rings,
And plovers hovering over him
In mazy, interweaving flight —
Until it made his young wits swim
To see them up against the light,
A dazzling dance of black and white
Against the clear blue April sky —
Wings on wings in flashing flight
Swooping low and soaring high —
Swooping, soaring, fluttering, flapping,
Tossing, tumbling, swerving, dipping,
Chattering, cawing, creaking, clapping,
Till he felt his senses slipping —
And gripped his corncrake rattle tight,
And flourished it above his head
Till every bird was out of sight:
And laughed, when all had flown and fled,

To think that he, and all alone,
Could put so many thieves to rout.

Then sitting down upon a stone
He wondered if the school were out —
The school where, only yesterday,
He'd sat at work among his mates —
At work that now seemed children's play,
With pens and pencils, books and slates —
Although he'd liked it well enough,
The hum and scuffling of the school,
And hadn't cared when Grim-and-Gruff
Would call him dunderhead and fool.

And he could see them sitting there —
His class-mates, in the lime-washed room,
With fingers inked and towzled hair —
Bill Baxter with red cheeks abloom,
And bright black eyes; and Ginger Jim
With freckled face and solemn look,
Who'd wink a pale blue eye at him,
Then sit intent upon his book,
While, caught a-giggle, he was caned.

He'd liked that room, he'd liked it all —
The window steaming when it rained;
The sunlight dancing on the wall
Among the glossy charts and maps;
The blotchy stain beside the clock
That only he of all the chaps
Knew for a chart of Dead Man's Rock
That lies in Tiger Island Bay —
The reef on which the schooners split
And founder, that would bear away
The treasure-chest of Cut-Throat-Kit,
That's buried under Black Bill's bones
Beneath the purple pepper-tree . . .
A trail of clean-sucked cherry-stones,
Which you must follow carefully,
Across the dunes of yellow sand
Leads winding upward from the beach
Till, with a pistol in each hand,
And cutlass 'twixt your teeth, you reach . . .

Plumping their fat crops peacefully
Were plovers, pigeons, starlings, rooks,
Feeding on every side while he
Was in the land of storybooks.
He raised his rattle with a shout
And scattered them with yell and crake . . .
A man must mind what he's about
And keep his silly wits awake,
Not go woolgathering, if he'd earn
His wage.   And soon, no schoolboy now,
He'd take on a man's job, and learn
To build a rick, and drive the plough,
Like father . . .
               Up against the sky
Beyond the spinney and the stream,
With easy stride and steady eye
He saw his father drive his team,
Turning the red marl gleaming wet
Into long furrows clean and true.
And dreaming there, he longed to set
His young hand to the ploughshare too.

THE OLD PIPER

With ears undulled of age, all night he heard
The April singing of the Otterburn.
His wife slept quietly and never stirred,
Though he was restless and must toss and turn —
But she kept going all the day, while he
Was just a useless bundle in a chair,
And couldn't do a hand's turn — seventy-three,
And crippled with rheumatics . . .

                         It was rare,
Hearing the curlew piping in the dark!
'Twas queer he'd got his hearing still so keen.
He'd be so bothered if he couldn't hark
To curlew piping, shrill and clear and clean —
Ay, clean, that note!

                 His piping days were done,
His fingers numb and stiff. And by the peat
All winter, or all summer in the sun,
He'd sit beside the threshold, in his seat,
Day-long, and listen to the Otterburn
That sang each day and night a different tune.
It knew more airs than he could ever learn
Upon the small-pipes. January to June,
And June to January, every hour
It changed its music. Now 'twas shrilling clear
In a high tinkling treble with a power
Of mellow undertones. And to his ear
Even the spates of winter over stones
Made no dull tuneless thundering; he heard
No single roar, but half a hundred tones
Eddying and swirling; blending, yet unblurred;
No dull-edged note, but each one razor-keen —
Though supple as the sword-blades interlaced
Over the morris-dancers' heads — and clean!
But, nay, there was no word for it. 'Twas waste
Of breath to try and put the thing in words,
Though on his pipes he'd get the sense of it,
The feel — ay, even of the calls of birds

He'd get some notion, though low-toned a bit —
His humming drone had not that quality
Of clean-cut piping.   Any shepherd lad
Upon his penny-whistle easily
Could mimic the mere notes.   And yet he had
A gift of feeling, somehow . . . He must try
To-morrow if he couldn't tune his pipes,
Must get his wife to strap them carefully . . .
Hark, a new note among the birds — a snipe's —
A small-pipe's note! . . .
                              Drowsing, he did not wake
Until his wife was stirring.
                              Nor till noon
He told her that he'd half-a-mind to take
His pipes and see if he could turn a tune
If she would fetch them.   And regretfully
She brought the pipes and strapped them on and set
The bellows under his arm, and patiently
She held the reeds to his numb fingers.   Yet
She knew 'twas worse than useless.   Work and years
Had dulled that lively touch: each joint was stiff
And swollen with rheumatics . . .
                              Slowly tears
Ran down his weathered cheeks . . .
                              And then a whiff
Of peat-reek filled his nostrils: and quite still
He sat remembering.   Memory was kind
And stript age off him.
                              And along the hill
By Golden Pots he strove against the wind —
In all his days he never again had known
A wind like thon — on that November day.
For every step that he took forward, blown
Half-a-step backward, slowly he made way
Against it, buffeted and battered numb,
Chilled to the marrow, till he reached his door,
To find Jack Dodd, the pitman piper, come
To play a contest with him . . .
                              Nevermore
There'd be such piping!
                              Ay, Jack Dodd had heard
That he could play — that up among the hills
There was a lad could pipe like any bird,
With half-a-hundred fancy turns and trills,

And give a lead even to Jack himself,
Jack Dodd, the pitmen's champion!

After tea
When they had smoked a while, down from the shelf
He'd reached his own small-pipes; and speedily
They two were at it, playing, tune for tune,
Against each other all the winter's night,
And all next morning till the stroke of noon,
Piping out bravely all their hearts' delight.

He still could see Jack, sitting there, so lean,
Long-backed, broad-shouldered, stooping and white-faced
With cropped black head, and black eyes burning keen;
Tight-lipped, yet smiling gravely: round his waist
His small-pipes strapped, the bellows 'neath his arm,
His nimble fingers lively at the reeds,—
His body swaying to the lilting charm
Of his own magic piping, till great beads
Of sweat were glistening on his low, white brow.

And he himself, a herd-lad, yellow-haired,
With wide eyes even bluer then than now,
Who sat bolt-upright in his chair and stared
Before him at the steady glowing peat
As though each note he played he caught in flight ·
From the loud wind, and in the quivering heat
Could see it dancing to its own delight.

All night the rafters hummed with piping airs,
And candle after candle guttered out;
But not a footstep climbed the creaky stairs
To the dark bedrooms. Turn and turn about,
They piped or listened; while the wind without
Roared round the steading, battering at the door
As though to burst it wide; then with a shout
Swept on across the pitchy leagues of moor.

Pitman and shepherd piping turn for turn,
The airs they loved, till to the melody
Their pulses beat; and their rapt eyes would burn
Thrilled with the sight that each most loved to see —
The pitman, gazing down a gallery
Of glittering black coal, an endless seam:
And through his piping stole the mystery

Of subterranean waters, and of dream
Corridors dwindling everlastingly.

The shepherd, from the top of Windy Gile
Looking o'er range on range of glowing hills,
A world beneath him, stretching, mile on mile,
Brown bent and heather, laced by flashing rills,—
His body flooded with the light that fills
The veins with running gold. And April light
And wind, and all the melody that spills
From tumbling waters, thrilled his pipes that night.

Ay, thon was playing, thon! And nevermore
The world would hear such piping. Jack was dead,
And he, so old and broken.
               By the door
All day he sat remembering; and in bed
He lay beside his sleeping wife all night,
Too spent, too weary, even to toss and turn.
Dawn found him lying, strangely cold and white,
As though still listening to the Otterburn.

THE NEWS

The buzzer boomed, and instantly the clang
Of hammers dropt, just as the fendered bow
Bumped with soft splash against the wharf,— though now
Again within the Yard a hammer rang —
A solitary hammer striking steel
Somewhere aloft — and strangely, stridently
Echoed as though it struck the steely sky
The low, cold, steely sky.
                  She seemed to feel
That hammer in her heart — blow after blow
In a strange clanging hollow seemed to strike
Monotonous, unrelenting, cruel-like —
Her heart that such a little while ago
Had been so full, so happy with its news
Scarce uttered even to itself.
                      It stopt,
That dreadful hammer.   And the silence dropt
Again a moment.   Then a clatter of shoes
And murmur of voices as the men trooped out:
And as each wife with basket and hot can
Hurried towards the gate to meet her man,
She too ran forward, and then stood in doubt
Because among them all she could not see
The face that usually was first of all
To meet her eyes.

                Against the grimy wall
That towered black above her to the sky,
With trembling knuckles to the cold stone pressed
Till the grit seemed to eat into the bone,
And her stretched arm to shake the solid stone,
She stood, and strove to calm her troubled breast —
Her breast, whose trouble of strange happiness
So sweet and so miraculous, as she
Had stood among the chattering company
Upon the ferry-boat, to strange distress
Was changed.   An unknown terror seemed to lie

For her, behind that wall, so cold and hard
And black above her, in the unseen Yard,
Dreadfully quiet now.   Then with a sigh
Of glad relief she ran towards the gate
As he came slowly out, the last of all.

The terror of the hammer and the wall
Fell from her as, a woman to her mate,
She moved with happy heart and smile of greeting —
A young and happy wife whose only thought
Was whether he would like the food she'd brought —
Whose one desire, to watch her husband eating.

With a grave smile he took his bait from her,
And then without a word they moved away
To where some grimy baulks of timber lay
Beside the river, and 'twas quieter
Than in the crowd of munching, squatting men
And chattering wives and children.   As he eat
With absent eyes upon the river set,
She chattered, too, a little now and then
Of household happenings: and then silently
They sat and watched the grimy-flowing stream,
Dazed by the stunning din of hissing steam
Escaping from an anchored boat hard-by,
Each busy with their own thoughts, who till now
Had shared each thought, each feeling, speaking out
Easily, eagerly, without a doubt,
As happy innocent children, anyhow,
The innermost secrets of their wedded life.
So as the dinner hour went swiftly by
They sat there for the first time, troubled, shy —
A silent husband and a silent wife.

But she was only troubled by excess
Of happiness; and as she watched the stream,
She looked upon her life as in a dream,
Recalling all its tale of happiness
Unbroken and unshadowed since she'd met
Her man the first time, eighteen months ago . . .

A keen blue day with sudden flaws of snow
And sudden sunshine, when she first had set
Her wondering eyes upon him — gaily clad

For football in a jersey green and red,
Knees bare beneath white shorts, his curly head
Wind-blown and wet,— and knew him for her lad.

He strode towards her down the windy street —
The wet grey pavements flashing sudden gold,
And gold the unending coils of smoke that rolled
Unceasingly overhead, fired by a fleet
Wild glint of glancing sunlight. On he came
Beside her brother — still a raw uncouth
Young hobbledehoy — a strapping mettled youth
In the first pride of manhood, that wild flame
Touching his hair to fire, his cheeks aglow
With the sharp stinging wind, his arms aswing:
And as she watched, she felt the tingling sting
Of flying flakes, and in a whirl of snow
A moment he was hidden from her sight.
It passed, and then before she was aware,
With white flakes powdering his ruddy hair
He stood before her, laughing in the light,
In all his bravery of red and green
Snow-sprinkled; and she laughed, too. In the sun
They laughed: and in that laughter they were one.

Now as with kindled eyes on the unseen
Grey river she sat gazing, she again
Lived through that moment in a golden dream . . .
And then quite suddenly she saw the stream
Distinct in its cold grimy flowing; then
The present with its deeper happiness
Thrilled her afresh — this wonder strange and new —
This dream in her young body coming true,
Incredible, yet certain none-the-less —
This news, scarce broken to herself, that she
Must break to him. She longed to see his eyes
Kindle to hear it, happy with surprise
When she should break it to him presently.

But she must wait a while yet. Still too strange,
Too wonderful for words, she could not share
Even with him her secret. He sat there
So quietly, little dreaming of the change
That had come over her — but when he knew!
For he was always one for bairns, was John,

And this would be his own, their own.   There shone
A strange new light on all since this was true,
All, all seemed strange, the river and the shore,
The barges and the wharves with timber piled,
And all her world familiar from a child,
Was as a world she'd never seen before.

And he, too, sat with eyes upon the stream
Remembering that day when first the light
Of her young eyes with laughter sparkling bright
Kindled to his; and as he caught the gleam
The life within him quickened suddenly
To fire, and in a world of golden laughter
They stood alone together: and then after,
When he was playing with his mates and he
Hurtled headlong towards the goal, he knew
Her eyes were on him; and for her alone,
Who had the merriest eyes he'd ever known,
He played that afternoon.   Though until then
He'd only played to please himself, somehow
She seemed to have a hold upon him, now.
No longer a boy, a man among grown men,
He'd never have a thought apart from her,
From her, his mate . . .
                              And then that golden night
When in a whirl of melody and light,
Her merry brown eyes flashing merrier,
They rode together in a gilded car
That seemed to roll for ever round and round
In a blind blaze of light and blare of sound,
For ever and for ever, till afar
It seemed to bear them from the surging throng
Of lads and lasses happy in release
From the week's work in yards and factories —
For ever through a land of light and song
While they sat, rapt in silence, hand in hand,
And looked into each other's merry eyes,
They two, together, whirled through Paradise,
A golden glittering, unearthly land,
A land where light and melody were one,
And melody and light, a golden fire
That ran through their young bodies, and desire,
A golden music streaming from the sun,
Filling their veins with golden melody

And singing fire . . .
           And then when quiet fell,
And they together, with so much to tell,
So much to tell each other instantly,
Left the hot throng and roar and glare behind,
Seeking the darker streets, and stood at last
In a dark lane where footsteps seldom passed,
Lit by a far lamp and one glowing blind
That seemed to make the darkness yet more dark
Between the cliffs of houses, black and high,
That soared above them to the starry sky,
A deep blue sky where spark on fiery spark
The stars for them were kindled, as they raised
Their eyes in new-born wonder to the night:
And in a solitude of cold starlight
They stood alone together, hushed, and gazed
Into each other's eyes until speech came:
And underneath the stars they talked and talked . . .

Then he remembered how they two had walked
Along a beach that was one golden flame
Of yellow sand beside a flame-blue sea
The day they wedded, that strange day of dream,
One flame of blue and gold . . .
           The murky stream
Flowed once again before his eyes, and he
Dropt back into the present; and he knew
That he must break the news that suddenly
Had come to him last night as drowsily
He lay beside her — startling, stern and true
Out of the darkness flashing. He must tell
How, as he lay beside her in the night
His heart had told him he must go and fight,
Must throw up everything he loved so well
To go and fight in lands across the sea
Beside the other lads — must throw up all,
His work, his home . . .
           The shadow of the wall
Fell on her once again, and stridently
That hammer struck her heart, as from the stream
She raised her eyes to his, and saw their flame.—
Then back into her heart her glad news came
As John smiled on her; and her golden dream
Once more was all about her as she thought

Of home, the new home that the future held
For them — they three together.   Fear was quelled
By this new happiness that all unsought
Had sprung from the old happiness . . .

                                             And he
Watching her, thought of home, too.   When he stept
With her across the threshold first, and slept
That first night in her arms so quietly,
For the first time in all his life he'd known
All that home meant, or nearly all — for yet
Each night brought him new knowledge as she met
Him, smiling on the clean white threshold-stone
When he returned from labour in the Yard . . .

And she'd be waiting for him soon, while he
Was fighting with his fellows oversea —
She would be waiting for him . . .

                                        It was hard
For him that he must go, as go he must,
But harder far for her: things always fell
Harder upon the women.   It was well
She didn't dream yet . . . He could only trust
She, too, would feel that he had got to go,
Then 'twould not be so hard to go, and yet . . .
Dreaming, he saw the lamplit table, set
With silver pot and cups and plates aglow
For tea in their own kitchen bright and snug,
With her behind the tea-pot — saw it all,
The coloured calendars upon the wall,
The bright fire-irons, and the gay hearthrug
She'd made herself from gaudy rags; his place
Awaiting him, with something hot-and-hot —
His favourite sausages as like as not,
Between two plates for him — as, with clean face
Glowing from washing in the scullery,
And such a hunger on him, he would sink
Content into his chair . . .
                                    'Twas strange to think
All this was over, and so suddenly,—
'Twas strange, and hard . . .
                                    Still gazing on the stream,
Her thoughts, too, were at home.   She heard the patter
Of tiny feet beside her, and the chatter
Of little tongues . . .

                Then loudly through their dream
The buzzer boomed : and all about them rose
The men and women : soon the wives were on
The ferry-boat, now puffing to be gone :
The husbands hurrying, ere the gates should close,
Back to the Yard . . .

                  She, in her dream of gold,
And he, in his new desolation, stood ;
Then soberly, as wife and husband should,
They parted, with their news as yet untold.

DAFFODILS

He liked the daffodils.   He liked to see
Them nodding in the hedgerows cheerily
Along the dusty lanes as he went by —
Nodding and laughing to a fellow — Ay,
Nodding and laughing till you'd almost think
They, too, enjoyed the jest.
                    Without a wink
That solemn butler said it, calm and smug,
Deep-voiced as though he talked into a jug:
" His lordship says he won't require no more
Crocks rivetted or mended till the war
Is over."
         Lord!   He'd asked to have a wire
The moment that his lordship should desire
To celebrate the occasion fittingly
By a wild burst of mending crockery
Like a true Englishman, and hang expense!
He'd had to ask it, though he'd too much sense
To lift a lash or breathe a word before
His lordship's lordship closed the heavy door.
And then he'd laughed.   Lord! but it did him good
That quiet laugh.   And somewhere in the wood
Behind the Hall there, a woodpecker laughed
Right out aloud as though he'd gone clean daft —
Right out aloud he laughed, the brazen bird,
As if he didn't care a straw who heard —
But then he'd not his daily bread to earn
By mending crocks.
               And now at every turn
The daffodils are laughing quietly
Nodding and laughing to themselves, as he
Chuckled: Now there's a patriot, real true-blue!

It seemed the daffodils enjoyed it too —
The fun of it.   He wished that he could see —
Old solemn-mug — them laughing quietly
At him.   But then, he'd never have a dim

Idea they laughed, and, least of all, at him.
He'd never dream they could be laughing at
A butler.
                    'Twould be good to see the fat
Old peach-cheek in his solemn black and starch
Parading in his pompous parlour-march
Across that field of laughing daffodils.
'Twould be a sight to make you skip up hills,
Ay, crutch and all, and never feel your pack,
To see a butler in his starch and black
Among the daffodils, ridiculous
As that old bubbly-jock with strut and fuss —
Though that was rather rough upon the bird!
For all his pride, he didn't look absurd
Among the flowers — nor even that black sow
Grunting and grubbing in among them now.

And he was glad he hadn't got a trade
That starched the mother-wit in you, and made
A man look silly in a field of flowers.
'Twas better mending crocks, although for hours
You hobbled on — ay! and, maybe for days —
Hungry and cold along the muddy ways
Without a job.   And even when the sun
Was shining, 'twas not altogether fun
To lose the chance of earning a few pence
In these days: though 'twas well he'd got the sense
To see the funny side of things.   It cost
You nothing, laughing to yourself.   You lost
Far more by going fiddle-faced through life
Looking for trouble.
                        He would tell his wife
When he got home.   But lord, she'd never see
What tickled him so mightily, not she!
She'd only look up puzzled-like, and say
She didn't wonder at his lordship.   Nay,
With tripe and trotters at the price they were
You'd got to count your coppers and take care
Of every farthing.
                        Jack would see the fun —
Ay, Jack would see the joke.   Jack was his son —
The youngest of the lot.   And, man-alive,
'Twas queer that only one of all the five
Had got a twinkle in him — all the rest

Dull as ditchwater to the merriest jest.
Good lads enough they were, their mother's sons;
And they'd all pluck enough to face the guns
Out at the front.   They'd got their mother's pluck:
And he was proud of them, and wished them luck.
That was no laughing matter — though 'twas well
Maybe if you could crack a joke in hell
And shame the devil.   Jack, at least, would fight
As well as any though his heart was light.
Jack was the boy for fighting and for fun;
And he was glad to think he'd got a son
Who, even facing bloody death, would see
That little joke about the crockery,
And chuckle as he charged.

His thoughts dropped back
Through eighteen years; and he again saw Jack
At the old home beneath the Malvern hills,
A little fellow plucking daffodils,
A little fellow who could scarcely walk,
Yet chuckling as he snapped each juicy stalk
And held up every yellow bloom to smell,
Poking his tiny nose into the bell
And sniffing the fresh scent, and chuckling still
As though he'd secrets with each daffodil.
Ay, he could see again the little fellow
In his blue frock among that laughing yellow,
And plovers in their sheeny black and white
Flirting and tumbling in the morning light
About his curly head.   He still could see,
Shutting his eyes, as plain as plain could be,
Drift upon drift, those long-dead daffodils
Against the far green of the Malvern hills,
Nodding and laughing round his little lad,
As if to see him happy made them glad —
Nodding and laughing . . .

They were nodding now,
The daffodils, and laughing — yet, somehow,
They didn't seem so merry now . . .

And he
Was fighting in a bloody trench maybe
For very life this minute . . .

They missed Jack,
And he would give them all to have him back.

BETWEEN THE LINES

When consciousness came back, he found he lay
Between the opposing fires, but could not tell
On which hand were his friends; and either way
For him to turn was chancy — bullet and shell
Whistling and shrieking over him, as the glare
Of searchlights scoured the darkness to blind day.
He scrambled to his hands and knees ascare,
Dragging his wounded foot through puddled clay,
And tumbled in a hole a shell had scooped
At random in a turnip-field between
The unseen trenches where the foes lay cooped
Through that unending battle of unseen
Dead-locked league-stretching armies; and quite spent
He rolled upon his back within the pit,
And lay secure, thinking of all it meant —
His lying in that little hole, sore hit,
But living, while across the starry sky
Shrapnel and shell went screeching overhead —
Of all it meant that he, Tom Dodd, should lie
Among the Belgian turnips, while his bed . . .

If it were he, indeed, who'd climbed each night,
Fagged with the day's work, up the narrow stair,
And slipt his clothes off in the candle-light,
Too tired to fold them neatly on a chair
The way his mother'd taught him — too dog-tired
After the long day's serving in the shop,
Inquiring what each customer required,
Politely talking weather, fit to drop . . .

And now for fourteen days and nights, at least,
He hadn't had his clothes off; and had lain
In muddy trenches, napping like a beast
With one eye open, under sun and rain
And that unceasing hell-fire . . .
                              It was strange
How things turned out — the chances! You'd just got

To take your luck in life, you couldn't change
Your luck.

        And so here he was lying shot
Who just six months ago had thought to spend
His days behind a counter.   Still, perhaps . . .
And now, God only knew how he would end!

He'd like to know how many of the chaps
Had won back to the trench alive, when he
Had fallen wounded and been left for dead,
If any! . . .
        This was different, certainly,
From selling knots of tape and reels of thread
And knots of tape and reels of thread and knots
Of tape and reels of thread and knots of tape,
Day in, day out, and answering " Have you got's "
And " Do you keep's," till there seemed no escape
From everlasting serving in a shop,
Inquiring what each customer required,
Politely talking weather, fit to drop,
With swollen ankles, tired . . .
        But he was tired
Now.   Every bone was aching, and had ached
For fourteen days and nights in that wet trench —
Just duller when he slept than when he waked —
Crouching for shelter from the steady drench
Of shell and shrapnel . . .
        That old trench, it seemed
Almost like home to him.   He'd slept and fed
And sung and smoked in it, while shrapnel screamed
And shells went whining harmless overhead —
Harmless, at least, as far as he . . .
        But Dick —
Dick hadn't found them harmless yesterday,
At breakfast, when he'd said he couldn't stick
Eating dry bread, and crawled out the back way,
And brought them butter in a lordly dish —
Butter enough for all, and held it high,
Yellow and fresh and clean as you could wish —
When plump upon the plate from out the sky
A shell fell bursting . . . Where the butter went,
God only knew! . . .
        And Dick . . . He dared not think
Of what had come to Dick . . . or what it meant —

The shrieking and the whistling and the stink
He'd lived in fourteen days and nights.   'Twas luck
That he still lived . . . And queer how little then
He seemed to care that Dick . . . Perhaps 'twas pluck
That hardened him — a man among the men —
Perhaps . . . Yet, only think things out a bit,
And he was rabbit-livered, blue with funk!
And he'd liked Dick . . . and yet when Dick was hit,
He hadn't turned a hair.   The meanest skunk
He should have thought would feel it when his mate
Was blown to smithereens — Dick, proud as punch,
Grinning like sin, and holding up the plate —
But he had gone on munching his dry hunch,
Unwinking, till he swallowed the last crumb.

Perhaps 'twas just because he dared not let
His mind run upon Dick, who'd been his chum.
He dared not now, though he could not forget.

Dick took his luck.   And, life or death, 'twas luck
From first to last; and you'd just got to trust
Your luck and grin.   It wasn't so much pluck
As knowing that you'd got to, when needs must,
And better to die grinning . . .
                                                  Quiet now
Had fallen on the night.   On either hand
The guns were quiet.   Cool upon his brow
The quiet darkness brooded, as he scanned
The starry sky.   He'd never seen before
So many stars.   Although, of course, he'd known
That there were stars, somehow before the war
He'd never realised them — so thick-sown,
Millions and millions.   Serving in the shop,
Stars didn't count for much; and then at nights
Strolling the pavements, dull and fit to drop,
You didn't see much but the city lights.
He'd never in his life seen so much sky
As he'd seen this last fortnight.   It was queer
The things war taught you.   He'd a mind to try
To count the stars — they shone so bright and clear.
One, two, three, four . . . Ah, God, but he was tired . . .
Five, six, seven, eight . . .
                                          Yes: it was number eight.
And what was the next thing that she required?

(Too bad of customers to come so late,
At closing-time!)   Again within the shop
He handled knots of tape and reels of thread,
Politely talking weather, fit to drop . . .

When once again the whole sky overhead
Flared blind with searchlights, and the shriek of shell
And scream of shrapnel roused him.   Drowsily
He stared about him wondering.   Then he fell
Into deep dreamless slumber.

    .   .   .   .

                                  He could see
Two dark eyes peeping at him, ere he knew
He was awake, and it again was day —
An August morning burning to clear blue.
The frightened rabbit scuttled . . .
                            Far away,
A sound of firing . . . Up there, in the sky
Big dragon-flies hung hovering . . . Snowballs burst
About them . . .
                Flies and snowballs!   With a cry
He crouched to watch the airmen pass — the first
That he'd seen under fire.   Lord, that was pluck —
Shells bursting all about them — and what nerve!
They took their chance, and trusted to their luck.
At such a dizzy height to dip and swerve,
Dodging the shell-fire . . .
                    Hell! but one was hit,
And tumbling like a pigeon, plump . . .
                        Thank Heaven,
It righted, and then turned; and after it
The whole flock followed safe — four, five, six, seven,
Yes, they were all there safe.   He hoped they'd win
Back to their lines in safety.   They deserved,
Even if they were Germans . . . 'Twas no sin
To wish them luck.   Think how that beggar swerved
Just in the nick of time!
                    He, too, must try
To win back to the lines, though, likely as not,
He'd take the wrong turn: but he couldn't lie
For ever in that hungry hole and rot.
He'd got to take his luck, to take his chance

Of being sniped by foe or friend.   He'd be
With any luck in Germany or France
Or kingdom-come, next morning . . .

       Drearily
The blazing day burnt over him, shot and shell
Whistling and whining ceaselessly.   But light
Faded at last, and as the darkness fell
He rose, and crawled away into the night.

STRAWBERRIES

Since four she had been plucking strawberries:
And it was only eight now; and the sun
Already blazing. There'd be little ease
For her until the endless day was done . . .

Yet, why should she have any ease, while he —
While he . . .
        But there, she mustn't think of him,
Fighting beneath that burning sun, maybe,—
His rifle nigh red-hot, and every limb
Aching for sleep, the sweat dried on his brow,
And baking in the blaze, and such a thirst,
Prickly and choking, she could feel it now
In her own throat. He'd said it was the worst,
In his last letter, worst of all to bear,
That burning thirst — that, and the hellish noise . . .

And she was plucking strawberries: and there
In the cool shadow of the elm their boys,
Their baby-boys, were sleeping quietly . . .

But she was aching too: her head and back
Were one hot blinding ache; and dizzily
Sometimes across her eyes the light swam black
With dancing spots of red . . .
        So ripe and sweet
Among their fresh green leaves the strawberries lay,
Although the earth was baking in the heat,
Burning her soles — and yet the summer day
Was young enough!
        If she could only cram
A handful of fresh berries sweet and cool
Into his mouth, while he . . .
        A red light swam
Before her eyes . . .
        She mustn't think, poor fool,
What he'd be doing now, or she'd go crazed . . .

514

Then what would happen to them left alone —
The little lads!
                    And he would be fair mazed,
When he came back, to see how they had grown,
William and Dick, and how they talked. Two year,
Since he had gone — and he had never set
His eyes upon his youngest son. 'Twas queer
To think he hadn't seen his baby yet,—
And it nigh fourteen months old.
                                    Everything
Was queer in these days. She could never guess
How it had come about that he could bring
Himself to go and fight. 'Twas little less
Than murder to have taken him, and he
So mild and easy-tempered, never one
For drink or picking quarrels hastily . . .
And now he would be fighting in that sun . . .
'Twas quite beyond her. Yet, somehow, it seemed
He'd got to go. She couldn't understand . . .
When they had married, little had they dreamed
What things were coming to! In all the land
There was no gentler husband . . .
                                    It was queer:
She couldn't get the rights of it, no way.
She thought and thought, but couldn't get it clear
Why he'd to leave his own work — making hay
'Twould be this weather — leave his home, and all —
His wife and his young family, and go
To fight in foreign lands, and maybe fall,
Fighting another lad he didn't know,
And had no quarrel with . . .
                                    The world was mad,
Or she was going crazy. Anyhow
She couldn't see the rights of it . . . Her lad
Had thought it right to go, she knew . . .
                                            But now
She mustn't think about it all . . . And so
She'd best stop puzzling, and pluck strawberries . . .

And every woman plucking in the row
Had husband, son, or brother overseas.

Men seemed to see things differently: and still
She wondered sore if even they knew why

They went themselves, almost against their will . . .

But sure enough, that was her baby's cry.
'Twas feeding time: and she'd be glad to rest
Her back a bit.   It always gave her ease,
To feel her baby feeding at her breast,
And pluck to go on gathering strawberries.

THE BLAST-FURNACE

And such a night! But maybe in that mood
'Twas for the best; for he was like to brood —
And he could hardly brood on such a night
With that squall blowing, on this dizzy height
Where he caught every breath of it — the snow
Stinging his cheek, and melting in the glow
Above the furnace, big white flakes that fell
Sizzling upon the red-hot furnace bell:
And the sea roaring, down there in the dark,
So loud to-night he needn't stop to hark —
Four hundred feet below where now he stood.
A lively place to earn a livelihood —
His livelihood, his mother's, and the three
Young sisters', quite a little family
Depending on him now — on him, Jim Burn,
Just nineteen past — to work for them, and earn
Money enough to buy them daily bread
Already . . .
         And his father on the bed
At home . . . gey sudden . . .
                 Nay, he mustn't think:
But shove his trolley to the furnace brink,
And tip his load upon the glowing bell,
Then back again towards the hoist. 'Twas well
He'd work to stop him thinking. He was glad
His mate to-night was not a talky lad —
But Peter, mum-glum Peter, who would stare
With such queer sulky looks upon the flare
When round the dipping bell it shot up high
With roar and flourish into that black sky.
He liked to hear it roaring, liked to see
The great flame leaping skyward suddenly,
Then sinking slowly, as the bell rose up
And covered it again with red-hot cup,
When it would feed more quiet for a time
Upon the meal of ironstone and lime
He'd fetched it in his trolley . . .

Ay, and he,
Trundling his truck along that gallery
High in the air all night to keep it fed —
And all the while his father lying dead
At home — to earn a livelihood. 'Twas strange
To think what it all meant to him — the change . . .

And strange he'd never thought before how queer
It was for him, earning his bread up here
On this blast-furnace, perched on the cliff-top —
Four hundred feet or so, a dizzy drop,
And he'd be feeding fishes in the sea!
How loud it roared to-night, and angrily —
He liked to hear it breaking on the shore,
And the wind's threshing, and the furnace' roar:
And then the sudden quiet, a dead lull,
When you could only hear a frightened gull
Screeching down in the darkness there below,
Or a dog's yelp from the valley, or the snow
Sizzling upon hot iron.   Queer, indeed,
To think that he had never taken heed
Before to-night, or thought about it all.

He'd been a boy till this, and had no call
To turn his mind to thinking seriously.
But he'd grown up since yesterday; and he
Must think a man's thoughts now — since yesterday
When he'd not had a thought but who should play
Full-back for Cleveland Rovers, now that Jack
Had gone to Montreal, or should he back
Old Girl or Cleopatra for the Cup.

In four-and-twenty hours he had grown up . . .
His father, sinking back there on the bed,
With glassy eyes and helpless lolling head . . .
The dropping jaw . . . the breath that didn't come,
Though still he listened for it, frozen numb . . .

And then, his mother . . . but he must not let
His mind run on his mother now.   And yet
He'd often thought his father glum and grim.
He understood now.   It was not for him,
His son, to breathe a word to her, when he,
Her husband, had borne with her patiently

Through all those years.   Ay, now he understood
Much, since he hadn't his own livelihood
To think of only, but five mouths to feed —
And the oldest, the most helpless . . . He had need
To understand a little . . .
                            But to-night
He mustn't brood . . . And what a golden light
The steady spurt of molten slag below
Threw up upon the snow-clouds — and the snow
Drifting down through it in great flakes of gold,
Melting to steam, or driven, white and cold,
Into the darkness on a sudden gust.
And how the cold wind caught him, as he thrust
His empty trolley back towards the hoist,
Straight from the sea, making his dry lips moist
With salty breath.
                    'Twas strange to-night, how he
Was noticing, and seeing suddenly
Things for the first time he'd not seen before,
Though he'd been on this shift at least a score
Of times.   But things were different somehow.   Strange
To think his father's death had wrought the change
And made him see things different — little things:
The sudden flashing of a sea-gull's wings
Out of the dark, bewildered by the glare;
And, when the flame leapt, mum-glum Peter's hair
Kindling a fierier red; the wind; the snow;
The unseen washing of the waves below
About the cliff-foot.   He could almost see,
In fancy, breakers, frothing furiously
Against the crumbling cliffs — the frantic spray
Leaping into the darkness, nigh half-way
Up the sheer height.
                        And now his thoughts dropt back
Into the valley, lying still and black
Behind him — and the mine where other men
Were toiling on their nightshift, even then
Working the ironstone for daily bread,
Their livelihood . . .
                        He saw the little red
Raw row of square brick houses, dark they'd be
And quiet now.   Yet, plainly he could see
The street he lived in — ay, and Number Eight,
His father's house: the rusty iron gate;

The unkempt garden; and the blistered door;
The unwashed doorstep he'd not seen before,
Or, leastways, hadn't noticed; and the bell
That never rang, though he remembered well
His father'd tinkered it, times out of mind;
And in each window, a drawn yellow blind
Broken and grimy — and that blind, to-day
Drawn down for the first time . . .

                         His father lay
In the front bedroom, quiet on the bed . . .
And he, upon his usual shift . . .

                        She'd said,
His mother'd said; he shouldn't take his shift
Before the undertaker'd been to lift . . .
'Twas scarcely decent: that was what she said —
Him working, and his father lying dead,
And hardly cold . . .

                And she, to talk to him,
His son, of decency, there, with that grim
Half-smile still on her husband's cold white face!

He couldn't bide a moment in the place
Listening to her chat-chatter, knowing all
That he knew now . . . But there, he had no call
To blame her, when his father'd never blamed.
He wondered in that room she wasn't shamed . . .

She didn't understand.   He understood,
Now he'd grown up; and had his livelihood,
And theirs, to earn . . .

                Lord, but that was a rare
Fine flourish the flame made, a bonnie flare
Leaping up to the stars.   The snow had stopt:
He hadn't heeded: and the wind had dropt
Suddenly: and the stars were shining clear.
Over the furnace' roaring he could hear
The waves wash-washing; and could see the foam
Lifting and falling down there in the gloam . . .
White as his father's face . . .

                      He'd never heard
His father murmur once — nay, not a word
He'd muttered: he was never one to blame.
And men had got to take things as they came.

IN THE MEADOW

The smell of wet hay in the heat
All morning steaming round him rose,
As, in a kind of nodding doze,
Perched on the hard and jolting seat,
He drove the rattling jangling rake
Round and around the Five Oaks Mead.
With that old mare he scarcely need
To drive at all or keep awake.
Gazing with half-shut, sleepy eyes
At her white flanks and grizzled tail
That flicked and flicked without avail,
To drive away the cloud of flies
That hovered, closing and unclosing,
A shimmering hum and humming shimmer,
Dwindling dim and ever dimmer
In his dazzled sight, till, dozing,
He seemed to hear a murmuring stream
And gaze into a rippling pool
Beneath thick branches dark and cool —
And gazing, gazing till a gleam
Within the darkness caught his eyes,
He saw there smiling up at him
A young girl's face, now rippling dim,
Now flashing clear . . .
              Without surprise
He marked the eyes translucent blue,
The full red lips that seemed to speak,
The curves of rounded chin and cheek,
The low, broad brow, sun-tanned . . .
                   He knew
That face, yet could not call to mind
Where he had seen it; and in vain
Strove to recall . . . when sudden rain
Crashed down and made the clear pool blind,
And it was lost . . .
            And, with a jerk
That well-nigh shook him from his seat,
He wakened to the steamy heat

And clank and rattle.
                              Still at work
The stolid mare kept on; and still
Over her hot, white flanks the flies
Hung humming. And his dazzled eyes
Closed gradually again, until
He dozed . . .
                      And stood within the door
Of Dinchill dairy, drinking there
Thirst-quenching draughts of stone-cold air —
The scoured white shelves and sanded floor
And shallow milk-pans creamy-white
Gleamed coldly in the dusky light . . .
And then he saw her, stooping down
Over a milk-pan, while her eyes
Looked up at him without surprise
Over the shoulder of her gown —
Her fresh print gown of speedwell blue . . .
The eyes that looked out of the cool
Untroubled crystal of the pool
Looked into his again.
                              He knew
Those eyes now . . .
                              From his dreamy doze
A sudden jolting of the rake
Aroused him.
                      Startled broad awake
He sat upright, lost in amaze
That he should dream of her — that lass! —
And see her face within the pool!

He'd known her always. Why, at school
They'd sat together in the class.
He'd always liked her well enough,
Young Polly Dale — and they had played
At Prisoners' Base and Who's Afraid,
At Tiggy and at Blindman's Buff,
A hundred times together . . .
                                        Ay,
He'd always known her . . . It was strange,
Though he had noticed that a change
Had come upon her — she was shy,
And quieter, since she left school
And put her hair up — he'd not seen

Her face, till from the glancing sheen
It looked up at him from the pool . . .

He'd always known her.   Every day,
He'd nod to her as they would pass.
He'd always known her, as a lass . . .
He'd never know her just that way
Again now . . .
               In a different wise
They'd meet — for how could he forget
His dream . . . The next time that they met
He'd look into a woman's eyes.

PARTNERS

He'd got to see it through. Ay, that was plain —
Plain as the damning figures on that page
Which burnt and bit themselves into his brain
Since he'd first lighted on them — such an age
Since he'd first lighted on them! though the clock
Had only ticked one hour out — its white face
And black hands counting time alone —
                                    The shock
Had dropped him out of time and out of space
Into the dead void of eternity,
Lightless and aching, where his soul hung dead
With wide set staring eyes that still could see
Those damning figures burning hugely red
On the low aching dome of the black heaven
That crushed upon his temples — glaring bright —
10,711 —
Searing his eyeballs . . .
                          Yet his living sight
Was fixed on the white ledger, while he sat
Before his office-table in his chair —
The chair he'd taken when he'd hung his hat
Within the cupboard door, and brushed his hair,
And stood a moment, humming " Chevy Chase,"
His hands beneath his coat-tails, by the grate,
Warming his back, and thinking of a case
They'd won outright with costs, and . . .
                                    Phil was late:
But Phil was Phil.   At home they used to call
His brother " Better-late."   At every turn
He'd had to wait for Phil.   And after all
There wasn't so much doing, now that concern . . .

And little thinking anything was wrong,
Laying his hand upon his own armchair
To draw it out, still humming the old song,
He'd seen the note from Philip lying there
Upon the open ledger.

Once, he read
The truth, unrealising, and again.
But only two words echoed through his head,
And buzzed uncomprehended in his brain —
" Embezzled " and " absconded."

                            Phil had spelt
His shame out boldly in his boyish hand.
And then those figures . . .

                        Dizzily he felt
The truth burn through him.   He could hardly stand,
But sank into his chair with eyes set wide
Upon those damning figures, murmuring " Phil! "
And listening to the whirr of wheels outside,
And sparrows cheeping on the window-sill —
Still murmuring " Phil!   Poor Phil! "

                            But Phil was gone:
And he was left alone to bear the brunt . . .
" Phil!   Little Phil! "

                    And still the morning shone
Bright at the window . . .

                        Callous, curt and blunt,
The world would call his brother . . . not that name!
And yet names mattered little at this pass.
He'd known that Phil was slack . . . but this!

                                    The blame
Was his as much as Phil's.   As in a glass
Darkly, he saw he'd been to blame as well:
And he would bear the blame.   Had he not known
That Phil was slack?   For all that he could tell,
If he'd looked after Phil, this might . . .

                                    Alone
He'd got to face the music.   He was glad
He was alone . . . And yet, for Phil's own sake
If he had only had the pluck, poor lad,
To see the thing through like a man, and take
His punishment!

                    For him, was no escape,
Either by Phil's road, or that darker road.
He knew the cost, and how the thing would shape —
Too well he knew the full weight of the load
He strapped upon his shoulders.   It was just
That he should bear the burden on his back.
He'd trusted Phil; and he'd no right to trust
Even his brother, knowing he was slack,

When other people's money was at stake.
He'd, too, been slack: and slackness was a crime —
The deadliest crime of all . . .

                        And broad awake,
As in a nightmare he was " doing time "
Already . . .

              Yet, he'd only trusted Phil —
His brother, Phil — and it had come to this!

Always before whenever things went ill
His brother'd turned to him for help; and his
Had always been the hand stretched out to him.
Now Phil had fled even him.   If he'd but known!

Brooding he saw with tender eyes grown dim
Phil running down that endless road alone —
Phil running from himself down that dark road —
The road which leads nowhither, which is hell:
And yearning towards him, bowed beneath his load,
And murmuring " Little Phil! " . . .

                     Again he fell
Into the dead void of eternity,
Lightless and aching, where his soul hung dead
With wide-set staring eyes that still could see
Those damning figures, burning hugely red
On the low aching dome of the black heaven
That crushed upon his temples — glaring bright —
10,711 —
Searing his eyeballs . . .

                When a ripple of light
Dappled his desk . . .

              And they were boys together,
Rambling the hills of home that April day,
Stumbling and plunging knee-deep through the heather
Towards Hallypike, the little lough that lay
Glancing and gleaming in the sun, to search
For eggs of inland-breeding gulls.   He heard
The curlews piping; saw a blackcock perch
Upon a dyke hard-by — a lordly bird
With queer curled tail.   And soon they reached the edge —
The quaggy edge of Hallypike.   And then
The gulls rose at them screaming from the sedge
With flapping wings.   And for a while like men
They stood their ground among the quaking moss,

Until half-blinded by the dazzling white
Of interweaving wings, and at a loss
Which way to turn, they only thought of flight
From those fierce cruel beaks and hungry eyes —
Yet stood transfixed, each on a quaking clump,
With hands to ears to shut out those wild cries.
Then the gulls closed on Phil; and with a jump
And one shrill yell he'd plunged into the lake
Half-crazed with terror. Only just in time
He'd stumbled after through the quag aquake
And caught him by the coat; and through black slime
Had dragged him into safety, far away
From the horror of white wings and beaks and eyes.
And he remembered now how Philip lay
Sobbing upon his bosom . . .

                      Now those cries
Were threatening Phil again; and he was caught
Blind in a beating, baffling, yelling hell
Of wings and beaks and eyes. And there was naught
That he could do for him . . .

                      Once more he fell
Into the dead void of eternity,
Lightless and aching, and his soul hung dead
With wide set staring eyes that still could see
Those damning figures, burning hugely red
On the low aching dome of the black heaven
That crushed upon his temples — glaring bright —
10,711
Searing his eyeballs . . . Then the pitchy night
Rolled by . . .

             And now that summer noon they sat
In the shallows of Broomlee lake, the water warm
About their chins, and talked of this and that;
And heeded nothing of the coming storm,
Or the strange breathless stillness everywhere
On which the dull note of the cuckoo fell
Monotonously beating through dead air,
A throbbing pulse of heat made audible.
And even when the sky was brooding grey
They'd slowly dressed, and started to walk round
The mile-long lake: but when they'd got half-way,
A heavy fear fell on them; and they found
That they were clutching hands. The still lough gleamed
Livid before them 'neath a livid sky

Sleek and unrippling . . . Suddenly they screamed
And ran headlong for home they knew not why —
Ran stumbling through the heath, and never stopped —
And still hot brooding horror on them pressed
When they had climbed up Sewingshields, and dropped
Dead-beat beneath the dyke.   And on his breast
Poor frightened Phil had sobbed himself to sleep.

And even when the crashing thunder came,
Phil snuggled close in slumber sound and deep.
And he alone had watched the lightning flame
Across the fells, and flash on Hallypike . . .

And in his office chair, he felt once more
His back against the sharp stones of the dyke,
And Phil's hot clutching arms . . .

                                        An outer door
Banged in the wind, and roused him . . .

                                        He was glad,
In spite of all, to think he'd trusted Phil.
He'd got to see it through . . .

                                        He saw the lad,
His little frightened brother crouching still
Beneath the brooding horror of the sky.
That he might take him in his arms once more!

Now, he must pull himself together, ay!
For there was some one tapping at the door.

THE ELM

The wind had caught the elm at last.
He'd lain all night and wondered how
'Twas bearing up against the blast:
And it was down for ever now,
Snapt like a match-stick.   He, at dawn,
Had risen from his sleepless bed,
And, hobbling to the window, drawn
The blind up, and had seen, instead
Of that brave tree against the sky,
Thrust up into the windless blue
A broken stump not ten feet high . . .

And it was changed, the world he knew,
The world he'd known since he, tip-toe,
Had first looked out beneath the eaves,
And seen that tree at dawn, aglow,
Soaring with all its countless leaves
In their first glory of fresh green,
Like a big flame above the mead.

How many mornings he had seen
It soaring since — well, it would need
A better head to figure out
Than his, now he was seventy-five,
And failing fast without a doubt —
The last of fifteen, left alive,
That in that very room were born,
Ay, and upon that very bed
He'd left at daybreak.
                              Many a morn
He'd seen it, stark against the red
Of winter sunrise, or in Spring —
Some April morning, dewy-clear,
With all its green buds glittering
In the first sunbeams, soaring sheer
Out of low mist.

           The morn he wed
It seemed with glittering jewels hung . . .

And fifty year, his wife was dead —
And she, so merry-eyed and young . . .

And it was black the night she died,
Dead black against the starry sky,
When he had flung the window wide
Upon the night so crazily,
Instead of drawing down the blind
As he had meant.   He was so dazed,
And fumbled so, he couldn't find
The hasp to pull it to, though crazed
To shut them out, that starry night,
And that great funeral-plume of black,
So awful in the cold starlight.
He'd fumbled till they drew him back,
And closed it for him . . .
                   And for long
At night he couldn't bear to see
An elm against the stars.
                     'Twas wrong,
He knew, to blame an innocent tree —
Though some folk hated elms, and thought
Them evil: for their great boughs fell
So suddenly . . .
                George Stubbs was caught
And crushed to death.   You couldn't tell
What brought that great bough crashing there,
Just where George sat — his cider-keg
Raised to his lips — for all the air
Was still as death . . . And just one leg
Stuck silly-like out of the leaves,
When Seth waked up ten yards away
Where he'd been snoozing 'mid the sheaves.

'Twas queer-like; but you couldn't say
The tree itself had been to blame.
That bough was rotten through and through,
And would have fallen just the same
Though George had not been there . . .
                         'Twas true
That undertakers mostly made

Cheap coffins out of elm . . .

                          But he,
Well, he could never feel afraid
Of any living thing.   That tree,
He'd seemed to hate it for a time
After she'd died . . . And yet somehow
You can't keep hating without rhyme
Or reason any live thing.

                        Now
He grieved to see it, fallen low,
With almost every branch and bough
Smashed into splinters.   All that snow,
A dead-weight, and that heavy blast,
Had dragged it down: and at his feet
It lay, the mighty tree, at last.

And he could make its trunk his seat
And rest awhile this winter's noon
In the warm sunshine.   He could just
Hobble so far.   And very soon
He'd lie as low himself.   He'd trust
His body to that wood.

                     Old tree,
So proud and brave this many a year,
Now brought so low . . .

                   Ah! there was he,
His grandson, Jo, with never a fear
Riding a bough unbroken yet —
A madcap, like his father, Jim!
He'd teach him sense, if he could get
Behind him with a stick, the limb!

THE DOCTOR

He'd soon be home. The car was running well,
Considering what she'd been through, since the bell
Tumbled him out again — just as his head
Sank in the pillow, glad to get to bed
After the last night's watching, and a day
Of travelling snowy roads without a stay —
To find the tall young shepherd at the door.

"The wife's gey bad in child-bed "— and no more
He'd said till they were seated in the car,
And he was asked, Where to? and was it far?
"The Scalp " he'd said —" Some fifteen mile or so."

And they'd set out through blinding squalls of snow
To climb the hills. The car could scarcely crawl
At times, she skidded so; and with that squall
Clean in his eyes he scarcely saw to steer —
His big lamps only lit a few yards clear —

But those young eyes beside him seemed to pierce
The fifteen miles of smother fuming fierce
Between the husband and his home — the light
In that far bedroom window held his sight,
As though he saw clean through the blinding squall
To the little square stone steading that held all
His heart — so solitary, bleak and grey
Among the snow-drifts on the windy brae,
Beyond the burn that, swollen, loud and black
Threatened the single plank that kept the track
Between them and the outside world secure.
If that were gone, when he got back, for sure
They'd have to plunge waist-deep in that black spate
And cling for life upon the old sheep-gate,
If it were not gone too, to cross at all . . .

And she! He saw the shadow on the wall
Behind the bed, his mother's as she bent

532

To comfort Mary, for a moment spent
By the long agony . . . That shadow seemed
So black and threatening, and the candle gleamed
So strangely in those wild bright eyes . . .

                                        They'd be
Lucky to reach the bank at all: for he
Had been through that burn once on such a night:
And he remembered how he'd had to fight
The frothing flood, rolled over, beaten, bruised,
And well-nigh dragged down under, though well used
To every mood and temper of the burn.

Yet, though he gazed so far, he missed no turn
In all those climbing miles of snow-blind way
Until the car stopt dead by Gallows' Brae,
And they'd to leave her underneath a dyke,
And plunge knee-deep through drift-choked slack and syke
Until they reached the plank that still held fast,
Though quivering underfoot in that wild blast
Like a stretched clothes-line. Dizzily they crossed
Above that brawling blackness, torn and tossed
To flashing spray about the lantern. Then
Setting their teeth, they took the brae, like men
At desperate hazard charging certain death:
And nigh the crest the doctor reeled — his breath
Knocked out of him, and sinking helplessly
Knew nothing till he wakened drowsily
Before the peat, and found himself alone
In a strange kitchen.
                        But a heavy moan
Just overhead recalled him, and he leapt
Instantly to his feet, alert, and crept
Upstairs with noiseless step until he came
To the low bedroom, where the candle flame
Showed the old woman, standing by the bed
On which the young wife lay. His noiseless tread
Scarce startling them, he paused a moment while
Those strained white lips and wild eyes strove to smile
Bravely and tenderly as the husband bent
Over the bed to kiss her, and then went
Without a word, closing the creaking door,
And crept downstairs on tiptoe, and once more
The room was filled with moaning.

   .   .   .   .   .   .

                                        When at last
His part was done, and danger safely past,
And into a wintry world with lusty crying
That little life had ventured, and was lying
Beside the drowsy mother on the bed,
Downstairs the doctor stole with noiseless tread,
And, entering the kitchen quietly,
Saw the young father gazing fearfully
Into the fire with dazed unseeing eyes.
He spoke to him: and still he did not rise,
But sat there staring with that senseless gaze
Set on the peat that with a sudden blaze
Lit up his drawn face, bloodless 'neath its tan.
But when the doctor stooped and touched the man
Upon the shoulder, starting to his feet
He staggered, almost falling in the peat,
Whispering " She's safe!   She's safe! "
                                     And then he leapt
Suddenly up the stair.   The doctor crept
Speedily after him without a sound:
But when he reached the upper room he found
He wasn't needed.   The young husband bent
Over his wife and baby, quiet, content:
Then the wife stirred, opening her eyes, and smiled
And they together looked upon their child.

The doctor drowsed till dawn beside the peat,
Napping uneasily in the high-backed seat,
Half-conscious of the storm that shook the pane
And rattled at the door . . .
                                And now again
He seemed to stand beside the lonely bed
He'd stood beside last night — the old man, dead
With staring eyes, dropt jaw, and rigid grin
That held the stark white features, peaked and thin —
The old man, left alone, with not a friend
To make his body seemly in the end,
Or close his eyes . . .
                         And then the lusty cry
Of that young baby screaming hungrily
Broke through his dream . . .

         .   .   .   .

                           The car was running well.

He'd soon be home, and sleeping — till the bell
Should rouse him to a world of old men dying
Alone, and hungry newborn babies crying.

THE LAMP

She couldn't bring herself to bar the door —
And him on the wrong side of it.   Nevermore
She'd hear his footstep on the threshold-stone . . .

"You're not afraid to lie all night alone,
And Jim but newly drowned?" they'd asked: and she
Had turned upon her neighbours wonderingly.
"Afraid of what?" she said.   "Afraid of him";
The neighbours answered.   "Me — afraid of Jim!
And after all these years!" she cried —" and he —
How can you think that he'd bring harm to me?
You know him better, surely, even you!
And I . . ."   Then they had left her, for they knew
Too well that any word that they could say
Would help her nothing.
                When they'd gone away,
Leaving her to her trouble, she arose,
And, taking from the kist his Sunday clothes,
Folded so neatly, kept so carefully
In camphor, free of moth, half-absently
She shook them out, and hung them up to air
Before the fire upon his high-backed chair:
And then when they were aired she folded them
Carefully, seam to seam and hem to hem,
And smoothing them with tender hands, again
She laid them in the kist where they had lain
Six days a week for hard on forty year . . .

Ay, forty year they'd shared each hope and fear —
They two, together — yet she might not tend
With loving hands his body in the end.
The sea had taken him from her.   And she —
She could do nothing for him now.   The sea
Had taken him from her.   And nevermore
Might she do anything for him . . .
                   The door
Flapped in the wind.   She shut and snecked it tight,

But did not bolt it.   Then she set a light
In the white-curtained window, where it shone
As clearly as on each night that he had gone
Out with the boats in all that forty year,
And each night she had watched it burning clear,
Alone and wakeful . . . and, though lonelier,
She'd lie to-night as many a night she'd lain
On her left side, with face turned towards the pane,
So that, if she should wake, at once she'd see
If still her beacon-light burned steadily,
Feeling that, maybe, somewhere in the night
Of those dark waters he could see the light
Far-off and very dim, a little spark
Of comfort burning for him in the dark,
And, even though it should dwindle from his sight,
It seemed to her that he must feel the light
Burning within his heart, the light of home . . .

From those black cruel waters sudden foam
Flashed as she gazed; and with a shuddering stir,
As though cold drowning waves went over her,
She stood a moment gasping.   Then she turned
From the bright window where her watch-light burned,
And, taking off her clothes, crept into bed
To see if she could sleep.   But when her head
Touched the cold pillow, such hot restlessness
She felt, she'd half-a-mind to rise and dress
Each moment, as she tossed from side to side.
The bed to-night seemed very big and wide
And hard and cold to her, though a hot ache
Held her whole body tingling wide awake
Turning and tossing half the endless night.

Then quieter she lay, and watched the light
Burning so steadily, until the flame
Dazzled her eyes, and golden memories came
Out of the past to comfort her.   She lay
Remembering,— remembering that day
Nigh twenty years since when she'd thought him drowned,
And after all . . .
                    She heard again the sound
Of seas that swept a solid wall of green,
Such seas as living eye had never seen,
Over the rock-bound harbour, with a roar

Rushing the beach, tossing against the door
Driftwood and old cork-floats, slashing the pane
With flying weed again and yet again,
As toppling to disaster, sea on sea
Beneath that crashing wind broke furiously
Almost upon the very threshold-stone
In white tumultuous thunder.   All alone
She watched through that long morn: too much afraid
To stir or do a hand's turn, her heart prayed
One prayer unceasingly, though not a word
Escaped her lips; till in a lull she heard
A neighbour call out that the *Morning Star*
Had gone ashore somewhere beyond Hell Scar,
Hard by the Wick, and all . . . and then the roar
Drowned everything . . .

                  And how she reached the door
She never knew.   She found herself outside
Suddenly face to face with that mad tide,
Battling for breath against a wind that fought
Each inch with her, as she turned North, and caught
Her bodily, and flung her reeling back
A dozen times before she reached the track
That runs along the crag-top to the Head.
Bent double, still she struggled on, half-dead,
For not a moment could she stand upright
Against that wind, striving with all her might
To reach the Wick.   She struggled through that wind
As through cold clinging water, deaf and blind;
And numb and heavy in that icy air
Her battered body felt, as though, stark-bare,
She floundered in deep seas.   Once in a lull
Flat on her face she fell.   A startled gull
Rose skirling at her; and with burning eyes
She lay a moment, far too scared to rise,
Staring into a gully, black as night,
In which the seething waters frothing white
Thundered from crag to crag, and baffled leapt
A hundred feet in air.   She'd nearly stept
Into that gully.   Just in time the wind
Had dropt.   One moment more, and headlong, blind,
She'd tumbled into that pit of death . . . and Jim,
If he were living yet . . .

                  The thought of him
Startled her to her feet: and on once more

Against a fiercer wind along the shore
She struggled with set teeth, and dragging hair
Drenched in the sousing spray that leapt in air
Spinning and hissing, smiting her like hail.

Then when it almost seemed that she must fail
To reach the Wick, alive or dead, she found
That she was there already.   To the ground
She sank, dead-beat.   Almost too faint and weak
To lift her head, her wild eyes sought the creek;
But there she saw no sign of boat or man —
Only a furious smother of seas that ran
Along the slanting jetty ceaselessly.
Groping for life, she searched that spumy sea
For sail or sign in vain: then knew no more . . .
Till she was lifted by strong arms that bore
Her safely through the storm, lying at rest
Without a care upon her husband's breast
Unquestioning, till she reached home, content
To feel his arms about her, as he bent
Over her tenderly and breathed her name.

And then she heard how, back from death, he came
Unscathed to her, by some strange mercy thrown
Alive almost upon his threshold-stone:
When, hearing where she'd gone, he'd followed her
Hot-foot . . .
                    The breath of dawn began to blur
The shining pane with mist . . . And nevermore
His foot would follow her along that shore.
The sea had taken him from her, at last,
Had taken him to keep . . .
                                    Then from the past
She waked with eyes that looked beyond the light,
Still burning clearly, into the lingering night,
Black yet, beyond the streaming window-pane
Down which big glistening drops of gentle rain
Trickled until they dazzled her; and she lay
Again remembering — how ere break of day
When she was young she'd had to rise and go
Along the crag-top some five mile or so,
With other lads and lasses, to Skateraw
To gather bait . . .
                          Again her young eyes saw

Those silent figures with their creels, dead-black
Against the stars, climbing the sheer cliff-track
In single file before her, or quite bright
As suddenly the light-house flashed its light
Full on them, stepping up out of the night
On to the day-bright crag-top — kindling white,
A moment, windy hair and streaming grass.
Again she trudged, a drowsy little lass,
The youngest of them all, across dim fields
By sleeping farms and ruined roofless bields,
Frightened by angry dogs that, roused from sleep,
Yelped after them, or by a startled sheep
That scurried by her suddenly, while she
Was staring at a ship's lights out at sea,
With dreaming eyes, or counting countless stars
That twinkled bright beyond the jagged scars:
Or stumbled over a slippery shingle-beach
Beneath her creel, and shuddered at the screech
And sudden clamour of wings that round her flapped.
Again she felt that cruel cold.   Though hapt
In the big shawl, the raw wind searched her through
Till every bone ached.   Then once more she knew
Brief respite when at last they reached Skateraw
And rested till the dawn.
                                        Again she saw
Those dark groups sitting quiet in the night
Awaiting the first blink of morning-light,
To set to work gathering the bait, while she
Sang to them as they sat beside the sea.
They always made her sing, for she'd a voice
When she was young, she had, and such a choice
Of words and airs by heart: and she was glad
To turn a tune for any lass or lad
Who'd ask her, always glad to hear them say:
" Come, Singing Sally, give us ' Duncan Gray,'
' The De'il among the Tailors,' ' Elsie Marley,'
' The Keel-Row ' or ' The Wind among the Barley ' ";
And always gladdest when 'twas Jim would ask.

Again, as they would settle to their task
Of gathering clammy mussels, that cold ache
Stole through her bones.   It seemed her back must break
Each time she stooped, or lifted up her head,
Though still she worked with fingers raw and red

Until her creel was filled.   But, toiling back,
Staggering beneath her load along the track,
Jim would come up with her and take her creel
And bear it for her, if she'd sing a reel
To keep their hearts up as they trudged along.
Half-numb with sleep, she'd start a dancing-song,
And sing, the fresh wind blowing in her face,
Until the dancing blood began to race
Through her young body, and her heart grew light,
Forgetting all the labours of the night . . .
Once more she walked light-foot to that gay air,
The wind of morning fresh on face and hair,
A girl again . . .
              And Jim, 'twas always he
Who bore her burden for her . . .
                   Quietly
With eyes upon the golden lamp she lay,
While, all unseen of her, the winter day
Behind the dim wet pane broke bleak and cold.

She seemed to look upon a dawn of gold
That kindled every dancing wave to glee
As she walked homeward singing by the sea,
As she walked homeward with the windy stir
Fresh in her flying hair, and over her
Jim leant — young lucky Jim — a kindly lad
Taking the creel; and her girl's heart was glad
As . . .
      . . . clasped within each other's arms, the deep
Closed over them . . .
              Smiling, she fell asleep.

THE PLATELAYER

Tapping the rails as he went by
And driving the slack wedges tight,
He walked towards the morning sky
Between two golden lines of light
That dwindled slowly into one
Sheer golden rail that ran right on
Over the fells into the sun.

And dazzling in his eyes it shone,
That golden track, as left and right
He swung his clinking hammer — ay,
'Twas dazzling after that long night
In Hindfell tunnel, working by
A smoky flare, and making good
The track the rains had torn . . .

                       Clink, clink,
On the sound metal — on the wood
A duller thwack!

             It made him blink,
That running gold . . .

                 'Twas sixteen hours
Since he'd left home — his garden smelt
So fragrant with the heavy showers
When he left home — and now he felt
That it would smell more fresh and sweet
After the tunnel's reek and fume
Of damp warm cinders. 'Twas a treat
To come upon the scent and bloom
That topped the cutting by the wood
After the cinders of the track,
The cinders and tarred sleepers — good
To lift your eyes from gritty black
Upon that blaze of green and red . . .
And she'd be waiting by the fence,
And with the baby . . .

               Straight for bed
He'd make, if he had any sense,

And sleep the day; but, like as not,
When he'd had breakfast, he'd turn to
And hoe the back potato-plot:
'Twould be one mass of weeds he knew.
You'd think each single drop of rain
Turned as it fell into a weed.
You seemed to hoe and hoe in vain.
Chickweed and groundsel didn't heed
The likes of him — and bindweed, well,
You hoed and hoed — still its white roots
Ran deeper . . .
     'Twould be good to smell
The fresh turned earth, and feel his boots
Sink deep into the brown wet mould,
After hard cinders . . .
      And, maybe,
The baby, sleeping good as gold
In its new carriage under a tree,
Would keep him company, while his wife
Washed up the breakfast-things.
        'Twas strange,
The difference that she made to life,
That tiny baby-girl.
      The change
Of work would make him sleep more sound.
'Twas sleep he needed.   That long night
Shovelling wet cinders underground,
With breaking back, the smoky light
Stinging his eyes till they were sore . . .

He'd worked the night that she was born,
Standing from noon the day before
All through that winter's night till morn
Laying fog-signals on the line
Where it ran over Devil's Ghyll . . .

And she was born at half-past nine,
Just as he stood aside until
The Scots Express ran safely by . . .
He'd but to shut his eyes to see
Those windows flashing blindingly
A moment through the blizzard — he
Could feel again that slashing snow
That seemed to cut his face.

                                But they,
The passengers, they couldn't know
What it cost him to keep the way
Open for them.   So snug and warm
They slept or chattered, while he stood
And faced all night that raking storm —
The little house beside the wood
For ever in his thoughts: and he,
Not knowing what was happening . . .

But all went well as well could be
With Sally and the little thing.
And it had been worth while to wait
Through that long night with work to do,
To meet his mother at the gate
With such good news, and find it true,
Ay, truer than the truth.
                              He still
Could see his wife's eyes as he bent
Over the bairn . . .
                        The Devil's Ghyll
Had done its worst, and he was spent;
But he'd have faced a thousand such
Wild nights as thon, to see that smile
Again, and feel that tender touch
Upon his cheek.
                        'Twas well worth while
With such reward.   And it was strange,
The difference such a little thing
Could make to them — how it could change
Their whole life for them, and could bring
Such happiness to them, though they
Had seemed as happy as could be
Before it came to them.
                              The day
Was shaping well.   And there was she,
The lassie sleeping quietly
Within her arms, beside the gate.

The storm had split that lilac tree.
But he was tired, and it must wait.

MAKESHIFTS

And after all, 'twas snug and weather-tight,
His garret. That was much on such a night —
To be secure against the wind and sleet
At his age, and not wandering the street,
A shuffling, shivering bag-of-bones.
                       And yet
Things would be snugger if he could forget
The bundle of old dripping rags that slouched
Before him down the Cannongate, and crouched
Close to the swing-doors of the Spotted Cow.
Why, he could see that poor old sinner now,
Ay! and could draw him, if he'd had the knack
Of drawing anything — a steamy, black
Dilapidation, basking in the glare,
And sniffing with his swollen nose in air
To catch the hot reek when the door swings wide
And shows the glittering paradise inside,
Where men drink golden fire on seats of plush
Lolling like gods: he stands there in the slush
Shivering, from squelching boots to sopping hat
One sodden clout, and blinking like a bat
Be-dazzled by the blaze of light: his beard
Waggles and drips from lank cheeks pocked and seared;
And the whole dismal night about him drips,
As he stands gaping there with watering lips
And burning eyes in the cold sleety drench
Afire with thirst that only death may quench.

Yet he had clutched the sixpence greedily
As if sixpennyworth of rum maybe
Would satisfy that thirst. Who knows! It might
Just do the trick perhaps on such a night,
And death would be a golden, fiery drink
To that old scarecrow. 'Twould be good to think
His money'd satisfied that thirst, and brought
Rest to those restless fevered bones that ought
Long since to have dropped for ever out of sight.

It wasn't decent, wandering the night
Like that — not decent.   While it lived it made
A man turn hot to see it, and afraid
To look it in the face lest he should find
That bundle was himself, grown old and blind
With thirst unsatisfied.
                                    He'd thirsted, too,
His whole life long, though not for any brew
That trickled out of taps in gaudy bars
For those with greasy pence to spend!
                                            The stars
Were not for purchase, neither bought nor sold
By any man for silver or for gold.

Still, he was snug and sheltered from the storm.
He sat by his own hearth secure and warm,
And that was much indeed on such a night.
The little room was pleasant with the light
Glowing on lime-washed walls, kindling to red
His copper pots, and, over the white bed,
The old torn Rembrandt print to golden gloom.
'Twas much on such a night to have a room —
Four walls and ceiling storm-tight overhead.
Denied the stars — well, you must spend instead
Your sixpences on makeshifts.   Life was naught
But toiling for the sixpences that bought
Makeshifts for stars.
                            'Twas snug to hear the sleet
Lashing the panes and sweeping down the street
Towards Holyrood and out into the night
Of hills beyond.   Maybe it would be white
On Arthur's Seat to-morrow, white with snow —
A white hill shining in the morning glow
Beyond the chimney-pots, that was a sight
For any man to see — a snowy height
Soaring into the sunshine.   He was glad
Though he must live in slums, his garret had
A window to the hills.
                            And he was warm,
Ay, warm and snug, shut in here from the storm.
The sixpences bought comfort for old bones
That else must crouch all night on paving-stones
Unsheltered from the cold.
                                    'Twas hard to learn

In his young days that this was life — to earn
By life-long labour just your board and bed —
Although the stars were singing overhead,
The sons of morning singing together for joy
As they had sung for every bright-eyed boy
With ears to hear since life itself was young —
And leave so much unseen, so much unsung.

He'd had to learn that lesson.   'Twas no good
To go star-gazing for a livelihood
With empty belly.   Though he had a turn
For seeing things, when you have got to earn
Your daily bread first, there is little time
To paint your dream or set the stars to rhyme:
Nay, though you have the vision and the skill
You cannot draw the outline of a hill
To please yourself, when you get home half-dead
After the day's work — hammers in your head
Still tapping, tapping . . .
                              Always mad to draw
The living shape of everything he saw
He'd had to spend his utmost skill and strength
Learning a trade to live by, till at length
Now he'd the leisure the old skill was dead.

Born for a painter as it seemed, instead
He'd spent his life upholstering furniture.
'Twas natural enough men should prefer
Upholstery to pictures, and their ease
To little coloured daubs of cows and trees.
He didn't blame them, 'twas no fault of theirs
That they saw life in terms of easy chairs,
And heaven, like that old sinner in the slush,
A glittering bar upholstered in red plush.

'Twas strange to look back on it now, his life . . .
His father, married to a second wife;
And home, no home for him since he could mind,
Save when the starry vision made him blind
To all about him, and he walked on air
For days together, and without a care . . .
But as the years passed, seldomer they came
Those starry dazzling nights and days aflame,
And oftener a sudden gloom would drop

Upon him, drudging all day in the shop
With his young brother John — John always gay
Taking things as they came, the easy way,
Not minding overmuch if things went wrong
At home, and always humming a new song . . .

And then she came into his life, and shook
All heaven about him.   He had but to look
On her to find the stars within his reach.
But, ere his love had trembled into speech,
He'd waked one day to know that not for him
Were those bright living eyes that turned dreams dim —
To know that while he'd worshipped, John and she
Had taken to each other easily . . .

But that was years ago . . . and now he sat
Beside a lonely hearth.   And they were fat —
Ay, fat and old they were, John and his wife,
And with a grown-up family.   Their life
Had not been over-easy: they'd their share
Of trouble, ay, more than enough to spare:
But they had made the best of things, and taken
Life as it came with courage still unshaken.
They'd faced their luck, but never gone half-way
To meet fresh trouble.   Life was always gay
For them between the showers: the roughest weather
Might do its worst — they always stood together
To bear the brunt, together stood their ground
And came through smiling cheerfully.   They'd found
Marriage a hard-up, happy business
Of hand-to-mouth existence more or less;
But taking all in all, well worth their while
To look on the bright side of things — to smile
When all went well, not fearing overmuch
When life was suddenly brought to the touch
And you'd to sink or swim.   And they'd kept hold,
And even now, though they were fat and old
They'd still a hearty grip on life . . .
                                        They'd be
Sitting there in their kitchen after tea
On either side the fire-place even now —
Jane with her spectacles upon her brow,
And nodding as she knitted, listening
While John, in shirt-sleeves, scraped his fiddle-string,

With one ear hearkening lest a foot should stop
And some rare customer invade the shop
To ask the price of some old Flanders' chest
Or oaken ale-house settle . . .
     They'd the best
Of life, maybe, together . . .
     And yet he —
Though he'd not taken life so easily,
Had always hated makeshifts more or less,
Grudging to swop the stars for sixpences,
And was an old man now, with that old thirst
Unsatisfied — ay, even at the worst
He'd had his compensations, now and then
A starry glimpse.   You couldn't work with men
And quite forget the stars.   Though life was spent
In drudgery, it hadn't only meant
Upholstering chairs in crimson plush for bars . . .
Maybe it gave new meaning to the stars,
The drudgery, who knows!
     At least the rare
Wild glimpses he had caught at whiles were there
Yet living in his mind.   When much was dim
And drudgery forgotten, bright for him
Burned even now in memory old delights
That had been his in other days and nights.
He'd always seen, though never could express
His eyes' delight, or only more or less:
But things once clearly seen, once and for all
The soul's possessions — naught that may befall
May ever dim, and neither moth nor rust
Corrupt the dream, that, shedding mortal dust,
Has soared to life and spread its wings of gold
Within the soul . . .
     And yet when they were told
These deathless visions, little things they seemed
Though something of the beauty he had dreamed
Burned in them, something of his youth's desire . . .

And as he sat there, gazing at the fire —
Once more he lingered, listening in the gloom
Of that great silent warehouse, in the room
Where stores were kept, one hand upon a shelf,
And heard a lassie singing to herself
Somewhere unseen without a thought who heard,

Just singing to herself like any bird
Because the heart was happy in her breast,
As happy as the day was long. At rest
He lingered, listening, and a ray of light
Streamed from the dormer-window up a height;
Down on the bales of crimson cloth, and lit
To sudden gold the dust that danced in it,
Till he was dazzled by the golden motes
That kept on dancing to those merry notes
Before his dreaming eyes, and danced as long
As he stood listening to the lassie's song . . .

Then once again, his work-bag on his back,
He climbed that April morning up the track
That took you by a short cut through the wood
Up to the hill-top where the great house stood,
When suddenly beyond the firs' thick night
He saw a young fawn frisking in the light:
Shaking the dew-drops in a silver rain
From off his dappled hide, he leapt again
As though he'd jump out of his skin for joy.
With laughing eyes light-hearted as a boy,
He watched the creature, unaware of him,
Quivering with eager life in every limb,
Leaping and frisking on the dewy green
Beneath the flourish of the snowy gean,
While every now and then the long ears pricked,
And budding horns, as he leapt higher, flicked
The drooping clusters of wild-cherry bloom,
Shaking their snow about him. From the gloom
Of those dark wintry firs, his eyes had won
A sight of April sporting in the sun —
Young April leaping to its heart's delight
Among the dew beneath the boughs of white . . .

And there'd been days among the hills, rare days
And rarer nights among the heathery ways —
Rare golden holidays when he had been
Alone in the great solitude of green
Wave-crested hills, a rolling shoreless sea
Flowing for ever through eternity —
A sea of grasses, streaming without rest
Beneath the great wind blowing from the west,
Over which cloud shadows sailed and swept away

Beyond the world's edge all the summer day.

The hills had been his refuge, his delight,
Seen or unseen, through many a day or night.
His help was of the hills, steadfast, serene
In their eternal strength, those shapes of green
Sublimely moulded.
                Whatsoever his skill,
No man had ever rightly drawn a hill
To his mind — never caught the subtle curves
Of sweeping moorland with its dips and swerves —
Nor ever painted heather . . .
                  Heather came
Always into his mind like sudden flame,
Blazing and streaming over stony braes
As he had seen it on that day of days
When he had plunged into a sea of bloom,
Blinded with colour, stifled with the fume
Of sun-soaked blossom, the hot heady scent
Of honey-breathing bells, and sunk content
Into a soft and scented bed to sleep;
And he had lain in slumber sweet and deep,
And only wakened when the full moon's light
Had turned that wavy sea of heather white:
And still he'd lain within the full moon blaze
Hour after hour, bewildered and adaze
As though enchanted — in a waking swoon
He'd lain within the full glare of the moon
Until she seemed to shine on him alone
In all the world — as though his body'd grown
Until it covered all the earth, and he
Was swaying like the moon-enchanted sea
Beneath that cold white witchery of light . . .
And now, the earth itself, he hung in night
Turning and turning in that cold white glare
For ever and for ever . . .
                She was there —
There at his window now, the moon.   The sleet
And wind no longer swept the quiet street.
And he was cold: the fire had burnt quite low:
And, while he'd dreamt, there'd been a fall of snow
He wondered where that poor old man would hide
His head to-night with thirst unsatisfied . . .
His thirst, who knows! but night may quench the thirst

Day leaves unsatisfied . . .

       Well, he must first
Get to his bed and sleep away the night,
If he would rise to see the hills still white
In the first glory of the morning light.

THE END

THE following pages contain advertisements of a
few of the Macmillan books of poetry.

The Road to Castaly

By ALICE BROWN

Author of " Children of Earth," " The Prisoner," etc.

$1.50

Readers of *Children of Earth,* and of many other of Miss Brown's books for that matter, must have seen many an evidence about them of the really natural poet. Some years ago, furthermore, she published a little collection of verse which was warmly received by the critics, and which served to intensify the desire for more. This volume, then, will be welcome to Miss Brown's admirers, and to literature lovers generally. It contains the earlier poems referred to, which were, as a matter of fact, also issued under the title of *The Road to Castaly,* and much new material as well — the poet's latest and most mature work.

A PLAY BY SIR RABINDRANATH TAGORE
The Cycle of Spring

Cloth, 12mo, $1.25
Leather, $1.75

This, the latest and richest of the author's plays, was recently performed in the courtyard of his Calcutta home by the masters and boys of Shantiniketan. The success was immense: and naturally, for the spirit of the play is the spirit of universal youth, filled with laughter and lyric fervour, jest and pathos and resurgence: immortal youth whose every death is a rebirth, every winter an enfolded spring.

THE MACMILLAN COMPANY
Publishers   64–66 Fifth Avenue   New York